Penguin Handbooks
The New Vegetable Grower's Handbook

Arthur J. Simons was born in London in 1893 and after a public school and university education entered the administrative civil service, from which, following air-raid injuries, he was compelled to retire prematurely on medical grounds. His garden had always provided him with his principal recreation, and in 1942 he was asked to collate and edit a large collection of kitchen-garden notes. These formed the basis of the original wartime *Vegetable Grower's Handbook*, published by Penguins. Subsequently he assisted in the management of a well-known firm of nurserymen in the Midlands and of other horticultural businesses. Later he devoted himself mainly to writing and lecturing, especially on the subject of greenhouses and frames, about which he wrote weekly in *Popular Gardening*. Arthur Simons died in 1958.

Brian Furner contributes regularly to gardening periodicals and has written several gardening books.

The New Vegetable Grower's Handbook

Arthur J. Simons

Revised by Brian Furner

Drawings by David Baxter

Penguin Books

Penguin Books Ltd, Harmondsworth,
Middlesex, England
Penguin Books, 625 Madison Avenue,
New York, New York 10022, U.S.A.
Penguin Books Australia Ltd, Ringwood,
Victoria, Australia
Penguin Books Canada Ltd,
2801 John Street, Markham, Ontario, Canada L3R 1B4
Penguin Books (N.Z.) Ltd, 182–190 Wairau Road,
Auckland 10, New Zealand

First published in Penguin Books as
The Vegetable Grower's Handbook in two volumes, 1945
Revised edition in one volume, 1948
Revised edition entitled
The New Vegetable Grower's Handbook, 1962
Further revised edition, 1975
Reprinted 1975, 1976, 1977

Made and printed in Great Britain by
Richard Clay (The Chaucer Press) Ltd, Bungay, Suffolk
Set in Monotype Plantin

Contents

Contents

The Reviser's Preface

The first edition of *The Vegetable Grower's Handbook* by A. J. Simons was published in 1945 in response to the 'Dig for Victory' campaign.

Times have changed, however, and today those of us who grow vegetables in our gardens do so by choice rather than by government invitation. For many, the growing of vegetables reduces household expenses; others claim that no vegetables are equal in quality and flavour to those grown by the gardener himself. There are a few, too, who grow vegetables for showing at local or national shows.

Before his death in 1958, Arthur Simons brought his original work up to date and the revised book was published in 1962. Now, more than ten years later, I have been asked to edit a second edition. I am very pleased to do this because of the special debt I owe to the author. Mr Simons's original book was my first handbook on the subject when I took up vegetable growing in 1947. Mr Simons was my first teacher – and a good one at that.

In 1950, however, I rejected the use of factory-made chemical fertilizers and pesticides in the production of my own garden food crops. I became what is known as an organic gardener. But Mr Simons remained convinced of the benefits of these chemical aids in the kitchen garden. So, in carrying out any necessary revisions, I have been on a tightrope, as it were. The majority of gardeners fall in line with Mr Simons's ideas as regards the uses chemical products have in vegetable growing; a growing minority both here and in the United States reject them. What I have done, therefore, is to follow a report to the Minister of Agriculture, Fisheries and Food that less persistent chemicals should be used wherever possible. So, in this edition you will find no references at all to persistent chemicals like B.H.C. and D.D.T. Mr Simons omitted all references to chemical weed killers in his own revisions, and I have followed suit. I have also, where possible, pointed out how, by organic methods, the gardener may avoid the use of all chemical fertilizers and sprays.

In the 1962 edition, it was assumed that the reader was familiar with the basic principles underlying the management of greenhouses, frames and cloches. For gardeners without this knowledge further reading was suggested. I have given a similar reading list and some extra books on organic methods (see page 360).

Organic Gardening

For the gardener who has no knowledge of organic gardening methods may I explain quite briefly how they differ from chemicalized gardening. The organic gardener is mindful that the topsoil is a shallow 'skin' which must be conserved if man has any future at all on planet Earth. He or she, therefore, is opposed to any destruction of the topsoil by faulty methods of gardening or farming. Organic gardeners consider that the chemicalization of garden and farm soils is a form of pollution and a faulty method of cultivation. Because the organic gardener is an opponent of pollution, he or she takes a personal interest in preventing it. Thus, no chemical potions and powders are used in the garden. Above all, the organic gardener is no waster of natural resources and he or she relies on the re-use of organic waste products for the fertilization of cultivated soils.

Soil is alive and not inert dust which may be dosed with all manner of chemical potions. Keeping it in good health, building up and maintaining its fertility are of the utmost importance. A healthy soil leads to healthy plants from which health-giving crops are gathered. Produce from organically-run farms and nurseries is known as and marketed as 'wholefood'.

All organic gardeners heed the work and advice of Sir Albert Howard (1873–1957), agriculturist and scientist. Instead of feeding food plants more or less directly with factory-made chemical salts, Sir Albert advocated the fermentation of mixed animal and vegetable wastes in heaps and the application of the resultant product, 'compost', to the soil. Because there are quite different sorts of composts – sowing, potting and other propagating composts – the sort of compost advocated by Sir Albert Howard is referred to in this book as 'garden compost'. There are many ways of making good garden compost which is not only a source of all necessary plant foods but is also an excellent soil conditioner or improver.

All compost-making methods call for a mixture of damp wastes, an activator and an air supply – without sufficient air, damp wastes will putrefy. Some compost-making methods call for larger quantities of animal dung than the average gardener is likely to come across; other methods include special activators which have to be bought.

My own preference is for the American Black Sheet method. This method permits sufficient air to reach the fermenting wastes, protects the heap from snow, heavy rain, hot sunshine and drying winds, and is a quick way of converting wastes into garden compost. It also avoids smells and flies, and, above all, the heap does not have to be turned.

What you put into a compost heap is really up to you. Wastes for composting can be anything and everything which has had life. I include garden weeds, lawn mowings, kitchen and general household rubbish including water-soaked torn newspapers and rags but omitting man-made fibres like nylon which do not rot down. I also omit prickly prunings from blackberry and rose bushes.

To make a compost heap first select a site fairly near the place where it will be later spread and alongside a garden path so that wastes can be wheeled to the site and the finished product taken away without too much effort. For a good ferment the base dimensions of the heap should be about 6 ft × 6 ft. Fork over the site to a depth of about 6 ins. and remove all weeds and their roots.

Have sufficient wastes to hand to build the first layer. If the wastes are on the dry side, moisten them with water; if they are loose, firm the layer gently with your boots. Each layer should be about 1 ft thick and covered with a sprinkling of animal manure if you can get it plus a few shovels of top soil from the garden. If your soil is slightly acidic, sprinkle a little lime (ground chalk) over the soil covering each layer. (A simple gadget like the Murphy Analoam Soil Tester, on sale at garden shops and large stores, is a useful guide to soil acidity/alkalinity.) After the first and subsequent layers cover the heap with a sheet of 500 gauge black polythene and wait until you have collected sufficient wastes for the next layer. Stop building when the heap is 5 ft high, add a few more shovelfuls of top soil to weigh the whole thing down, cover with polythene sheet and anchor securely with scrap iron poles or stakes. Although 500 gauge black polythene is pretty tough, it can be damaged if your wastes include twigs. This can be prevented by covering the heap with an old carpet, rug or discarded clothing before the polythene sheet is draped over.

A heap made in early spring or early summer takes a month to six weeks to rot down well. Winter weather delays the process so that autumn-made heaps take months to rot down. A heap completed in November is just right for use as a thick, rich mulch on the potato bed at Easter.

At one time I thought that garden compost should resemble the crumbly, earth-like matter that one finds on the floor of an ancient wood. Although I saw what a wonderful job it did to the soil and crops, I was disappointed that it was often rather rough and not as sweet-smelling as I had anticipated. For readers who still have this sort of worry let me say that, though garden compost may often appear rough, it is still excellent for the job it has to do.

To rejuvenate a worn-out garden soil, garden compost should be used liberally. It is far better to treat a small part of the garden with a large barrow load per square yard than to spread it over a large area.

Organic manures and fertilizers are made from the waste products of meat, fish, fruit and mushroom industries; chemical fertilizers are sometimes added to give balance. Dried blood, bone meal and other all-organic packeted fertilizers are also sold. These are all useful though they do put up the cost of home-grown produce.

Chinese Artichokes

The name Chinese (or Japanese) artichokes is applied to the tubers of the plant *Stachys affinis* which is a native of the temperate regions of the Far East. This plant is not an artichoke nor is it in any way related to the artichoke family; its tubers have come to be called artichokes merely because of some fancied resemblance between their taste and that of the true artichokes; but actually the flavour is more akin to that of salsify. In this country there is some difference of opinion regarding their table qualities; some people like them and some people don't. It is certainly an acquired taste to be able to eat them raw, as is occasionally done. They enjoy much greater popularity in France where they are known as *crosnes*. In appearance the curious tubers, which are spirally twisted, are somewhat reminiscent of bed springs: old gardeners used to call them 'spirals'; they vary in length from 1 in. to 3 ins. and are about ½ in. thick at the centre, which is the widest part. The tubers are light in weight and ½ lb. is more than sufficient to plant a 30-ft row.

It is easy enough to grow this crop provided that you give it a sunny, well-drained position: in shade it makes far too much top growth. A light soil is best and should have been dug 1 ft deep; preferably it should have been manured for a previous crop; but the Chinese artichoke will give a good account of itself in poorish soil of a heavy nature if a little compost or organic fertilizer is employed to liven it up. Plant in March or April, 9 ins. apart and 4 ins. deep; if you want more than one row, space the rows 15 ins. apart so that you have plenty of room to hoe constantly during the growing season and keep down weeds. Give plenty of water in July and August if the weather is droughty. The only pest likely to trouble the plants is greenfly which must be controlled by periodical spraying with a suitable insecticide.

The tubers should have matured by November and should remain in good condition until February. They should not, however, be dug until the actual day on which they are to be used in the kitchen and, with this point in mind, during severe frost the rows should be protected with straw or bracken so that the ground does not get so hard that you cannot drive a fork into it for lifting purposes. Immediately you have dug up sufficient spirals to make a meal, wash them thoroughly before sending them to the kitchen; if you don't do this and let the soil dry on them you will find them hard to clean, and they may begin to shrivel. Another point is that they must not be exposed to light or air for any appreciable period before cooking, otherwise they become discoloured and unfit to eat. If it should be essential for any reason to lift them some time in advance they must at once be covered with damp soil or sand until they are wanted; but no attempt should be made to store them because they are then almost certain to throw out shoots and lose their flavour.

Few cookery books appear to give recipes for cooking this vegetable and most of those that do so recommend that the spirals should be peeled. One is bound to conclude that the authors have never themselves done what they advise. Ask any cook who has ever tried to peel the things what she thought of the job and you may be quite shaken by the answer. If you are cooking Chinese artichokes for the first time, I suggest that you boil them till they are tender, then fry them till they are crisp and serve them with parsley sauce and slices of lemon.

Globe Artichokes

Cynara scolymus, the globe artichoke, is the only plant entitled to the name of 'artichoke' which is derived through the Italian *articiocco* and *alcarcioffo* from the Arabic *al harshuf* which means 'rough-skinned'. It is a very ornamental herbaceous perennial, looking somewhat like a super-thistle, about 5 ft tall, with coarse leaves 3 ft long, grey on the upper side, covered with white cottony down on the underside. Although it is cultivated extensively in gardens throughout the Mediterranean area, it has never been found growing wild, and in the opinion of present-day botanists it is simply a domesticated form of the cardoon (*Cynara carduncwlus*).

If it were allowed to bloom, the globe artichoke would produce large purple thistle-like heads in autumn but in practice the unopened, bluish-green flower buds are eaten and provide a dish which is highly appreciated by connoisseurs and gourmets; the taste is, however, an acquired one, and those who have not previously tried globe artichokes should hesitate before they go to the trouble of growing a plant which takes up a lot of room and may only disappoint when the produce is brought into the kitchen. You do not wish to find yourself in the position of the old coachman who was given some surplus 'globes' by his employer and later reported that they were well named artichokes because 'they well nigh choked I and the missus'. I suggest to those who are unfamiliar with this vegetable that they should first try it out at one of the high-class restaurants where it is served in its season or, alternatively, that they should buy a few of these artichokes from one of the more exclusive greengrocers, cook them according to recipes given in the more up-to-date cookery books, and see how they like them. A third method of making the acquaintance of the distinctive taste of the globe artichoke is to buy the fleshy bases of the buds (which the French call *fonds d'artichaut*) in tins: these can be obtained from grocers who specialize in exotic and luxury produce.

Assuming that you enjoy eating these artichokes and would like to grow your own, you have still to consider whether you have room for them, seeing that each plant occupies 16 sq. ft of space, and also whether your garden is warm enough for them. The plants are not impeccably hardy, and I myself would not attempt to grow them in the northern counties or indeed in any except the warmer gardens of the south and west. They will not tolerate frost pockets or heavy, cold, wet, badly-drained land, so here are two other factors that may have a bearing on your decision.

However, we will take it that you are prepared to go ahead with this crop, in which case you should start off with rooted plants which are available in spring for April planting from leading nurserymen and seedsmen specializing in unusual varieties. In calculating your requirements you can estimate the yield from each plant as from 12 to 18 buds and its useful bearing life as three years. You will therefore make one third of your total planting each year for the first three years and thereafter you will destroy the third-year plants at the end of each season.

Propagation from Seed

When I wrote the original *Vegetable Grower's Handbook* early in the Second World War no globe artichoke plants were obtainable and I therefore dealt only with the raising of stock from seed. I no longer advocate this method because, like all perennials, *Cynara scolymus* does not come true from seed and the seedlings differ widely in their varietal characteristics, some of them being useless for food production purposes, whereas purchased plants, which are raised from suckers, come from parent plants of known high productivity. However, if you wish to raise your own plants from seed because it is cheaper to do so, I advise you to sow in heat in February and put the plants out in April in a reserve bed where they will bear some buds in August, September, and October, when the best specimens can be selected and marked for planting out finally the following spring. If you have no heated glass and must wait until you can sow in the open ground in March or April the plants will not form buds until the following year and valuable time will be lost before the process of selection can be carried out. However, if an open ground sowing is unavoidable, the seedlings should be thinned to 6 ins. and left undisturbed till the following April.

Preparation of the Soil

Although globe artichokes will grow in any medium to light soil, you have got to do them really well or the globes will be too small to be really worth eating. Prepare the land therefore by taking out a trench 3 ft wide and 18 ins. deep and putting a good layer of well-rotted stable or farmyard manure at the bottom. If you cannot get animal manure, the best substitute for it in this case is composted seaweed because the cardoon (from which the artichoke is derived) is found in nature growing on sandy seashores, especially those of North Africa. Failing any composted seaweed, use garden compost. As you return the excavated soil to the trench, give it a liberal dusting of bonemeal.

Planting and After-cultivation

In this prepared ground you set your plants 4 ft apart with 4 ft between the rows. They will need a great deal of water during the summer: in dry seasons a mulch will help to conserve moisture in the soil. Ordinarily, the buds appear in June and July and, after they have been taken, the flowering stems are cut right out. On the approach of winter the question of protecting the plants will arise. In mild districts where the soil is light and well-drained it is usually sufficient to shorten the leaves by one half and then tie them together with string, thus giving some protection to the crowns. But in the average garden and on retentive soil it will be necessary to cut off the large leaves and partially earth up the inner leaves with soil from between the rows, or bank them round with sifted ashes, and, in addition, if sharp frost threatens, to cover them with dry bracken or dry leaves or strawy litter. Some discretion is needed here, however, because you must not coddle the plants so that they break into early growth and then get cut by later frosts and you must not leave them buried under wet straw or strawy manure because, if you do, you will assuredly rot their crowns and kill them. The implication conveyed by so many writers that mulches can be left on automatically until spring should be entirely disregarded: as soon as the frost goes take the litter off and replace it again later if necessary. It is only if your garden, like mine, is almost invariably frozen hard for at least one long spell in winter that you should cover the plants permanently, and in this case the only satisfactory covering consists of fine weathered ashes sifted over to a depth of one foot. All ashes must be removed, and earthing soil restored to its proper place, in March, when a liberal dressing of manure should be forked in around each plant.

Propagation from Suckers

During the growing season up to fifteen or more suckers will be produced round the base of each plant. Do not leave more than five of these to grow: pull the others off. Those that are left will develop into large shoots and can be removed to form new plants when they are from 9 to 12 ins. long. Simply scrape back the soil with a trowel until you can break or cut them off from the parent plant with a portion of the old stock and as many small roots as possible attached; trim back the leaves and replant very firmly down to their original depth. This operation can be performed in October, November, or April. In places where the winters are usually mild there is everything to be said in favour of autumn propagation because the suckers can establish themselves in their final positions during the rainy season and will be less liable to suffer check from late spring droughts. Water is of prime importance when raising plants from suckers, as these will not endure anything like the same amount of drought as seedlings will. In less favourable areas it may be necessary to overwinter the suckers either 1 ft apart in a nursery bed where they can have the protection of cloches or in 5-ins. pots in a frame: much depends on their size. In both cases the final planting will take place some time in April and there should be a fair crop of buds the first year. During this season it is usually possible to take a catch crop of lettuce, turnips, or carrots from between the rows but this cannot be done in the second or third years because the spread of the leaves of the artichokes will be too great. It is beneficial to give newly planted suckers a dressing of nitrogenous fertilizer before the first hoeing.

Gathering the Heads

As has already been stated, the edible parts of the plant are the 'heads' or immature flower buds. In order to obtain large heads, it is desirable to remove each lateral bud surrounding the main heads when it is about the size of a hen's egg and either eat it raw (as the Italians do) or pickle it or fry it – the main heads are usually boiled. Some people twist a piece of wire round the stem 3 ins. below the head, in order to increase the size, but this should not be necessary if the plant has been liberally treated and carefully disbudded. As a rule the buds are gathered with about 6 ins. of stem attached just before they are due to open, when the still tight heads are beginning to spread at the base. They are useless if allowed to expand beyond this stage: therefore, if too many are ready at once, cut them with longer stems which can be pushed into damp sand: this will keep them in good condition in a cool place for a week. Wash your hands immediately after cutting globe artichokes and tell your cook to do the same before she handles any other vegetables which are to be eaten raw: otherwise she will impart to them an intense bitterness and, if her fingers come into contact with milk, she may curdle it. The heads themselves should be soaked in cold water for at least half an hour, the stalk having been cut away, before being drained and boiled in salted water until they are tender. For the benefit of the uninitiated I would say that the portions you can eat are the fleshy base (the *fond d'artichaut*), the centre bud leaves, and the bases of the large outer leaves: the spiny centre or 'choke' cannot be eaten.

Production of 'Chards'

When a plant is three years old and all the current year's heads have been taken it can be regarded as exhausted from the point of view of artichoke production and is due to be thrown away and replaced by a young sucker. But before this is done it can be made to provide a crop of young blanched growths, known as 'chards', which make very good eating when cooked in the same way as seakale beet (Swiss chard). Cut back the leaves in July to within 6 ins. of the ground and water the plants weekly until the end of September. New growth will soon appear and when it is about 2 ft high the leaves should be drawn together, tied with raffia, wrapped round with thick paper or with clean dry hay or straw, and then neatly earthed up with dry soil or sifted ashes. Blanching takes about six weeks and no growth takes place during the blanching process: hence it is essential that growth should be well forward before the earthing up is done. If any chards remain uneaten when winter sets in, remove all wrappings, lift the plants, and pack them in dry sand. It may be added that the large leaves which are cut off at the commencement of this process should not be thrown away there and then as they will last for a fortnight and look very decorative if placed in big vases stood at a sufficient height above the ground to enable the underside of the foliage to be seen.

Jerusalem Artichokes

These are not artichokes and they do not come from Jerusalem. The tubers which we eat are those of a sunflower, *Helianthus tuberosus*, which was found growing in Nova Scotia by the French about the beginning of the seventeenth century. When samples were brought back to Europe, there was much speculation as to what they really were. Some people thought they were merely a variety of potato, which latter vegetable had been discovered about the same time; others were under the impression that they could detect in the tubers a flavour similar to that of the globe artichoke and concluded that the plant must also be an artichoke. In Paris the first tubers were imported for sale to the public simultaneously with the arrival of a party of Nova Scotian aborigines who were exhibited as curiosities; Parisian costermongers, not knowing what the tubers were called, gave them the name of the tribe to which the unfortunate captured natives belonged and thus what we call Jerusalem artichokes have remained *topinambours* in France to this day.

The Italians alone showed any common sense by calling the tubers Canadian sunflowers (*girasole del Canada*), which followed closely the native name for them, 'sun roots' (*Kaischuc penauk*). The Dutch imagined them to be artichokes, grew them in large quantities at Ter Neusen, and exported them to Britain where they were also called artichokes. There is no certainty how the prefix 'Jerusalem' originated: the common explanation is that it represents a corruption of the Italian *girasole*. But some think that it was a contemporary barrow boy's effort to make some sense out of the labels on the boxes from Holland which read: *Artischokappeln van Ter Neusen*. Anyhow the tubers became 'Jerusalems' and the Victorians with typical humour christened the soup made from them Palestine Soup.

It would be idle to pretend that Jerusalem artichokes are popular in this country. Many people complain that they are apt to discolour and go black on cooking and have a smoky taste, besides being knobbly and difficult to prepare; but these strictures apply only to the old, unnamed stocks which should never be bought. The improved modern strains of this vegetable can make excellent eating provided that the tubers are both well grown and properly cooked. In this connection it may be mentioned that although the nutritive value of the Jerusalem artichoke is equivalent to that of the potato it ought not to be cooked like a potato, and readers who have found it unsatisfactory when cooked would do well to consult a modern recipe book and then give it another trial. At the same time, however, it must be admitted frankly that there are some people whom the Jerusalem artichoke 'does not like', although they may actually enjoy eating it. This is no new thing. As long ago as 1622 Dr Venner of Bath wrote of the 'artichoke of Jerusalem' that 'it breedeth melancholy and is somewhat nauseous and fulsome to the stomache, and therefore very hurtful to the melancholick, and them that have weak stomackes'. About the same time John Goodyer, who grew them in Hampshire, wrote, 'But in my judgement, which way soever they be drest and eaten, they stir and cause a filthy loathsome sticking wind within the body, thereby causing the belly to be pained and tormented; and are a meat more fit for swine than man. Yet some say that they have usually eaten them, and have found no such windy quality in them.' Over a century later Phillip Miller in his *Gardener's Dictionary* (1754) also referred to this 'windy Quality which hath brought them almost into Disuse'.

Modern medical science is more explicit. The plain fact is that some digestive systems are allergic to the Jerusalem artichoke and on these the vegetable has the effect of a strong dose of castor oil, which is most pronounced in freshly dug tubers which have been grown on well-manured soil, especially if these are eaten unaccompanied by a leaf vegetable and either crisp toast or crusty rolls. I do not propose to enter into the scientific reasons for all this beyond saying that the tubers, unlike those of the potato, contain no starch but store all their carbohydrates in the form of inulin which is more easily converted into sugar and apt to digest rapidly. Some people are similarly affected if they eat freshly dug new potatoes.

Soil Preparation

The Jerusalem artichoke will grow in any soil from hungry sand to heavy clay and in any odd corner, open or shady, provided that sufficient lime is present and that it does not get waterlogged: the plant is impeccably hardy. Nevertheless it pays to do it reasonably well because, if starved, it will tend to produce only undersized tubers at the base of a forest of leafy tops. I advise therefore that plenty of good ripe compost and coarse leafmould should be dug into the bed, which can then be dressed with wood ashes to remedy any deficiency of potash in the soil which might otherwise cause the tubers to go 'soapy' on cooking. A nitrogenous fertilizer is definitely not needed because the plants seem capable of accumulating on their own account much more nitrogen than they could possibly obtain from the soil.

Planting

Tubers are planted in February or March about 15 ins. apart and from 4 to 6 ins. deep according to the nature of the soil. If there is more than one row of them the distance between rows should be 2½ ft. About 4 lb. of tubers will be ample to plant a 30-ft row; but many seedsmen do not sell a smaller quantity than 7 lb. so that, if you have too many, you should select the most shapely small specimens for planting. Large tubers may be divided, leaving three eyes to each portion.

Cultivation

Periodical weeding and hoeing are the only cultural attentions needed; but towards the end of summer the plants, which attain a height of 8 ft or more, should be tied to wires strained between posts, otherwise they may be blown flat by autumnal gales. I have seen it recommended that the tips should be pinched out to prevent flowering; but in fact flowers are never borne in this country except when the summer is abnormally hot and dry. (I have only twice had *Helianthus tuberosus* bloom in my gardens in the Home Counties, once in 1921 and again in 1947.) On the approach of winter cut off all stems fairly close to the ground.

Lifting and Storing

Jerusalem artichokes should be removed from the soil in the same way as parsnips by digging a deep hole up against the end plant in the row and drawing the tubers sideways with a fork into the hole, and so on from plant to plant. Great care must be taken to remove all the underground portions of this subject, for anything that remains will grow and become troublesome in the following year. A fair average yield from each root is about 3 lb. of tubers and for culinary purposes preference should be given to those which are free from knobbliness and of even size (about twelve to the lb.). Ordinarily, the tubers are best left in the ground until they are wanted, some protection being given to prevent the soil from becoming too hard to dig during severe frost. Owing to their thin skins the tubers do not store as well as potatoes but, if desired, some of them can be lifted towards the end of November and stored in dry sifted soil or ashes or in sand in a cool shed where they will remain in good condition for up to a couple of months. The best of the latest dug tubers should be set aside for replanting to provide the next season's crop.

It may be added that the Jerusalem artichoke is invaluable as a windbreak. Even if it is not wanted to use the plant for human consumption, it is an excellent idea to plant a row of artichokes on the north side of the tomato rows and ridge cucumber beds as a protection against cold winds. Such a line will also provide welcome shade in summer for such things as lettuces and radishes.

Asparagus

This is one of the oldest of cultivated vegetables and was held in great esteem by the Romans as long ago as 200 B.C. The name 'asparagus' is Greek and appears to refer to the immature shoots, which are eaten: it is not clear what the ancients called the actual plant. In this country which is one of its native habitats it was known as 'sperage' in the sixteenth century, although Samuel

Pepys called it 'sparrow-grass'. It still grows wild on Asparagus Island off Kynance Cove in Cornwall.

Assuming that you like asparagus, three conditions must be satisfied before you start to grow it. Firstly, you must have room for it. The plants do not throw up their shoots all at once; they bob up here and there over a period of about seven weeks and in order to be certain of securing bunches of adequate size the average household will need at least fifty plants occupying a bed approximately 5 ft wide by 65 ft long (about 36 sq. yds). Secondly, you must possess patience and not expect quick results: it will be from three to five years before your asparagus bed begins to bear. Thirdly, you must have a more or less permanent residence to make the planting of an asparagus bed worth while to you, having regard to the fact that the life of such a bed will be at least fifteen to twenty years with the biggest return during the latter half of that period.

Soil and Situation

Contrary to general belief, asparagus will succeed in a wide range of soils, anything in fact except the very heavy clays, thin chalkland, and acid peat. The bed should be in an open spot but not so exposed that high winds can wreak havoc on the haulm: it may be desirable to plant a windbreak. While the crop must not lack moisture in summer, it will not tolerate waterlogging in winter: effective drainage is therefore of great importance and any necessary work in this connection should be undertaken in the autumn of the year previous to planting. A sunny aspect is an advantage. Avoid frost pockets unless you are prepared to see the earliest young shoots turned to jelly. If the existing soil is wholly unsuitable but the drainage is satisfactory, you can excavate and remove the top spit, dig decayed vegetable matter, lawn mowings and seaweed (if available) into the subsoil, then replace the original top spit with a mixture of fibrous loam, leafmould, wood ashes, lime rubble, and sand with the addition of a little bonemeal. If on the other hand the drainage is unsatisfactory, the present top soil can be treated as subsoil and the new bed made up on top of it.

Preparation of the Bed

The asparagus plant is capable of developing an enormous root system and will penetrate easily to a depth of 4 ft and a similar distance sideways. It is therefore necessary to double-dig the ground and this operation must not be confined to the actual width of the bed, which is normally 5 ft, but must be extended to an area 2½ ft wide on either side of it, making a total width of 10 ft. While digging is in progress, the soil must be liberally enriched by the incorporation of stable or farmyard manure, composted seaweed (which asparagus much appreciates because it is a native of the sea coast), and other wholly organic materials such as leafmould and garden compost. This work must be completed by the beginning of February and the surface left rough until planting time when the whole area is raked level, the actual bed is marked out 5 ft wide in the centre of the dug portion, and trenches 1 ft wide and 1 ft deep are taken out along its whole length for the reception of the plants.

There are two systems of growing asparagus, the 'flat bed' and the 'ridge'. In the former you have four rows of plants (i.e. four trenches) 15 ins. apart; in the latter you have only two rows of plants, digging your trenches along each edge of the bed. Whichever method is adopted, along the centre line of each trench you must form a ridge 9 ins. high with some of the excavated soil. Since, however, I myself strongly favour the ridge system, *all further cultural instructions will relate primarily to that system.*

Obtaining Plants

Should you have difficulty in obtaining plants locally, Jackmans of Woking offer two-year plants of the popular variety, Connover's Colossal. During the 1960s, Marshalls of Wisbech introduced an F.1 hybrid asparagus; Marshalls claim that the plants have far more vigour and produce much earlier crops. Asparagus plants are unisexual and male plants yield an earlier crop as well as being almost twice as productive as the female plants. Unlike the females, male plants do not litter the bed with unwanted seedlings. As a rule the sex of a seedling asparagus plant cannot be determined until it is at least in its second season and no supplier could, therefore, guarantee to supply you with all-male plants. You can recognize male and female plants quite easily – the females disclose their identity by producing the green 'berries' which are, in fact, the seed capsules.

Since no shoots should be cut from any asparagus plant until it is four years old, and full bearing does not start until the fifth to seventh years, many amateurs are tempted to buy three-year-old roots despite their high cost. But it is as true of asparagus as of any other plant that the younger it is the better it will recover from the shock of transplantation. If it were possible to identify the sexes in them, I would advise you to save money and plant only one-year-old roots despite the fact that this will involve a wait of three years before cutting commences: one-year-old roots are sold by the actual growers, though seldom offered by seedsmen. In all circumstances, however, two-year-old roots are probably the best investment and everybody sells those.

It is of course quite possible to raise your own plants from seed if you are hard up and in no great hurry for results. You can then pick out the males for yourself in the second season, though you may not be as successful as the professional in selecting only the best types: even the finest strain of seed will show some variation in the seedlings and, when it comes to planting time, you must discard all plants with weak crowns and thin, straggling roots. Seed is sown thinly in April in drills 2 ins. deep and the seedlings are thinned to 6 ins. apart the first summer and again to 1 ft apart the second summer. They are planted out permanently in the April of the third year when exactly two years old. There are 1,500 seeds to the ounce and normally they will produce 50 per cent males and 50 per cent females. The seeds germinate more quickly if first soaked in water. The seedlings must be kept weeded, watered, and hoed until finally planted out.

Planting the Bed

The planting season is late March or early April according to district; this applies whether you buy roots or are planting out your own seedlings. Whichever you are doing, it is most important that the roots should not be exposed to the air for a moment longer than is necessary. Particular care must be taken with purchased plants; you must be ready for them and, once you open a package, you must get the plants into the trench and covered with soil as quickly as possible. Keep the unplanted roots covered with sacks and place soil over each crown as you go; don't wait until you get to the end of the trench. More asparagus plants are killed or permanently injured by being left about after unpacking than from any other cause. The roots travel perfectly well: the danger starts only after the wrappings have been removed.

The business of planting is a little complicated because the roots of the asparagus plant resemble the legs of a spider – and they are very long legs too. It is necessary to set each plant in the centre of the trench so that its roots fall down the sides of the ridge, half on one side and half on the other, like a man bestriding a horse. The distance between the crowns should be 18 ins. and when all the plants are in position and the soil has been put back, the crowns should be about 3 ins. beneath the surface. Soak the bed with water immediately after planting.

It is wise to keep a few plants in reserve to mend any gaps which may result from odd roots here and there having failed to take on.

Cultivation

No sticks must be cut in the year of planting, the top growth (which is of course the familiar asparagus 'fern') being allowed to grow unchecked. When it is nearing its full development it will need to be supported and this is best done by driving in stiff canes on the slant so that each stem can be tied in clear of its neighbours instead of being bunched up with others on a vertical stake. The space between the two rows on a ridge bed can be catch-cropped with lettuce, carrots, turnips, or dwarf beans. Give water freely during the summer if there is a shortage of rain. When the fern has turned yellow in autumn, about November, cut it off at about an inch above ground level and, if necessary, mark the position of each plant with a short stick. Rake the bed clean and apply well rotted manure or garden compost. In February fork the bed over very lightly, not more than a couple of inches deep, and apply to each square yard a trowelful of wood ashes; in March apply 4 oz. weathered soot or ½ oz. nitro chalk to each square yard.

The foregoing instructions apply in their entirety only to plants which are but one year old, having been sown the previous year. In the case of plants which are two or more years old there is one important variation in treatment, namely that after applying the autumn dressing of manure or garden compost you dig a shallow layer of soil from the centre of each ridge bed between the rows and heap it on top of the crowns to form low ridges. The following spring, before growth commences and usually about March at the time of application of the nitrogenous fertilizer, these ridges must be forked over lightly and moulded up neatly with a draw hoe. In July the ridges are levelled out and pea boughs are pushed in all over the bed to prevent the frail stems from being blown down and snapped off. If you have no pea boughs, use tarred twine tied to stakes. This routine is continued year after year as long as the beds exist and may be briefly recapitulated:

Autumn Cut down growth; clean the bed; apply manure or compost; ridge.
Winter Give dressing of potash in form of wood ashes.
Spring Give dressing of nitrogenous fertilizer as weathered soot and tidy up ridges.
Summer Cut; level out ridges; stake; water.

No catch crops must be taken from any bed in which the plants are three or more years old.

Some growers, taking into account the fact that asparagus is a seaside plant, use agricultural salt as a fertilizer. Salt is not required on new beds, but may be applied to established beds at the rate of 2 oz. per yard run in the middle of April; a second and third dressing may be given at three-weekly intervals following the first. It is important not to apply the salt too early, for, in the event of snow or bitter weather, it would form a freezing mixture and seriously damage the crop.

A warning is perhaps necessary that the roots of asparagus grow very near the surface and will be injured by deep cultivation either in or between the rows. Manure and fertilizers must be distributed over the whole bed and not merely along the line of the rows.

GIANT ASPARAGUS

The cultural directions just given apply to the production of ordinary asparagus for domestic consumption. The production of giant heads, such as are sold in bottles, demands the use of large quantities of stable manure; it is unlikely that many readers will have the facilities for its cultivation despite the fact that it has a flavour all of its own, much esteemed by connoisseurs. Briefly, the system consists in excavating wide trenches and building up the soil at the sides until you have something resembling a railway cutting 3 ft deep. The bottom 12 ins. of the trench should be filled with leafmould, wood ashes, and more or less well decayed vegetable matter; over this is put about 4 ins. of good garden soil and on this are set one-year-old crowns at least 2 ft apart, which are then covered with 3 ins. of a well-matured mixture of soil and rotted manure. The rows must be 5 ft apart. In autumn a further dressing of soil and manure is given and in the spring of the following year the top inch or two of soil is scraped off to allow a thick dressing of manure to be applied; then the soil is replaced. In the autumn of the second year the trench is filled to the top with manure which is dug out again in spring and replaced by a soil–manure mixture. The ridges can then be levelled off. In this year the first cutting will take place; thereafter the bed will bear annually provided that you continue the routine of applying manure in autumn and the soil-manure mixture in spring.

Cutting

The season of cutting begins on about 20 April in the south and at about the beginning of May in the Midlands. The same person should always do the cutting, and do it systematically, taking every shoot that is the proper length and sorting to thickness afterwards. You can soon spoil an asparagus bed by allowing any and every member of the family to have a go – for each will usually go for the fattest sticks only. No sticks may be cut from three-year-old plants in the year of planting; but in the case of three-year-old plants which have been in the ground for at least a year it is permissible to take up to three shoots from each strong plant provided that none is taken after the middle of May. In established beds cutting must cease about the middle of June so that the plants have an opportunity of putting up some top growth for the remainder of the season. If they were kept cut back for the whole of the year, they would obviously die, because no plant can continue to grow without leaves. If you wish to be able to judge the quality of your sticks by commercial standards, the finest must be not less than $\frac{7}{10}$ in. thick and nothing less than $\frac{1}{4}$ in. thick deserves consideration.

It is an open question whether asparagus should be white right up to the coloured bud at the top or whether several inches of the stem should be allowed to acquire the natural green colour. In the U.S.A. they like it green; on the Continent they prefer it blanched. In this country tastes vary, though I myself often wonder whether green asparagus is not best in made-up dishes because the sticks are not easy to handle at table and the green tops are more likely to fall off just as you are trying to put them into your mouth. From the gardener's point of view it is merely a matter of how much of the stem he allows to be affected by light before he cuts it. If he cuts immediately the tip shows through the soil, he gets it white; if he wants it green, he allows three or four inches to emerge above the ground before cutting. As regards the length when cut, your greengrocer sells two grades, 'long' and 'short', but the former merely looks more imposing and is harder to manipulate with decency at table. In my humble opinion it is sufficient if a blanched shoot is cut 6 ins. long and a green shoot 8 ins. long, the latter being made up of 4 ins. green and 4 ins. white.

The actual cutting of the shoots calls for a combination of skill and judgement. If you wish to sever them several inches below the surface you must use either the special type of asparagus saw sold by sundriesmen for this purpose or one of the narrow-bladed 'kitchen' or 'vegetable' knives which are now so popular among housewives. Either of these can be quite tricky to manage. It is no use making a blind jab into the ground for, if you do, you will almost certainly decapitate one or more of the shoots which have not yet shown up at the surface. You must remember that the shoots are clustered round the plant in different stages of development and that their points of origin are often very close together, so that if you run amok with a knife in securing the first shoot of the season it may well prove to be also the last that you will get from that plant until the following year. It is therefore necessary to feel your way, as it were, down the length of the shoot you intend to take and to cut it with the least possible to-and-fro movement of the saw or knife. Some people manage to detach the shoots by a sort of combined twist and pull, without using a knife, but this requires considerable knack. The difficulty is of course greatest when you wish to cut a fully blanched shoot from a flat bed, which means going down a good 6 ins. For this reason some gardeners like to cover the bed with about 4 ins. of granulated peat when the first shoots are due to show; it is then possible to scrape the peat away from individual shoots, as required, so that they can be severed almost at ground level. (This peat mulch must not be confused with the covering of clean hay or straw which is sometimes applied to flat beds at the same season: this is quite a light, loose covering and its purpose is to protect the first shoots from early morning frosts when it is desired to cut them green.) In America they let green asparagus attain a height of from 6 to 12 ins. above ground before cutting it off a bare inch below the surface; but this practice has absolutely nothing to commend it as the resultant sticks are quite unmanageable at table. If the art of cutting below ground level entirely eludes you, the best course is to heap a pile of leafmould over each crown; or you can do as they do in France to get blanched sticks, and put bottomless wine bottles over the sticks as they rise – or, in the case of giant asparagus, use seakale pots. The tips of the blanched sticks will colour up if placed in ordinary bottling jars full of water with the points just above the rim and left in full daylight for a day or so. The jars themselves must be wrapped round with brown paper held in position by rubber bands. It should be clear, however, why I am addicted to the ridge system of culture because under it no difficulties arise in regard to the colouring of the tips or any desired length of stem and you can then cut on the level at the base of the ridge or, if the soil is really friable, you can often scrape it away from the base of the shoot which can then be neatly snapped off by slight pressure of the forefinger instead of being cut.

Forced Asparagus

If you grow your asparagus on the flat bed system you can bring on a section of the bed in advance of the remainder by placing one or more portable frames in position, filling them with loose littery material such as clean hay or straw, and covering the lights with thick mats. This produces a blanched sample. Cutting must cease, and frames and litter must be removed, while there are still several sticks left on each root, and the same section must not be forced in two successive years.

In France they force asparagus by laying hot water pipes on the surface of beds which have been cut naturally for three years and then covering with a run of frames. The beds are forced thus for three years, little ventilation being given and mats being used to promote blanching. Then frames and pipes are moved to another section, leaving the first section to grow naturally again for three years. Some market growers in this country have attempted to achieve similar results by using fermenting manure in trenches and on the surface of the beds. In both cases the roots are planted closer together than usual, not more than 9 ins. apart. One well-known grower in Surrey plants roots in frames over a system of buried hot-water pipes; others in the southern counties lift roots and force them in hothouses. In both cases the roots have to be thrown away after forcing. Few private gardeners are in a position to follow their example or would wish to lose several pounds' worth of good asparagus plants for the sake of one year's forced crop. Nevertheless, if any reader is so minded and has a greenhouse heated to 70° F., he can plant three- or four-year-old roots closely together on 4 ins. of soil in deep boxes and cover with 5 ins. of soil, then place the boxes under the staging and throw sacking over them which must be kept moist (as must also the soil). A better method, however, is to use frames set over a good manure hotbed or fitted with electrical soil-warming. Carefully lift three- or four-year-old roots from the asparagus bed at the end of October or during November and replant immediately in the frame, packing the roots closely together on a 4-ins. layer of leafmould, then working light, rich, sifted soil in among the crowns until they are just covered. A fortnight later cover the whole bed with 6 ins. of similar soil and surface with a layer of granulated peat. The first shoots should appear in about three weeks and cropping should continue throughout December. The temperature required is 60–65° F. and must not exceed 70° F., or the quality of the sticks will be spoiled. Very little air should be given. One frame will accommodate 100–50 crowns. The roots are of no value after forcing and should be destroyed.

Asparagus Beetles

The only pests that attack asparagus are the red, yellow, and black asparagus beetles, which, with their larvae, gnaw the young shoots and foliage during July and August. They can be controlled by means of derris dust provided that action is taken in good time before the stems are beginning to look stripped.

Asparagus Rust

This fungoid disease covers the stems and foliage of the plants with reddish 'dust' which in turn gives rise to black pustules on the shoots of the following year which of course you want to eat. It ought not to bother you if from time to time you dust the top growth with flowers of sulphur and later, when you cut it down, burn it. You must also burn any infected shoots.

Asparagus Pea (Tetragonolobus purpureus)

This is not a pea and it has nothing to do with asparagus. It is a vegetable appreciated by epicures for its curious rectangular pods which are eaten whole when about an inch long. The reddish-brown flowers which precede the pods are reminiscent of those of the purple clover.

Plants should be raised under glass in gentle heat by sowing the fairly large seeds in April 2 ins. apart in boxes 4 ins. deep. Germination and growth should both be rapid and there ought not to be any difficulty in getting the seedlings hardened off ready for planting out during the latter half of May about 15 ins. apart in rows 2 ft apart.

The natural habit of the plants is spreading or sprawling but you will be wise to keep this under control by means of stakes and twine stretched taut on either side of the rows. The height varies from 12 to 18 ins. according to season. No attention is necessary beyond hoeing and watering when the weather is dry.

Some people use brushwood to give support but this makes picking very difficult. It is essential to gather the pods whilst they are still quite small, otherwise they become stringy and unpalatable. Care must be taken not to overcook them.

In warm districts it is possible to grow this vegetable from an outdoor sowing in May; but it then comes into use rather late, whereas if started early under glass, it is usually ready several weeks before the runner beans come in, when it is as a rule much more appreciated.

Aubergines

These are the fruits of *Solanum melongena ovigerum*, a relative of the tomato, commonly known as the egg plant because in one of its varieties (which is seldom, if ever, eaten in this country) the aubergines are white and look very like goose eggs. Although a native of South America, the egg plant was unknown in the U.S.A. until about 1850; but it reached England towards the end of the sixteenth century when its fruits were christened Jews' apples or rind

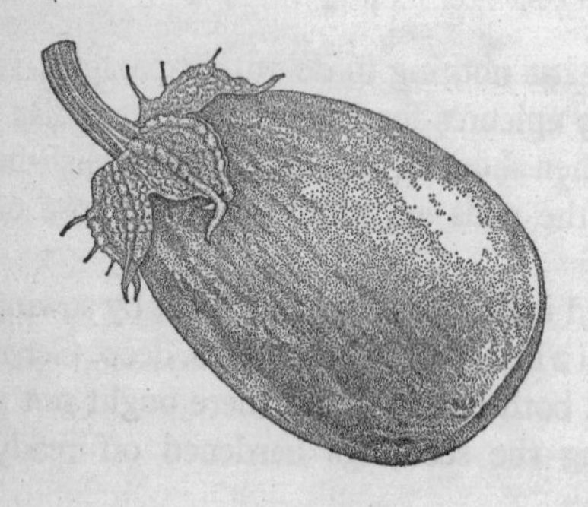

apples and regarded with the greatest suspicion from the point of view of edibility. It can hardly be said that they are popular over here even today; it is in India (where they call them brinjals or egg apples), in the Balkans, and in France that you will most frequently be served with a dish of aubergines – indeed this name for them comes from France.

Although the average Englishman is always slow to welcome any innovation in his vegetable diet, it has to be admitted that it is not everybody who regards aubergines as 'highly delicious' (a phrase beloved by most of the writers on gardening who refer to them, and have themselves probably never eaten them!). They are certainly in the nature of a luxury vegetable and possess no special food value. Nevertheless I, who have both grown and eaten them, consider them to be most palatable and to make a very pleasant change from the other vegetables available in late summer *provided that they are properly cooked*, which is very far from always being the case in this country. In the larger towns it is usually possible to buy aubergines in season from high-class greengrocer's and, if you have not already tried them, I suggest that you buy a few of the long purple kind and cook them according to one or other of the recipes from the Balkans which are to be found in books on continental cookery such as can be consulted in most good public libraries. I think you will like them.

One of the reasons of course for the comparative unfamiliarity of the egg plant in Britain is that it is really too tender for our climate. It is essential to raise the plants in heat and you must do this job yourself because young plants are not ordinarily available from nurserymen, as they are in the case of tomatoes. Furthermore, although in the south of England in a good summer the plants will fruit satisfactorily outdoors under the shelter of a sunny wall, cultivation in the open is, generally speaking, even more of a gamble in this country than it is with tomatoes. The best place for the egg plant in summer is an unheated greenhouse; but it should do quite well plunged to the rim of the pot in ashes in a warm glass-sided frame raised on a brick plinth or set over a pit so as to afford a good 2½ ft of headroom. It can also be grown in the warmer parts of the country under large barn cloches provided that these are capable of being raised up as the plants grow.

Sowing must take place in a heated greenhouse, or heated propagating frame, in which it is possible to maintain soil and air temperatures around 60° F. by means of artificial heat until such time as the same temperatures can be maintained by sun heat. Sow in February or March for growing on in pots in either a greenhouse or a frame but, if for planting out under cloches, delay sowing until mid-April so that the young plants, after due hardening, can be set out 2 ft 6 ins. apart early in June when about six weeks old. Do not sow on a manure hotbed as the high humidity would not suit the seedlings: a dry atmosphere and sterilized soil are both essential for the prevention of damping off. Take great care not to allow the seedlings to become drawn or spindly, as they will then be worthless.

When the seedlings are 2 ins. tall, prick off singly into 3-ins. pots and, when these are beginning to fill with roots, shift the plants to the 6-ins. size. If they are to be fruited in pots, transfer finally to the 8½-ins. size using a compost of 3 parts loam to 1 part old mushroom bed manure, if obtainable. (If there is no manure to be had, substitute granulated peat and add a 5-in. potful of bonemeal to each bushel of the mixture.) Pinch out the growing point to induce bushiness when the plants are 6 ins. tall and give each one a 3-ft stake.

The egg plant, when in full growth, demands ample supplies of water at the root and liberal doses of liquid manure. But despite this thirstiness it thoroughly dislikes any excess of atmospheric moisture which, even if it does not lead to damping off, will most certainly cause sappy, elongated growth and poor cropping. Unfortunately, endeavours to keep the atmosphere on the dry side can encourage the red spider mite – this must be controlled by syringing the foliage, especially on the underside, with warm water during the morning and afternoon of every bright, warm day, and by spraying occasionally with derris or soft soap as well. (This applies even when the plants are grown under cloches.)

The period from seed-sowing to the commencement of fruiting is about 4½ months. Do not allow more than five aubergines to mature on each plant, otherwise they will all be too small to be of any real value for table use. Half a dozen plants are quite enough to satisfy the needs of an average family of four persons. Pick the fruit as soon as they are fully coloured and while they still bear a polished gloss.

It may be added that the egg plant is most ornamental when in fruit.

Broad Beans

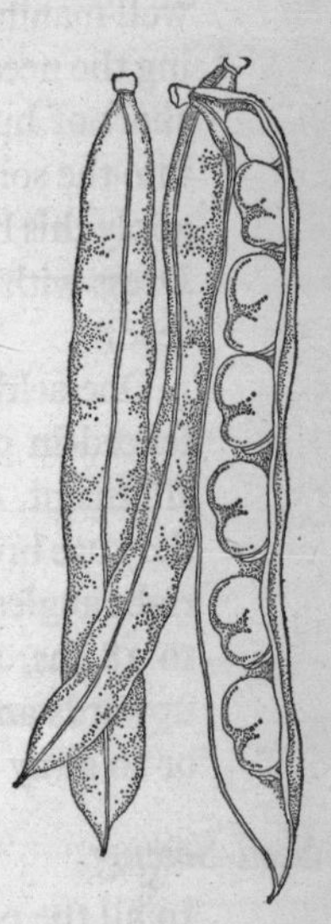

The broad bean (*Vicia faba*) is one of the oldest of cultivated vegetables. It is the bean of the ancients and of the Bible, the bean that makes horses 'full of beans', and the only bean commonly grown in England until about the beginning of the present century. It is still comparatively little grown in America where it is known as the fava, giant butter, or horse bean and is less esteemed than the tender lima bean which produces seeds similar to those of the broad bean.

When I was a child, I much disliked broad beans; but I think that the reason for this dislike was that in those days the choice of vegetables in summer was far more restricted than it is now and therefore the broad-bean season was extended for so long that a goodly proportion of the later pickings yielded seeds that were tough-skinned, mealy, and not very palatable. There can also be little doubt that the strains then grown were much inferior to those in cultivation today. Modern parents do not seem to be troubled by any general dislike of broad beans among their offspring and every gardener ought therefore to grow the crop if he has room for it. Unfortunately it does not give a big return for the land occupied: a 30-ft row will yield only 15 lb. of Windsors or 11–12 lb. of Longpod type (these weights include the pods); and you need at least 2½ lb. of unshelled beans to make a meal for four people.

Soil Preparation

The broad bean has a preference for fairly heavy land but it will do well on all soils except those which are badly drained, and become waterlogged in winter, and those which dry out in summer. It is always more satisfactory if you can arrange for the bean crop to follow a crop such as autumn cauliflowers for which the ground was well manured with animal manure or garden compost, thus avoiding the need for a further application of these materials. If the soil is short of humus, wool shoddy or coarse peat may be incorporated into the soil during any winter digging. If the soil is lacking in lime, apply this by itself in the form of carbonate of lime (½ lb. per sq. yd). Dress with superphosphate (2 oz. per sq. yd) just before sowing the seed.

One seldom gets a first-class crop of broad beans from a small, fenced-in garden: they do far better on an open site, such as an allotment. As a matter of interest I have heard that in New Zealand they use broad beans as a windbreak, setting three rows 2 ft apart at right angles to the prevailing wind and dwarfing the two outermost to 18 ins. and 24 ins. respectively, so that the wind is diverted upwards and considerable protection is given to crops up to 10 yds or so away on the leeward side of the beans.

Seed Sowing

In all the older and far too many of the current books and articles upon gardening you will find it recommended that broad beans should be sown in autumn. This advice originated long ago with the gardeners of large estates which were favourably situated for the purpose. It has been copied blindly by one writer after another; but it was never intended for general application. I have known such sowings fail in four years out of five either because the seed rotted in the ground or because the seedlings were killed by alternate freezing and thawing, excessive wet and searing winds. The total wastage of seed over the years must have been colossal. It is true that a seed dressing can now be employed to prevent rotting and that cloches can be used to protect the seedlings from the elements; but there is a snag about the use of cloches because, in our uncertain climate, if the winter turns out to be mild, the bean plants may be hitting the tops of the cloches by the middle of February. If you then remove the cloches, the chances are that a sudden icy spell will cut the plants to the ground. You can guard against this of course by raising the height of the cloches but, frankly, I consider this a shocking waste of cloches, adaptors, and extra glass at a season when cloches are in great demand for covering more important crops and seeing that the only advantages to be gained by sowing broad beans in autumn are that they come into pick about a fortnight earlier and that, since the growth is more advanced, it will offer a greater resistance to black fly.

My advice is therefore that, if you live in a district where the winters are normally mild and have a patch of well-drained land in a sheltered position on a south-facing slope and can get the soil prepared in time, then by all means sow a hardy variety early in November and take a chance with it. Again, if you live in one of the inhospitable regions of the north, you may sow under large barn cloches in November and growth is likely to be so slow that you will not have to uncover dangerously early in the year. In all other circumstances the sowing times should be (a) about mid-January in the south and mid-February in the north for sowing under cloches and (b) from mid-February to the end of March for unprotected outdoor sowings. (If the nature of your soil and local weather conditions ordinarily make it impossible to sow in the open ground before April, you can start the seeds in 5-ins.-deep boxes in a heated greenhouse in February or in a warm frame in March for planting out about mid-April.) Picking from the earliest sowings will begin in June and from the later ones in July. You can sow in April for gathering in August and at the beginning of June for a late crop in September.

The principle of sowing is the same in every case. Single seeds should be inserted 2 ins. deep and 8 ins. apart, this being the distance at which the plants will mature; a few extra seeds may be sown at the end of the row to provide plants to fill gaps, but usually every sound seed germinates. Sow a double row, i.e. two lines spaced 6 ins. apart counting as one row; if more than one such row is sown, a full 2½ ft should be left between them to prevent them from overshadowing one another. By placing the seeds in one line opposite the gaps between the seeds in the other line, you get an effective distance of 4 ins. between each two plants in the staggered row, making ninety plants to the row, which calls for ½ pint of seed. (There are about 200 seeds to the pint.) The best method of sowing consists in taking out a flat-bottomed drill 2 ins. deep, spacing out the seeds along each edge of the drill and then filling in again: but in light land where there is a tendency for the upper layers to dry out rapidly the drill can be made 6 ins. deep and the seeds are then covered to a depth of 3 ins., leaving a channel 3 ins. deep to receive water in dry weather. It is possible, and saves much time, to cut out drills entirely and simply place each seed in position with the aid of a blunt-ended dibber and a garden line; but this is a business that calls for a lot of skill and experience if you are to get your seeds in dead straight lines and all at exactly the same depth.

In gardens and on allotments where mice are a nuisance it will be necessary to set traps for them; they have been known to clear ¼ acre of land of bean seeds, which they placed in store, before a single one had had a chance to commence germinating.

Cultivation

Watch for the first appearance of the seedlings and dust promptly with derris dust to deter the bean weevil from eating semi-circles out of the leaves. Hoe regularly and remove all basal suckers so that each plant is confined to one stem. In the case of autumn sowings which are unprotected draw soil up the stems to a height of about 3 ins. before the worst of the winter sets in; and on light land which is exposed to strong winds support the plants with stakes and lines of string when they are 2 ft high – it is true that broad beans make an excellent windbreak but they are of little use for this purpose if they have themselves already been blown flat.

Cut off the tops of the plants as soon as four clusters of bloom are showing. This last operation, apart from encouraging the early development of the pods, is one step in the campaign against the black fly, which in some districts is called dolphin or collier or other names and is equally repulsive under any name. It can however be controlled quite easily by the use of modern insecticides and is no longer the menace that it used to be. It does not appear until early summer, and an attack can frequently be prevented altogether by spraying regularly with liquid derris during May: the odour of this fluid appears to repel the egg-laying females. If the fly actually appears on the plants, spray promptly with liquid derris before the attack has become severe; and repeat on successive days if necessary, until the plants are completely free from the pest.

Apart from the fly the only trouble likely to be experienced with broad beans is the appearance of tiny chocolate-coloured spots on the leaves, stems, and pods. These are signs of a disease which can cripple the plants and completely spoil the chance of a crop. It is most prevalent in areas where there is heavy rainfall accompanied by mild weather conditions in spring but it can also be due to frost damage. It can readily be checked in the early stages by spraying with Bordeaux Mixture and is seldom met with on well-drained soil which has been adequately manured.

Chocolate Spot must not be confused with ordinary rust on the leaves which may look unsightly but seldom causes any serious damage. I have heard it said that green-seeded varieties are less susceptible to rust than white-seeded varieties, but I have no definite proof of this.

Gathering

Gather broad beans when the pods are well filled but while the seeds are still soft. Test a specimen pod here and there by opening it to see if the crop is ready. Never let the pods hang until the eyes of the seeds go black as the seeds will by that time have lost their palatability.

Root out all plants as soon as the beans are gathered; if left they throw up suckers and exhaust the soil and the value of the secondary crop from these suckers in October is really negligible as compared with the shocking waste of land which could be put to so much better use in producing worthwhile winter or spring crops.

It may be added that broad beans cannot be grown in a greenhouse as an out-of-season crop because the flowers refuse to set under greenhouse conditions in winter. It is nevertheless possible to secure a small but very early crop of the dwarf varieties from a frame equipped with soil-warming by sowing in December or

January either direct into the soil of the frame at 6 ins. apart or by putting four or five seeds in each large pot and then plunging the pots to the rims. It is essential however not to coddle the plants: indeed the light should be removed as often as possible so that they may receive as much fresh air as is consistent with their making vigorous and unchecked growth.

French (or Kidney) Beans

These beans are in no way related to broad beans; they belong to the botanical species *Phaseolus vulgaris* and are tender annuals highly susceptible to even a single degree of frost. They appear to have originated in sub-tropical America and to have been first cultivated by the Peruvian Incas and later by the American Indians. Like so many plants which are natives of the New World they first reached this country by way of the Continent. At the outset, during the reign of Queen Elizabeth I, they were known as Russian beans and were assumed to have originated in that country, but later the name was changed to French beans because most of the imports of them came from France where, as in Holland, much work was done to improve the strains.

In those early days French beans were cultivated exclusively for their seeds which were eaten green as *flageolets* or dried as *haricots* – in each case we imported the French names with the beans but we also christened them 'kidney' beans from the shape of the seeds. (Actually some varieties have round seeds and may then be known as 'pea beans'.) It was not until the beginning of the present century that it became customary to eat the pods which are considered by gourmets to be of much more delicate flavour and finer texture than those of the runner bean. This view seems to be shared in the north where French beans are much more popular than they are in the south of England. In the U.S.A. these beans are known as 'snap' or 'shell' beans according to whether they are grown to provide pods or seeds.

Cultivation Outdoors

French beans will grow well in almost any soil except one that is very heavy and wet, provided that it is not acid and provided that it is warm enough. The seed needs a higher soil temperature to start it off than that of almost any other vegetable; on the other hand it needs comparatively little moisture during germination (and ought never to be soaked before sowing) and the plants will tolerate shade during part of the day and will endure drought in summer better than any other kitchen-garden crop. It ought not to be necessary to do any special manuring as the beans will do best on a site which was well manured for a previous crop (other than peas or beans) and it is a good plan to let them follow the brussels sprouts. However, in view of the importance of plenty of phosphate, a dressing of bone flour can do nothing but good; and sufficient lime should be applied to give a pH reading of between pH 7 and pH 8.

If the beans are to grow in a border backing on to a warm wall or fence, sow in a single row: but if they are to be grown on an open plot sow in a double row, i.e. in two lines 12 ins. apart. Leave at least 2 ft between any two double rows to allow ample room for picking. The minimum authorized percentage of germination for French beans is only 75 per cent, and it is wise to assume that not more than three out of every four seeds will come up. The correct method of sowing, therefore, is to draw drills 2 ins. deep and press in two seeds, scar downwards, side by side at intervals of 6 ins. for the early and late crops and 9 ins. for the main crop. If both seeds germinate, cut off one seedling at soil level with a sharp knife. It is most important that the surface soil shall have a fine tilth, free from caking and lumps, throughout the period of germination: otherwise there will be losses resulting from breakage and deformity as the seedlings push their way upwards and the rows will be gappy. Do not spill any seeds and leave them on the surface of the soil as this will advertise the fact that you have sown beans to the birds and they may soon locate the rows and unearth all the beans. If jackdaws are around it may be necessary to cover the sown rows with wire pea guards: otherwise they will steal all the seeds of which they are inordinately fond.

The size of French bean seeds varies considerably according to the variety and there may be anything from 86 to 180 seeds in 1 oz. On the basis of about 14½ oz. to the pint, assuming the seeds to be fairly large, you ought to be able to make a ¼-pint packet sow one 30-ft double row. The estimate of the amount of seed required which appears in most seedsmen's catalogues (usually 1 pint to 60 or 80 ft of row) would seem to be based on an assumption that the seeds will be sown continuously and fairly thickly along the row, the seedlings then being thinned to stations; but this is unnecessarily wasteful.

On no account should you follow the advice given in many text-books to sow single seeds 3 ins. apart and thin the seedlings to 6 ins.; such a practice is just silly because it will be obvious at the outset that every alternate plant, if the seed germinates, will have either to be destroyed or transplanted. If you are prepared to transplant to fill gaps, you should sow extra seeds at the end of the row specially for this purpose. But, although with care it is possible to transplant seedling beans successfully, it is not a practice that I recommend because the transplants never catch up with the others.

Under good cultivation a double row will give you up to 4 lb. of green beans per yard run from dwarf plants in successive pickings over a period of four to five weeks, while climbing plants should yield at the rate of at least 5 lb. per yard. When the plants are grown for their seeds, which may be eaten either as green flageolets (*haricots verts*) or as dried haricots, a good average yield would be 6 oz. of seeds per yard run. These figures should help you to decide how many plants to grow.

In view of the French bean's refusal to germinate in cold soil and its extreme vulnerability to even one degree of ground frost, it is useless to sow before the third week of April in the warmer parts of the south and before the beginning of May elsewhere unless you can protect the sowings with large barn cloches which afford sufficient headroom to allow the plants to remain covered until all danger of spring frosts has passed. (The latest frost date may be taken to be 15 May in Devon and Cornwall, 23 May in the rest of the south, and 8 June in all other parts of the country.) Sowing times under cloches are mid-March in the south, the end of March in the Midlands, and mid-April in the north. In the case of all these early sowings the seed should be treated with a seed-dressing as a safeguard against rotting in the ground. When local conditions make early outdoor sowings an impossibility, seeds may be started 3 ins. apart in boxes of turf soil or in cubes of turf or in soil blocks either in a greenhouse or in a warm frame and planted out, as weather permits, during May.

The main crop of French beans is sown during May in the warmer half of the country and during June in the colder half. If desired, successional sowings may be made at intervals of two to three weeks. A late sowing may be made early in July or, if cloches are available to finish off the crop, as late as 20 July. These dates apply to green beans only: if the plants are to be grown for their seeds, there is only one sowing during May and this should only be attempted in the warmer areas of the country, and in the case of haricots preferably those which have been found to be favourable for commercial seed growing.

Once the seedlings are up, provided that you protect them from slugs, they will more or less look after themselves and call for little attention except hoeing with the Dutch hoe to keep them weed-free and, during spells of drought, an occasional good watering followed by mulching. The climbing sorts will of course require support and this is best given by the same twiggy boughs as are used for peas. Although the climbing French bean will twine around a pole in the same way as a runner bean it takes much longer about it and seldom goes up beyond 5 ft; it will climb much more rapidly on pea boughs but, if these are not available, it will find its way up large-mesh string netting.

Dwarf sorts also require support, as a rule, otherwise they are apt to be blown over or knocked down by heavy rains and then the beans get muddy and unfit to eat. Moreover, if the plants lean so that the pods touch the soil, the slugs will have them. Short green-dyed split bamboo canes, secured to the stems by means of split rings or twist-its, will keep the plants vertical but the more usual practice is to earth them up to the lower leaves, this giving protection as well as support and showing up the beans to be picked.

In a bad season some strains of dwarf beans may throw out runners in an endeavour to climb; these runners should be promptly removed.

Cultivation under Glass

It is possible, subject to certain limitations, with the aid of frames and a heated greenhouse, to pick French beans at any time from October, when outdoor supplies usually come to an end, until mid-June when the earliest sowings under cloches come into bearing. Anybody who possesses good stout frames of brick, concrete, or timber and who lives in a warm district which gets plenty of winter sunshine can make the first sowing in late August and the last in early March since no artificial heat is required for either. It is merely necessary to make up a bed of fairly rich soil in the frame, 1 ft deep, and sow seeds in pairs to stations, as recommended for outdoor sowings, in rows 12 ins. apart. For the August sowing the stations can be 6 ins. apart, a 6 × 4 ft frame will take thirty-five plants (i.e. the equivalent of about 12 ft of double row), and cropping may be expected to take place in November; for the March sowing the stations should be 9 ins. apart (twenty-five plants to a light) and picking should commence before the beginning of June. It must be emphasized that success with French beans in cold frames is possible only in districts where natural sun heat in winter and early spring can be expected to assist in maintaining the temperature at about 55° F. It will be necessary to protect the frames on all chilly or cold nights and it is important that there shall be adequate headroom for the plants, although in the case of the spring sowing it is customary to remove the lights entirely about midday so that the crop may finish without any overhead protection. Watering needs careful management, since the plants must not suffer from dryness or chill: in the case of the spring-sown crop a thorough syringing should be given on all suitable occasions.

If you can obtain the requisite materials and possess the necessary skill to make up a really good fermenting hotbed capable of taking something like a 12 ft 6 ins. by 5 ft Dutch light frame and maintaining in it a heat very little below 70° F., then by all means plant it up either about mid-December or around 7 to 10 January with French bean seedlings raised in a heated greenhouse to provide pickings in February or March. A frame of the size stated will take sixty plants and the bed of soil need not be more than 6 or 7 ins. deep. Once again the crop is not worth trying for unless you get a fair amount of winter sunshine, as on the Sussex coast; heat is useless without adequate light. Ventilation must be given under all suitable circumstances but the lights must be covered with warm mats every night and the sides of the frame must be banked up with warm manure right to the top. The frame will have to be raised up on bricks as the plants grow and the bank of manure must be renewed and heightened at the same time. A catch crop of radishes can be taken while the beans are settling down after planting.

Forced Beans for Christmas Picking

These can only be considered a practicable proposition if you possess a first-class greenhouse with a highly efficient heating apparatus in a district with a good winter light-factor and if you yourself have a fairly high degree of skill and experience in greenhouse management. You must bear in mind that it is not natural for the plants to make growth during the period of shortening days which is really nature's resting season and that it must be reckoned something of a feat to be able to induce them to do so. The crop cannot be regarded as a cheap one to produce since it calls for a temperature of 60° F. throughout the night and 60° F. to 70° F. by day. In this case, 60° means 60°; if it falls to 55° F. by day the flowers will drop and the pods go yellow; if it rises above 65° F. at night, you will get all leaves and no pods.

If you decide to attempt this crop, it will follow conveniently after the house has been cleared of tomatoes and I advise sowing a dwarf variety about the second or third week in September. These early forced beans are best grown in large pots from 12 to 16 ins. in diameter, about 8 seeds being sown round the rim of the pot, 1 to 1½ ins. deep, and the resultant plants thinned to three or four, those retained being of course the most sturdy and the healthiest of the seedlings. The compost employed should consist mainly of loam to which should be added not more than a quarter of its bulk of leaf-mould and old rotted manure with sufficient sand to keep it open. It should include some bone flour in addition to a sprinkling of lime and should be just moist but not moist enough to 'ball' when squeezed at the time when the seed is sown. At the outset the pots are only half filled. More compost is added at intervals as a top-dressing, 2 ins. deep, until the pots are almost full, commencing when the plants are 8 ins. high and ending when they start to flower; but any roots which show on the surface at any time should be covered at once.

Stand the pots on ashes, shingle, or chippings and water freely once the plants appear above soil level. In no circumstances must water be given during the period of germination or the seeds may rot. Over-watering must be avoided at all stages of growth: the plants must never be dry at the root, but there must never be water in excess of their requirements. Maintain a fairly humid atmosphere by spraying the foliage overhead and damping the floor and staging; this also helps to keep away red spider. But exercise discretion: on a sunny November day you may have to spray and damp down twice, while on many dank days it would be folly to spray or damp at all – it is rather a case of drying the already saturated atmosphere.

Some support for the plants will be necessary: a few twigs of brushwood will serve, but I prefer to put three split bamboos in each pot with ties of raffia round to keep the plants from sprawling. In the darkest days there is a tendency for the plants to grow over-leafy and to throw out runners. Nip off the latter and, if the centre of the pot is becoming congested, take a few leaves away also.

Begin to feed when the first flowers form. Sootwater and liquid manure made from animal dung are best, but dried blood will do. Never use an artificial fertilizer, and use all stimulants very dilute on the 'little and often' principle. If any surplus of liquid manure is poured into zinc trays fixed over the heating pipes, so that ammonia is produced, the crop will benefit and the red spider will be discomfited.

As a rule cropping commences about ten weeks after sowing and will continue throughout December.

After-Christmas Sowings

These are much less difficult to manage than autumn sowings and when the greenhouse is of a type glazed to ground level and has really good borders I strongly recommend that a climbing variety of French bean be grown. The reason why I have not advised the sowing of the climbing sorts in autumn is that they then tend to lose their leaves through damping off if there is any excess of humidity in the house. This difficulty usually ceases with the turn of the year when a high degree of humidity is essential subject to a slightly drier atmosphere being maintained while the flowers are setting. The regular syringing, spraying, and damping down with aired water, which the cultivation of these beans involves, will be welcomed by early cucumbers which can therefore share the house with the beans if this is otherwise convenient; but it would be unwise to plant a French bean crop which would have to carry on alongside the earliest tomatoes because the humidity favoured by the former might prove altogether too much for the latter.

Seed can be sown in 3-ins. pots of John Innes Seed Compost or in soil blocks about mid-January in districts where light is usually good during the early months of the year; in less favoured areas it would be a mistake to sow before the middle of February. Remembering the rule about 'no watering during germination' it is a good plan to cover the pots with moist hessian (which should be damped daily) until top growth appears.

Assuming that the borders have been well manured for previous crops, it is better not to manure for the beans but to wait until cropping starts and then apply dried blood at the rate of 1 oz. per sq. yd in solution. A too rich soil tends to produce excessively leafy plants which drop their flowers. It should be understood that the forcing of French beans and other vegetables is not in harmony with more natural, hardier ways of growing food crops. With dwarf beans, for example, dull weather leads to bud-dropping if plants are in a greenhouse. Should this occur, substitute nitrate of potash for the dried-blood solution.

The seedlings are ready for setting out when they have made their first true leaves and should go 9 ins. apart in a double row consisting of two rows 12 ins. apart. But it is useless to plant unless the temperature of the soil is at least 55° F. If the greenhouse has been well heated throughout the winter, it may be assumed that the borders are warm enough but, if this is not the case, the most economical way of bringing them up to the required temperature will be by means of electrical soil-warming. The air temperature must be kept between 60° F. and 70° F. and repeated overhead damping will be needed to maintain atmospheric humidity. Watering calls for the same care as before. Too much may prevent the flowers from setting; too little will check the growth of the plants. It will be fatal if insufficient moisture allows the red spider mite to establish itself on the plants.

Provide strings up which the plants can climb, stretching them from wires running under the roof to a second set of wires running about 4 ins. above soil level. Do not leave the lower ends of the strings free and twist them round the bean plants as you do in the case of tomatoes, because the growth of the bean is much too brittle to withstand the strain and in any case it climbs best up a string that it taut. It is quite in order to allow each two plants to climb one and the same string – they will sort themselves out when they reach the top.

Gathering

French beans are in prime condition when the pods snap cleanly between the fingers. Unless they are to be eaten as flageolets, you must gather before the seeds begin to swell in the pods and give them a bulging appearance – and do this whether you want the beans or not. The swelling of a few seeds in neglected pods will cause the plants to cease bearing. The plants should be gone over carefully three times a week.

If the beans are to be eaten shelled as flageolets, the pods must be gathered semi-ripe in a state intermediate between the green pod (*haricot vert*) stage and the ripe seed stage (*haricot sec*): at this stage the seeds will be found not to have developed their final colour.

Exhibitors of French beans often gather them with as long a stalk as possible up to ten days before the day of the show and stand them on end with their stalks in about ½ in. of water in a cool, dark cellar. Every day this water is changed and twice a week a little piece is nipped off each stalk. Then two days before show day the beans are laid out flat on a level surface, covered with brown paper and a piece of moist flannel, and straightened by placing a piece of board or other suitable material on top to provide a minimum of essential pressure.

Harvesting for Use as Haricots

The pods are left on the plants until they are ripe and have begun to turn yellow. As they will not all be ready at once, some skill is necessary to enable you to judge the best moment. You get a bigger yield if you pick each individual pod as it ripens, thus encouraging the plants to continue bearing and to develop more pods. But this is hardly practicable if you have more than a hundred plants. If the weather turns wet or cold, pull the plants up while they are dry, tie them in small bundles, and hang them up in a cold greenhouse or anywhere under cover where a good current of air can reach them and they will receive any sun that there is. It is sometimes possible to dry them successfully under cloches. When the pods are quite brittle, shell out the bean seeds and spread them on clean paper to complete their drying either on a greenhouse staging or on the floor of a sunny room. Hand-shelling is a tedious business and, if the quantity of beans is very large, it may be better to remove the biggest haulms and lay the rest out on a clean sheet on the floor where they can be threshed with an old-fashioned wicker carpet beater, the chaff being afterwards blown away with the aid of a pair of bellows. The resultant haricots should be rock-hard.

If the atmosphere is at all damp, as is often the case in autumn, it may be wise to give the seeds a final drying by leaving them overnight either in a cooling oven or in front of a dying fire, but do not allow them to become really hot. Then store, preferably in screw-topped glass jars or alternatively in tins with tight-fitting lids or in stout paper bags tied tightly round the neck – but in the latter case the place of storage must be absolutely dry or the beans may go mildewed and will certainly taste musty.

Runner Beans

The runner bean, *Phaseolus multiflorus*, is in a sense the perennial counterpart of the kidney bean, which is an annual. It forms tuberous roots on the same lines as a dahlia and, if these roots are lifted and stored in the same way as dahlia tubers before they can be frosted, they can be replanted the following May. No useful purpose is served, however, by this practice under normal conditions because better and more certain crops can be secured by annual sowing.

Although introduced into England in 1633, the runner bean was treated solely as an ornamental climber until some time in the eighteenth century when it was discovered that the pods were edible; and certainly the plants are decorative enough with their scarlet, white, or bicoloured flowers and their green pods. As compared with the kidney bean the runner will climb to a greater height, has larger leaves, and produces many more flowers which in due course turn to longer and much coarser pods. Despite this coarseness, which leads all epicures to prefer the French bean, the British public, at any rate in the southern half of England, will not touch French beans so long as runners are available. From the gardener's point of view runners are attractive because they give an immensely heavy crop, in the region of 10 lb. per yard run, over a very long period which is terminated only by the onset of the frosts of autumn: and of course the fact that extremely long pods can be grown makes them dear to the hearts of exhibitors.

It is possible to grow white-flowering, white-seeded runners for their seeds, which are dried as haricots.

Soil and Situation

Runners succeed on any average soil that is well supplied with moisture; provided that the upper layers are well drained, the higher the water table the better. But it is really not worth while growing them on heavy clay which is generally much too cold at sowing time or on light shallow land which usually dries out in summer. The crop is not suitable for windswept sites or low-lying frost-pockets. Acid soil results in poor yields and the pH should be between 6·0 and 7·0. In most gardens and allotments the runner bean has to be relegated to the end of the plot because of its height and must occupy the same site annually. Careful and thorough preparation of the ground is therefore of the greatest importance. It is essential that there should be an adequate supply of organic matter in the soil and there is no better way of ensuring this than by incorporating every winter as much well rotted material from the compost heap as can possibly be spared.

Manuring

Too much nitrogen is often a cause of bean flowers failing to set. It is best avoided by feeding the soil with garden compost rather than manures or fertilizers known to have a higher nitrogen content. If necessary 1½ oz. superphosphate and ½ oz. sulphate of potash per sq. yd should be applied at the time the ground is prepared in March. If a soil test shows that your soil is short of lime, up to 4 oz. ground chalk (calcium carbonate) per sq. yd may be applied. But be careful not to over-lime.

Sowing

The normal time for sowing in the southern half of England is between 4 and 15 May according to the nature of the season but in specially warm areas it is possible to sow during the last week in April. Since the plants are very tender and extremely susceptible to frost, it is not worth while attempting the crop in Scotland and the colder districts of the north of England unless initial glass protection is available. This can take the form of continuous cloches, or seedlings may be raised in squares of turf in boxes in a greenhouse or frame for subsequent hardening off and planting out when the first pair of rough leaves has formed. Runner and other beans may be raised in pots, too; because there is no disturbance to the rooting system at planting out time, peat pots are admirable – though make quite sure that all dry parts of the pot are removed at planting out time. In either case the earliest sowing date will be somewhere about the end of April or early in May. When a specially early crop is desired in the south seed may be sown under cloches about mid-April, while in the south-west it is sometimes possible to sow as early as mid-March. Everything depends on when the last spring frost usually occurs as the plants must be adequately protected until this danger period is over.

Runner bean seeds differ in size according to the variety but are always much larger than those of French beans – the average is about 80 seeds per ¼ pint. The minimum percentage of germination authorized by the E.E.C. regulations is 80 per cent. Germination of runner seeds is usually higher, however, but it is wise to sow a few extra seeds at one end of the row. You will then have a few seedlings with which to fill any gaps in the row caused by poor germination or by pest damage to the germinating seedlings. Runner seeds ought not to be soaked in water before sowing as this encourages the development of the disease known as Halo Blight.

It is standard practice to sow seeds 9 to 12 ins. apart in a double row consisting of two lines spaced 9 to 18 ins. apart, the seeds in one line being placed directly opposite those in the other line. This assumes, however, that the plants are to be trained up poles in the orthodox manner; if unorthodox training methods are adopted, it may be necessary to alter the spacing of the seed. Each drill should be V-shaped and 2 ins. deep. Sow the seeds 1 in. deep in the bottom of the drill and, immediately germination has taken place, fill in the drill so as to protect the young seedlings from possible frost damage. If by misfortune they do get frosted, the only satisfactory course is to scrap the sowing and, if not too late, sow all over again; frosted runner beans never grow away properly.

In order to escape the glut which is apt to occur at the peak of the season, it has been suggested that the seed in each row should be sown in successional batches. Nevertheless I feel compelled to point out that there would be no gluts if only amateurs would limit their sowings in accordance with their estimated household requirements. Many of them sow far too long a row and, since they are bound to pick regularly to keep the plants in bearing, find themselves with periodical surpluses. If you have a freezer, these come in very handy for the winter. For gardeners without a freezer, there are always kind neighbours and retired folk who welcome home-grown produce.

Few private gardeners have occasion to grow more than one double row of runners; but, if you do have occasion to do so, the rows must be spaced a good 5 ft apart.

Training

If you are an American gardener do not confuse the English runner bean with your own Pole beans. Pole beans are a climbing variety of French bean and, of course, you have Pole limas, too. But in Britain poles were the traditional way of providing supports for runner plants to climb. Bean poles are straight, bare, 8-ft sticks, about 2 ins. thick at the butt end and entirely free from the twiggy brush-wood which is characteristic of pea boughs. If you are a country-man you may be able to cut your own bean poles from a local copse. Nowadays 8 ft bamboo canes are frequently used instead. There are many ways of erecting the poles or sticks but the orthodox (and still the best) method in the average kitchen garden consists in inserting one pole against each bean and tilting the poles in each line so that they cross those in the other line to form a V-shaped trough at the top, about 2 ft deep. A third line of poles is then laid horizontally in the trough and lashed to the other two at the points of intersection. Lateral stability is assured by straining wires from the endmost poles to pegs driven into the ground, in much the same way as a tent is secured by guy ropes. Alternatively, it is sometimes possible to secure the end poles to conveniently situated trees or permanent clothes posts. In any case absolute rigidity is of the greatest importance, not merely because of the risk of the whole affair collapsing in a high wind. All poles should be inserted into the ground to a depth of 9 to 12 ins.

There are other methods of erecting and securing bean poles and sticks, either singly or in groups of three or four, as well as many ways in which runners can be trained up strings or string netting supported on a framework of posts and wire. The two main advantages of these latter methods are, firstly, that some of them facilitate the growing of runners in small gardens where space is limited and, secondly, that the work of erection is less strenuous than in the case of poles, which may commend 'stringing' to weak sisters. Having regard to the present high cost of timber for frameworks, however, I am not impressed by the claim that stringing is a cheaper method of providing support; and I would emphasize that any method by which the vines are induced to climb at a slope is superior to one in which they are trained vertically because it allows the pods to hang clear of the leaves and makes picking much easier. Another objection to stringing is that in very high winds the string may break and then you are landed with a simply appalling tangle. This objection also applies where nylon bean netting is used. Sometimes advertisements for runner bean kits appear in the gardening press. The suppliers' instructions should be followed carefully so that the metal supports are well anchored into the ground.

It is often advised that runners should be dwarfed and grown without poles by pinching out the growing points at the first joint or when the plants are a foot high by nipping off the tips of the resultant trailers at the first or second joint once a week so that the plants grow into something like bushes and can be grown in rows only 3 ft apart. There is little to be said in favour of this practice which is sometimes adopted commercially partly because of the greater area required for poled beans and the labour and cost of erecting the poles and partly because the beans come into pick earlier and thus fetch a higher price on the market. These considerations do not apply to the ordinary gardener. Nature intended runner beans to climb, and if they are maltreated by pinching the yield will be less because the crop cannot be kept in bearing right up to the end of the season and the beans themselves will be liable to be short, curved, and twisted and a perfect nuisance to the cook, besides being in many cases dirty from contact with the soil or partially eaten by slugs. There are, of course, the two bush forms of 'runner beans' which form plants about 16 ins. high and bear pods 8–9 ins. long. These should be cultivated as dwarf French beans. But going back to the more popular climbing sorts of runner bean, even though you have none of the usual supports, why not let the plants climb the garden fence? Many ugly wire mesh dividing fences can be converted into 'living walls' of runner bean plants in summer. One enthusiast is said to have let his runners climb up the stems of tall annual sunflowers – I suppose that the stems of Jerusalem artichokes would do equally well!

Mention might be made of a system of combining pinched beans with poled beans which has been evolved by market gardeners under cloches. Two rows of cloches are set side by side with two lines of beans sown under each. The outermost rows are pinched and the inner rows are trained up poles or strings. This method is rather untidy and the job of disentangling the two sets of plants at decloching time is a bit of a nightmare. But you do get a big return, the pinched plants being scrapped as soon as the others begin to come into full bearing.

Routine Cultivation

When the plants are to be grown up poles or string they require to be directed at the outset to their individual supports, otherwise they are liable to wander around rather aimlessly until you get half a dozen of them all rushing up the same pole. Twisting the shoots round the poles seldom does the trick, especially if you try to make them twist in the opposite direction to that intended by nature. The best thing is to loop each shoot to its allotted support with a loosely tied string, although sometimes it is sufficient to steer it to its destination with the aid of a few bits of stick. The general rule is one plant one pole, stick, or string; but some growers allow two (or even four) plants to climb the same support. Once started on their way up, they need no further attention until they reach the tops of the supports when you must pinch off the growing points. Don't let them grow on any further so that they wave about wildly in the air, as this will merely diminish the crop. And don't use such tall supports that you cannot easily reach all the beans at picking time. 'Stopping' leads to the production of more lateral growth lower down. Incidentally, a similar result can be achieved by changing the angle at which the vines climb and thus impeding the flow of sap to the higher levels.

When started under cloches, which must not be removed until all danger of frost has passed, runners are usually in full flower and right up to the roof glasses when decloching time arrives. They will then in all probability have twined round the handles of the cloches and you will find it almost impossible to get the latter off without breaking off the points of the plants also. I myself find this most exasperating but actually it does no harm as the plants will promptly send out a side-shoot which will become the new climbing leader. Some experts actually stop their plants deliberately on these lines because they think that a better crop results.

Pinched beans are another matter entirely. Unless the necessary stopping is carried out each week with unfailing regularity, the plants sprawl and the yield is reduced. Even though less pinching is required after flowering commences, I consider the amount of attention demanded by pinched beans to be a tedious waste of the gardener's time.

Apart from training, the principal requirements of runner beans are warmth and moisture. A warm summer with plenty of fairly heavy showers at intervals is to their liking and will save you a great deal of labour. A cold summer is just the reverse and there is nothing that you can do about it. Unless you have a sprinkler system, a hot dry summer involves you in plenty of work with the hose and watering can if you are to secure a good crop. During spells of drought the rows must be given a thorough soaking at least twice a week, the quantity of water applied being sufficient to reach right down to the lowest roots. Mere surface sprinklings do nothing but harm, since they encourage the feeding roots to come to the surface where they are killed by hot sun and drying air. Just as important as watering is mulching which checks the rate at which water is lost from the soil. Although many people use lawn mowings to a depth of not more than 2 ins., the best of all materials for mulching is bark fibre which allows water and liquid feeds to run through it. This should be applied in June.

Liquid feeding should occasionally take the place of ordinary watering as soon as the plants have begun to flower freely. You cannot do better than use soot water alternatively with a very dilute liquid manure feed made by soaking a bag of animal dung in a tank of water applied as a very weak solution. Non-flowering may be due to excess nitrogen which may be counteracted by dressing with sulphate of potash ($\frac{1}{2}$ oz. per yd) immediately after watering. Failure to set is almost invariably due to dry atmospheric conditions or in other words dry weather. If you have a hose and a young child, it will pay you to pay him to give the bean rows a mist-like spray both under and over the foliage every fine morning and evening. This may help fertilization and will certainly discourage attacks by red spider mite. But nothing is really effective in a severe heatwave because what happens then is that the flowers droop and close up so that neither insects nor moisture can penetrate them.

Use liquid derris to control black fly if this pest should move over to the crop from the broad beans.

Runner Beans for Exhibition

There is no purpose in growing beans of immense length unless you wish to exhibit them. It is true that, since all runners are sliced up before cooking, it makes little difference to the cook how long the pods are provided that they are fairly straight. But, on the principle that you cannot have your cake and eat it, you cannot produce beans of first-class exhibition quality without at the same time sacrificing much of the total weight of crop which you would otherwise have obtained.

Except that many exhibitors like to allow their runners more space than usual – up to 2 ft between the two lines in the double row and 18 ins. between the plants – no special treatment is called for until the bines have been stopped two leaves above the last flower truss on reaching the tops of their supports. It is then necessary to stop all laterals at two leaves above a flower truss. About a fortnight before the show date, look over the plants carefully and mark the most promising and straight pods with a strand of raffia. Thin the trusses to two or three pods and tie in lightly to support the weight of the beans and prevent the truss from snapping off. At all times keep the other beans well picked, allowing no stringy or poddy specimens to remain on the bines and steal nourishment from the others. Experts have a knack of running their fingers down the pods and applying slight pressure where the seeds are forming, the idea being both to stretch the pods and at the same time render them free from any trace of 'beaniness'.

The longest beans are not necessarily the most prizeworthy, as length depends to some extent on the variety. You should aim to secure pods at least 15 to 20 ins. long and 1 in. wide; but they must also be young, fresh, brittle, of a rich dark green colour, and displaying no evidence of swelling seeds. A dish of runner beans is usually regarded as consisting of twenty-four beans and these ought to be as nearly alike as possible. Therefore you must cut your beans with scissors, leaving an inch of stem, as soon as they attain the size you want and while they are still in prime condition. This cutting may commence several days before the show and the beans can be kept until wanted stalk downwards in a jam jar containing ½ in. of water which is changed daily. Any final straightening can be done by wrapping in a damp rag as in the case of the dwarf beans.

Some leading exhibitors grow their runners only from home-saved seed and have their own selected strain, special plants being reserved for seed production and used for no other purpose. This, however, is not a course I would recommend to the ordinary amateur because only experts can distinguish the signs of the two dreaded seed-borne diseases, Anthracnose (*Colletotrichum lindemuthianum*) and Halo Blight (*Pseudomonas phaseolicola*), which can quickly put paid to any prize-winning hopes.

Picking the Crop

It is essential to look over the plants every fourth or fifth day throughout the season and pick off every young and succulent pod whilst the developing seeds are still small and juicy. This must be done whether or not the beans are wanted in the kitchen. At the same time every slug-damaged, muddied, distorted, or badly curled pod should be removed and destroyed. If even a handful of pods is allowed to remain to become old, stringy, and seedy, the further production of beans will cease. For this reason it is most important to search thoroughly since it is so easy to overlook a few pods that are well hidden among a mass of dense leafiness. In hot weather pick either early in the morning or in the cool of the evening, and, if you cannot use them immediately, store the beans in a cool larder away from sun and drying winds for not more than a couple of days, after which period they will deteriorate rapidly. The beans will store even better in a fridge but do not forget that you are growing your own beans for that special freshness and quality which only a home-grown product has. So do not make it a practice to store harvested beans. Share any surpluses and pick and enjoy more freshly-picked runners within a few days.

Beet, Seakale (or Silver)

See Swiss Chard

Beet, Spinach

See Spinach, Perpetual

Beetroot

Beetroot (*Beta vulgaris*), which comes from Northern Africa and Western Asia, was used as a food plant at least 2,000 years ago. It has naturally fleshy roots and must not be confused with our native

Beta maritima which has a very poor root system and yields only leaves to be eaten like spinach. The growing of beetroot in this country seems to date back to 1546 but modern strains owe their origin to the selections made by the famous French seed-grower, M. Vilmorin, during the first half of the nineteenth century. The principal aim of modern selection is to produce a shapely root free from 'rings' so that, when cut, it is an even red throughout.

Soil Preparation and Manuring

Long beet will grow satisfactorily only in really deep, sandy loams such as is seldom to be found in private gardens; and I see no reason why any amateur should want to grow it unless he is a keen exhibitor, in which case he should grow his beetroots in holes bored with a crowbar and filled with John Innes Potting Compost. From the culinary aspect the big drawback of long beet is that few households possess utensils large enough to accommodate it for boiling purposes and baking takes too long and uses up far too much gas or electricity. Globe and tankard beetroots on the other hand can be cooked in most of the pots you find in an average small kitchen and in many types of pressure cooker. They can be grown on almost any land which does not dry out completely in summer and is not so clayey and badly drained that it is unworkable for long periods and incapable of being reduced to a fine tilth. Nevertheless in the case of a heavy soil it always pays, before sowing a beet crop, to do everything practicable to lighten it, especially by the incorporation of old mortar rubble and wood ashes from the bonfire.

Preferably beet should follow peas or celery or some other crop for which the ground was deeply dug and well manured in the previous season. Do not manure specially for the beet but, if the soil is shallow, stony, or lacking in humus, dig it in winter a full spade's depth, sieve out all stones from the upper layers, and then mix into the top 6 ins. plenty of well-decomposed garden compost. In other cases it will be sufficient to incorporate hoof and horn meal (1 lb. per sq. yd) during the winter digging. A general fertilizer should be added in March prior to sowing.

Beet will not tolerate acid soil and no plant indicates more readily when a soil is deficient in lime, so make a point of giving any necessary dressing before the crop is sown.

Sowing

Although beet is strictly a hardy biennial, many of the cultivated sorts can be badly checked by frost when they are in the seedling stage and are then very likely to bolt in the first season, even if they continue to grow. For this reason it is generally unwise to sow before the middle of April, although with cloche protection it is often possible to sow from the beginning of March onwards according to district and season. This applies to beet for salads which ought to be sown in small batches successionally about once a month until the beginning of July to ensure a regular supply of young roots. Beet for storage ought not to be sown until June, otherwise it may grow too large and coarse.

Although it is the practice to squeeze in three rows under cloches, wider spacing – about 12 ins. between rows – is desirable when sowing in the open ground as it makes it easier to keep the crop weed-free. Drills should be 1 in. deep. Each 'seed' of beet is actually a capsule containing several seeds; it is therefore wasteful to sow continuously along the row. You need only plant two or three capsules at intervals of 4 ins., if for salad purposes, or 6 ins., if for storage, and thin to one plant at each station.

Cultural Attentions

The seedlings of beet are particularly liable to be attacked by birds and must therefore be protected from them. The rows must be kept weeded and, if a hoe is used for this purpose, great care is necessary to avoid damage to both the foliage and the swelling roots. No feeding is necessary but, since beet grows naturally near the sea coast, it not only tolerates but appears to appreciate a dressing of agricultural salt (1 oz. per yard run) which should be hoed in during June or July. Apart from this the most important thing is to see that the crop does not lack water during July and August because dry soil has an adverse effect upon the eating quality of beetroot.

It is occasionally necessary to take measures against black fly or leaf-mining maggots but generally beet is free from the attentions of insect pests. As a rule it is also free from disease attack provided that the seed is purchased from a reputable source. Beet is, however, abnormally sensitive to any shortage of trace elements in the soil and, if you find that the heart leaves become dead and black and that the roots become cankered on the outside and full of black spots on the inside, the crop is suffering from Heart Rot. This indicates a deficiency of boron in the soil and is most likely to occur on light land in a dry season. An attack can be alleviated by watering over the plants at the rate of 1 quart per sq. yd a solution of 1 oz. of borax in 5 gallons of water.

Heart Rot is likely if the garden soil has been over-limed. If this happens, do not apply lime but put on heavy dressings of garden compost containing a large proportion of waste products not derived from your own garden. In addition to any local wastes, you may be able to obtain a load of leafmould or several loads of autumn leaves for rotting down, seaweed or treated sewage sludge. Municipal composts sold by some local authorities contain boron and all other trace elements so necessary for the good plant growth. Straight fish fertilizers – unless 'laced' with factory-produced chemicals – are also recommended as good sources of trace elements.

If the leaves of globe beet become abnormally red with numerous small, pale red, irregular areas between the veins which later become brown and dead, this is a form of Speckled Yellows caused by deficiency of manganese. It is most likely to occur on chalky or over-limed soil but, if detected in the early stages, it can be cured within a fortnight by watering the plants overhead with a solution of 2 oz. manganese sulphate (or chloride) in 5 gallons of water with the addition of a spreader at the rate of 1 gallon of solution to every 6 sq. yds of land. Both Heart Rot and Speckled Yellows are, as has been explained, diseases due to deficiences of trace elements. You should prevent such deficiences from occurring by building up and maintaining the fertility of the garden soil by regular applications of garden compost prepared from many varied wastes. These wastes will include such oddments as the peelings and other inedible portions of bought vegetables, orange and grapefruit peel, egg shells, discarded cotton and woollen clothing, and the daily newspaper.

Because these waste products come from different parts of the world the wastes contain various trace elements as well as the more well-known plant foods – nitrogen, phosphorous, and potassium.

Misshapen, forked, or fanged roots are due to growing beet on unsuitable land or in soil that has been too recently manured. Split roots are caused by irregularities in watering, usually by giving a lot of water after the ground has been dry for some time.

Forced Beet

Fresh young beet is frequently appreciated in late spring and early summer, even though mature roots may still be available from storage. It is quite easy to force an early crop if you have a mild hotbed available in a warm, well-constructed frame, facing south. Sow in February or March, placing two seeds ½ in. deep and 4 to 6 ins. apart in rows 8 to 9 ins. apart, and thinning the seedlings of course to one at each station. No great warmth is required; air should be given on every suitable occasion. Any globe variety is suitable for this crop.

Beet for Exhibition

Very large roots will not win prizes: these go to the roots of medium size which are of perfect shape, free from blemish, uniformly dark in colour, and tender and sweet. Globe beet should be the size of a cricket ball with a smooth, symmetrical outline and a tap root that is clearly defined as a single unit. Long beet can be as long as is consistent with lack of coarseness but must taper perfectly from the shoulder to a single tap root. Except that long beetroots are best grown in holes bored with a crowbar 1 ft apart and filled with John Innes Potting Compost, no special treatment is needed to grow beetroot to a prize-winning standard. But it is useless to enter roots which are fanged or have corky crowns or gall marks or which have been nicked by the hoe or nibbled by slugs or other pests. What is more, the skin must be free from roughness and the flesh must be as dark as possible and free from rings – the judges will cut one of yours in half for inspection so you will do well to anticipate them and do the same yourself with a spare root, noting if it is free from rings and tasting a bit raw, when it should be tender and of sweet, true flavour. Wash your selected roots very carefully with a clean, soft rag – don't use a brush; trim off any tiny rootlets but do not interfere with the tap root. Unless the show schedule specifically lays down that the leaves are to be left on, all leaves must be removed from beet before it is exhibited, leaving not more than 3 ins. of leaf-stalk. Some exhibitors on the day before the show soak their beetroots for fifteen minutes in a solution of table salt (1 oz. to a gallon of water) in the hope that this will deepen the colour. It should be noted that beetroot does not count as a salading but as a salad vegetable, i.e. a vegetable commonly eaten in salads in the cooked state.

SUGAR BEET

It is quite practicable to grow sugar beet in an ordinary garden, its high sugar content making it an excellent vegetable for children. From this point of view it is a profitable crop because the roots are much larger than those of common beet; incidentally they are white, not red. The roots are so large that they take a great deal of boiling and are better baked wrapped in greased paper in a hot oven for about an hour. Sugar beet also makes a delicious soup.

Pulling Salad Beet

The first pulling of globe beetroot for use as a salad vegetable, which is what is known to the greengrocer as 'bunched beetroot', should be made when the roots are 1½ ins. in diameter. This pulling takes the place of thinning. The remaining roots are then allowed to develop until they are between 2 and 3 ins. in diameter but they must of course be pulled whilst they are still young and tender and before the crown goes hard, crinkled, and leathery. Pulling is best done during dry weather, and the leaves should be removed by twisting them off by hand, not cutting them off. Some people dispute the need for this practice and I do not deny that it is feasible to cut off the tops with a knife. The object, however, is to avoid bleeding or loss of sap from the root: if a beetroot is allowed to bleed badly, all the goodness and colour will run out of it. If you care to strip off the leaves of a beetroot one by one you will find that the curvature of the root is continued to the extreme tip of the crown. This tip is the most vulnerable part of the root from the point of view of bleeding and it is most difficult to avoid slicing it off when you are cutting off the leaves as low down as you dare because appearances are deceptive. Hence all the old hands in gardening still prefer to play for safety and screw the leaves off about 2 ins. above the top of the root; very little sap is lost through the broken-off leaf-stalks.

Harvesting Maincrop Beet

If it was sown at the proper time and has been well cultivated, maincrop beet for winter use is generally ready to lift some time between the end of September and the beginning of November; but it is often left in the ground far too long and ought to be lifted as soon as it has attained its full size, even if this should mean lifting during August. The signs of maturity are a general falling away from the upright position on the part of the outer leaves and a certain loss of freshness in the foliage which indicates that active growth has ceased. Although it is possible in some districts to leave beet in the ground during the winter it is not immune from frost damage and ought always therefore to be lifted before severe frost occurs and at the very latest immediately after the first touch of autumn frost has been experienced.

Lift the roots when the soil is fairly dry by thrusting a fork in vertically about 6 ins. from the row and then levering backwards until they can be pulled out by the left hand gripping the leaves fairly close to the crown, taking great care to avoid any breaking or bruising. Twist the tops off and shake the soil from the roots, being careful not to expose them to sun or a drying wind. It does no great harm to shorten the long fang-like roots of the long varieties of beet, if these have been grown, for at that end of the root any slight bleeding that may occur will not affect more than ½ in. next to the cut part. It may also be remarked that, if it is essential to cut these long beetroots in order to boil them, bleeding can be avoided by first bringing the water in the pot to the boil and then, whilst it is boiling rapidly, holding the beet over the pot and cutting it into two or three pieces so that each piece falls into the boiling water and has its cells instantly sealed.

It should hardly be necessary to add that you must not remove the skin from a beetroot until *after* it has been boiled.

Storing Beetroot

It is quite practicable to store beetroot in a circular, conical clamp outdoors on the same lines as potatoes. This clamp must be in a convenient corner which is not a frost-pocket and where rainwater does not collect; it must also be away from the drip of overhanging trees. The base can consist of a 1-in. layer of sifted ashes or of a layer of clean, dry straw, 3 to 6 ins. thick, in a 6-ins.-deep depression. Arrange the roots, clock-face fashion, in circles of diminishing diameter, crowns to the outside, tap-roots to the centre; some people cover each layer with sifted ashes as they go. Broken, bruised, scratched, and pest-damaged roots must not be stored as they may decay and infect the rest. Cover the heap with a 4-ins. layer of straw and a week later with a 4-ins. layer of moist, sifted soil, after inserting a tuft of straw at the top for ventilation. Many readers are, however, unlikely to have enough beetroots to warrant the trouble of making a clamp and they should store what they have under cover in sifted ashes, sifted dry soil, sand, or peat in any frost- and damp-proof place, preferably in deep boxes where the roots can stand upright or be laid flat top to tail, sandwich-fashion, each layer of roots alternating with a layer of storage material. Dry and cool conditions are essential for the storage of beet. If it gets damp mildew will set in, while if it gets too warm it will start to grow.

Borecole

See Kale

Brassicas

The term 'brassica' in its strict botanical sense covers not only the cabbage and its related green crops but also such vegetables as horseradish, kohl-rabi, radishes, rape, seakale, turnips, and watercress. In ordinary horticultural parlance, however, when we speak of brassicas, we refer only to those green vegetables which are popularly regarded as members of the cabbage family and are cultivated either for their green leaves or for their succulent immature flower heads; these are broccoli, brussels sprouts, cabbages, cauliflowers, and kale. All of them have sprung from a common wild ancestor and have developed along individual lines without the aid or intervention of man. Nature alone has produced all the widely diversified types we know today and scientists have merely worked to improve them from the point of view of their consumption as food by human beings.

Some scholars hold that the family name of 'brassica' comes from the Latin *praeseco*, meaning that you cut the top off to eat it. I prefer to take the view that the Romans borrowed the name from the Celts of Ireland, northern Scotland, and Wales who called a cabbage a *bresic*. For the cabbage was essentially the food of the European races living north of the Mediterranean who later on christened it cole or kale, a name which is still in common use and seems to be allied to the Latin *caulis*, a stalk – and the earliest cabbages were probably more stalk than anything else. Generations ago the Scots still ate custocks, the pithy stalks of kale, and for all I know some of them may still do so today.

Now the procedure for raising young plants is more or less the same whatever type of brassica is being grown and in order to avoid a lot of needless repetition I shall deal with it fully under the present heading so that, when we come to the individual vegetables, apart from giving sowing dates, I can start off from the planting out stage. I shall do the same as regards those pests and diseases which are common to all members of the cabbage tribe.

Although there are exceptions which will be noted in the appropriate places, the general rule is to sow all brassicas in a specially prepared seed bed and to transplant them to a nursery bed before setting them in their final positions. Some people hold that, since brassicas respond readily to surface dressing of manures and fertilizers, transplanting encourages the development of fibrous feeding roots in the topmost layer of soil. But against this it is obvious that the double transplanting must subject the young plants to checks in growth which may be severe if the operations have to be carried out during spells of unfavourable weather. However, little purpose will be served by entering into the pros and cons of this matter because the plain fact is that in the average garden or on a standard allotment it is just a waste of land to sow brassicas where they are to mature. The point is that most of them take a very long time from the date of sowing until they are ready for eating – in the case of some broccoli over a year – and during a great part of this period they do not occupy anything like the space they will need when they are approaching maturity. Therefore it is merely common sense and good husbandry to delay the final planting for as long as is reasonably possible so that the land can be used for some other crops before the brassicas take over. This practice also saves much labour in weeding and, since as a rule the number of plants of each kind that can be accommodated is quite small, it enables the gardener to pick out the best and most promising seedlings, which would be impossible if the seedlings were merely thinned in the rows.

Sowing

A seed bed 6 ft by 4 ft is large enough to raise all the seedlings of all the cabbages, cauliflowers, and greens that a fair-sized family has room to grow and appetite to eat. Since a dozen or more different kinds are required to ensure a regular succession it is easy to see what a waste of seed takes place if every gardener, true to the British spirit of individualism, insists on buying a packet of each all to himself. The rule should be either to buy one packet, sow the whole of it, and distribute the resultant seedlings among your neighbours, receiving in exchange from them seedlings of the kinds you haven't raised yourself – in this way a dozen keen gardeners can raise sufficient brassica plants for a whole district; or to pass on the packets from house to house until they are empty; or to buy plants from a nurseryman. In the last case you may have to order more than you actually require because the plants are sold only in minimum lots of twenty-five; but you must bear in mind that a nurseryman does not transplant the seedlings but sells them direct from the seed rows as dug, so that all will not be of the same quality and the price is based on the assumption that you will pick out and plant only the best specimens.

The essentials of a good seed bed are that it shall be in a sunny spot well away from any hedge and that the soil shall be in good tilth, very friable, free from even the smallest clods, and thoroughly consolidated by trampling. If you know from a soil test or if you feel from your own observations of previous brassica crops that lime is needed, then give the seed bed a dressing of garden lime at the rate of 4 oz. per sq. yd but do not apply any manure or fertilizer. Since you want only a few plants, there is no excuse for thick sowing. Space the seeds individually as nearly as possible about ⅛ in. apart in drills ¾ in. deep. Protect from birds, unless the sowings are made under cloches, either by covering the drills with wire netting guards or by collecting lawn mowings and spreading them lightly over the bed.

Owing to the exceptional vulnerability of all brassicas to attack by certain soil-borne pests and diseases it is important to avoid making the seed bed on the same site in two successive years. If a definite system of rotation is practised the change of site comes about automatically and each year's site should contain a carry-over of plant nutrients from the previous crop. But if you are forced to use a patch of ground which has not received any manure or fertilizer for years it would be wise to cover the prepared seed bed with a 1 in. mulch of sieved garden compost. Levington Compost can be used, too, if you don't mind buying it.

In some small gardens it is almost impossible to find a suitable spot for the brassica seed bed and it is then preferable to sow in well-drained boxes, 6 ins. deep, filled with John Innes No. 1 Potting Compost. If these boxes are stood on a low wheeled platform (such as a trolley kneeler), they can be kept on a path without causing any obstruction since it is an easy matter to move the trolley to another position if it is in the way where you want to work.

Good, well-developed, mature, mite-free seed, such as is sold by the leading seedsmen, will give excellent germination under suitable conditions of temperature and moisture; but it is interesting to note that the finest plants come as a rule from two-year-old seed, not from the younger and fresher yearling seed. If therefore you have a part-used packet of new seed, it should pay you to keep the remnant for sowing next year, provided of course that you store it under cool, dry, and airy conditions.

Flea Beetles

Brassica crops sown during the latter part of April and the beginning of May, or during late July and throughout August, have usually to be protected against flea beetles. These tiny pests, measuring about $\frac{1}{10}$ in. long, are black with either yellow stripes or a blue, green, or bronze metallic sheen. They jump with great agility when disturbed; when undisturbed, they bore circular holes in the seed leaves of seedlings of any type of brassica. They confine their attentions exclusively to brassicas. If you have never spotted the actual beetles, you will almost certainly have seen examples of the damage they do. Seed leaves are to the tiny plant what an egg yolk is to the embryo chick; if they are destroyed either in whole or in part the plantlet cannot develop normally and, even if it does not die, is bound to start life as a weakling. The pest hibernates in rubbish and refuse in the bottoms of hedges, ditches, and haystacks, as well as in shrubberies and copses; in spring it awakes and feeds on weeds of the cabbage tribe, such as charlock, preparatory to flying to the nearest patch of newly germinated brassicas where its activities usually reach their peak about mid-May and are particularly troublesome in hot dry weather. After the end of May the original beetles lay eggs on the soil and then die; the eggs hatch, the maggots feed on the roots of the plants, then pupate in the soil and emerge as a new lot of beetles about the end of July, so a new attack on seedlings may be expected to break out at the beginning of August and continue until mid-September when the beetles retire to their winter quarters.

It will be clear therefore that normally trouble with flea beetles is unlikely to occur in the case of sowings made up to the end of

March and during June and the early part of July; attention must be given to all sowings made during April, May, August, and the early part of September – and this covers almost all sowings for winter and spring consumption. Fortunately, flea beetles are seldom troublesome if the seedlings are growing in a healthy, fertile soil and are receiving adequate supplies of water. It is slow-growing, obviously unhappy brassica seedlings which often suffer from flea beetles. Encourage rapid growth by watering when necessary and hoe to disturb the beetles. Should the seed leaves show some circular holes, dust with derris when the seedlings are dry. Once the young plants have grown well out of the seed leaf stage the beetles seldom trouble them, probably because they are too tough.

Transplanting

Commercial growers in this country plant out finally direct from the seed drills; but in France they first prick out into nursery beds and no private gardener who has ever had an opportunity of comparing the quality of English and French seedling brassicas can be left in any doubt regarding the advantages of intermediate transplanting which, incidentally, also permits later planting in permanent quarters – and this can be a great help. The time to transplant is when the plants have made four true leaves and are about 2 ins. tall. They should have been previously thinned so that no two neighbours touch one another. The distance between the plants in the nursery bed should be 4 ins. and they can remain in the nursery bed for between four and six weeks. When transplanting throw out any plants with bent stems and those which lack growing points or are otherwise defective; plant only perfect specimens. In order to prevent flagging in dry weather I find it excellent practice to dibble the seedlings, as lifted, into a bowl containing vermiculite which has been saturated with water to its limit. After eight hours in such a medium the plants are turgid with water and require the minimum of watering in the nursery bed to prevent them from checking.

Final Planting

Planting dates and planting distances are given under the headings of the particular vegetables concerned. The following notes apply to all brassicas. While it may prove fatal early in the year to set out plants raised under glass until suitable weather conditions obtain, it can prove equally disastrous, as the season advances, if planting out is allowed to fall badly behind schedule. Although, therefore, in theory, all planting out should be done, if possible, when the barometer is falling and the sky is cloudy with a prospect of rain, it often happens that there is no option but to plant during a hot, dry spell. In such circumstances ordinary watering in will not prevent the plants from checking badly. Some old gardeners soak the nursery bed with soot water made by actually stirring soot into the water until it becomes a thick liquid sludge. Several applications are given during the twelve hours prior to lifting, so that the plant roots are turgid with nourishing liquid which enables them to withstand the shock of removal without wilting. This is good gardening, but very messy.

Another way of keeping the roots of the plants moist until they have settled down is known as 'puddling'. This consists of mixing clay (or very tenacious soil) and, if obtainable, cow dung with water in equal proportions in a bucket so as to produce a liquid of the consistency of thin mortar, which will make a 'mud pie'. Dip the roots of each plant in this compound immediately before planting. Some people add soot and 1 lb. of agricultural salt to each bucketful of puddle compound: that is quite good practice.

The alternative to these rituals (and the practice I always follow myself) consists in making a deepish hole for each plant with a crowbar or dibber, filling it up to the top with water and then planting the seedling as soon as the water has drained away. The nursery bed has of course been flooded with water on the evening before lifting; and if, in addition, screening material erected along the row to keep off hot sun for a few days, there will be none of that ghastly business of a row of wilted cabbage plants lying flat on the ground for a week after setting out and losing half their leaves in the process.

Plant firmly right down to the lowest leaves that remain on the stalk so that these leaves practically sit on the ground. Firm planting is imperative; this does not mean that wet, pasty soil should be rammed into a solid mass around the plant's roots; it means simply that the soil must be made so firm and compact that you cannot pull the plant out again. Never plant between potato rows unless these have been deliberately spaced more widely so that the potato haulm will stand entirely clear of the cabbage plants. Always use a line when planting out and employ a yard stick to check the spacing in the row.

General Notes on Cultivation

All members of the cabbage family prefer a heavy clayey ground. This does not mean that you can grow them successfully in virgin yellow clay; it simply means that a well-worked clay will give you finer crops than you will get off light soil. Another characteristic of all brassicas is that they require an alkaline (i.e., well-limed) soil having a pH value of between pH 7 and pH 8. This might involve the application of as much as ½ lb. carbonate of lime per sq. yd and such a heavy dressing might lead to mineral deficiencies about which I shall have something to say a little later in this section.

All brassicas again prefer an open, airy position, free from draughts; that is why they do better on allotments than in private gardens. One explanation of this is that in the shelter of a garden the plants are more exposed to attack by pests. I have actually seen a garden in which the plants were infested with cabbage caterpillars whereas on the same owner's allotment, barely fifty yards away, the same types of vegetable were free from caterpillars, the explanation being that the prevailing breeze on the open allotment prevented the butterflies from alighting to lay their eggs.

Brussels sprouts, cauliflowers, autumn and winter cauliflower-broccoli, and, to a less extent, summer and autumn cabbage must have deeply-dug, richly-manured ground which is in good heart (i.e., of excellent texture and free from any trace of sourness). Cauliflowers in addition must have ample sun and moisture; if you can't provide something approaching these conditions it is a waste of time to grow the things, as the weight and food value of the crop will be so small that the ground could have been better used for other vegetables. In such cases the quality is also usually poor. We all know the heartless cabbages, the blowsy, open sprouts, and the button cauliflowers produced by well-meaning amateurs who do everything strictly in accordance with instructions except get the ground right before they plant. Spring cabbages, late cauliflowers and sprouting broccoli, savoys, and kales on the other hand do not need such rich, deeply-dug soil: that is presumably why beginners are often more successful with them than with the summer- and autumn-cropping brassicas.

Cultivation after planting consists mainly of persistent hoeing and weeding, prompt removal of dead and decayed leaves, which should be hurried to the compost heap, and vigilant warfare against diseases and pests. Further details will be found under the headings of the vegetables concerned.

Pests and Diseases

Certain pests and diseases specialize in attacking brassicas exclusively and I will therefore deal here with the worst of these nuisances.

The Cabbage Root Fly (*Erioischia brassicae*)

This looks like a grey house-fly. It lays eggs at the base of any plant belonging to the brassica family and these eggs hatch into maggots any time from the beginning of May until about the end of August. These maggots work downwards into the soil and chew off all the side roots, leaving only the tap root; they are able to cripple or destroy any plants of the cabbage family which may be set out during the period of the flies' activities and unfortunately it is not always possible to secure evidence of their activities until too late. In bad cases the leaves wilt and go purple and ultimately the plant collapses: but in milder cases the crops merely fail to give a good yield or come up to expectations – cauliflowers 'button', cabbages won't heart, and so on.

It is the smell of freshly-planted brassicas which appears to attract the egg-laying female flies. The best preventive measure is to plant out firmly and in soil which has just received a mulch of garden compost – the smell of the compost is stronger than that of the brassica transplants.

There is no fly-free period during the summer and since the pupae of the pest overwinter in the soil the importance of controlling it and of moving the cabbage crop around will be readily appreciated.

The Cabbage Aphis (Brevicoryne brassicae)

This can be an appalling nuisance in some districts and in some seasons; the infestations by this pest do not occur by any means regularly. It is only in very hot and dry seasons, and particularly after a mild winter, that they are really troublesome. The aphis is of course a form of greenfly, but in this case it is greyish-green with a mealy covering and is usually found in colonies on the underside of the leaves. Its presence can be detected by the resultant curling, blistering, and discoloration of the foliage, which in the case of young plants just set out may be completely destroyed.

It is on the stalks of the previous year's plants that the eggs of this aphis are laid in autumn and, if they survive the winter, they hatch in April to produce wingless aphids. In May winged forms appear and migrate from the old stumps to the current season's crop of young plants. If there were no old stalks left to flower on neglected land there would be very few cabbage aphids. Therefore the first step in coping with this pest is not to leave the stumps of cabbages or brussels sprouts in or on the ground after the crops have been gathered grub up and burn the lot.

Derris and pyrethrum give some control but unfortunately the aphids are in positions where insecticides cannot reach them and multiply so rapidly during August and September that the buttons of sprouts, particularly, swarm with aphides; where aphis infestation is bad, it may take up to six soakings in salted water to clean Brussels sprouts before they may be cooked. Even if one manages to halt an infestation on one's own brassicas, more aphids can arrive from neighbouring gardens and allotments. Fortunately, really nasty outbreaks of aphis trouble are seldom.

Cabbage Caterpillars

These are much more familiar to most beginners than are cabbage aphids. But it is not generally realized that there are two sorts of caterpillars, those of the cabbage butterfly and those of the cabbage moth. The cabbage white butterfly which flies by day is too well known to need any description; the cabbage moth which flies only by night is not so often seen and is a dingy greyish-brown colour with white markings. The large white butterfly first appears in spring and early summer, having passed the winter in the chrysalid stage suspended from fences, buildings, and other suitable positions. It lays yellow eggs in patches of twenty to 100 and the caterpillars which are hatched from these eggs are dark bluish- or greenish-black with a yellow line down the back and yellow along the sides, and are slightly hairy. The eggs are laid, and the caterpillars feed on the outer leaves not only of cabbages but of flowering stocks, nasturtiums, and weeds such as charlock and shepherd's purse; in addition to eating the leaves until they are skeletonized the caterpillars foul the plants with their excrement. After a month, when they are fully fed, they become chrysalids and emerge as butterflies in July. These are responsible for producing a second brood of caterpillars during August and September and this lot usually does even more damage than the first lot. Losses are often most severe in coastal districts because hordes of large white butterflies sometimes cross the Channel from the Continent and give rise to an absolute plague of caterpillars over here.

The caterpillars of two other butterflies are sometimes found mixed up with the caterpillars of the large white: these are the caterpillars of the small white and green-veined white butterflies. They are green with a peculiarly velvety appearance and do not always have the yellow line down the back.

The cabbage moth lays globular eggs as compared with the oval pointed eggs of the cabbage butterfly, and the resultant caterpillars are light green when young but brown, dark green, or even black on the upper surface as they get older; they have smooth bodies, no hairs, and no velvety appearance. These caterpillars are much more objectionable than those of the butterflies, because they burrow into the hearts of the plants to feed and make a filthy mess in places where they cannot possibly be got at. They are also liable to attack tomatoes, nicotianas, lettuces, onions, sweet corn, and many flowering plants. They are active from June to October. It is not much use shooing and chasing the butterflies or even catching them with a net, as some people do, seeing that you cannot chase the equally troublesome moth in the middle of the night, although possibly some moths could be caught by 'treacling'. By far the best course is to keep a close watch on your cabbage plants and destroy the eggs, especially on the undersides of the leaves, where they are conspicuously visible owing to their bright colour and the fact that they appear in large clusters (except in the case of the small white and green-veined white butterflies, which have a vexatious habit of laying their eggs singly so that they need a lot of looking for). It is a simple matter to crush the eggs with your finger, and then if you make a point of walking round every other night looking for small holes in the leaves, you will have little difficulty in catching the caterpillars which have hatched out of any eggs which you have missed. Do this early in the season while the caterpillars are young. When searching for the eggs take care that you do not crush the larger and egg-shaped cocoons of ichneumon wasps – also known as ichneumon flies. Ichneumons are internal parasites and the grubs devour the caterpillars. It is during the pupal stage of the ichneumon's life that the gardener comes across egg-shaped cocoons on the leaves of brassicas and other plants and even suspended on the wall of the garden shed. Derris and pyrethrum may also be used in the battle against cabbage caterpillars. But if you do nothing until the caterpillars are bigger and have found their way into the more inaccessible parts of the plants, it is unlikely that you will ever be able to eradicate them, and you will have to leave it to the cook to clean up your messy plants and make the remnants into a presentable dish free from any corpses.

Cabbage White Flies (*Aleurodes brassicae*)

These which do *not* belong to the same family as the greenhouse white fly (*Trialeurodes vaporariorum*), can be a great nuisance in a hot, dry summer in the south of England. They do not check the growth of the plants but they are capable of rendering the produce most unattractive – this applies especially to brussels sprouts which turn black when attacked by the fly. Unfortunately this pest is just as elusive and hard to kill as the greenhouse type of white fly: it is continually laying eggs and giving rise to fresh generations and, since you cannot fumigate outdoors, your only hope of keeping it under control consists in spraying the underside of the leaves early in the season, before a build-up of the fly population has developed, with a derris/pyrethrum mixture such as is sold by The Henry Doubleday Research Association, Bocking, Braintree, Essex. The one consolation is that this particular pest is by no means a regular visitor.

Club Root Disease

This is not nearly so prevalent as many gardeners believe. If your soil is well cultivated and well limed and you have never been troubled with club root, you probably never will be, so long as you don't grow brassicas on the same patch year after year. Accordingly you need not worry your head over precautions against club root. For the benefit of those who are dubious about whether they have got Club Root in their gardens, it may be stated that the mere presence of knobs or swellings on the roots of their brassicas is no indication in itself that the disease is present. The roots of wild cabbage have knobs on and the fact that these knobs appear in the cultivated type may be a characteristic of a new strain, though it may also be due to poor soil, careless cultivation, or inferior seed. Then there is a little beetle called the gall weevil which is responsible for swellings on the roots. It is simple to determine the cause of any malformation. Cut the swelling across; if the interior tissue is clean and healthy there is nothing to worry about; if the cut brings to view the small white grub of the gall weevil there is little to worry about, since a healthy plant growing in good soil is not appreciably inconvenienced by the presence of the maggot; if, however, the cut flesh shows a marbled or mottled appearance there is a lot to worry about, because the plant is definitely infected by Club Root (also called Anbury or Finger-and-Toe). In due course the tissues will go rotten and stink, the roots of affected plants in the ground will become distorted, and the tops will grow stunted and sickly and may die away completely.

Club Root is caused by a slime fungus that lives in the soil; it can only be eradicated by starving out the very small parasitic organisms which enter the plants through the tips of the root hairs and this means that you must not grow any vegetables of the cabbage family in the garden for two or three years; neither must you grow turnips or radishes. You must rigorously weed out charlock and shepherd's purse, which act as host plants, and you must apply slaked lime annually for two years at the rate of anything up to 2 lb. per sq. yd (56 lb. per rod). It is of little use merely to relegate cabbages to another and as yet uninfected part of the garden, since the infection can be spread by the soles of your boots, by the tyre of the wheelbarrow, and by your tools. All diseased plants must be pulled up and the roots of them burnt *before* the swollen roots start to decay; under no circumstances must they be placed on the compost heap. No acidic chemical fertilizers should be applied because their acidity would counteract the beneficial effects of the liming. Very heavy dressings of garden compost should be applied. Not only will the compost very probably contain minute predators able to attack Club Root fungi, but garden compost, being prepared from many varied wastes, will contain plenty of trace elements which the heaving liming of the infected soil may well have displaced. You may also need to improve the drainage of the land, as bad drainage increases sourness and encourages the fungus which always spreads most virulently in a wet season.

Other Diseases

Many other diseases of brassicas are known to scientists and to those who cultivate these crops on a commercial scale; but it is most unlikely that the ordinary amateur will be troubled by any of them if he is a reasonably good gardener and takes certain common-sense precautions. In such cases as I have noticed outbreaks of the less usual diseases in private gardens it has often turned out that the owner has saved his own seed. This practice is never worthwhile. Brassica crops readily cross-pollinate one another so that home-saved seed from an ordinary garden or allotment is likely to produce only mongrel plants, wholly unrepresentative of the plants from which it was harvested; and, apart from this, it is often in the second year of their existence that the biennial brassicas develop diseases which are then transmitted to the offspring through the seed. Therefore it should be a rule among all private growers to raise their brassica plants only from high-quality seed purchased from a leading seedsman and under no circumstances to leave stumps in the ground to grow on into the second season and, incidentally, to serve as breeding places for all manner of pests.

Amongst the other causes of disease in brassicas are failure to observe a satisfactory system of rotation so that the same crop occupies the same site at too frequent intervals; the use of the same site in the garden for seed and nursery beds year after year; the location of these beds too close to hedges, trees, buildings, and mature crops of brassicas; the intemperate application of too much fertilizer (and often the wrong kind of fertilizer as well); a badly-drained, acid soil which readily becomes waterlogged in winter; and a stuffy, walled-in, airless garden. It is within the power of every gardener to avoid the hazards just described and, though he cannot control the weather and do away with very warm moist summers, cold, rainy spells, and periods of severe frost accompanied by drying wind, which encourage outbreaks of disease, or give rise to damage, in all classes of plants, he is unlikely to have much to worry about if he raises his brassicas in the shelter of his garden but grows them on to maturity on an open allotment.

If disease does occur, and is of a fungoid nature, it can often be controlled by a copper spray or dust; but if it is due to a virus or bacterial infection nothing can be done except uproot and burn every badly affected plant.

Mineral Deficiencies

Some diseases and ailments are, however, directly attributable to a shortage of certain elements, especially trace elements, in the soil. These are most likely to occur where a grower persists in using nothing but inorganic (chemical) fertilizers or has been compelled to apply large quantities of lime to counteract acidity. Some brassicas are more sensitive to these shortages than others. Cauliflowers, for example, react quickly to any shortage of boron which leads to the production of a small, bitter-tasting curd (or head), disfigured by brown water-soaked patches and surrounded by stunted, deformed leaves; in bad cases the head may even rot and become a stinking, slimy mass. Apply 1½ oz. borax with 10 oz. steamed boneflour to each rod of land immediately before planting.

A curious mottled yellowing of the areas of the leaves between the veins (which remain bright green) usually indicates either iron or manganese deficiency, whilst if the patches turn brown and die and the plants are attacked by mildew the trouble is due to magnesium deficiency. Troubles of this sort can be rectified in the short term by chemical powders or sprays – but it is better to ensure that your soil is replete with all necessary trace elements. As has been explained already, these are present in abundance in garden compost prepared from a varied selection of waste products. Magnesium deficiency mostly affects sprouts and cauliflowers grown on light, sandy soil.

The Problem of Succession

Whether you like cabbage or whether you don't, the fact is that the members of the cabbage family represent the backbone of the all-the-year-round supply of fresh green vegetables and there are times when there is nothing else to be bought at the greengrocer's except roots from store and a few glasshouse-raised vegetables selling at fabulous prices. In a bad season even the prices of 'greens' soar, and they are sometimes unobtainable, so that housewives are constrained to use tinned or frozen produce. It is hardly to be wondered at, therefore, that I regularly receive requests to draw up cropping plans which will ensure that there will be no month of the year in which there will be no green vegetables available on which the cook can rely when other things fail.

Accordingly I have drawn up such a 'round-the-calendar' plan designed to meet the needs of a household of four persons of which every member can be relied upon to enjoy eating his whack of greens if they are properly cooked and attractively served. At the same time I must make it clear, however, that the production of green vegetables, even on the limited scale envisaged by the tables, will mean devoting two thirds of a standard allotment (about seven rods of land) exclusively to brassicas each year; and, since you do not want to use the same plot for brassicas more frequently than once in three years, the maintenance of a proper rotation will call for a total kitchen garden area of at least twenty rods (or two standard allotments) exclusive of areas devoted to permanent crops, such as asparagus and rhubarb. This is in no sense a disadvantage because it will automatically allow a sufficient breadth of potatoes to be grown to render the family independent of bought supplies throughout the year. But many readers just will not have so much land available for the cultivation of vegetables and these will have to scale down the tables to suit their gardens in accordance with their individual tastes.

Table A lists the varieties of seed that will be needed, the number of seedlings that will be required at planting time, the number of rows they will occupy, and the yield of produce that may reasonably be expected in each case. Table B is a time-table for sowing and final planting out. Table C shows what greens will be available in each month of the year.

It will be noted that no fewer than 22 different packets of seed are required to produce this succession. The reason for this is that brassica varieties are now so highly specialized that each variety matures at a particular season of the year and cannot be induced to change its habit merely by altering the dates of sowing and planting. By and large there is no single variety of any one type of brassica that can be sown successionally in the same way as, for example, dwarf kidney beans. It should be obvious, therefore, that only the smallest packet of each recommended variety of seed will be required to provide plants for a single household; but this does not mean that you should attempt to cut your initial outlay by buying cheap and inferior seed. Only the best strains, as offered by leading seedsmen of repute, are worth buying; and, as previously suggested, the proper way to economize in seed costs is by collaborating with your friends and neighbours and sharing the contents of the packets.

Broccoli

(See also Brassicas and Cauliflowers)

The word *broccoli* is Italian for 'stalklets' and refers to the soft young stalks terminating in clusters of flower buds set among the leaves which are characteristic of what the seed catalogues call 'sprouting broccoli' and most housewives include under the general

TABLE A

VEGETABLE	VARIETY	NO. OF PLANTS	NO. OF 30-FT ROWS	PROBABLE YIELD
1. broccoli, sprouting	Green (Calabrese)	12	1	
2. broccoli, sprouting	Early Purple	12	1	1½ lb. per plant
3. broccoli, sprouting	Late Purple	12	1	
4. brussels sprouts, early	Cambridge No. 1	15	1½	2 lb. per plant
5. brussels sprouts, late	Cambridge No. 5	15	1½	
6. cabbage, early summer	May Star (Suttons)	15	½	2 lb. each
7. cabbage, late summer	Greyhound	8	½	2½ lb. each
8. cabbage, autumn	Winnigstadt	15	1	3 lb. each
9. cabbage, winter	January King	20	1	2–3 lb. each
10. cabbage, spring	Wheeler's Imperial	40	2	1–1½ lb. hearted or ¾ lb. per plant when cut as greens
11. cabbage, spring	Flower of Spring	60	2	
12. cabbage, savoy, early	Dwarf Green Curled	8	½	
13. cabbage, savoy, midseason	Ormskirk Medium	8	½	2–3 lb. each
14. cabbage, savoy, late	Ormskirk Extra Late	15	1	
15. cauliflower, early summer	Early London	15	1	
16. cauliflower, late summer	Improved Snowball	15	1	
17. cauliflower, autumn	Autumn Giant	15	1	heads weigh between 1 lb. and 2 lb. each
18. cauliflower, early spring	(Suttons) Snow White*	15	1	
19. cauliflower, late spring	St George*	15	1	
20. kale, maincrop	Half-tall Scotch	40	2	½ lb. per plant
21. kale, late	Hungry Gap	30	2	
22. turnip tops	Hardy Green Round	—	2	15 lb. per row

* winter cauliflower (cauliflower – broccoli or heading broccoli)

TABLE B – SOWING AND PLANTING GUIDE

The numbers in this table refer to the corresponding numbers of the different varieties in Table A.

JAN	FEB	MAR	APRIL		MAY		JUNE	JULY		AUG		SEPT	OCT
sow	sow	sow	sow	plant	sow	plant	plant	sow	plant	sow	plant	sow	plant
4†	6†	1	2	6	3	4	1	10	3	11	9	15†	10
	16†	7†	5	7	9	8	2	21*	13	22*			11
		8	13	15	19	16	5		14				
		12	14				12		19				
			17				17		20				
			18				18						
			20										

* Not transplanted – sown and thinned *in situ* † Sown under glass

TABLE C – KEY TO PRODUCE AVAILABLE

	JAN	FEB	MAR	APL	MAY	JUN	JUL	AUG	SEP	OCT	NOV	DEC
broccoli, sprouting		X		X	X				X	X		
brussels sprouts	X	X	X								X	
cabbage, hearted	X	X			X	X	X		X	X		
cabbage, spring			X	X	X	X						
cabbage, savoy	X	X	X							X	X	X
cauliflower			X	X	X	X	X			X	X	
kale		X	X	X	X	X						
turnip tops			X	X								

and rather vague title of 'greens'. This vegetable, as you may note from the name of the green variety, Calabrese (from Calabria), was developed from the original wild 'break' in Italy and must be carefully distinguished from the hearting type which, although botanically it also belongs to the broccoli group, is to all intents and purposes a cauliflower and will be dealt with under that heading in this book.

Sprouting broccoli is really very easy to grow provided that it is planted *firmly* in well-drained land which does not get waterlogged under the conditions of an average winter. In strictness manuring should follow the lines laid down for brussels sprouts but in practice the crop will give quite a good account of itself even in comparatively poor land and it is certainly not desirable for the soil to be so rich that there is any risk of the plants growing soft and sappy and thus being unable to survive hard winter weather.

The green and white varieties do not withstand frost as well as the purple. The former should therefore be sown during the second half of March and the latter at the beginning of April. The purple sorts ought all to be sown during the remainder of April except the late purple which can wait until the early part of May. Plants (raised in accordance with the instructions given under the heading Brassicas) should be set out in their final positions in June with the single exception of the late purple which will not be ready until July. The planting distance is 2 ft 6 ins. every way (i.e., the distance between the plants in the rows is the same as the distance separating the rows).

No cultural attentions are required beyond regular hoeing and the removal of weeds. The plants must of course be kept free from caterpillars, and on the approach of winter it is a good plan to draw earth up the stems, thus affording additional protection to the roots as well as helping to support the plants and preventing them from rocking or being blown over.

Calabrese differs from the other sorts in that it first produces in late summer a large green central head which must be cut and eaten before the plant will send up the more typical shoots from each leaf joint, each shoot having a small curd on top and a few leaves beneath it. These 'greens' are available throughout September and October, sometimes continuing into November, and should be cut with about 6 ins. of stem

Plants of the other varieties do not form any central head but start off by sending up about half a dozen strong shoots and, soon after these have been cut, you will get a picking of a score or more shoots with smaller curds which will be succeeded by third and fourth pickings. All these shoots should be taken when they are 9 to 12 ins. long, the top portions being severed or snapped off about one third of the way down the stem and all large leaves being allowed to remain to shelter the shoots still to come. By the time of the last picking almost the whole of each plant will have been used up.

In the case of well-grown plants of all varieties except Calabrese you may expect an average yield of about 6 oz. from each plant at each picking; but Calabrese yields more heavily than this, doubtless because it makes its growth at a more favourable season of the year.

Brussels Sprouts

(See also Brassicas)

Although most members of the cabbage family are biennial and do not form the buds in the axils of the leaves (from which flowering heads later appear) until the second season of their growth, the brussels sprout develops these buds during the first year after planting and it is these hard knobs, resembling miniature cabbages, which are eaten under the name of 'sprouts'. Most people now drop the epithet Brussels which merely serves to remind us that it was in the vicinity of that city that sprouts were first developed into a vegetable worth eating over 600 years ago. Curiously enough, although the Belgians have eaten them ever since the year 1213, it was not until the late nineteenth century that sprouts began to be grown in this country, except in the gardens of the rich, and even today they are not grown commercially to any extent in the United States where most greengrocers would look at you in astonishment if you asked for a couple of pounds of sprouts.

Sprouts need a long season of growth and fairly liberal manuring. Unless you can do the crop well it is not worth growing, for you will merely get a few miserable loose buttons instead of the heavy crops of close-set sprouts that you ought to have. One seldom sees a well-grown sprout plant in an amateur's garden or allotment, but when such a plant is available, you should notice that it is covered from the ground level to the top with buttons set so closely that once you have cut a few off it is impossible to put them back where they came from because others will have closed up and taken their space.

One of the most common causes of failure is the use of inferior or unsuitable seed. It is extremely difficult to keep a named strain true to type; only the leading seed growers are qualified to cope with the problems involved and it follows therefore that the name of the variety on a packet of sprout seed is often less important than the name of the seed merchant who offers it for sale. If you buy cheap seed from unreliable sources, you may well find that such sprouts as do form are merely open, leafy 'blowers'. Apart from this, it is essential to grow a variety which suits your district; it is no good going by the seedsman's catalogue and choosing a much praised sort, probably with a well-known name, unless you also get a guarantee that it is capable of giving a good account of itself in your particular patch of country – if you live in Cornwall you will be wise to give sprouts a miss altogether because in that county all varieties are extremely liable to develop a disease known as Ring Spot.

Above all, unless you are an amateur expert in these matters, do not attempt to save your own seed. Sprouts cross freely with most other brassicas grown within the distance of a bee's flight and may then yield worthless offspring, while self-pollinated plants seldom produce anything bearing any reasonable relation to the parent.

Soil and Situation

The brussels sprout plant will grow satisfactorily on any medium heavy soil that has reasonably good drainage. It does particularly well on the flinty clay that overlies the chalk in many southern areas around London. I would not recommend anybody to grow this crop on sticky, raw clay, however, because it is the object of every good gardener to improve such soil and this object will be largely defeated if the ground is repeatedly trodden, while wet, by persons tramping up and down the rows in winter gathering sprouts. On light land sprouts are seldom a success, not only because it is difficult to make the soil firm enough about the roots but also because such land usually dries out in summer when the plants ought to be growing most strongly.

A sunny site is not essential: excellent crops can be taken from land sloping to the north provided that it is open and not overshadowed by trees or buildings. Such land does not get sun-caked in summer and therefore there is less risk of any check during the growing period. Nevertheless due regard must be had to the district and the normal severity of the winters: although sprouts are comparatively hardy, there is a limit to what they will stand in the way of frost and snow, particularly if the site is exposed to the east wind.

Manuring

The rotation of crops is vital in the production of good vegetables; you can grow this season's sprouts on land which in the previous year was devoted to main-crop potatoes or to carrots or beet for storage. Such a site is cleared of the previous crop in time to allow digging and manuring to be completed by the end of the year, after which it should be left fallow until planting time, except possibly for catch-cropping with quick-growing, shallow-rooting crops such as radishes and salad onions. I am well aware that some gardeners like to snatch a crop of early peas or lettuce under cloches from the sprout site because they cannot bear to see it vacant and idle for three months or more. But this is not the way to get good 'buttons'. Sprouts require extremely firm soil and all the most successful growers find that it pays them not to disturb the planting site by digging after the end of January. Since the sprout plant makes a tap root it is essential to dig deeply; but since all the feeding roots form quite near the surface the stable manure or garden compost should be applied to the top spit. It is not necessary to compost during autumn or winter digging – excellent crops can be obtained by giving a generous mulch of compost just before the young plants are set out in their final growing positions.

Sowing and Planting

It has always been a matter of surprise to me that the British public demands sprouts at the end of August and during September when runner beans, cauliflowers, and many other delicious green vegetables are available. The result of starting on sprouts so early can only be that one gets heartily sick of them by Christmas. It is still more surprising to me that many otherwise sensible gardeners concentrate on the production of early sprouts to the exclusion of late sprouts which can often prove to be the only alternative to savoys and stored roots during the lean period from January to April.

Admittedly, many books of reference still advocate sowing either in autumn or in January but their writers are merely copying from earlier books published in the days when all strains of sprouts took a very long time to reach maturity and it was deemed to be necessary either to sow in a heated greenhouse early in the new year or, if no greenhouse was available, to sow the previous August and over-winter the seedlings in a frame.

These considerations no longer apply. If you really must have sprouts by the end of the summer, then by all means sow an early variety from the beginning of January to early in February according to district and season; but for goodness' sake do not sow in a heated greenhouse or even in a heated propagator. Old-time gardeners all laboured under a delusion that their plants needed more warmth than we now know to be necessary. You can sow in an *unheated* greenhouse in boxes placed on a shelf close to the glass, pricking out the seedlings 2 ins. square into other boxes as soon as they can be handled and placing these boxes also on shelves; but, even so, you will find it extremely difficult to avoid drawing and spindling and you would do far better to sow in a cold frame or under cloches.

If you sow in a frame, make the soil sufficiently moist to render subsequent watering unnecessary. Sieve soil over the seed to a depth of ⅛ in.; cover the light with a mat and keep it on the frame until germination takes place, after which it can be removed altogether on all dry days when there is no frost. Prick out 2 ins. square as before; and, although you will have to replace the light at night and during heavy rain (and to replace the mat also on freezing cold nights), you must always leave a gap for ventilation. If this results in the seedlings getting frozen on occasion, you must shade the frame lightly and ventilate freely during the thawing out period. As the weather warms up, the light can be taken away once and for all.

Sowing under cloches involves less trouble; you can get four or five rows 5 to 6 ins. apart in ½-in. drills under a low barn cloche. Prick out 2 to 4 ins. apart under other cloches, observe the same precaution as regards shading (e.g. with tiffany) in the event of the seedlings getting frozen, and remove the cloches altogether as soon as the first warm spell comes along.

Plants from greenhouse, frame, and cloche sowings are put in their final positions during April.

You will note that I have said nothing about autumn sowing because I consider it to be unnecessary. However, if you want to try it, sow seed about 10 August in the north and 21 August in the south, preferably making two small sowings on different dates so that you have two batches of plants from which to select. Prick out either into frames, using the lights only to protect from heavy rain or frost, or under cloches which should be set to give full ventilation whenever possible. Plant out towards the end of February or very early in March, according to conditions, and keep a good stock of plants in reserve to make good losses as a result of bolting. As a rule at any rate some plants run up to seed as soon as they begin to grow after planting out and I have known a whole batch to bolt in a bad year, which is another reason why I take a poor view of autumn sowing.

So much for very early sprouts. Most of us are, however, quite satisfied if our sprouts are ready for picking about the end of November and are in plentiful supply around Christmas and the New Year, and for this purpose it is sufficient to sow an early sort in the open ground at the end of February or during March, according to locality. Provided that seed is sown before 21 March, at any rate in the southern half of the country, and the plants are in their final positions before the end of May, there should be no fear of the crop being too late for the festivities. Maincrop sorts to produce sprouts in February and March and into April should be sown at the beginning and end of the previous April for planting out in June. Sowing and planting follow the lines laid down under the heading Brassicas except that it should be noted that, while seedlings raised in frames and under cloches are planted out when 6 ins. tall, sprout plants from outdoor sowings ought not to be put out until they are much larger, say to 8 to 10 ins. tall – and this height refers to good, stocky, close-jointed plants, not to such as have been drawn up and become lanky.

The minimum planting distance is 2 ft 6 ins. square; but strong, well-grown plants will do better if given a whole square yard apiece (i.e. set 3 ft apart in rows 3 ft apart). It is quite a usual thing to see sprouts in private gardens and allotments planted much too closely together.

Cultivation

Apart from regular hoeing and the usual counter-measures against diseases and pests (see Brassicas), the crop will need little attention beyond watering if the summer is dry. Considerable care is necessary, however, to avoid damage with the hoe as the plants become fully grown, because the rooting system, which lies shallowly below the surface, has by then become extremely widespread. It is also necessary to discontinue hoeing as soon as the leaves begin to meet in the row, otherwise they would be damaged. On the approach of autumn draw soil around the bases of the stems up to the level of the lowest leaves; this helps to support the weight of the plant, protects the feeding roots, and keeps the bark of the stem from hardening. If the ground on which the plants are grown is very much exposed, it is desirable before the onset of winter to stake the taller varieties, placing the stake on the windward side. All decayed basal leaves should be removed by carefully detaching them from the stems. It is inevitable that some of them should fade and wither as winter sets in and, if left to turn mouldy, they would infect the buttons with the mould fungus and discolour them. An excessive amount of yellow, slimy foliage indicates that the plants were raised too early and for lack of good cultivation have been unable to support the huge leaves that have formed during the summer. Wholesale loss of leaves should be a matter of grave concern to the grower because it is the leaves that protect the sprouts from the effects of alternate freezing and thawing and, although sprouts make better eating after they have been frosted, prolonged exposure to the elements in a hard winter due to the absence of leaves may spoil the outer layers of the buttons which have then to be discarded as waste.

If most of your buttons turn out to be 'blowers' (i.e. open, flabby, and spongy) this is probably due to a lack of firmness in the soil. Many amateurs seem to be under the impression that if the surface of the soil is hard and compressed all is well, but this is quite wrong – the actual surface soil should always be kept friable by hoeing after heavy rain. Another cause of blowers is lack of moisture during early growth, leading to the formation of an over-deep tap root at the expense of the feeding roots. Some old-time gardeners used to remedy this by levering the whole plant upwards with a fork, at a time when the top spit was fairly moist, until the tap root was heard to snap, then treading the soil firmly back into position. This, however, is an operation demanding great skill and experience and cannot be recommended to the average gardener who is far more likely to give his plants such a check that the remedy is worse than the disease. If by any chance despite good cultivation a few sprouts do burst open they should be cut at once and not left upon the plant to grow more blowsy and impede the development of the remaining sprouts.

The growth of sprouts can be stimulated, so that they become edible at an earlier date and are of better quality, by resorting to the practice known as 'cocking'. This consists in nipping out of the heart of the plant a piece of the growing point not larger than a cob nut and the operation is usually carried out at the end of August or the beginning of September by those who want their sprouts really early in the season. Great care must be taken not to remove too big a piece, particularly if the plants are not too well forward, as this would result in the production of open, loose, and deformed sprouts instead of hastening the development of early sprouts. Cocking at a later date, i.e. up to the end of November, will assist late sprout plants and stimulate the development of sprouts at the top of the stem; many failures on the part of sprouts to button could be avoided in a bad season by cocking. Naturally, the later the cocking is carried out, the larger may be the piece removed, because the plants themselves will be larger; in the latest cocking from the most forward plants, the piece removed may be as big as a sprout. But all cocking must be carefully distinguished from cutting off the cabbage-like head which is known as the sprout top. This is fatal to the production of solid buttons and the top should be left in position until all the sprouts have been picked, and then cut and eaten at the end of March when the stumps are dug up, chopped in sections and added to the compost heap.

Feeding

Plants growing in soils which have been well enriched with heavy dressings of garden compost need no extra feeding during the summer months. But if the soil is not as fertile as it should be for sprouts, then fertilizer feeds will be necessary. It is generally agreed that the fertilizer used must contain nitrogen but great care is necessary to avoid an excess of that element which would result in over-leafy growth and a high proportion of blowers. For these reasons I dislike the use of straight nitrogenous fertilizers, such as sulphate of ammonia and nitrate of soda, especially the latter which is liable to ruin the flavour of the sprouts, and I advise you to stick to Chilean nitrate of potash applied (½ oz. per sq. yd) when the plants are 1 ft high, well established, and growing strongly. Then about August you should dress with weathered soot (4 oz. per sq. yd) worked in with the hoe.

Gathering

Always gather sprouts systematically, starting from the bottom and snapping a few sprouts off each plant after first stripping the leaves from the stem up to the point to which you intend to pick. Begin to gather when the lowest sprouts are of the same diameter as a 10p. piece which is the ideal size for cooking and eating. (In the opinion of all lovers of good food, the large elephantine sprouts often sold by greengrocers are simply horrible, and I agree with them!) Don't leave the lower sprouts to grow while picking those above them or they may turn yellow and go slimy. Don't strip all the sprouts regardless of size from individual plants. Spread your picking evenly. Cut the head last of all. I would like to add that, if you have grown your sprouts well, it should be perfectly easy to snap them off by a slight downward pressure; but, if they do not respond to this treatment, use a sharp kitchen knife rather than maul them about and damage the stems.

A good average yield for the beginner would be 2½ lb. per plant but many experienced gardeners succeed in getting a much bigger weight than that.

Exhibiting Sprouts

The brussels sprout is one of the few vegetables of which it may be said that there is no distinction to be drawn between table and exhibition quality. No special method of cultivation is therefore called for: if the sprouts are of really fine eating quality, as they should be, they should also be prize-worthy when exhibited. In other words they must be fresh, of medium size, solid as a nut, and tightly closed, also of good colour. The usual pointing is 6 points for condition, 5 for solidity, and 4 for uniformity, bearing in mind that a 'dish' of sprouts means fifty buttons. Judges have no business to award prizes to monster sprouts, which are inferior to the smaller buttons, and in my opinion and that of some other judges early sprouts exhibited in September ought not to be awarded priority points in a mixed collection merely because they are harder to grow than, say, cabbages. Regard should be had to the season when this vegetable is more properly in demand, especially having regard to the fact that more skill is needed to exhibit good sprouts at a late show when the plants have had to endure the rigours of autumn and a touch of winter too, perhaps.

Cabbage

(Including Savoy Cabbage)

The father-and-mother of all cabbages (*Brassica oleracea*) can be seen growing wild on the seacoast at Dover, on the rocks of Glamorgan, on the dunes of East Lothian, and in hundreds of other places. But hearting cabbages as we know them today, are of the cultivated variety, *B. oleracea* var. *capitata*, and take their name from the Latin *caput* (head) which becomes in French *caboche*: they are the coles with a head on which have formed a staple article of diet for many centuries – we read in a recipe book dated 1440: 'Take caboches and cut hom on foure . . . and let hit boyle.'

Savoys, although similar to cabbages, in many ways belong in fact to a different branch of the family and are more closely allied to the brussels sprout. Botanically, the savoy is a *Brassica oleracea* var. *bullata major*. It was developed in the French Department of Savoy in the Middle Ages but remained unknown in Britain till the seventeenth century. Its habit in growth is more dwarf than that of a true cabbage, it is more hardy, and it has puckered or crimped leaves owing (it is believed) to the fact that the spongy tissue between the veins grows more rapidly than the veins themselves.

Both cabbages and savoys have one essential feature in common: the terminal bud is surrounded by leaves which turn inward and clasp it tightly, thus forming the 'head', of which the solid inner portion is termed the 'heart'.

Varieties of cabbage belong to one or other of several highly specialized types according to the season of the year at which they are required to mature and, since each type demands a certain amount of individual treatment, it will be best for me to deal with each group separately.

SUMMER CABBAGE

This falls into two sections. Early summer cabbage is sown during January or at the beginning of February in a frame or under cloches for planting out in late March or early in April: or it may be sown very sparingly in rows under cloches at the beginning of March and allowed to mature without transplanting. The object in both cases is to secure hearted cabbage in June if the autumn-sown crop of spring cabbage has failed because of a severe winter or was for some reason or other omitted altogether. Maincrop summer cabbage on the other hand aims to produce supplies of this vegetable during July, August, and September and, even though cabbage stands better than most other brassicas when mature, it is always wise to make several sowings, using different varieties, and to plant out in more than one batch, rather than all together, from each sowing. This is the only way to avoid an unwanted glut because you can never be sure just how long cabbage will take to turn in and, when it does so, all the plants in each batch usually turn in together. This is one of the cases in which the cooperative raising of plants by a group of neighbours saves much labour and expenditure on seed. On this basis a first sowing should be made early in March and planted out in April for July cutting; a second sowing in April for May planting should be ready in August; and a final sowing at the end of April, if planted early in June, will come into cut in September. It is not everybody who wants cabbage in July when many other green vegetables are usually available, but as a rule it is welcome from late August onwards. (All the dates given relate to the southern half of the country where summer cabbage can usually be induced to grow quickly; in the north it takes much longer to reach maturity and the usual practice is to concentrate on one late summer crop only. In some areas the savoy is preferred to the ordinary cabbage for this purpose.)

Planting distances for summer cabbage are governed entirely by the size of the variety chosen, but, generally speaking, the small early summer sorts can go 12 ins. apart in rows 18 ins. apart, while the maincrop summer sorts demand on an average a good 2 ft on each side.

Although cabbages can be grown successfully on most types of soil that are well drained, yet reasonably retentive of moisture, the fact remains that they are by nature most at home on medium light land and this raises obvious difficulties with the summer crop because of the increased risk of drying out. Cabbages withstand drought better than most brassicas but it does them no good to go short of water and, since the summer crop demands rich soil, the need for adequate manurial treatment with humus-forming materials raises certain problems of rotation. You cannot expect any soil to settle down again and acquire its original firmness of texture within a few weeks of the incorporation of bulky organic manures; on the other hand, land that has been plain dug can readily be reconsolidated by trampling or light rolling when it is in a suitable condition. Since few gardeners have so much land to spare that they can readily afford to leave the summer cabbage patch fallow from late autumn onwards, it will be appreciated that there is everything to be gained by growing the cabbages on land which was well manured for a previous crop due to be cleared by March (e.g., summer cabbage might well follow leeks).

If the soil where leeks or some other crop were grown the previous season was well enriched with garden compost, there is nothing more to do than to fork over the site as soon as it is vacant and, later on, when your cabbage plants are ready for setting out in the bed, hoe through the soil to remove annual weed seedlings. But many soils are not as highly fertile as they ought to be for vegetables and many gardeners therefore continue to use chemical fertilizers. It must be understood that these chemical products can lead to acidic soil conditions necessitating further liming which itself can lead to an unbalanced soil condition. If you have to provide by chemical feeding, a dressing of Growmore fertilizer can be put on as soon as the soil has been dug (or for the earliest crop, which requires extremely rich soil, 3½ lb. hoof and horn, 2 lb. superphosphate, and 1½ lb. sulphate of potash, all per square rod).

All applications of fertilizer must, however, be related to the state of fertility of the soil to begin with and this applies equally to top dressings during growth. Nevertheless it is reasonably safe to assume, as regards the latter, that a dressing of nitro-chalk (¾ oz. per sq. yd) a month after planting and a similar dressing three weeks later can do nothing but good, while if watering is resorted to during drought it will be wise to add 1 oz. sulphate of ammonia to each 4 gallons of water.

It might be noted that savoys root less deeply than cabbages and will do better on the less fertile soils, so that they will be content with smaller dressings of fertilizer kept strictly to the surface layers of soil.

A word of warning is perhaps necessary regarding nitrate of soda. Never use it as a top dressing for cabbages as it is apt to impart to them a most disgusting flavour. (I have heard of a farmer who declines to use it even on brassicas grown for cattle feed and who has many other things to say about this chemical which cannot possibly be set down on paper.)

Apart from top dressing, all that summer cabbage demands is to be kept weed-free and regularly hoed; but you must of course be prepared to deal with caterpillars and other pests (see under Brassicas). Bolting after a spell of dry weather can sometimes be prevented if the early signs of the trouble are spotted in good time when the plants show their first tendency to become long-jointed and rise up in the air. The procedure that frequently proves successful is to pierce the stem of the plant with a penknife about an inch above ground level and insert a match stalk or small piece of stone in the slit to keep the hole open and so check the flow of sap.

AUTUMN CABBAGE

This is sown at the end of April for planting out early in June. It can be treated in all respects similarly to summer cabbage and should be ready in October. If early savoys are grown in place of cabbage for October cutting, sowing should be delayed until early in May and the plants set out about the middle of June. In some parts of the north it is a common practice to plant this lot of savoys in small mounds of soil drawn together between the rows of second early potatoes. This is good practice provided that the potatoes are of a variety with an upright growing haulm and that the rows are sufficiently widely spaced. If a chemical potato fertilizer is being used for the potato plants, the same fertilizer may be used as a dressing for the savoys.

WINTER CABBAGE

Two types of cabbage can be made to cover the period from November to February inclusive, but only three sowings are necessary. The Christmas Drumhead type, sown early in May and planted out at the end of June, will turn in during November, while a second sowing made a fortnight later and set out early in July should provide cabbages throughout December. Unfortunately it is not uncommon for the late June/early July period to suffer from drought, which checks the plants at the outset, so some growers prefer to sow short runs of seed at intervals along the row, thin to single plants and so avoid transplanting. This can be a good plan provided (a) that in the 'chopping out' of unwanted seedlings just as much care is taken to retain only top quality plants as would be taken in selecting plants from a nursery bed; and (b) that sowings are postponed until mid-May and end May respectively. For supplies during January and February a single sowing of the long-standing variety January King will be sufficient. This should be made about the middle of May and planted out mid-July.

As an alternative, or in addition to cabbage, savoys can be grown except in industrial areas where the puckered foliage encourages contamination with soot, rendering the produce inedible. Since, however, the savoy is so highly specialized as regards dates of maturity, a different variety must be sown for each month in which supplies are required. Thus a medium variety, sown mid-May and planted early July, will be needed for November cutting whilst the lates will be sown in early May and planted mid-July for December/January cutting and again in mid-May for end-July planting to produce heads in February and March. The last sowing ought to be made in every garden and on every allotment, using one of the very latest sorts, because savoys are the only type of cabbage that is available in March.

Sowing and planting dates given above apply to the south of England where winter cabbage can usually follow any late spring crop (e.g., cloche-grown lettuce, peas, or broad beans) for which the ground was well manured in autumn; but in the north, where planting dates must be brought forward by several weeks, it is not possible to take a previous crop from the same land in the year of planting. Most of what has been said about preparing the land for summer cabbage applies equally well to winter cabbage; but it must be emphasized that the land must be sufficiently well drained to prevent it from getting sodden wet in winter. Winter cabbages also require less nitrogen and more potash than summer crops because you want a harder type of growth. I have found that a tomato fertilizer (or even John Innes Base Fertilizer) is better than an ordinary vegetable fertilizer for this crop and in addition I advise dressing the land just before planting with extra sulphate of potash (¾ lb. per rod) which helps the lates to withstand hard weather and with soot (14 lb. per rod) which promotes a good, healthy, dark colour.

Winter cabbages must be spaced not less than 18 ins. apart in rows 2 ft apart and will often need 2 ft each way. It is a wise precaution to earth them up to some extent, without in any sense moulding them up as was suggested in the case of sprouts; this is just to firm the plants and assist them to stand up against the autumn gales.

SPRING CABBAGE

This is a very different proposition from summer, autumn, or winter cabbage. It aims to produce, as it were, two different types of vegetable namely (i) spring greens (which are actually loose un-hearted cabbages) during March and April and (ii) ordinary hearted cabbage during April, May, and June.

The principal difficulty with spring cabbage is the uncertainty, not to say perversity, of our climate. At the time when the seed is due to be sown there may quite well be a drought which can result in irregular germination and weakly seedlings which are promptly attacked by the flea beetle. This is the first problem that has to be tackled. It is unwise to soak the ground just prior to sowing as this will tend to make it lumpy and, if it is at all heavy, it will clog; but it is an excellent plan to give it a thorough soaking a week or so beforehand and then, at sowing time, to re-moisten the surface layers only, using the spray nozzle of the hose to produce the effect of a refreshing shower of rain. After sowing, tread the drills very firm, mulch lightly with fresh lawn mowings to prevent trouble with sparrows, and use a flea-beetle dust.

Drought conditions may also obtain at the time of transplanting. The young plants must therefore be made turgid with water before they are lifted and should be puddled into their final quarters.

Contrary to the general rule that cabbages prefer an open situation, those sown in autumn do often succeed best in private gardens where they receive some shelter from cold winds, especially those from the east. But this very protection may prove to be the undoing of the plants in a mild autumn because they will tend to grow soft and proud so that either a bitter spell in winter will kill them outright or, if the winter also is mild, they will be upset by the first cold winds of spring, will promptly turn blue, and will ultimately bolt.

Errors in manuring can also lead to failure. Spring cabbage must not be given the generous manurial treatment accorded to summer and autumn cabbage. The ground should have been well manured for a previous crop, such as peas or beans, but manuring at the time when the site is being prepared for planting the cabbages should be confined in the main to the application of a single organic fertilizer, preferably fish guano (14 lb. per rod or ½ lb. per sq. yd) with, as alternatives, either hoof and horn meal (10 lb. per rod or 6 oz. per sq. yd). Gardeners who are relying more on bought fertilizers than on home-made garden compost should also add a dressing of sulphate of potash (1 oz. per sq. yd). Really first-class spring cabbages may be had if the soil in which the plants are to be set out is generously mulched with garden compost beforehand. No other feeds, whether organic or chemical, are needed. The whole job of growing spring cabbage is to secure a plant which is strong enough to stand the winter and yet not so far advanced as to bolt when spring arrives, and any dressing with fertilizer containing mineral nitrogen in the autumn is liable to defeat both these objects. It is a different matter when the plants have suffered from frost damage after a very hard winter. In fact, if the plants are not being grown by organic methods their rate of recovery and the ultimate yield will then be wholly dependent on the application of nitrogenous fertilizers. The first application is made at the beginning of February and then repeated (a) a month later for hearted cabbage and (b) twice at fortnightly intervals for the production of spring greens. Nothing is better for the purpose than Chilean potash nitrate (¾ oz. per sq. yd) but nitro-chalk can be used as an alternative at the rate of 1½ oz. per sq. yd.

The choice of a suitable variety or varieties for your particular locality is a most important factor in the cultivation of spring cabbage. The correct date of sowing is also important and it pays the beginner to take advice on this point from successful growers in his own area. Undoubtedly the best plan is to make two sowings of each of two different varieties between 20 July and the end of August and to plant out finally from mid to end September (and not a day later than 25 October), putting the first batch of each variety 2 ft apart and interplanting with the later batch, the rows being

18 ins. apart. Since all sowings must be to some extent experimental and growth will vary according to weather conditions, it is probable that plants from one or other of the two sowings will not be up to the standard that is required for hearting; so every alternate plant can be drawn young for consumption as spring greens, leaving the hearting crop a couple of feet apart. When the heads of these have been cut, the stumps can be left for a period to sprout and yield a supply of late spring and early summer 'greens'.

A useful tip is to put some of the spring cabbage plants in a frame during the third or fourth week in October or alternatively to cover them with cloches in case a particularly severe winter cripples those left unprotected out of doors. The plants in the frame will come in about fourteen days after the other kinds or they can be used to fill gaps.

Another useful hint is to use any surplus seed of a very quick-maturing autumn-sowing variety to make a July sowing in rows without transplanting for the production of small-hearted cabbages for cutting about the third week in December. If on the other hand you prefer to make your sowings for spring cutting in this manner, you should not sow before the first half of August. The rows for all these sowings should be 15 ins. apart for hearted cabbage and 12 ins. apart for spring greens, and the plants should be thinned to 9 ins.

When all the plants being set out are of the same batch, and there is no interplanting, the rows should be 15 ins. apart and the plants set 12 ins. apart in the rows if the whole crop is to be cut as spring greens. But if the whole crop is to be left to heart up these distances must be increased to as much as 24 ins. between rows and 18 ins. between plants according to the size of the variety.

Waterlogging, such as occurs in low-lying gardens, is fatal to spring cabbages; they are indeed unlikely to succeed in any soil that retains so much moisture that it cannot be hoed in early spring. If you have the least doubt about the effectiveness of your drainage, you will be well advised to plant on ridges or on mounds of soil ('cobs', as commercial growers term them); alternatively, you can earth the plants up lightly in November, forming a continuous ridge which will drain away surplus water from the crowns as well as prevent damage in winter gales. Incidentally, the better the drainage, the earlier the maturity of spring cabbage, other things being equal.

One might add one more tip, and that is that savoys may be sown in late July and made to serve the purpose of spring cabbage. It is true that many people consider them inférior to true spring cabbage, but that does not alter the fact that they are less of a gamble, because they suffer few casualties in a severe winter and are extremely unlikely to bolt.

Pickling Cabbage

All the best pickling (i.e. red) cabbages come from sowings made in August and wintered either in a cold frame or under cloches. The young plants grown from these sowings are set out not less than 2 ft apart in rows 2 ft 6 ins. apart in March or April in the south and in late April or early May in the north. If you cannot sow in autumn, you can do so in northern districts in a frame or under cloches from mid-February to late March and plant out between mid-May and mid-June; but in the south you should sow in the open in March and plant out as early as the weather permits in order to get the longest possible growing season. In either case the heads will be much smaller than those from autumn sowings. Manuring and general cultivation of autumn-sown red cabbage is exactly the same as for winter cabbage, while the spring-sown stuff can be treated as if it were ordinary summer cabbage. The crop is usually cut and pickled about the middle of August; late sowings can be left to continue growing for another month or so but under no circumstances should cutting be delayed until cold weather sets in.

How to Cut Cabbages

When cutting hearted cabbages in summer and autumn (or in winter and spring if you want to clear the ground), lift the entire plant with a fork, take it to the compost heap, where you may cut off the stalk and root and the outer leaves. But if you do not want to clear the ground in winter and spring, cut the main heart out of the cabbage, leaving the large outer leaves attached to the stump. In due course shoots will appear and the old leaves can be cut away, leaving the young growths to grow into 'greens'. When, however, spring cabbages are deliberately cut in a semi-hearted condition for use as spring greens the whole of the top is cut off and the stalk and roots are then disposed of as soon as convenient.

Exhibiting Cabbages

If you go in for exhibition work, it is a good thing to grow some cabbages as a stand-by because good cabbages are worth more to you than not-so-good cauliflowers if the latter crop should let you down – and I say this with the full realization that you can get a total of 20 points for cauliflowers as opposed to a maximum of only 15 points for green cabbages (whether green or red) and savoys. The art of growing cabbages to the exhibition standard of quality consists largely in choosing the right variety and sowing it at the right time so that it is at its best at the time of the show. Failure to do this involves at any rate a lot of extra fuss and bother, especially if the plants are too forward. It is possible to retard them by driving a fork in beneath them and levering them up just sufficiently to break the feeding roots; but if the date of the show is close at hand and you lack confidence in the ability of your plants to stand even those few days longer I would prefer to lift the plants completely and hang them upside down in a cool dark cellar or shed. In both cases you must spray them regularly with cold water twice daily to prevent any sign of wilting from manifesting itself. Freshness is one of the factors that accounts for many points in the judges' marking.

It is of course essential to keep exhibition produce free from pests, particularly caterpillars and aphis, and this can be an art in itself in some seasons. But where any damage is confined to the outer leaves which have served their purpose and have already begun to deteriorate there is no reason why these leaves should not be carefully removed provided that this does not upset the symmetry of the cabbage and, in the case of collections or dishes of cabbage, leaves the three specimens required for this purpose still evenly matched. The remaining leaves surrounding the heart must however be perfect.

Although the firmness of the heart accounts for one third of the maximum points that can be gained for cabbage, the heart must still be fresh and tender and free from splitting; the judges will probably cut one of your exhibits in half so that they may be able to satisfy themselves on this point.

Great size is of no merit in green cabbages which should be of a weight of about 2 lb. apiece, i.e., sufficient for one cooking for an average family. A 4-lb. cabbage has usually to be cut in half and the second half retained uncooked for use on another occasion and this practice has nothing to commend it. In the case of red cabbage, however, it is the large heads which win the prizes: 3 points being allocated to size, while 4 points are allocated to excellence of colour which must be a good deep red throughout.

Capsicums (or Peppers)

These are tropical plants from South America and in this country are best treated in the same way as tomatoes and grown in a greenhouse where they are very decorative and get on quite well among tuberous begonias and the other flowering plants which are commonly grown under glass during summer. It is only in the very warmest districts and gardens that capsicums can be fruited outdoors, preferably against a south wall, and even then they can be a flop in a bad season in the same way as outdoor tomatoes were before the introduction of earlier ripening cultivars; while, although it is quite practicable in most areas to fruit them under cloches, it is a bit of a nuisance because the cloches have to be elevated to give sufficient headroom and, seeing that the plants have to be raised in a heated greenhouse, there is little point in moving them outside unless of course, lacking you own greenhouse, you obtain your plants from a neighbour with the necessary facilities. The same considerations apply to frame culture.

It is the large 'sweet' peppers that are usually grown by amateurs. These have long been popular in the U.S.A. but it is only in recent years that they have become at all well known in Britain, largely as a result of the publicity that has been given to them in the cookery pages of women's magazines. In addition to their piquant and unusual flavour their brilliant colouring makes dishes more attractive to the eye. If you want to find out whether you like the taste, you can now buy the fresh fruits from most of the better-class greengrocers in autumn or you can buy them in tins at any time under the name of 'pimentos' – but be on your guard that the grocer does not foist upon you instead of sweet peppers a tin of 'allspice' which is also called pimento but comes from a Jamaican tree and is no relative of the capsicum. The small 'hot' peppers, known to most cooks as chillies or in the form of cayenne pepper or tabasco sauce, are quite different from the 'sweet' varieties and are hardly worth growing except for fun, as few households have a use for any substantial quantity of these highly pungent little capsicums which created such a sensation when Christopher Columbus first brought them from America at a time when only the oriental black pepper was known in Europe.

Capsicums want a long growing season, and one of the principal factors in their successful cultivation is early sowing. The end of February is not too soon if the plants are to be grown throughout in the greenhouse but if they are to be fruited under cloches or outdoors it is better to delay sowing until the end of March. Space the seeds 1 in. apart in trays of John Innes Seed Compost, push them just beneath the surface and germinate in a temperature of 60–65° F. Prick off when three leaves have been formed either direct into 3-ins. pots or, if for outdoors, into soil blocks, using John Innes Potting Compost No. 1. The plants in pots must be shifted before they become root-bound into 6-ins. or 7-ins. pots of John Innes Potting Compost No. 3 in which they will fruit; but if any of this batch are intended for planting under cloches or in frames or open ground the 5-ins. size will be large enough. Plants in the 5-ins. pots and those in soil blocks can be put out under cloches or in frames from the end of April to the end of May, according to district and season, but, if to be grown on without protection, they had better wait until the beginning of June since it is imperative that they should not get frosted. Set them 18 ins. apart. Under cloches (which must be of the large barn type), plant them in a shallow trench and keep covered throughout growth, raising the cloches on cloche raisers.

All the capsicums form bushy plants about 2½ ft tall with leaves similar to those of lilac. They bear white flowers rather like those of the mock orange, and the fruits, with one or two exceptions, start off by being green and then turn red or yellow when ripe. The plants must be kept reasonably moist at the roots at all times (and those under cloches must be well soaked at the time of transplanting); in addition it is usually necessary to syringe them twice a day, in the morning and late afternoon, on both sides of the leaves, using tepid water, in order to prevent a foothold being gained by red spider mite which seems to be particularly attracted by capsicums. Plants growing in the open ground and exposed to normal rainfall are naturally less troublesome in this respect except during periods of drought.

It is unnecessary to pinch the plants when 8 ins. high, as is sometimes recommended; I find that they do just as well if allowed to develop naturally. It is wise, however, to nip off the earliest flowers, as this will increase the total crop of fruits, and you should feed regularly as soon as the fruits begin to swell. The feed can be a liquid manure solution – made by suspending a sack of animal dung in a tub or tank. Always dilute the liquor to the colour of weak tea before applying it. Alternatively, a good liquid tomato fertilizer may be used.

The fruits of sweet peppers can be picked and eaten green and unripe; the Italians prefer them that way. Or you can wait until they are red (or yellow) and fully ripened. It is not true that you are bound to pick them green, as some books state, but, whereas in the greenhouse cropping will begin about the third week of August and with the aid of artificial heat will continue into early winter, plants under cloches, in frames, or outdoors will seldom yield pickable fruits until September, and the fruits will cease to develop as soon as the weather turns chilly, so that in these cases you are almost bound to have to pick a big proportion of the fruits green.

Hot peppers must always be allowed to ripen before picking and for this reason are best grown in a heated greenhouse throughout. *Do not however grow them in the same greenhouse as sweet peppers as cross-pollination may bring about some queer and most unpleasant results.*

Most good cookery books give recipes for making chilli vinegar, cayenne essence, and so on. If you want to dry your chillies and cayenne peppers put them in a wire basket in a mild oven for about twelve hours, leaving the door open to prevent the heat from rising too high; for you are trying to dry them, not cook them. If you then wish to convert the cayenne fruits into cayenne pepper weigh the pods and measure out ¼ of their weight of salt. Dry the salt in the oven and, while it is still hot, pound the pepper pods up with it very finely. In this way you will produce a perfect sample of cayenne pepper which can be bottled and kept in the larder. But I warn you to protect your face with cold cream and your eyes with glasses while you do your pounding and to perform this operation near the open back door where a draught will carry the finer dust away from you, or otherwise you will end up with a scarlet and inflamed countenance and weeping eyes, as members of my own family did when they first 'made pepper' without taking any precautions.

Cardoons

It is generally supposed that the wild cardoon (*Cynara cardunculus*), which is found growing in Spain and Sardinia, is the parent type from which the globe artichoke (*Cynara scolymus*) has been developed by cultivation. The cardoon is, however, not grown for its buds but only for its blanched stalks which resemble to some extent the 'chards' produced from globe artichokes.

At one time cardoons were grown in most large gardens but they do not ever seem to have become well known among ordinary gardeners and therefore have not achieved general popularity. Nevertheless they make an attractive winter vegetable and anybody who can grow good celery can grow even better cardoons. Seed is obtainable from several of the leading seed-merchants.

The best plants undoubtedly come from March sowings in a heated greenhouse or propagator, three seeds being sown in each 3-ins. pot and the seedlings later thinned to one per pot. In April, as soon as the first true leaves have formed, move the plants to an unheated frame, keep them fairly close, and do not give them a lot of water. Harden off at the beginning of May and plant out a good 2½ ft apart. If you have no glass, then do not sow outdoors until the first week of May, when you should sow three or four seeds at intervals of 18 ins. and thin each group to a single plant when the seedlings are 2 ins. high.

Cardoons demand a rich soil and an abundance of water. If planting out from pots, prepare sites as for marrows, taking out holes and putting in a mixture of old, rotted manure or some garden compost with a few handfuls of fresh lawn mowings, then covering this with 6 ins. of old potting soil and leaving the level such that after all the stuff has settled there will be a saucer-shaped hollow for the retention of water. If sowing on the site, it will be easier to take out a continuous trench 18 ins. wide and 12 ins. deep, put a thick layer of good animal manure or rich compost into the bottom, and mix it with the subsoil, then return the excavated soil to a depth of 6 ins. after mixing it liberally with old leafmould. As before the finished surface should be below the level of the surrounding ground. If more than one row is grown, the rows must be 3 ft apart to allow space for subsequent operations.

From May to September the principal attentions called for are watering and feeding. The trenches or depressions must be flooded at regular intervals in the absence of adequate rainfall, towards the end of July a mulch will be helpful, and throughout August the plants must be fed weekly with dilute liquid manure. Keep the hoe going to prevent the surface soil from caking and to keep down weeds. When each plant is 1 ft high, tie it lightly to a 2-ft cane.

Blanching can commence at the beginning of September; but this is rather a waste of good vegetable because cardoons are much more appreciated in winter than when plenty of other fresh produce is still available. There are two methods. One consists in bunching all the leaves together and tying them at the top with raffia or string, then proceeding exactly as you would with celery, either tying corrugated paper round the stems or winding them round and round with strips of brown paper from soil level upwards, leaving only the leafy tops exposed and finally packing earth round to exclude all light. By this method blanching takes from six to eight weeks. The other method, as practised in France, dispenses with earthing up and results in a quick blanch in less than a month. By this method each plant is secured to its stake by three ties and then thatched with a 3-ins. layer of straw from tip to toe so that it resembles a bottle-straw, the tied straw top being turned over like a nightcap.

Whichever method is adopted the cardoons must be absolutely dry at the time the wrappings are applied. Precautions must also be taken to keep the crop free from slugs. Some strains of cardoons are exceedingly thorny and one can easily get torn to pieces wrapping them up even if gloves are worn. This difficulty can be overcome by arming a friend with two sticks joined by a length of string which he can twist round the leaves to gather them together and hold them in a bunch while you do the tying.

If frosts threaten before blanching begins, throw some light protective litter over the plants at night and remove it in the morning. Once wrapped they will be safe enough until hard winter weather sets in when any plants still in the ground must be dug up with as much soil as possible around the roots and transferred to a shed, garage, or cellar where more soil, peat, or sand should be heaped over the roots. So long as you keep the roots moist, the cardoons will remain in good condition for several weeks and the stems ought not to go limp. If the place of storage is completely dark (e.g. a cellar) you can remove all the wrappings, but otherwise leave them on.

When cut for use and trimmed up, cardoons look like celery and are used like celery. The white stalks and thick leaf ribs can be eaten raw in salads, or they can be stewed or braised in accordance with any recipe for cooking celery.

Carrots

The carrot is the most recent of all root vegetables to be used as human food. The carrots we eat today have been developed from a wild biennial plant, *Daucus carota*, which is a member of the parsley family and a native of Europe and the British Isles. This plant, however, is deadly poisonous so that our forefathers could hardly be expected to eat it with avidity. French and German plant breeders eliminated the poisonous element and gave us the field carrot of which the roots have been fed to cattle both on the Continent and in this country from the days of Queen Elizabeth I onwards. The French also used them in the manufacture of sugar – for carrots have a fairly high sugar content – and for distilling alcohol.

In the meantime horticulturists laboured to improve the type by getting rid of the fibrous texture of the field carrot and the hard central yellow core. Thus we get the garden carrot of which the best strains today are red throughout, although the root of the wild carrot is white, and on the Continent both white and purple carrots are still grown and eaten.

It was not until the Second World War that the value of the carrot as a highly nutritive vegetable was brought home to the people of Britain. It is particularly rich in vitamin A and is a cure for night blindness.

Soil

The ideal soil for carrots is a sandy loam with a high water table which will never dry out in summer even during spells of drought. Such a soil is found naturally in the alluvial sands of the Fens, in the Nottingham area, in Yorkshire, and in the moss lands of Lancashire. Unless you live in one of these areas it is wholly impracticable to grow long carrots except in small numbers and by artificial methods solely for exhibition, as will be described later. It is also useless to attempt to grow any kind of carrot in a raw, sticky clay or in gravelly soil (unless you are prepared to sift out the stones). Light, sandy soils which hold no moisture in summer can be utilized for only the earliest 'bunched' carrots; but in between these extremes any soil will grow the short and stumpy and the intermediate types of carrot provided that you make it fine and even textured, free from grit and stones, and so friable that the roots can penetrate and expand without effort. You cannot grow any good root crops in lumpy, stony ground. This means that a heavy soil must be lightened by the addition of sand, peat, and garden compost – don't use boiler ashes, which would scratch the roots – and you must fork it and hoe it and rake it until you have reduced it almost to powder. It is a laborious job on some soils; the depth to which you must carry your improvement schemes depends on the length of the roots you intend to grow. But even though you confine your attentions to the uppermost layer, do the job thoroughly while you are at it – it will pay you. If your soil is already on the light side, then of course you will omit the sand but should dig in as much sifted leafmould and wood ashes as you can possibly get hold of.

Manuring

It is an accepted rule that the ground for carrots must not have been recently treated with animal manure which goes on in lumps and causes the roots to stray from their rightful path in order to feed in a specially rich 'pocket'. This causes them to fork and become unfit to eat. There is no objection to your using, prior to sowing, plenty of well-rotted garden compost so well decomposed that it mixes evenly throughout the soil. All the same it is better if you can arrange to grow your carrots on land which has been well-fed with garden compost for a previous crop, such as garden peas. All that is needed is a dressing rich in phosphate and potash applied in the form of 2 oz superphosphate, 1 oz sulphate of potash and 1 oz steamed boneflour per square yard.

Sowing and Thinning

All the best seed merchants now treat carrot seed so as to remove the hairs which render it difficult to sow, so it is no longer necessary to mix it with sand, as recommended by some of the older gardening books. There are 18,500 seeds in an ounce and, if properly stored under cool, dry conditions, they will remain 'live' for five years. The seed rows are usually spaced about 1 ft apart and the drills must be very shallow, not more than ½ in. deep, the seed being hidden by only the very lightest covering of fine, sifted soil. During dry weather this can result in the seed rows drying out at frequent intervals so that germination is very poor. This can often be avoided by soaking the drill thoroughly before sowing and then, after the seed has been sown and covered, carefully drawing earth from either side of the drill or sifting peat over it, to form a narrow ridge from 1 to 3 ins. deep according to the nature of the soil – the lighter it is, the deeper the covering. This ridge must not be left in position for much more than a week, otherwise the seed will suffocate; so on the assumption that germination will have taken place in seven to ten days, you should then rake the ridge away so as to leave the seed no deeper than it was covered originally. Some people sow the seed at intervals along the row and then thin each group of seedlings to one plant when they are about 1 in. high; but it is less trouble and far more profitable to sow continuously and use the thinnings in the kitchen. The first lot of thinnings will of course be too small to be eaten but later thinnings will yield delicious little roots for immediate consumption. The surface soil after sowing must be made very firm and even and after each thinning it must again be pressed back firmly where it has been disturbed. Loose soil encourages the carrot fly. It is easier to sow seeds in pellet form, though pelleted seeds must always be sown in really moist soil, so soaking the seed drills is very necessary unless the ground is quite moist. Sow the pellets at about 1 in. apart. Pelleted carrot seeds also eliminate overcrowding of the seedlings.

Carrot Fly

This pest is most likely to be met with in large gardens, on allotments, and in districts where lots of carrots are grown year after year. Where a small crop is grown in a private garden here and there it may never be met with at all. The fly is ½ in. long and of ½-in. wing span, shiny black with a brown head and yellow legs. It turns up any time from mid-April to June and proceeds to lay eggs in crevices in the soil right up against the carrot plants. The eggs hatch into maggots which first eat off the tip of the main root and then bore into the upper portion. The first sign of their presence is the wilting of the foliage in hot sunshine; then the foliage turns reddish and in due course may become yellow and wither away altogether. The carrots themselves may grow forked and misshapen and of a rusty red colour. Sometimes they go rotten; sometimes they develop deep cracks right across the root, and these cracks are invaded by slugs, millipedes, and woodlice, which are blamed for the trouble caused by the carrot fly. After about three weeks the maggots pupate and the second generation of flies does not appear until the end of July at the earliest. Flies continue to emerge until September but their number at any one time in August and September is considerably less than in early summer; hence carrots sown early in July are exposed to less risk of attack than those sown in May or early June.

Maggots of the second generation pupate at varying times during autumn and winter, but do not emerge from the soil as flies until spring. They then take shelter in hedges, ditches, and clumps of weeds adjoining the site of the previous crop, biding their time until a new carrot crop shows up when, if it is within smellable distance, they will soon move over and start work on it.

The first step in keeping off the carrot fly is to keep down weeds and as far as practicable deprive it of its spring hiding-places. We have already seen that the disturbance of the soil when thinning is favourable to the operations of the carrot fly. You should therefore not only make the soil firm after thinning, but also water it copiously in order to consolidate the earth round the remaining roots. Never thin carrots if the soil is dry. To do so would lead to the breaking of foliage and roots during thinning and the carroty odour is bound to attract a carrot fly or two. Immediately after you have thinned your carrots, bury all unwanted tiny plants and all carrot foliage, cut from usable thinnings, inside the compost heap. Growing onions alongside carrots is said to deter the carrot fly which is confused by the stronger onion smell. Carrot fly is rare in organic gardens. Possibly, with so many other odours arising from the garden compost used in such gardens, the smell from the carrot bed is too weak to attract it.

Carrots for Storage

Carrots for storage are usually sown in May or early June; but a sowing made early in July will provide sizable roots by the beginning of November, and this sowing will escape the attentions of the first generation of carrot flies. It is most important to keep the crop weed-free: groundsel, fat hen, and other broad-leaved weeds will soon choke a bed of seedling carrots. Apart from this, keep the plants growing rapidly by watering often in dry weather. Drought not only stunts growth, it also leads to an infestation of aphids.

Carrots for storage should be lifted during dry weather not later than the end of October. By that date you should have observed the usual signs and indications of maturity in the form of a natural curling (not shrivelling) of the foliage, a falling away of the outer leaves, and a change of colour from rich lustrous to dull listless green. There is no point in leaving them longer because carrots are only moderately frost-resistant and, even if they survive outdoors, they run the risk of being spoiled by slugs and other soil pests; or of cracking. Where there has been an attack by carrot fly, the sooner the roots are taken up the better while the grubs are still inside them and before they have escaped to pupate in the surrounding soil.

Lift the roots by driving a fork in at the side of the row in order to loosen them and then pulling them up with the free hand. After throwing out all that are badly damaged, cut off the leaves as near the crown as possible. Take care not actually to cut the crown for, if you do, the root will shrivel and perhaps rot. But unless you cut as close to the crown as possible, the carrots will almost certainly produce shoots and become useless for cooking purposes.

If you have only a small crop, you can store the roots in sand or peat either in boxes or bins or on the floor of a cellar or shed. Put down a 2-ins. layer of sand or peat and follow this with alternate layers of carrots and storage material. Arrange the roots alternately, top to tail, with the root end of one carrot between the crowns of the two adjoining carrots. If your crop is a large one it can be clamped outdoors in a circular pile of haystack type.

One objection to clamping is that it is a great nuisance to have to open up a clamp for the sake of getting out an odd carrot or two. In that case, if you have a really dry patch of vacant ground fairly close to the kitchen door, you can dig out a hole of sufficient size to take a box or small barrel almost up to the rim. Line the hole with roofing felt or pieces of surplus linoleum, put in the box or barrel, pack your carrots into it without any storage material, and put on a lid of wood, asbestos sheeting, or any suitable material out of which you have cut a hole large enough to enable you to put your hand and arm in and draw the carrots out. Close this hole with a piece of flat paving stone or a couple of bricks, easily removable when you want to take some roots out of store. Then cover all the rest of the lid, first with a layer of straw, bracken, or the dried stalks of golden rod or michaelmas daisies, then with 6 ins. of soil. Finally, erect a tent-shaped roof of corrugated iron or any suitable material that is handy, or stand a cloche over the site to throw off rain. Please note however that this type of storage is no use on wet land where the hole can fill up with water in winter.

'Bunched Carrots'

The term 'bunched' is applied to the small succulent carrots which are sold in the shops tied together in bunches around the base of the foliage, which is left on. A bunch is either 24 carrots of equal size or 1½ lb. weight of carrots. The roots vary in size from ½ to 1½ ins. across early in the season, increasing to ¾ to 1¾ ins. later in the year.

While many private gardeners do not consider it worth while to grow maincrop carrots, seeing that they can be bought quite cheaply from the greengrocer and an average household would not use more than 56 lb. in a year, everybody ought to grow some 'bunched' carrots because these are not only more expensive but have a much wider range of uses in the kitchen.

Bunched carrots can be grown in hotbed frames, in cold frames, under cloches, and in the open. All sowings that mature before mid-May escape the carrot fly.

Culture in Heated Frames

Make up a bed 10 ins. deep early in the New Year, using a light soil rich in organic material such as spent mushroom-bed manure. Bring the surface to a fine tilth, level it, dust with lime, and sow seed broadcast and very thinly any time after 21 January, working the seed into the soil with a handfork; ¼ oz. of seed will fill a frame 4 × 4 ft. After sowing, firm the bed with a board or 'float'. Water freely, ventilate as weather permits, mat up on frosty nights, aim at a night temperature of 45–50° F., spray overhead from mid-March onwards, and remove the lights altogether in April. Pulling should commence about mid-April.

This crop can also be grown as part of a mixed scheme of intensive cultivation in hotbed frames, which are sown successionally with carrots between 15 January and 1 March and planted with Cheshunt Early Giant lettuce four days later. Sometimes carrots are sown in conjunction with radishes in soil-warmed frames during

February, the radish seeds being spaced 1 in. apart. In this case the crop receives less water until the radishes are pulled which will be several weeks before the carrots are ready.

In Cold Frames

Carrots can be grown on exactly the same lines in cold as in heated frames, either alone or with radishes or as part of a scheme including lettuce; but sowing is delayed until mid-February and the crop will be a month later than that from heated frames. In this case also, unless the carrots have the frame to themselves, liberal watering to make good any lack of moisture will be necessary immediately the other crops have been cleared.

Under Cloches

It is sometimes possible to sow as early as January if we get any decent sowing weather during that month. But as a rule it will be nearer the middle of February before you can sow. You can get five rows 4 ins. apart under barn cloches or two rows under tent cloches; or you can sow carrots on either side of a row of cloched peas or broad beans or in between two rows of cloched lettuce provided that the lettuces are sown or planted at the same time as the carrots. The crop can be decloched, as weather conditions permit, some time between the beginning and middle of April.

In the Open

It is possible to pull in June from a sowing of a quick-maturing 'Early Horn' type made in early March in the open on light soil in a sheltered border under a south wall. The intermediate types, which take about three months to attain a good size, are sown monthly from March to the end of July, while early varieties can be sown again in August in cold districts, and in September or October in warm ones, for pulling in November and December, provided that you are in a position to put cloches over them at the beginning of October. All these sowings should be made on strips of land which were well manured organically for a previous crop of some early vegetable which has been cleared in time to permit the soil being dug over and dressed with, say, fish manure, then allowed to settle down before the carrots go in. Rows should be 12 ins. apart and the most important item in their cultivation is the control of weeds.

When to Pull Young Carrots

Early carrots may be pulled as soon as you consider that they are big enough for immediate use. Preferably they should be about the thickness of a man's thumb; but thinnings of usable size will obviously be much smaller. Search the beds for the best roots at each pulling and always water the night before so that you pull when the soil is moist, otherwise the foliage may come away in your hand.

Do not leave late 'bunching' carrots in the soil when winter comes in the hope that you can go on pulling after Christmas – the roots are almost certain to become hard, colourless, and inedible.

Carrots for Exhibition

If you wish to win prizes with long carrots, then, unless you have a perfect deep 'carrot soil' – and you almost certainly haven't! – you must bore deep holes with a crowbar, 1 ft apart, and fill them up with fine compost. The soil from last year's chrysanthemum stools, sieved and mixed with a balanced fertilizer is ideal for the job. If your ground is not well drained it will be better not to bore holes but to put your compost in large drain pipes or barrels and grow your carrots in these above the general level of the garden. Some people dislike such methods as being artificial; but unfortunately they will have been adopted by most of your rivals and you are more or less compelled to try and beat them on their own ground. For the early autumn shows seed must be sown not later than the beginning of April, putting a pinch of seed at each station and thinning the resultant seedlings to one. If the weather is bad invert a glass jam jar over each clump of seedlings until they are well away.

Short carrots for exhibition can be drawn from normal sowings provided that you thin to not less than 6 ins. apart and provided that your soil is by nature, or has been rendered, light and sandy. It must also have an exceedingly fine tilth throughout its depth because, in addition to the fleshy, edible root, a carrot makes a mass of exceptionally long, hair-like feeding roots and if these cannot find their way easily through the soil distortion is almost certain to result.

Roots growing in drainpipes or barrels must of course be watered regularly during growth. Unless you keep carrot rows uniformly moist during dry weather, you will risk splitting the carrots if you apply water once the soil has dried out a lot. It is better to rely on hoeing instead. As a matter of fact the best carrots are those grown in a position where they will be shaded by adjacent crops during summer – this not only delays drying out in hot weather but also helps to keep down the temperature. The deepest colour comes from growing the plants at about 65° F. by day and 45° F. by night, and in autumn it may be helpful to use cloches to prevent the day temperature from falling below 65° F.

Draw soil over the crowns of the carrots, or mulch them with peat, to prevent greening, corkiness, or canker. Leave the roots in the ground as late as possible except when a wet spell threatens to cause them to split, when it may be necessary to lift some time before the date of the show and store in sand or peat.

Carefully excavate the long roots and lift short ones with a trowel. Unless the schedule definitely requires you to leave the foliage on, cut it off an inch above the crown – it serves no useful purpose and can be an untidy hindrance on the bench. Wash with a sponge and plenty of water with a little shredded soap added – never scrub with a brush and take care not to bruise. Trim off all small rootlets but leave the main root intact with the tap root as a clearly defined unit. Throw out all specimens with slug or worm holes or showing signs of damage by carrot fly

Six carrots make up a dish and should be spread out fanwise with the whip end to the front. But in a collection you usually have to stage ten roots and these look best arranged as a pyramid and garnished with parsley.

Carrots are marked high – up to 20 points – because they are not easy to grow to perfection. Under R.H.S. rules 3 points go to shape which must be good without side roots or fangs, 6 points to uniformity, 6 points to colour which must be clear and bright, not dull, wishy-washy, and anaemic, and 5 points for condition – a well-grown carrot should be tender, juicy, and sugary when tasted raw.

If you want to exhibit your prize carrots at a second show, store them in sand with the green remnant of the top growth sticking out and before staging again pare off a little of the top and remove any bit of stalk that may have become discoloured.

Cauliflowers

(See also Brassicas)

Cauliflowers, as sold by the greengrocer, come from two different types of plant. The cauliflower plant proper is not hardy and can therefore be made to supply heads only during summer and autumn, unless, of course, it is forced under glass. As the Cole-Flower it was known and grown in the south of Europe long before we had it over here. It is first mentioned in 540 B.C.; the Moors grew it in Spain in about the twelfth century; and improved strains were developed in Cyprus and in Naples. Almost inevitably, as a result of being coddled, it became less hardy than the cabbage, and we have never been successful in restoring its hardiness. It came to England before the eighteenth century when Dr Johnson said: 'Of all the flowers in the garden, I like cauliflower' – we trust that he was referring only to the kitchen garden. Enterprising London market gardeners put acres of land under cloches to grow cauliflowers and for a time Britain exported them to the Continent. Then the Dutch, Danish, and German growers got busy and many of our modern strains owe much to them. It remains a fact nevertheless that the cauliflower does not like our climate and that is really the reason why it is so difficult to grow well here.

Most of the cauliflowers which we eat between October and June come from the broccoli plant, which is generally fairly hardy and in some cases extremely hardy. The cauliflower-broccoli, if one must use such a cumbersome term, is the most artificial of all the Brassicas. It has been so bred that the varieties fall into four groups, each maturing at a different season, though all sown at the same time. Some of these, such as the Roscoff types from north-west Brittany, are not hardy enough for our climate and will grow only within twenty miles of the sea coast in the maritime area from

Chichester to Penzance; others, such as those from Anjou, are hardy but fail if grown in mild areas. The best hybrids are those evolved by our own growers in England and Scotland. Unfortunately none of them head up before April whereas the French sorts head up from mid-December onwards.

Both types of cauliflower have certain disadvantages from the amateur's point of view. Each plant occupies an appreciable amount of space and produces only one head which has got to be cut and eaten as soon as it is ready. Small private gardeners and allotment-holders have space for only a comparatively few plants, and these plants have an annoying habit of 'turning in', or forming their heads, all at one and the same time. Accordingly, there is apt to be a glut of cauliflowers and then no more for a considerable period; for if left upon the plants, the heads will open and become unfit for eating, and although the plants can be pulled up by the roots and hung head downwards in a cool dark place, the heads will not keep in good condition for longer than a week. It therefore all too often becomes a case of cauliflower with every meal and cauliflower *au gratin* just to use the things up, although some of the surplus can, on occasion, be turned into piccalilli.

Obviously it cannot pay the small grower to buy a selection of packets of seed for succession unless he is raising plants for neighbours and friends; for he will only want a pinch of seed from each packet for his own requirements. As an alternative in the case of summer cauliflower it is suggested that the amateur should buy a packet of one variety only, All the Year Round; while as regards cauliflower-broccoli the small grower's best plan is to confine himself to the varieties which form their heads in the late autumn and early winter, before the worst frosts come, and to rely on 'spring greens' after Christmas.

SUMMER (OR TRUE) CAULIFLOWERS

The true cauliflower will not grow in districts where extremely hot summers and dry soil are experienced, and it must have a deeply dug, rich soil. If you are unable to provide it with its requirements in the matter of district and soil, it is a waste of time and space to attempt to grow it. Gravel soils and heavy clays, especially if the latter are waterlogged, will never produce good summer cauliflowers. On the other hand, where the soil is otherwise suitable, summer cauliflowers will often give a good account of themselves on newly broken up grassland, replacing potatoes as a first crop, provided that the turves are well buried and the ground thoroughly consolidated. Suitable precautions must also be taken to deal with soil pests.

The site for the early summer crop must be in full sun with some protection from cold winds: under no circumstances must this crop be planted in a frost pocket. But the late summer and autumn cauliflowers appreciate a cooler position where they are sheltered from hot sun and drying winds. In neither case, however, must they be set close to trees or tall hedges because they are then likely to draw up and become spindled and weakly, producing only small heads.

These cauliflowers are gross feeders. When digging the site you must incorporate cow manure at the rate of 4 cwt per rod. This is also the minimum rate at which good ripe garden compost should be used, whether dug in or spread onto the soil surface at planting time. If you are short of both of these, substitute hoof and horn meal (6 lb. per rod) but bear in mind that this organic fertilizer lacks the 'body' of manure or garden compost and will not help at all to moisture in the soil during dry weather. If you use chemical fertilizers, too, hoe in a dressing of Growmore. During their period of growth the plants will also take all the manure water and soot water you have time and patience to give them.

Early Cauliflowers

By far the best early summer cauliflowers are those sown in autumn and wintered in frames in a bed of old potting soil. But it may be of interest to record that seedling cauliflowers in my garden in Oxfordshire were frequently wintered under cloches and came through just as well as those in frames – this was doubtless because they were grown hard in poor soil on purpose to enable them to withstand the rigours of winter, although they are of course, by nature, tender plants.

For the purpose of this crop seed is usually sown about the end of September in the south of England, and somewhat earlier in colder areas, using 3-ins.-deep boxes from which the best seedlings are pricked out 3 ins. apart in a cold frame during October. The soil in the frame must not be rich but it should not lack lime. Once the seedlings have settled in, the light is removed from the frame during the day and is replaced only at night or during heavy rain or frost. If air is admitted at all times at the bottom of the light it is generally unnecessary to cover with mats during frost. Towards the end of March the light is removed permanently in order to harden off the plants and they are set out in their final positions outdoors, 20 ins. apart each way as weather permits, not later than mid-April, if possible. If they can be covered with barn cloches till they reach the top of the glass, so much the better. It is also a good plan to take a catch crop of lettuce from the cauliflower rows, using February-sown seedlings, two cabbage and one cos lettuce being planted between each two cauliflowers. The latter should form curds from late May onwards throughout June.

Some growers do not plant their seedlings in a frame-bed but prick them off direct into 3½-ins. pots or soil blocks which are stood 'pot thick' (or 'block thick') in the frame. Others lift their plants from the frame-bed and transfer them to pots or blocks in January, when they are either returned to a frame with an ash base or taken into an unheated span-roofed greenhouse where they are easier to manage. The object in both cases is to reduce root disturbance at planting out time.

If you have a heated greenhouse and wish to avoid the responsibility of overwintering plants in frames, you can sow seed in boxes in gentle heat early in January, prick off into boxes, pots, or blocks, grow on for a period on a shelf close to the glass, then remove to a cold frame, harden off, and plant out during April or May. Plants from this sowing may mature about the same time as the autumn-sown crop or they may be up to a month later – it all depends on the district and season.

If you wish to overwinter under cloches, sow three rows under them early in September in the north or at the end of September in the south, thin to 1 in. apart in October or November, and plant out 1 ft apart in late March or early April, covering with barn cloches until the plants touch the roof glasses; or, alternatively, if conditions permit, plant 1 ft square without covering. In the very warmest parts of the country it is sometimes possible to sow four or five rows under a barn cloche in January, prick out 4 ins. square under barn cloches, and plant out 18 ins. apart in rows 2 ft apart in late April. This sowing should mature in July.

Whichever method is adopted, provided the young plants are kept healthy and free from slug damage, the real test comes when they have to be set out in their final positions in spring. All cauliflowers are extremely sensitive to check and one of the first results of checking is what is known as 'buttoning' which is the premature production of small useless heads or curds only one or two inches across. It is of course our climate that is responsible for most of our troubles with early summer cauliflowers. It happens over and over again that just when the plants are ready to be set out we get a parching east wind or a scorching spell of drought or a run of unexpected late frosts. If we delay planting until weather conditions improve, the seedlings which have been growing in frame-beds or under cloches may become too big – it is always noticeable that if a cauliflower is transplanted after it has made five or six leaves the risk of buttoning is much increased, however much care is taken to lift with a good ball of soil. Similarly, plants in pots may become pot-bound whilst they are waiting and will take much longer to catch on to new soil after transplanting. It would seem that plants in soil blocks have by far the best chance provided that you give them any necessary protection and keep them well watered after they have been set out.

Cultivation in Frames

Many people grow early cauliflowers in frames throughout but only as part of a scheme of intensive cropping: it is uneconomical to devote a frame solely to cauliflowers. The plants are raised in one of two ways: either seed of All The Year Round is sown the first or second week in September, pricked out in October or November and overwintered in a frame; or seed of an upright-growing forcing type is sown in heat during the first week in January and then pricked off and hardened in a frame. Plants from either sowing are set out about 31 March 18 ins. apart in two rows, each 6 ins. from the front and back respectively, either in heated frames containing lettuce with carrots (and sometimes also turnips) or in cold frames containing lettuce and carrots. The lettuce is about two thirds grown when the cauliflowers go in and the lights are kept closed until it is ready to cut. Then ventilation is given every day, water is given in increasing quantities as the cauliflowers grow and form buds and finally the lights are removed altogether and the cauliflowers finish without protection.

Cultivation in a Greenhouse

It is possible to grow cauliflowers in winter in a slightly heated greenhouse. If you possess a house of suitable type in which you grow tomatoes during summer in the permanent borders, you can follow the tomatoes with cauliflowers planted 18 ins. apart. If you use staging, you can grow the plants in pots of from 6 to 9 ins. in diameter. In either case you sow outdoors in August, prick out 4 ins. apart into a nursery bed at the third rough leaf, and put them in their final quarters by the end of October when they have formed six or seven leaves. The variety All The Year Round is suitable and no attempt should be made to maintain a high temperature: 45–50° F. is ample. The greenhouse must of course be thoroughly cleaned out by washing down after the tomatoes have been cleared. Borders should be dressed before planting with steamed bone flour (3 oz. per sq. yd). A good compost for pot plants will consist of a mixture of 5 parts loam with one part each of spent mushroom bed compost, old mortar rubble, and coarse sand. Add a 5-ins. potful of bonemeal to each barrow load of compost.

Maincrop and Autumn Cauliflowers

The season of the early cauliflower ends in July. In order to obtain cauliflowers in August and September, seeds of such varieties as All The Year Round and Autumn Giant can be sown successionally in the open during March, April, and May and planted out 27 ins. apart each way from May to July, following the instructions for plant raising given under the heading of Brassicas. Similarly the slower-growing autumn and self-protecting types are sown in March for planting out in June to crop from September to November. Australian cauliflowers are now becoming popular for autumn growing. If you go in for them, check the instructions on the seed packet as to whether seed of the variety you have chosen should be sown in April or delayed until May. The cultivation of these later crops calls for no special comment as it is merely necessary to keep them weed-free, hoe between the rows, and feed and water as required. Take care not to damage the surface roots when you carry out the hoeing.

WINTER CAULIFLOWER (HEADING BROCCOLI)

The term 'winter' is used merely to distinguish the broccoli-cauliflower from the true cauliflower which is called 'summer' cauliflower because summer is its main season of maturity. The distinction is however rather misleading because winter is the one season of the year in which most readers of this book are unlikely to be able to cut any cauliflowers of any kind. The point is that, although the 'summer' cauliflower is definitely a more tender plant than the 'winter' cauliflower, the latter will not withstand an unlimited amount of frost and snow and I can remember winters in which, after a mild autumn, alternations of frost, snow, and thaw killed off the winter cauliflower crop in wholesale fashion all over the country. What is more, even if the plants survive, it does not follow that the heads or curds will do so, and it is no use having the plants if there are no cauliflowers on them.

Now one of the principal distinctions between the two types of cauliflower plant is that in the true summer cauliflower the leaves grow upright and keep clear of the curd whereas in the other type they fold over the curd to protect it from the weather. Therefore, if you want to cut cauliflowers as late as November and you live in a district of early frosts, you would be wise to grow a winter (i.e. broccoli) type, sown mid-March and planted in June, rather than an autumn-heading variety of true cauliflower simply because there is less risk of the curd being damaged. There is not much to choose between the two types from the culinary point of view: the true cauliflower gives you on the whole a larger, whiter, and softer head than the cauliflower-broccoli but many housewives would never notice the difference.

But when it comes to growing cauliflowers for cutting between December and the beginning of March, take my advice and do not attempt it unless you live in the maritime region of the south-west already referred to, where certain varieties normally succeed if sown in April and planted out during June or July. The rest of us have to be content with those strains which are sown from late April to May, planted out in July and produce their heads in March, April, May, or June according to the variety. The latest of these, as you will observe, overlap the early summer cauliflowers and it is entirely up to you to decide which you will grow: early summer cauliflower calls for more work and cultural skill but at least it only occupies the land for a few months, whereas late 'winter' cauliflower is on the ground for pretty nearly a whole year.

So far as cultivation is concerned there are several important differences between the two types. One of the main tasks with summer cauliflower is to ensure that it never lacks moisture whereas with winter cauliflower it is usually necessary to take steps to ensure that it does not get too wet. If the time of planting out coincides with a dry spell, you will of course have to water assiduously for a few weeks, afterwards either hoeing the caked surface or covering it with loose, dry soil. But it will not be long before the autumnal and winter rains set in and then there may be a risk of waterlogging. Although all cauliflowers appreciate the extra protection that is usually afforded by a private garden, especially if it is walled, it is unfortunately the case that the ground in such gardens has usually been levelled and allows standing water to collect to a much greater extent than does an allotment which is often on a slope. Cauliflowers will not tolerate wet feet and it is an almost universal custom among market-gardeners, before the plants get too big, to bank them up with continuous ridges of soil running from north to south (unless a fall in the ground makes this direction undesirable). These ridges support the plants, prevent water from collecting round the main stem and, if there is a slope, make it easier for any surplus to run right off the plot.

Winter cauliflowers will not succeed in a frost pocket but, except for this, they are much less pernickety about soil and situation than their summer relations. Any garden soil other than the very heavy and the very light can be rendered suitable for the crop. Manuring must, however, follow different lines from those followed in the case of the summer crop. Summer cauliflower consumes vast quantities of food over a comparatively short period; winter cauliflower takes up food slowly over a period that may be as long as ten months. It is also necessary to avoid any excess of basic nitrogen which might cause growth to become too forward in autumn and early winter – a similar precaution has to be taken in the case of spring cabbage. Therefore the plot should be manured with either farmyard manure or composted straw (4 cwt per rod) *or* matured poultry manure (¾ cwt per rod) plus shoddy (½ cwt per rod) *or* hoof meal (7 lb. per rod); and these manures should be applied when preparing the land for the previous crop which the cauliflowers are to follow. This crop may be either early potatoes, early broad beans, peas, early turnips, winter lettuce, or spinach. Of these undoubtedly the best from the rotational aspect is potatoes and if a balanced potato fertilizer was used no further fertilizer need be applied when the plot is dug over for the cauliflowers. If you garden all-organically, then just use as much garden compost as you can spare for the potato crop. There will be sufficient plant foods available later on for the cauliflower plants. Apply municipal composts or proprietary organic fertilizers at the rates suggested by the suppliers.

For gardeners who use fertilizers the following information should be noted. Since cauliflowers stock up with phosphates while they are still tiny plants, the seed-bed must be dressed with superphosphate (1½ oz. per sq. yd) and sulphate of potash (¾ oz. per sq. yd). At the time of ridging a very light dressing may be given of fish guano (½ lb. per rod) and sulphate of potash (¼ lb. per rod); and in very wet districts or on extremely poor land it may also be desirable to dress with nitrate of potash (1 lb. per rod) as soon as the plants begin to grow again after the turn of the year. Always bear in mind that while nitrogen hastens development of the curd it also renders it soft and easily damaged, whereas potash makes the curd later but firmer and more frost resistant.

All cauliflowers are acutely sensitive to acidity in the soil. If insufficient lime is present, the plants may suffer from molybdenum deficiency which leads to the condition known as Whiptail and in which the leaves have practically no blades and look like narrow straps while the growing points may go blind and the bud, if it ever develops, will be small with leaves growing through it. (Somewhat similar symptoms can be produced by low temperatures or drought conditions or excess of nitrogen while the plants are still small.) Do not, however, attempt to remedy acidity by excessive dressings of lime, as this may lead to boron deficiency in the form of browning (and perhaps stunting) of the curd, distorted leaves, and a hollow stem – a condition best remedied by applying a fertilizer containing boron.

Since by reason of the time of sowing, young winter cauliflowers are exposed to attack by a wide range of pests, precautionary measures are particularly necessary (see under Brassicas).

The best average distance apart for planting, to allow for the formation of 4½-ins. heads, is 2 ft 3 ins. apart every way. Greater or lesser distances make for larger or smaller heads, as the case may be.

Hoeing should be carried on until ridging necessitates its discontinuance.

In districts where there is a definite risk of frost whilst the heads are finishing, it is an old practice to take out a trench 12 ins. deep on the north or west side of the plants and then lever the plants over into the trench with a fork so that the curd faces north or west. Soil from the trench dug along the second row is heaped over the plants in the first row so that only the leaves are uncovered. The object of this procedure is to make it impossible for the sun to shine on a frozen curd and thaw it rapidly which would render it inedible. It must be emphasized, however, that there is no point in carrying out this operation except in gardens where the type of weather experienced and the earliness of the variety chosen make the risk of such damage extremely likely; and in any case the operation should be delayed as long as possible.

GENERAL

Roguing of Plants

It is very necessary to exercise great care in the selection of cauliflower seedlings for planting out. Those of a bluish tint are likely to develop button hearts and should be rejected. Blind plants with no growing point must also be thrown out – they are usually the result of buying cheap, poor quality seed but may also have become blind as the result of pest damage. Do not set out plants which have more than six leaves and check up that the selected plants have bright green leaves and short, straight stems with plenty of fibrous roots. Apply the same criteria to plants bought from a nurseryman as you would to those of your own raising

How to Cut Cauliflowers

If summer cauliflowers begin to turn in during very sunny weather, snap one of the inner leaves, without breaking it off, and bend it over to protect the head from the sun. Bright sunshine has the effect of turning the mature curd yellow. A modification of the same idea can be applied at an earlier stage of development by tying leaves loosely together to form a sort of umbrella over the curd, thus protecting it from thundery rain as well as from sun. A summer cauliflower cut with the dew on it soon after daybreak is very much finer than one cut after the dew has evaporated. The same method of protecting the maturing curds with a leaf can be employed to minimize weather damage in the case of winter cauliflower. During periods of frost cut the heads only in the middle of the day when the temperature is rising – this is the only way in which you can avoid damage to the growing crop and the keeping quality of the heads. When a spell of frost looks like being of long duration, it will pay you to cut all heads which are of usable size without waiting for them to get larger; no cauliflower ever escapes damage if left to weather a really prolonged frost.

The proper way to cut cauliflowers is to make a level, not slanting, cut through the stem with a really sharp butcher's knife just below the point where the head joins the second ring of basal leaves, thus allowing two or three bottom leaves to remain on the stump.

It is not advisable to leave mature heads on the plants for any length of time because they will continue to develop and the individual sprigs of curd will separate and open out as part of their natural process of evolution, so that what had been a tight head becomes a 'ricey' one. If several summer cauliflowers are ready at once, lift them with the earth attached to the roots and hang them head downwards in a cool, dark, dry shed or garage. If they are lightly syringed every evening, they will keep in good condition for a week. If frost threatens before the autumn cauliflowers are finished, lift the plants whole just before the curd reaches maturity, and plunge them into moist sand or soil on the floor of a cool shed or cellar where the temperature is between 33° F. and 40° F. The sand or soil should entirely cover the roots and the leaves should be tied up over the head. So treated, they will remain in good condition for a month. If it is desired to protect winter cauliflowers, it is better to lift them, with good balls of soil attached, when the heads are forming and replant them in a frame or even pack them in a cellar: the heads will finish fairly well, but of course not so well as if the plants had remained undisturbed.

It may be noted that when cauliflowers are grown solely for the kitchen the size is immaterial because all the best cooks break the curd up before cooking it. If cauliflowers are to be cooked whole, they should be very small.

Special Types of Cauliflower

The Danish Giant strains, which have been specially developed for pickling, are sown in late April or early May and planted out finally in late June or early July. Since the heads are quite small, about ¾ lb. each, the plants are set out 18 ins. square. They are cut during the autumn. Similarly, the Cape Broccoli, which is a winter cauliflower with a purplish head ready to cut during late March or April, is sown the previous April in drills 12 ins. apart and planted out 18 ins. apart in rows 30 ins. apart during late June or July. Nine Star Broccoli is a semi-perennial plant which yields in spring anything from 5 to 15 cauliflower heads, from 6 to 10 ins. in diameter, which compare favourably in texture and flavour with true winter cauliflowers; the yield and size increase as the plants get older. Seed may be sown in heat early in the year or in the open ground in April or May for planting out in June, July, or even August. The plant requires a considerable amount of room, a good 4 ft every way, and its presence as a semi-permanent occupant of the kitchen-garden may prove embarrassing in later years if it interferes with rotational cropping schemes. But it is an excellent novelty to try if you have a suitable place and sufficient spare ground for it.

Exhibiting Cauliflowers

By reason of the dates of the shows only summer cauliflowers and the very earliest winter sorts are exhibited. A first-class strain of seed is essential and there is much to recommend the variety All The Year Round because it can usually be had ready for most show dates. Correct timing is half the battle and you can usually reckon from nineteen to twenty-two weeks from sowing to maturity. Nothing will hasten a backward head but it is sometimes possible to save a too-forward head by digging the plant up and heeling it in under a north wall (or hang it in a cellar as previously suggested in connection with cutting). Nevertheless the best heads from the judges' point of view are the freshest, cut very early on the morning of the show. As three heads make up a dish and six heads a collection, and 4 points are awarded for uniformity, you will have to grow quite a lot of plants from which to select. You should syringe the heads a few days beforehand to remove dust and then tie the leaves over to protect them. For a single dish remove all but the inner circle of leaves and cut these back severely at the last moment to expose the curd. For a collection it is best to remove all leaves and secure the heads with nails in one of the special triangular exhibitors' boards used for the purpose, packing them round with fresh green moss and curled parsley.

When transporting to the hall, with the leaves only roughly trimmed, cover the curd with crumpled tissue paper and put each head in a polythene bag. Always keep cauliflowers covered up to the last possible moment before judging. Then give a last minute spraying. Take great care not to exhibit any caterpillars as well and, whilst the heads are still growing, remember not to use any insecticides which could stain the curd.

The best size for show cauliflowers is from 5 to 6 ins. in diameter. Out of a total of 20 points, 10 are awarded for condition and 6 for solidity. Heads must be symmetrical, close, solid, pure white, unstained, and free from frothiness. Heads of irregular shape which are yellowed or stained or beginning to blow do not win prizes; neither do those which show any trace of leaf in the curd.

Celeriac

If you cannot grow winter celery, and if you are one of those people who always grabs the 'heart' or solid core of the celery that appears on the dining-table, leaving the stalks to your fellow-eaters, then grow celeriac in which the swollen, turnip-like body at the base of the stems is the equivalent of the heart of ordinary celery. If you want to try it before you grow it, you can usually buy roots in winter from the better-class greengrocers.

The history of celeriac or turnip-rooted celery, known in America as knob celery, is obscure. Its cultivation in private gardens can be traced back as far as the middle of the seventeenth century; but in this country at any rate it only came into prominence during the Second World War, largely on account of the fact that it will succeed on shallow and stubborn soils and can be grown with the expenditure of far less time and trouble than ordinary celery. Celeriac is a true celery, but instead of putting its energies into the manufacture of stems alone, the plant forms a basal knob or swollen turnip-like root which may be eaten raw, thinly sliced, or grated, as a substitute for celery in salads, or boiled like a beetroot. The leaf-stalks may be eaten as seakale. Every bit of the plant is a valuable poultry food; the bulbous portion can be cut in half and fed raw to fowls or it can be cooked and kneaded in with the mash, using the water in which it has been boiled for mashing the meal.

Sow in heat not later than the beginning of March; celeriac requires a long season of growth and, though I have heard of it being raised successfully under cloches from an early March sowing, I would not like to take the risk that the seedlings would be late in appearing. If therefore you have no heated greenhouse or hotbed frame, I advise you to buy plants from a nurseryman if you know of one who goes in for this less common vegetable.

Use John Innes Seed Compost for sowing and, when the seedlings are 1½ ins. high, prick them off into boxes of John Innes Potting Compost No. 1 where they should stand 3 ins. apart. You may prefer to use soil-less composts or your own special mixture. After carefully hardening off, plant out at the end of May or the beginning of June, 12 ins. apart in rows 18 ins. apart. The soil should have been well dug and enriched with garden compost. The rate at which you use your garden compost is up to you. Bear in mind that both celery and celeriac are greedy feeders. If the soil is very heavy, however, the whole of the top 6 ins. should be intimately mixed with an abundance of sifted leafmould or old mushroom-bed compost, with the addition of a little hop manure. No trenches are required, but in dry districts it helps if the plants are set in a shallow drill to facilitate watering.

Do not plant deeply and at all times water copiously. If you use chemical fertilizers you may have dressed the site with Growmore or a similar balanced mixture and you may also care to encourage early growth with nitrate of soda (½ oz. per sq. yd) if the plants lag and, as the season progresses, feed them liberally with liquid manure and soot water. The process of cultivation consists in keeping the plants to a single stem and continually drawing soil away and removing lateral shoots and suckers from the basal knob, as it forms, so that this knob stands out of the ground as bald as a coot; but you must not of course remove or expose the fibrous roots by means of which the plants feed. Towards the end of the season, when growth is complete, the plants should be lightly earthed up as a protection against frost – this should not be done before mid-October.

Celeriac should, as a rule, be lifted in November though it is reasonably hardy and in light soil can remain in the ground and be drawn upon as wanted provided that the knobs are covered during severe weather with soil taken from between the rows. When lifting for storage remove all the leaves *except* the little tuft in the centre; if you cut that off the root will waste all its energy in producing another set of leaves. Then trim off the fibrous roots and store in sand in a cool, dry shed.

It might be added that, when eaten raw, the basal knob cannot be scrunched whole with the teeth, as this is bad for dentures. Either slice it thinly as if it were cucumber or grate it up on a bread-grater.

Celery

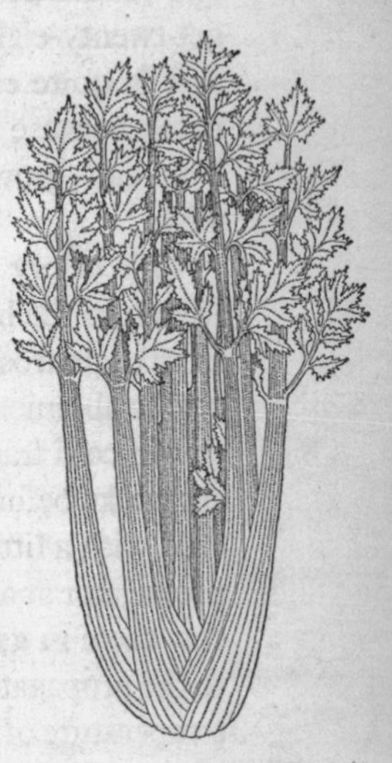

Wild celery or 'smallage' is a biennial plant which grows in ditches and other moist places near the sea in almost all parts of the world. It sometimes crops up as a weed in cultivated watercress beds. Garden celery, which is derived from it, was known to the Romans and most of the basic work in the production of improved strains was carried out in Italy. It was not until after 1800 that celery came into common use as a vegetable in other parts of Europe and in this country. For a long while it was confused with parsley which in its wild form has very similar foliage.

Today we have two main types of cultivated celery, 'summer' and 'winter': and, since each has to be cultivated in an entirely different way from the other, I shall deal with them separately.

SUMMER CELERY

Summer or self-blanching was introduced into this country from America. When well grown from a first-class strain of seed, it is excellent stuff, crisp, nutty, and never stringy.

The essential characteristic of this late summer and early autumn celery is that its stalks are naturally of a creamy white colour. It is rather misleading to imply that it blanches itself. There is not much chlorophyll in the stems to bleach out anyway but what little there is will not disappear unless the plants are grown in solid blocks so that they shut out the light from each other.

I regard self-blanching celery as essentially a frame crop. If grown in the open it must be in square blocks of at least forty-nine plants (7 × 7) and there is some risk that the outermost plants on each side of the square (i.e. nearly half the crop) will be slightly sub-standard in the matter of blanch. In a 6-ft × 4-ft frame you can get twenty-eight plants at 9 ins. apart, all perfectly blanched, and that is quite enough for ordinary household consumption in one batch because the plants will not stand long once they are ready. You can grow a successional batch in another frame if you wish.

This celery grows quickly and must not be sown before mid-March in the hope of getting an earlier crop because a single check from a late frost can cause it to bolt. Germination on the other hand can be abominably slow and I strongly advise you not to attempt to sow in cold frames or under cloches since it may well be more than six weeks before anything shows up. The best course is to mix the seed with a little moist sterile sand or vermiculite and place it in a propagator at a temperature of 70° F. Immediately the seeds sprout sow them in a tray of John Innes Seed Compost and either return to the propagator or plunge in a hot bed frame, still maintaining the temperature of 70° F. As soon as the seedlings can be handled, prick them out 2 ins. apart into boxes and keep under glass at a temperature of 60° F. until established, then gradually harden off in preparation for final planting which can take place from mid-May to the end of June according to district and date of sowing. If you have no facilities for raising your own plants, you can buy excellent ones from leading nurserymen.

The soil in the frames must be made extremely rich and retentive by incorporating old hotbed or mushroom-bed manure, vegetable compost, and peat; outdoor beds must be prepared in the same way. If, owing to shortage of organic manures, a dressing of fertilizer is considered necessary, hoe in Growmore before planting.

No overhead protection is required and the lights are not used on the frames. It is a common practice to interplant the celery with

Feltham King lettuce, sown a month previously, which will come into cut during July.

Cultivation consists mainly in keeping down weeds and seeing that the soil does not go dry. Once the lettuces have been cleared, abundant supplies of water will be needed and the plants should be dressed twice at an interval of ten days with a mixture of 1 part soot (over twelve months old) and 3 parts lime which should be dusted over them early in the morning when the dew is on the foliage and washed off twenty-four hours later with a hose or a rosed can. Use a slug bait at regular intervals, otherwise every stick is likely to have small slugs in it when it reaches the kitchen. If you are not growing in frames, you can improve the blanch by working clean, dry straw to a depth of 9 ins. all over the bed and in between the plants; but dust it well with pyrethrum powder as you go to discourage woodlice from taking up residence in it. A point to remember about the use of straw is that after heavy rain it will consolidate and will damage the plants unless you take a fork and loosen it again.

Summer celery is dug through September and into October. It must always be cleared before the autumn frosts begin as it is not hardy and its height will as a rule prevent you from putting the lights back over frame-grown stuff. Once you start to dig, you will of course expose the outermost plants in the frame to full light: but you can preserve the blanch either by using straw or by erecting a screen of old lino, held in place by canes, hard up against the nearest plants.

American Green celery is eaten green and, because no blanching has to be undertaken, it is pointless to grow the plants in frames. Raise young plants in the manner indicated for self-blanching celery and set out hardened-off plants in the garden during early June or when you consider there is no risk of a late spring frost at night. Do not set the plants in trenches, though if your soil is sandy and dries out rapidly it could be an advantage to place the plants in a shallow depression for watering purposes; 9 ins. between plants is a suitable distance, with a foot between rows. Harvest the heads in September and in October and, of course, before the first autumn frost.

WINTER CELERY

The growing of good winter celery calls for an immense amount of labour and attention and it is all too often frozen in the trenches when you most want a head for the table; so that often enough the only return you get for a great deal of trouble is a little pre-Christmas celery in mixed salads (because the rest hasn't been frosted and is not at its best for eating raw) and a small glut of stewed and braised celery when the thaw comes about March. Nevertheless it is a crop the cultivation of which brings out all that is best in a gardener and gives him a real glow of satisfaction when it is successful.

Ordinary winter celery may be 'white', pink, or red, and it may be dwarf or tall. I have never been able to detect any pronounced difference in flavour due to the presence of the pink or red tinge in the stalks but the so-called white sorts (which are actually green-stemmed until blanched) are rather tender and less tolerant of winter rains and frost, so that it is usual to sow them about 1 March, plant out towards the end of May, and eat before Christmas, whereas the pink and red sorts are sown and planted about a month later to provide after-Christmas supplies. The choice between dwarf or tall must be governed by household requirements; a head of celery ought not to be larger than can be consumed while still fresh. No attempt should be made to copy the exhibitor and grow plants to a size larger than the natural average of the variety – the result, however beautiful, is likely to be merely tough and tasteless.

Seed sowing and the raising of the plants follow in general the same lines as I have already laid down in the case of summer celery. The jobs call for either a heated greenhouse or a hotbed frame and, if you do not possess either, you should buy plants from a nurseryman. It is in my opinion far too big a gamble to sow in the open ground or even under cloches. Buy your seed only from a seedsman who guarantees it to be fresh and disease-free (or at any rate to have been treated against Leaf Spot). Don't prick the seedlings out in one operation; prick out the most forward ones first and plant out finally in the same order, thus obtaining a longer season.

Cultivated celery is true to its parentage in requiring an abundance of water at the roots and must therefore be grown in trenches. It does best in fertile soil overlying peat ('moss land'); it cannot be cultivated on light, sandy soil or heavy clay. It is also a gross feeder and, like the cauliflower, has on occasion been grown to perfection in rotted manure or good ripe compost without the admixture of any soil at all. I do not believe that it is possible to produce first-class celery without the aid of plenty of stable or farmyard manure or their nearest practicable organic equivalent. The abominable frothy stuff, unfit even for stewing, sold on our local markets (and bought at high prices by the undiscriminating) is the outcome of attempts to grow celery with the aid of inorganic fertilizers only by commercial growers without conscience or, in many cases, even horticultural knowledge. The only fertilizer I would allow would be superphosphate (2 oz. per sq. yd) applied shortly before planting time.

The task of preparing the celery trench must be undertaken well in advance: the standard practice is to dig it in February. Since, however, one alternative to the use of stable or farmyard manure is to half fill the trench with lawn mowings, you may have to wait until April before the first mowings are available and you will then have to move quickly if you are to allow sufficient time for the rotting mowings to lose some of their heat before you plant out in June.

The width of the trench should be 15 ins. if you are planting a single row and 18 ins. if you are planting a double row. In the latter case, don't plant zigzag or staggered: put the plants side by side in pairs – otherwise you will have trouble when earthing up.

If there is more than one trench, the distance between them must be 4 ft.

No definite depth for the trench can be recommended: circumstances alter cases. Ideally, celery should have 18 ins. of good soil under it and another 18 ins. of drained subsoil beneath that. But finished depth is another matter. On lightish soil and in dry districts 10 ins. is a good finished depth; in cold soil and a cold district 6 ins. is enough. But the later the planting, the shallower should be the trench; otherwise the plants will get waterlogged in winter and may rot. My own preference is for a trench 3 ins. deep when finished because I want after-Christmas celery. You will note the phrase 'when finished': the point is of course that you dig a foot or two deep to start with and then return some of the soil after mixing it with peat, compost, and manure. Alternatively, if the bottom of the trench, a foot below normal soil level, is covered with a layer of manure not dug in, or if grass mowings are used, obviously these must be covered with a layer of good soil. The finished depth in either case will be the depth after you have put back some of the original soil. The surplus soil is made into neat ridges on either side of the trench, and these ridges can be used for growing lettuces and dwarf beans during summer, provided that this will not interfere with the management of the celery and that the nature of the soil is such that the catch crops will not quickly dry out.

Plant 9 ins. apart and water each plant in as you go. Earthing up is a long-drawn-out ritual. You cannot do it in one go, and the soil must be moist and crumbly and the plants dry, so choose the day after a rainy day for each stage of the operation. Start in August by heaping about 4 ins. of soil loosely round each plant with a handfork, so that it lightly presses the outer leaves. A fortnight later make the soil fine and heap it with a spade on each side of the plants; then go down on your knees and, holding the plant bunched together with one hand, sweep the earth round it with the other hand, like a plumber wiping a joint, but taking care that no crumbs fall into the heart of the plant and refraining from pressing the soil close. This should add another 4 ins. to the earthing. Repeat the performance a fortnight later and finish off, roughly a week after that, provided the plants appear fully grown, by tying the stems together with raffia and carrying the earthing up to the top of the stalks so that only the very tips of the leaves are left showing. The resultant ridge should be finished off neatly with a spade and the sides left nicely sloping.

Remove all side-shoots or suckers before earthing, also any small outer leaves which would be buried entirely. Watch out for slugs and use a slug bait at each earthing. Never press the soil against the plants: they want darkness but not imprisonment. It is also essential to keep earth out of the hearts of the plants as this may cause rotting.

I have dealt at length with the technique of earthing up because I consider that it is good gardening practice and represents the most natural method of obtaining the required blanch and indeed the only one so far as late celery is concerned. Nevertheless it has been truly said that celery is only as good as its blanch and the private gardener ought to be able to do better than the commercial grower whose sticks, however well grown, are barely blanched at all nowadays, judging by much of the stuff one sees in the shops. Therefore, I feel that there is much to be said to copying the exhibitor whose methods of blanching pre-Christmas celery fully justify the labour involved both from his own point of view and that of the consumer. I will confess that when the soil available for earthing celery is insufficiently friable, I confine myself to the early sorts and use paper collars as well. The special celery collars sold by sundriesmen are 6 ins. wide and can be tied loosely round the plants with raffia, though many people prefer to use $\frac{3}{16}$ inch rubber bands (which I dislike and distrust because they are usually either too tight or too slack, require two hands to stretch them on, and often perish and bust!). You add a fresh collar every fortnight or so until you have encased the whole plant and will probably find it necessary to secure the upper collars to a cane to prevent them from sliding downwards. Even so, you will not get as good a blanch as by the more natural method unless you do a certain amount of earthing up as well. Most people seem content to heap a small quantity of soil roughly round to prevent the wind from rocking the plants; but I prefer to mix dry leaf-mould or coconut fibre with such sieved soil as is available and then pack it round each collar after it has been fixed, so as to give a tolerable imitation of earthing up and also protect the collars themselves. In this connection, if you wish to save money and make your own collars, cut 12-ins. × 6-ins. pieces from tar-backed paper which discourages worms and slugs and does not disintegrate into a soggy pulp when it gets wet as do ordinary brown paper and corrugated wrapping paper. One last point about the use of collars is that some light is bound to enter down the top of the tube and reduce the length of blanch unless you plug it with cotton wool about 3 weeks before you expect to dig the celery – then keep an eye on the wool in case earwigs colonize it for you.

If after all this you consider the work of producing a perfect blanch in a fair-sized plantation of celery rather too much for you, why not be content with a lesser degree of perfection in part of the crop and reserve that part for braising? Good celery, well braised, with brown sauce, is an ambrosial dish!

In the interval between planting and earthing the grower's main tasks are to keep weeds down by routine hoeing, to remove all side-shoots and suckers, to see that the soil never lacks moisture, and to wage continual war against slugs which seem to regard the heart of a celery plant as the nearest approach to heaven on earth. Although the leading firm of fertilizer manufacturers recommends a pre-planting dressing of a 9:7:6 fertilizer, I adhere to my previous recommendation of superphosphate only because I dislike a high nitrogen content in celery land. Excessive nitrogen is responsible for those frothy sticks in which the leaf stalks crack open and expose their inner tissues, sometimes also developing soft rot. The same consideration applies to feeding which begins about the end of July and continues until the time of final earthing in September. I have had much success with weekly and alternating feeds of dried blood in solution (½ oz. per gallon of water and 3 pints per plant) and superphosphate (½ oz. per plant) applied close to the stems and watered in if the weather is dry. But everything depends on how much nitrogen there is in the soil to start with and in some gardens the quantity of dried blood I have instanced would be far too much. It is not possible to give exact instructions to suit every case, but one thing that is certain is that it is useless to go on feeding when the final earthing time approaches since earthing up stops growth. You must also be extremely careful not to apply fertilizers in any form to the soil used for earthing up as this will damage the stalks.

Once earthing up is complete there is nothing more that you can do to your early celery prior to digging it – and, by the way, try and get all the early white celery eaten within six weeks of blanching because it is very susceptible to frost damage and then becomes extremely brittle, so that it is almost impossible to handle it. There is still a possibility, however, of trouble with the late celery in a very wet winter if rain succeeds in trickling down into the hearts. One method of preventing this is to bend the tops of the plants to one side at the final earthing; another is to cover the tops of the ridges with strips of waterproof packing paper folded along the centre to make a tent-shaped roof and held in position by crossed canes. A more permanent arrangement, which cannot blow away, is provided by setting two boards on edge along the ridge so that rain is thrown off.

Dig your celery carefully or, after all your trouble, you will damage it and probably chop off some of the stems. The proper way is first of all to scrape away cautiously all the earthing soil on one side of the ridge and continue down into the original trench until you can see the whole stick right down to the roots. Then drive your spade right under the plant and lever it out.

It is sometimes desired to lift a few roots of celery in advance when severe frost threatens in case it may not be possible later on to dig the plants out of the open ground. This can be done quite successfully if the plants are lifted with the roots intact and stacked in an upright position in boxes containing several inches of moistened sand. All unnecessary outside leaves should be removed before placing the plants in the boxes and the latter should be stored somewhere where the temperature is only a few degrees above freezing point. The sand will require to be re-moistened at intervals.

Celery for Exhibition

The main point in connection with the growing of celery of show quality is that only the winter sorts can be grown up to the standard of quality required and these have to be ready anything up to a couple of months earlier than you would expect them to be forthcoming for ordinary domestic use. This means that for an August show you must sow in January, and for the later shows about mid-February, in a well-heated greenhouse (55–60° F.) The seedlings must be pricked out into 5-ins.-deep boxes and grown under glass until it is possible to harden them off in frames; planting must take place in May, preferably with cloche protection for a few weeks; and blanching must commence correspondingly earlier. It is of course essential to use an early maturing sort. If you have no greenhouse facilities and wish to buy plants in from a nurseryman, make sure that he caters for the exhibitor and has got his plants sufficiently far advanced to enable him to give early delivery.

It is only in respect of blanching that there is any difference between the methods of the exhibitor and the ordinary gardener. Few, if any, exhibitors earth up their celery and by no means all of them dig any sort of trench, some preferring to plant on the flat. Their methods of blanching are many and various: some rely on the paper collars already described; others use tubes of tar-free roofing felt, land drain pipes 4 to 6 ins. in diameter of varying lengths filled with sawdust or tall round sweet tins cut lengthwise into two halves, tied together round the plant and filled up with hay or moss. I have even come across plutocrats who have lined a whole trench with boards held in position by pegs and then filled the space between them with river or silver sand, sifted leaf-mould, or granulated peat. I have also heard of a case of an exhibitor who grows his celery in 12-ins. pots raised up on bricks near a water butt, filling the pots with a mixture of half manure and half sterilized soil and putting two plants in each. As soon as these plants have begun to grow, he binds them round with 6 ins. strips of corrugated paper, continuing till they are about 3 ft high and then putting a second layer of paper round the other. By keeping his plants well watered and fed with liquid manure and soot water he wins many prizes.

Anyway, once you have lifted your celery with great care, do not ruin it by exposing it to the light for any length of time so that your beautiful blanch becomes green again. Wrap it in clean, damp paper and stand the roots in water till you are ready to prepare for the show. Then trim the roots back to the hard base, remove the outside leaves, if damaged, hang upside down, and flush with running water from the tap until all soil has been washed away – do not on any account scrub celery. Search each stick for small slugs with a keen eye and a darning needle; then tie with raffia at the top of the blanch, which must be at least 12 ins. long, and wrap up again.

In a collection you stage six heads of celery but only three are required for a dish. Celery counts as a salading (not a salad vegetable). In judging 4 points can be awarded for size – the larger the better – 4 for uniformity, 5 for solidity, and 7 for condition, including blanching. The judges ought to test for quality by satisfying themselves that the sticks are brittle and not soft, pithy, and stringy; but they do not always do so because it spoils the look of the exhibit! The chief causes of lost marks are blemished or pest-damaged leaf stalks, poor blanch, dirt, visible flower stems, small size, coarseness, and looseness of the heads.

Pests and Diseases of Celery

The Celery Fly

This is one of the plagues of the celery crop. It is active in some years from May to December; in other years it never puts in an appearance. The fly lays eggs on the leaves; the eggs hatch into grubs which tunnel into the leaves, making blistery trails till the whole leaf shrivels. Lacking many of its leaves celery cannot grow properly and the sticks are small and bitter. You may be able to deter the fly from visiting your crop to lay its eggs by dusting *weekly* and *very lightly* with a mixture of three parts well weathered soot and one part lime. Do it in the early morning when the dew is on the plants. As a change you may spray occasionally with derris or with quassia extract. If nevertheless the leaves are attacked, crush the maggots between finger and thumb; remove and burn badly blistered leaves. Another preventive measure is to hang rags dipped in paraffin alongside the plants.

Leaf Spot

Is another plague of celery. It is a fungoid disease which is transmitted with the seed and can blight the whole crop. You will not get it if you buy guaranteed clean seed and you are unlikely to get it if you buy seed which has been treated either by steeping it for three hours in a solution of 1 part formalin to 300 parts water or by immersing it for twenty-five minutes in water at 122° F., then rinsing and drying it. The treated seed must be young or it will germinate badly (and you must not try to make celery tea out of it!). But treated seed is not as good as clean seed. The disease first takes the form of small brown patches populated with black specks: but the fungus soon spreads over the leaf stalks and into the heart of the plant, which is killed. The only safe policy if you are doubtful about your seed is to spray with Bordeaux mixture or a copper fungicide in the seed-bed, before pricking out and before planting out: in moist summers further sprayings may be necessary every two or three weeks before rain if Leaf Spot actually appears.

Chard, Swiss

See Swiss Chard

Chicory

Chicory is a perennial plant, *Cichorium intybus*, which grows wild in the neighbourhood of chalk pits in England and bears beautiful blue flowers in summer. The cultivated sort that we grow as a salad, however, has been developed in Belgium. Do not confuse this chicory (Witloof) with Magdeburg chicory the roots of which are dried and roasted and used as an adulterant to coffee. It was this use of chicory which was best known in Britain until comparatively recent years and it is rather gratifying to me, therefore, that as a result of the publicity which this vegetable received in the original *Vegetable Grower's Handbook* salad chicory is now familiar to almost everybody and can be readily bought in the shops when in season. There seem to have been few readers who, having once sampled them, have not acquired a permanent liking for the delicious and unusual flavour of the blanched 'chicons' or chicory heads which in shape somewhat resemble the compact close heart of a cos lettuce.

For the purposes of cultivation we treat chicory as a biennial, sowing it in summer, lifting the roots in autumn, and then inducing them to send up their second season's growth in complete darkness so that it is blanched. Since you cannot buy dormant roots you must raise your own from seed; but this is a simple enough matter because the crop will give a good account of itself in any reasonably light but really fertile soil. Recent manuring is not desirable.

Sow at the beginning of June in drills ½ in. deep and 1 ft. apart. It is unwise to sow earlier because of the risk of the plants running to flower the first season. Thin to 9 ins. apart. Hoe and weed. No other cultural attention is required. Any time from the beginning of October to mid-November lift the plants and heel them in, just as they are, tops and all, close together, in a deep trench in a convenient corner; then mound soil over them to such a depth as will rule out any risk of the roots being actually frozen. From December to March, take up plants as required, cut the tops off to within 1 in. of the crown, allow to dry on a shelf in a frost-proof shed for a week; then trim off all side-shoots, cut back the tap-root to leave the root exactly 8 ins. long, pack in moist peat in deep boxes, cover the crowns with a 7-ins. layer of sand, and put where the temperature will keep around 55–60° F. – in a cellar or garage or under the greenhouse staging, or you can take the box indoors and stow it near the domestic boiler. Absolute darkness is essential, but by covering the crowns with sand you save yourself the trouble of finding a dark place in which to put the boxes and ensure that you get a tight head and not a loose one with spreading leaves. As an alternative to using boxes, you may make a sort of trough with a couple of long 9-ins.-wide boards stood on edge and supported on the outside with pegs on one of the soil borders beneath the staging of a heated greenhouse. Plant the roots 1 in. apart in rows 2 ins. apart in the soil; give a thorough watering then fill in with absolutely dry sand, peat-moss, or light powdery soil to a depth of 7 ins.

Avoid too much heat in forcing: it makes the stuff taste woolly. The chicons are ready to cut when the points are just beginning to appear through the surface of the covering layer of sand or soil. The best time to take them is when they are just lifting up the covering material and are about ½ in. below the surface. You then have to cut the chicon off with a sharp knife low enough to preserve the crown intact but with no vestige of root attached – this is much better than twisting it off, as I have seen some people do. If the roots are in a box, some rather awkward excavation is involved (unless you remove one end of the box). The trough method has the advantage that, with the aid of two movable ends, you need only plant successionally, a section at a time, and at cutting time have merely to take out one end and draw your covering material sideways to expose the chicons. Once cut, keep them in a dark, not too cold, larder till you eat them.

It might be added that for the best chicons you require roots 1 to 1¾ ins. in diameter. Smaller ones are no good; larger ones give you a selection of small loose heads instead of one large fat chicon.

Chillies

See Capsicums

Chinese Cabbage

This belongs to the mustard, rather than to the cabbage, section of the brassica family and forms an oval or elongated head resembling a cos lettuce with shining leaves and none of the bloom present on an ordinary cabbage. Some have compared it in size and general appearance to a Swiss chard. The tender, crisp heart can be eaten raw like lettuce and has a delicate celery-like flavour. Some housewives use only the thinner parts of the leaves in salads as a substitute for lettuce and cream up the midribs like asparagus. Others treat it as a cooked vegetable and after removing the outer leaves either boil it whole or chop it up and fry it with a little fat.

Although this crop has been the staple food of the Chinese peasantry for forty centuries, it was little known outside that country until about 50 years ago when it suddenly acquired popularity in the U.S.A. – it is now listed by all American seedsmen. Because it will not travel Chinese cabbage is not sold by many greengrocers.

Briefly, the trouble with this crop is that it will not tolerate hot, dry weather and it will not stand frost. Furthermore it will not remain in good condition once the heads are fully developed but will immediately throw up flower heads. The only method of growing it successfully therefore is to delay sowing as late as possible, allowing seventy to eighty days from sowing to maturity, and trust that the weather will be sufficiently wet to discourage bolting. The Americans call this a 'fall' crop and over here the best sowing period is probably from about mid-July to mid-August.

Obviously the more retentive medium to heavy soils offer far better prospects of success than the light, sandy ones. Try to find a semi-shaded spot between a widely spaced crop for which the ground was well supplied with humus and plant foods at the beginning of the season and sow the Chinese cabbage on this without any further dressing of artificials which might only promote bolting. Set out your rows 3 ft apart and sow pinches of seed at 15-ins. intervals, successionally, thinning the seedlings to one at each station. Do not attempt to transplant. If we get a warm, wet August, you will find that the crop grows itself: the whole trick consists in growing it rapidly without the suspicion of a check due to extreme heat or lack of moisture. You may have to watch out for caterpillars and aphids; but ordinarily, except for weeding and, whenever necessary, watering, there is nothing for you to do except to put two raffia ties round the outer leaves, top and bottom, shortly before maturity, to ensure a better blanched heart.

Cut the heads just as you would cabbages and use them at once. Although the Americans claim that they can keep them in the fridge for as long as a couple of months, my experience of Chinese cabbage is that it starts to wilt and lose its freshness after a couple of hours. It must of course all be used before the frosts set in.

Chinese Mustard

Under the names of 'tender green', 'mustard spinach', and 'mustard greens' this is a popular vegetable throughout the southern states of the U.S.A. and is being grown in increasing quantities in the gardens of North America where it is also available canned. If you wish to grow either Chinese mustard or Chinese cabbage and have difficulty in buying seeds, drop a line to Samuel Dobie & Son, Llangollen. Chinese mustard is really only another form of Chinese cabbage from which it differs by reason of its loose, open habit of growth, its much greater resistance to hot, dry weather, and its comparative hardiness. It is a substitute for spinach but grows rather more rapidly than that vegetable, and its leaves, which are larger than the largest spinach leaves, are frilled and waved in some varieties and curled after the manner of curly kale in others. The flavour is mild both when cooked as spinach and when eaten raw in salads.

Sow in rows 15 ins. apart any time from April to August and thin the plants to stand 6 ins. apart. The crop should be ready for cutting in about 6 weeks' time and ought not to be left to stand as it will only run up to flower. It is for this reason that you cut off the entire plant at soil level instead of picking off the older leaves as you do with ordinary spinach.

Chinese mustard thrives best in a rich, moist soil with some shade from hot sun. It is a good plan to encourage the plants with a quick-acting nitrogenous fertilizer, such as dried blood, when they are about 2 ins. tall.

Chives

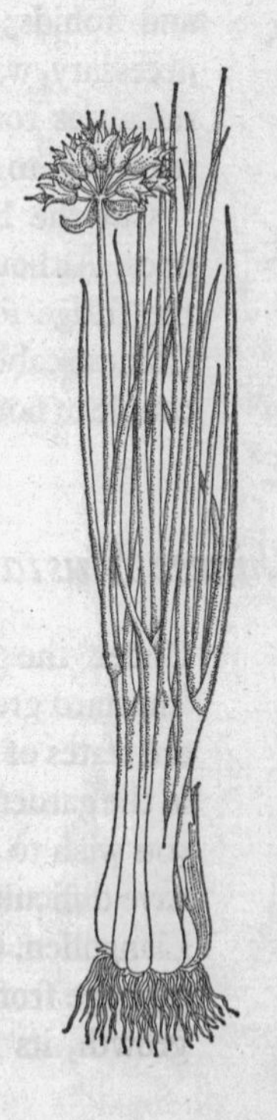

The chive is a miniature onion (*Allium schoenoprasum*) which can be used as a substitute for 'spring' onions but is more usually grown solely for the sake of its foliage which is grasslike and imparts a delicate flavour of onion to omelettes, salads, and soups. The plant is perennial and a native of northern Europe, occasionally found growing wild in Northumberland, Wales, and Cornwall. It forms 'tufts' or clusters of bulbs, whence seedsmen (who generally persist in listing it under the heading of Herbs) always refer to it in the plural as 'chives', a name which derives from the Latin *cepae*, meaning onions, and suggests that this was the first type of onion with which the Romans came to be acquainted.

Chives will grow in any decent soil and the quickest way of acquiring a stock is to buy growing plants (clumps or tufts of several bulbs) from your seedsman. These are put out 6 ins. apart in autumn or spring; they make a good edging to a bed. Lift, divide, and re-plant on fresh ground every three or four years, by which time each original bulb will have become a cluster, the plantation will be overcrowded, and the soil exhausted. If, when lifting in autumn, you have more divisions than you wish to re-plant, you can take the surplus bulbs indoors, dry them off, and store for use as tiny onions. Cut the 'grass' regularly close to soil level whether wanted in the kitchen or not; this ensures a continuous growth of young and tender shoots and prevents flowering (though the mauve flowers are very pretty and it does no harm to the plants to let them bloom). It should be clearly understood that it is the leaves which are ordinarily used for flavouring, not the roots or bulblets. Some people prefer to gather leaves from the outside of each cluster, but it is better to cut the whole plant back – the younger leaves are the best from the cook's point of view.

A stock of chives can also be raised from seed sown in March or April outdoors, in drills ¼ in. deep. The seedlings are thinned to stand 6 ins. apart. Thinnings can be transplanted, if well watered. This is of course a much cheaper method of obtaining plants but you must be prepared to wait for a year or two for the seedlings to grow into clumps from which leaves may be taken.

Coleworts (or Collards)

Coleworts are little cabbages no bigger than an average lettuce which were formerly much used for the production of 'spring greens' but were replaced for this purpose by the improved strains of quick-maturing cabbage and then largely forgotten. Interest in them revived during the Second World War when it was realized that coleworts still have their uses, largely because of their hardiness and the rapidity with which they mature or at any rate reach an edible stage. Coleworts are no longer popular amongst British gardeners. Seeds may not be listed in your seedsman's catalogue but he can probably obtain seeds for you. Farmers grow collards for what is known as the 'spring greens bagging trade'. American readers may order seeds of the variety Georgia from W. Atlee Burpee Co., Philadelphia, Pa.19132. Seeds may be sown in May to provide 'greens' in late summer; they take up no room of their own because they can be interplanted during June and July between slow-maturing members of the cabbage family. But it is far better to sow in July and plant in August and have them available in late autumn and early winter. Most people sow in a seed-bed for planting out; others find that they do better sown in drills, thinned to 10 ins. and not disturbed until cut. There is no rule about this: it depends on the district and season.

Three rows of thirty coleworts spaced 1 ft apart each way will keep you going with nice little 'cabbages' from the time the last savoy is cut to the time the first spring cabbage becomes available. Another method of growing the coleworts is to space your spring cabbage plants 2 ft apart each way, place one colewort between each two cabbages in the row, and run a complete row of coleworts between each two rows of cabbage; the coleworts will be cut before the spring cabbages need all the room.

Although often cut as 'greens', if left to mature, coleworts make nice little round or flat hearts, reasonably solid which will stand in usable condition from January right through the winter.

Corn Salad

Corn salad (*Valerianella olitoria*) grows wild in cornfields in various parts of Great Britain and also on the Continent; it is much appreciated by grazing sheep hence its other name of lamb's lettuce. The wild stuff which looks rather like a large dandelion is very coarse and we eat only the cultivated types with larger and more succulent leaves which have a somewhat earthy taste, stronger than a cos lettuce but milder than the leaves of dandelion. Some people dislike the flavour but it is generally much appreciated by those who have visited Switzerland during the winter season and encountered it in salads under the name of *Nüsslisalat*, freshly picked as its green leaves pushed through the covering snow. It has also long been a staple ingredient of salads served in restaurants specializing in continental fare in the Soho district of London.

Any soil that is in good heart and has been well treated and enriched for a previous crop will grow excellent corn salad provided that the site is sunny, well drained, and reasonably well sheltered. Although sowings can be made any time from February onwards, there is little point in sowing before July because corn salad is most in demand during the season of the year when lettuce is both expensive to buy and usually cannot be had from your own garden. It can be used to provide the whole of the green part of a salad or it can be mixed with other saladings. Incidentally, it has the reputation of being the best of all salads to eat with game.

In the north, seed should be sown before the end of July: but in the south fortnightly sowings can be made up to the latter part of September. An August sowing is usually ready for eating when the crocuses are in bloom. Draw drills 6 ins. apart and, unless you live in an area of heavy summer rainfall, make them 2 ins. deep but cover the seed with only ½ in. of soil – this facilitates watering whilst the plants are small and must not be allowed to suffer from dryness at the root. Thin to 6 ins. apart. It is an advantage if you can cover with cloches from October onwards – you can get four rows under a barn cloche. Lacking cloches, you can keep the leaves fresher during severe weather by means of a loose covering of hay or straw. You can also, if you wish, partially blanch selected plants by inverting large flowerpots over them – it is not necessary to cover the drainage hole.

The crop can be gathered by cutting off the whole plant at the root. But, as this may lead to other plants growing too large and tough before they can be used, it is better practice to pick a few leaves from each plant and spread picking over the whole plantation, just as if you were gathering spinach. You can begin by taking one leaf from each plant that has made four leaves and then increase the number of leaves taken as the plants grow larger: but you must never take more than half the leaves from any one plant at any one picking. Some folk, who lack the patience to pick methodically, cut over the whole tuft of each plant with a large pair of scissors, as if they were using shears on long grass.

Use corn salad as soon as possible after gathering and do not omit to wash it thoroughly to get rid of any grit.

Couve Tronchuda

(*Portugal Cabbage*)

Often known as the Braganza cabbage, this brassica is cultivated in northern Portugal and the province of Tras-os-Montes and has been grown in private gardens in this country for over a century but at the present there appears to be no supplier of seeds here. It grows to an impressive size and needs at least 3 ft of space. It produces a spread of great leaves of which the mid-ribs, cooked after the manner of seakale, form an excellent dish. When a goodly number of these leaves has been taken, there remains in autumn at the top of the plant a very good loose-hearted cabbage. Seed is best sown in heat in February or March, so that the plants can be set out after due hardening as early in the season as possible. But in warm districts an outdoor sowing before mid-March should give good results. The general principles of raising the plants have been dealt with under the heading of Brassicas to which reference should be made. A rich fertile soil is necessary in a sunny, well-drained position, and plenty of organic manure should have been dug in during the previous winter. In dry weather the plants will need frequent and generous supplies of water, otherwise both growth and quality will suffer.

Couve tronchuda has the distinction of being extremely resistant to Club Root disease and can be grown with success on infected soils. It may also be mentioned that the cabbage-like head is more tasty if left on the plant until it has been slightly frosted.

Cress

Up to the beginning of the nineteenth century nobody spoke of cress: it was always 'cresses', and 'cresses' meant water cresses. ('Cress' by the way means 'creeper'.) For the purpose of this book,

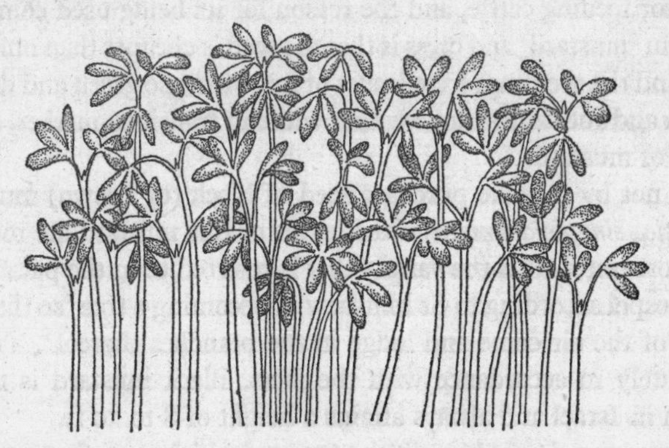

however, I am including four different salad crops under the heading of Cress. They are: (1) and (2) Mustard and Cress taken together in the reverse order; (3) American or Land Cress; and (4) Watercress.

MUSTARD AND CRESS

The cress that we use in this mixture (always referred to in Covent Garden as 'hot and cold') is the garden or pepper cress, *Lepidium sativum*, a native of Persia which does not grow wild in this country. It is an annual plant and it is quite a modern idea to grow it and cut it in the seed-leaf stage of development for use as a salading and it is still regarded as a novelty in the U.S.A. If allowed to mature, it would grow 1½ ft high and bear white flowers. The 'mustard' which is grown and mixed with garden cress is a member of the cabbage family. If you grow it yourself you sow seed of white mustard (*Brassica alba*); if you buy it at the greengrocers you may well be given rape (*Brassica napus*), which is allied to the turnip section of the cabbage family and cannot be distinguished from mustard in the seed-leaf stage. White mustard is a native of waste land in Britain, an annual plant, growing from 2 to 4 ft high and bearing yellow flowers: as a child, holiday-making on the east coast, I can remember field after field of it in bloom, the crop being grown by a well-known firm of mustard manufacturers. Rape is not a British plant: its seeds are the source of colza oil and the oil cakes used for feeding cattle, and the reason for its being used commercially in 'mustard' and cress is that the seed is cheaper than mustard seed and the seedlings have leaves of more intense green and do not soften and rot during hot weather while in transit to market, as do those of mustard.

Do not by mistake purchase seed of black (or brown) mustard (*Brassica sinapioides nigra*) – the leaves of this mustard are too hot for most tastes. It is the variety that is referred to in the parable in the Gospel according to St Matthew as becoming a tree 'so that the birds of the air come and lodge in the branches thereof'. This is absolutely in accordance with the facts. Black mustard is much grown in Israel and always attains a height of 8 to 10 ft.

In case you do not know it the mustard which is used as a condiment is prepared from the seeds. The Romans were great mustard-eaters and pounded the seeds with wine. In this country they used to be pounded and mixed with cinnamon and vinegar or honey, then made into large pills which were dissolved in vinegar for use as mustard. In Shakespeare's *Henry IV* we are told that the best mustard came from Tewkesbury; but it was Mr Clements of Durham who discovered the modern method of preparing mustard flour so that 'Durham Mustard' replaced 'Tewkesbury Mustard'.

Mustard and cress would undoubtedly be grown in greater quantity by gardeners if it were more acceptable to their households; and the reason for its non-acceptability is usually its poor quality as compared with the commercial article. Lack of sensible guidance is responsible for this situation – there can be no vegetable about which more nonsense has been written. Yet the principles of cultivation are perfectly simple. Whereas in the case of every other known plant raised from seed the grower's object is to prevent the seedlings from drawing to the light and spindling, here is a case in which he actually wants to make them 'draw' so as to display an unnatural length of stem; but apart from that his only requirement is that they shall shed their seed cases and remain free from soil.

Now the first essential requirement is fresh, high quality seed. This may surprise many readers who imagined that any old seed will do for such a humble crop. Actually, however, unless the seed germinates absolutely evenly and develops at a uniform rate, you get backward low-growing patches in the trays which are smothered by the remaining growth and therefore damp off and cause moulds to grow which quickly ruin the whole sowing. This sort of thing happens when the seed is old or has been harvested or stored under bad conditions. Never preserve remnants of mustard or cress seed until a second season. Commercial growers attach so much importance to this aspect of culture that every batch of seed is subjected to careful germination and growth tests before each sowing.

The second essential is that you must treat this crop as a subject for protected cultivation: in other words you must grow it in a greenhouse or frame or in boxes stood outdoors under cloches which are in a sense equivalent to very small frames. It is just a waste of seed to sow in outdoor beds as a catch crop in summer because either you will have to water or the rain will do the watering for you so that the whole crop becomes spattered with soil even if it is not beaten down flat. Those who advocate this method have either never given it a practical trial themselves or are perverse creatures who actually enjoy eating dirt. By all means hand over surplus cress seed to your young children so that they may grow pretty green geometrical patterns of hearts, butterflies, and lovers' knots as did their Victorian great-grandparents but for goodness' sake do not try to consume the result.

The temperatures required to grow good mustard and cress are a maximum of 65° F. by day and a minimum of 50° F. by night. If the thermometer falls to 45° F. or lower the crop will be stunted, if it rises above 65° F. the stems will be crooked and exceptionally weak and thin. In order to provide the requisite temperatures a heated greenhouse or frame is necessary from the beginning of

October to the end of March but no artificial heat is needed at other times of the year. The best arrangement in a greenhouse is to have a made-up bed in a small propagating frame on the staging: the best type of frame for outdoors is a single-light Dutch frame. If boxes must be used either in a greenhouse or frame or outdoors, you have a choice between a single box 6 ins. deep only half-filled with soil (and with one corner left unsown to enable you to get your hand in to commence cutting) or the much preferable combination of two boxes each 3 ins. deep, one inverted over the other to form a lid which is dispensed with as soon as the hessian is removed (see below). Single boxes stood outdoors can be protected from rain by placing a sheet of glass over the top.

It has long been the custom for amateurs to stretch canvas over the surface of, and in contact with, the soil in the beds or boxes and having saturated it with water, to sow the seed on the fabric. This practice, reminiscent of the childhood game of sowing mustard seed on pieces of wet flannel, while affording less root-hold, nevertheless does certainly eliminate all risk of the crop being gritty; but it does not necessarily get rid of the tendency of the seed cases to remain on top of the plants, which is due to the air being too dry and causing the cases to shrink on to the cotyledons. The modern practice, which disposes of this difficulty, is to lay a clean, sterilized, wet sheet of hessian, cut to size, on top of the sown seed and to keep it continuously moist until the seedlings are 1 to 1½ ins. high, when it is removed and the crop exposed to full light.

Soil

While the growing medium must be sufficiently porous to ensure perfect drainage, it must also be retentive so that no watering will be required during the whole period from sowing to cutting. Obviously no nourishment is needed in the soil since the crop is to be cut in the seed-leaf stage. Nothing meets these requirements so well as discarded John Innes Compost (or similar) which should be allowed to accumulate under cover after it has been thrown out, then sterilized with a 2 per cent solution of formaldehyde. This material should form the top 2 ins. of frame beds or the whole filling of boxes over the usual drainage layer. It should be put in through a sieve so as to ensure a surface that is fine, even and dead level which must them be firmed with a block of cork or wood. At this stage it must be as moist as good potting compost ready for use. After the seed has been evenly distributed over this level surface it is not pressed in but is simply moistened with a fine spray and then covered with the wet hessian which in turn is kept moist solely by light but frequent overhead spraying, never by the use of a watering can. When the crop has been cut, the soil in the boxes is discarded altogether; so are the top 2 ins. of soil in frame beds. In the latter case, if more mustard and cress is to be grown on the same bed, the remaining soil is forked over, watered and levelled, then topped up again with a fresh 2 ins. of sterilized compost, which is well firmed.

How Much to Sow

Once they have reached the stage of being ready for use, cress and mustard do not remain in good condition for more than a week and it is usually best to consume each sowing within three to four days of maturity. You can get a dozen ¼ lb. punnets of cress, as sold by the greengrocer, from an area equivalent to that of a standard seed tray (14 × 8½ ins.). The contents of the purchased punnet, if mixed, will probably consist of 4 parts mustard to 1 part cress, though sometimes the cress and the mustard are sold in separate punnets. You can of course vary the proportion to please yourself if growing at home. The quantity of seed used to sow a standard seed tray is (a) during autumn and spring ¾ oz. of mustard or ½ oz. of cress, (b) during winter 1 oz. of mustard or ¾ oz. of cress. From these particulars, knowing the rate at which your household will eat the stuff, you ought to be able to work out how much seed to sow and over what area without overproduction or wastage. For your information, however, to get a couple of punnets for my own small household, I sow a strip about 12 ins. long by 2½ ins. wide; this uses about ⅙ of a 1 oz. packet of seed. By the way some seedsmen sell the seed by measure instead of weight; but you can take it that 1 pint will weigh (very roughly) ½ lb.

When to Sow

Mustard and cress is most appreciated from November to May and greengrocers say that the peak period of popular demand is from March to May. I must say that I do not think it worth while growing it in summer but you are of course free to grow it all the year round if you like. Given the temperatures previously specified the times taken for the crop to reach 1 in. (when the hessian is removed) are (a) in autumn and spring, mustard four days, cress seven days, (b) in winter, mustard seven days, cress ten days from time of sowing. After this you have to allow time for the seed-leaves to develop fully and become a good green which will be about twenty-four hours during the lighter days of autumn and spring, and up to seventy-two hours during the rest of the winter period after the sacking has been removed. Accordingly you have to allow from eight to thirteen days from sowing to cutting according to weather and time of year and you will note that, as mustard germinates and grows more quickly, it must be sown three days *after* the cress in order that both may end up level. The frequency of sowing may be anything from twice a week to once a fortnight to suit the household requirements.

How to Cut

The crop should be cut when just over 2 ins. high by using a pair of sharp scissors in the right hand and holding tufts of mustard or cress in the left hand. As each handful is cut put it directly into a punnet. Make the cut ¼ in. above soil level and take the greatest care not to pull the roots up or otherwise disturb the soil.

AMERICAN OR LAND CRESS

The so-called American or land cress, *Barbarea praecox*, is not American and is not even cultivated in America; it is a native of Britain and wants almost as much water as watercress to enable it to grow well. It is a brother of *Barbarea vulgaris*, the Yellow Rocket, which was once used as a salading but has been ousted from favour by our native watercress which is a nasturtium.

This cress looks and tastes very much the same as watercress but has a smaller leaf; it is perennial; and it is most likely to succeed in a north-facing border where the soil remains reasonably moist at most seasons of the year – but this does not mean that it will tolerate sour, stagnant conditions due to lack of proper drainage. Although it *can* be sown in spring, it will be obvious that by reason of its predilections, it is not an easy subject to establish during the summer months; I advise you therefore to make your sowing during the early part of August. You may sow either broadcast or in drills; but it is desirable to confine the seed to an area which can be covered with a light portable frame in winter because, although the plants are perfectly hardy, you cannot eat frosted cress and must therefore take all reasonable steps to prevent the leaves from getting frozen.

Any decent soil will grow this crop which needs only to be thinned to about 4 ins. apart and kept weed-free. The plants yield a continuous supply of leaves once the growing points have been taken out; but I would like to emphasize the need for keeping them constantly supplied with an abundance of water, otherwise the produce is likely to turn out to be unpleasantly tough.

WATERCRESS

Watercress (*Nasturtium officinale*) is an aquatic plant which grows wild by the sides of shallow streams and as a rule only in sluggish water: in a fast-running stream its leaves tend to resemble those of the poisonous water parsnip. In bygone days it used to be collected and sold in town in spring, meeting with a ready sale because of its health-giving properties and high vitamin content – there were few saladings or green vegetables available in winter in those days. Goldsmith speaks of stripping 'the brook with mantling cresses spread'. It was also the custom to mix wild watercress with the leaves of the brook lime, *Veronica beccabunga*, in order to improve the flavour.

It was not until about 1808 that any attempt was made in this country to cultivate watercress in areas where suitable streams existed, although this had been done earlier in Germany. Today, of course, we have a flourishing and ever-expanding watercress industry, and supplies are available all the year round and especially during the season of greatest demand which is still in spring from March to May and includes Easter.

When grown commercially, watercress is planted in artificial beds which are in effect shallow, concrete-sided, gravel-bottomed troughs through which passes a controlled flow of water of unimpeachable quality usually about 4 to 6 ins. deep. During summer the watercress grows out of the water (i.e. the growth rises above the surface) and is cut with a knife; but from October to March it grows *in* the water and is gathered by pulling out one plant in every three, a system of thinning.

If any reader has a sufficiently large garden in association with a suitable and adequate natural water supply and, possessing also some capital and either leisure or paid labour, desires to grow his own watercress *in water*, I advise him to purchase and study Bulletin No. 136 of the Ministry of Agriculture, Fisheries and Food published by H.M. Stationery Office and entitled *Watercress Growing* (27p. plus postage). The cultivation of watercress is not as easy as it might sound and the details and snags are beyond the scope of this book.

Since, however, when growing wild, the plant seems to be more concerned with having its roots in water than with being immersed in it, it follows that it is quite possible to grow watercress in the average garden (and good watercress too), provided that you have plenty of water available and also plenty of spare time. But frankly I regard the home cultivation of watercress as uneconomic and best suited to those retired folk who are also enthusiastic gardeners always wanting to fuss about with something out of the ordinary. I myself would confine myself to land cress, if I could not buy decent watercress from the greengrocer. This is not to say that I have not grown my own watercress: I have – but it was in a sunken bed which was kept continuously half-flooded by a leaking water butt in a very wet summer (and we had to add lime to the water because watercress doesn't like soft water). We had a splendid crop the first year, but the second year was a dry one and we had a big enough job preventing our water butts from going dry without letting the precious stuff run out all the time on to the watercress bed. So we got a new water butt which did not leak and, as soon as it became dependent on watering with can or hosepipe, the watercress bed ceased to thrive.

However, for those who wish to try, here are the necessary instructions. Select a site which receives a fair amount of sun but is otherwise reasonably well sheltered, though experience has shown that it must be clear of overhanging trees – all manner of complications arise if you have your watercress buried beneath fallen cherry blossom or the June drop of apples. Since watercress does not grow in *stagnant* water, your site must not be one that gets waterlogged in winter and the natural water table must be at least 2 ft below the surface. If you can find a suitable spot close to a garden standpipe, so much the better. On this site mark out an area equivalent to that occupied by a couple of frame lights: I used lights measuring 4 × 3 ft, giving me two beds each just over 1 sq. yd in extent which proved ample for my household needs, but you can use Dutch lights if you prefer. Excavate 18 ins. deep; make a firm, levelled bottom of rammed hardcore; put in a 6-ins. layer of good ripe garden compost well trodden down; cover this with 4 ins. of peaty soil mixture, such as John Innes Seed Compost; top up with 2 ins. of a mixture of equal parts of good soil and coarse vermiculite; dress with superphosphate (2 oz. per sq. yd), which is the only fertilizer that watercress needs; make all firm, and soak thoroughly with water. Now line the bed on all four sides with treated boards on edge and fit a cross piece so that you have bearers for your frame lights. Your seedsman probably won't have watercress seeds in his catalogue but he should be able to tell you where to get them. The seeds you get will almost certainly be of the green, or summer, type which makes no growth in winter and is unfortunately easily damaged by sharp frost. Therefore you should sow one half of your bed with this in April, scattering the seed thinly along very shallow drills spaced 3 ins. apart and giving only the lightest covering of sifted soil. Place one of the frame lights in position and shade with sacking until germination has taken place; then remove the light and thin the seedlings by stages to about 4 ins. apart. This bed should give supplies until about Christmas. In order to get water-cress during winter and spring, you must plant the remainder of the bed with cuttings of the *brown* variety in July. If you live near any of the commercial watercress beds, you should have no difficulty in cadging a handful of cuttings at this season. Failing this, go to a first-class greengrocer who sells branded watercress supplied by a grower in the area, if possible, and arrange with him to supply you with a few bunches immediately they reach his shop, so that you can get your cuttings planted within twenty-four hours or so of the cress leaving the beds. The best cuttings are 3 ins. long, cut through squarely just below a joint, the bottom half stripped of leaves, and planted firmly 2 ins. apart with 1½ ins. of stem buried in the soil. Shade heavily from the sun until rooted but do not exclude air.

Once started off, the only attentions the watercress will demand are watering and weeding. If ever there were a strong case for trickle irrigation it is provided by the amateur watercress bed; and even though some local authorities insist on charging you for the water used for trickle by means of a water meter it could still be worth while running trickle tubes in lines 3 ins. apart all down the bed and connecting up to a nearby standpipe. The alternative is to flood the beds with the aid of a hose pipe at least once a day and this calls for very careful manipulation because anything in the way of too much pressure can create a small tidal wave and wash the whole of the cress to the end of the bed! Of course you *can* water by hand if you have the time and energy; but I advise you to turn a deaf ear to all the folk who tell you that you need only water once or twice a week – leave those tales for the Marines! If you have to carry a 2-gallon can any distance from the tap, you will soon curse the day when you decided to try to grow watercress. As regards weeds, aquatic weeds grow only in summer and remain on or below the surface of the water while the watercress grows above it; the commercial grower has therefore merely to cut above water level to ensure weed-free produce. But when watercress is grown in soil instead of water and has to compete with land weeds it is a very different picture and you must keep an eagle eye on the beds to enable you to spot and eradicate weeds before they can develop to any size. This particularly applies to chickweed which, if once it gets hold on a watercress bed, will completely ruin it in a matter of weeks so that there is nothing for it but to dig the crop in.

It has, I hope, been made clear that no lights are required on the bed (except for brief spells following sowing and planting) until cold weather sets in. When growing in water, watercress sinks below the surface in winter because the water is warmer than the air. Since it cannot do this in a garden bed it has to be protected from the cold by means of frame lights which may need to be matted up during frosty nights, a procedure which corresponds in a way to the action of the commercial grower in closing his sluices and increasing the depth of the protective water on such occasions.

Cut your watercress with scissors, carefully (so as not to pull it up), and not too low down so that the stems that are left will branch and produce side-shoots to continue the supply. Incidentally, there should be far less wastage than there is with commercially grown produce because there will be no yellowed leaves and fewer white adventitious roots such as always occur when the crop is actually grown in water.

Do not keep a watercress bed in being for more than nine to twelve months. It is far more satisfactory to dig up all the plants and make an entirely new bed with fresh compost and everything from the hardcore base upwards. But there is no need to start all over again with seed or cuttings: simply heel in your stock while you are making the new bed and then replant at once with divisions from the old plants obtained by pulling them to pieces and planting the best of the bits, each with a few roots, 2 ins. apart. This work can be carried out any time during spring and summer.

Finally, for the benefit of those who feel that they could not possibly face up to all the work involved in growing watercress properly, I would say that I have seen it successfully grown in large clay pans stood in a galvanized bath containing 2 to 3 ins. of water constantly replenished and placed where it would receive shade from trees or hedges; and I have even heard of it being grown in pots stood in saucers of water. These things are only possible in summer; some people enjoy this type of recreation, but I do not regard it as either serious gardening or vegetable growing.

Cucumbers

(*Including Gherkins*)

The cucumber plant is a tendril-bearing creeper or trailer, occasionally met with as a self-supporting climber, and its fruits are among the oldest cultivated vegetables. It seems to have been a native originally of either the East Indies or of India. It is not certain that the cucumbers which the Israelites enjoyed so much in Egypt were not actually Persian melons. Whether they were melons or cucumbers they seem to have been regularly stolen when they ripened (as happens with melons today), so that each field had to have a watcher who sheltered from the heat in a booth or 'lodge' as the prophet Isaiah calls it.

There is no doubt that cucumbers as we know them were ordered to be served daily at the table of the Roman Emperor Tiberius. Our ancestors called them 'cowcumbers' and grew them as long ago as 1584 when it was written: 'The cowcumber loveth water.' Over a century ago the spiny (or prickly) ridge kind was grown outdoors in huge quantities commercially for pickling: one market-garden in Bedfordshire is said to have sent 10,000 bushels of them to London in a single week. Most people now favour only the straight, refined, smooth-skinned sorts (though some say they lack flavour). These are at their best when grown in greenhouses or frames but in many districts they can now be grown with some success in the open ground under continuous cloches. (The Slavonic word for a cucumber is gherkin and that is the name we apply to the smallest species of ridge cucumber which is used so much in pickles.

The cucumber is a tender plant and its fruits have the highest water content of any vegetable (96·1 per cent). It follows therefore that warmth and moisture, both in the soil and in the air, are the main essentials to the successful cultivation of this salad vegetable.

Raising the Plants

It is most important that cucumbers should be got off to a flying start by reducing to a minimum the time taken by the seed to germinate and by ensuring that, after germination, growth proceeds at a rapid rate without any check. This involves sowing in a very warm greenhouse unless one is prepared to wait until the weather becomes so genial that it is possible to sow without heat under glass or outdoors; this, however, causes lateness in the crop and a risk that the plants may be cut down by bad weather when they have only just begun to bear fruit.

Far too many amateurs raise cucumber plants at too low a temperature and then are perplexed by the poorness of the crop and other troubles that arise. The explanation is that with this species the fact that the seeds do 'come up' is not enough; they must not have been too long in coming up, and the same applies if subsequent development is slow. If therefore you do not have the facilities to raise your own plants in the proper manner, I do strongly recommend you to buy good plants from the nearest nurseryman of repute provided that you can ensure that they reach you without chill or check – never buy plants which have been exposed for sale in the open or stood in draughts, as they seldom recover properly. Above all, do not be misled by the 'stunt' writers on gardening and germinate cucumber seeds in a heated airing cupboard or similar place. Of course the seeds will come up all right but since you will have no equally warm place where the seedlings can be grown in full light, you will derive no benefit whatever from your ingenuity.

Cucumber seeds should be sown singly, point downwards, ½ in. deep, in 3-ins. pots filled with John Innes Seed Compost or Levington Seed Compost. Before sowing, look through the seeds in the packet and test each for plumpness between your thumb and forefinger. Sow only the plumpest and discard any that are hollow or very small – there is always some slight variation even in the best quality seed. A soil temperature of 70° F. is needed to ensure quick germination but the temperature of the air in the greenhouse may be permitted to fall to 60° F. during the hours of darkness. At these temperatures the seedlings should start showing up from 36 to 48 hours later. Adequate moisture in the sowing compost is most important because in a season of bad harvesting conditions, or if it has been slightly over-dried, the seed casing of the cucumber seed may become so tough that it is reluctant to allow moisture to pass through to the germ and then the germ cannot grow. This defect does not manifest itself during laboratory germination tests and can cause much perplexity to the grower whose only fault is that he uses his compost a little too dry.

The young plants must not be allowed to become potbound and, when well rooted, will need to be moved to 4½-ins. or even 6-ins. pots. The ideal stage of development for planting out is when the second rough leaves are the size of a 5p piece. This stage should be reached within a month of sowing and the plants, whether raised by yourself or bought in, should then be deep green in colour, short-jointed, with a strong growing point and stems which are straight and succulent, not thin and hard. It is permissible to encourage any laggards by giving dilute liquid manure every three days or by adding a little soot or bonemeal to the compost used for 'potting on'. If there is any uncertainty whether you will be ready to plant out before your seedlings begin to starve in pots, you may prefer to put the seedlings into soil blocks; in that case sow in a small seed box and block up within 48 hours *before the seed leaves have fully unfolded and before any lateral feeding roots have been produced.*

Plants intended for outdoor cultivation must be gradually and thoroughly hardened off to withstand the lower temperatures to which they will be subjected and this hardening should commence quite early in the life of the seedlings. If seeds are sown outdoors, put them (point downwards as before) 1 in. deep and 3 ins. apart, two or three at each final station, thin to one plant (and that the best) at each station and keep covered as long as possible with a cloche or jam jar. Do not under any circumstances transplant outdoor-sown seedlings.

Since the roots of cucumbers are extremely fine and fragile and very easily damaged by ordinary methods of planting which tend to alter the shape of the soil ball, you should always adopt this special method. Instead of planting the cucumber straight away, first of all 'plant' an empty pot of the same size as that in which the cucumber is growing. After firming, remove this pot with a slight twist, turn the cucumber out of its pot and drop it into the formed cavity. Slight pressure on the sides will bring the surrounding soil into intimate contact with the ball of roots which cannot then possibly be damaged.

It may be added that all new soil into which cucumber plants are moved and all water used in watering them must have been previously warmed to a temperature of 60° F.–70° F. – it must never come straight from the tap or hose pipe.

Cultivation Outdoors

There is no getting away from the fact that the outdoor cultivation of cucumbers is more than a bit of a gamble in this country. If we get a dull summer, which usually means that temperatures are below normal for the time of year, outdoor cucumbers do not get sufficient warmth and are a flop whatever preparations are made; if we get cloudless skies, hot sunshine, and no rain, the plants will not grow because they lack adequate moisture – it does not matter how much water you give them at the root, you are still up against the difficulty that all the syringes, sprinklers, and rainers in the world cannot re-create that humid atmosphere which is essential to the proper growth of the cucumber.

The only type of cucumber that can be grown outdoors at all without glass protection is the 'ridge', which will thrive at a lower temperature and under drier atmospheric conditions than the frame or greenhouse sorts. It will not, however, tolerate exposed situations and strong winds and the first essential, if you aspire to grow it, is to satisfy yourself that you have some suitable place for it in your garden where it will get the shelter and protection that it needs while still receiving full sun. It gets its name from the practice in market-gardens of putting down manure in trenches and then turning soil over on top of it with the plough to form ridges on the south side of which the cucumber plants are set out. If your soil is a medium to heavy loam which has been liberally treated with bulky organic manures for previous crops, is in good heart, well drained, and free from acidity, having been suitably limed, you cannot do better than follow the commercial practice.

Neither planting nor outdoor sowing can take place until the second half of May or early June when the soil has warmed up;

in a backward season it may be still later. Obviously it is preferable to start with greenhouse-raised plants, sown in the latter part of April, and well hardened, because if you sow outdoors the crop will not come into cut before the middle of August. In a normal season the natural heat of the soil after the beginning of June should be sufficient to enable you to dispense with use of fermenting material, though the young plants will appreciate the protection of a handlight or some bushy twigs in chilly weather until they are well established. In this case all you need do is to take out a shallow trench about 8 ins. deep, fill it with old rotten manure, heaped up and lightly mixed in with the soil at the bottom of the trench, and then put back the excavated soil on top of the manure to form a low, flat-topped ridge, after mixing it with half its bulk of good imported loam and half its bulk of moss peat so as to emphasize its spongy, moisture-retaining texture.

On the other hand if you wish to undertake either sowing or planting before the summery weather can be relied upon to have set in, the bed will have to be warmed by the use of half-fermented manure mixed with leaves; otherwise the plants may not keep moving. The best plan is to dig out the soil to a depth of a foot or more and fill the trench with fermenting material; then spread a foot layer of good loamy soil on top to make the ridge as before.

It will be appreciated, I hope, that ridge cucumber plants, if they succeed, crop very heavily during their comparatively brief season, so that in the average household not more than two or three plants will be needed with perhaps one plant of the gherkin type for pickles. In view of this some people make separate mounds for each plant a yard apart but I think this wasteful because you can do little or nothing with the spaces between the mounds. My own practice is to do as the market-gardeners do and make up a continuous ridge 3 ft wide, backing, if possible, on to a south-facing fence, and take a crop of lettuce off it while the cucumbers are still small.

If the soil in your garden is of a light nature, the ridge system will not work and you must dig a hole for each plant 2 ft across and a foot deep. The excavated soil will not be used but can be neatly piled round the north side of the hole where it will act as a windbreak. In its place put into the hole first a large bucketful of fresh manure which has been spread and turned in the open for a few days to get rid of the ammonia and then mixed with its own bulk of last year's tree leaves and secondly a 4-ins. layer of John Innes Potting Compost No. 3. This, when firmed, will leave you sufficient headroom to place a sheet of glass flat over the hole after the cucumber has been planted. Leave this in position at night and during chilly periods by day until the plant is well established but ventilate whenever possible by propping the glass up on one side and, in the event of a spell of unfavourable weather most unfortunately following planting, replace it as the plant grows by a large barn handlight. Plants on ridges may appreciate similar protection and, if no handlights are available, you may find it desirable to cover them with large inverted flower pots or with boxes every night while the weather remains cold.

Opinion differs concerning the distance the plants should go apart when on ridges. The truth is that ridge cucumbers will make small plants or great ramping ones according to the season, the soil, and the grower's skill and experience. There cannot be any rule about spacing therefore but you will probably not go far wrong if you allow 18 ins. between plants.

An American method of growing outdoor cucumbers may appeal to some readers. A small barrel or keg, measuring not more than about 2 ft across its widest part, is sawn in half, after knocking out the ends, and one half is placed on the site, smaller end upwards, packed almost full of well-rotted manure and covered with a board or a piece of coarse canvas. The cucumbers are planted on low mounds or hills, 1 ft apart, in a circle close up against the barrel on three sides – no plants on the shaded side. Every day, unless there is heavy rain, a 2-gallon bucket of water is emptied on to the manure in the barrel; this water of course seeps through and supplies the plants with moisture and nourishment at the root, thus cutting out other forms of watering.

The plant food requirements of cucumbers are essentially nitrogen and phosphates – they want comparatively little potash. Proprietary cucumber fertilizers are available but not in small packs so that the least quantity an amateur can buy is likely to last him about fourteen years, if he can keep it in good condition for such a lengthy period of time! It is better therefore to rely on the ordinary straight fertilizers that most keen gardeners will already have available. On the whole I am against base dressings and suggest that you wait until the plants are beginning to grow well and then top dress at the rate of 2 oz. per sq. yd with a mixture compounded of 2 oz. hoof and horn meal, 1½ oz. steamed bone flour, and ½ oz. sulphate of potash. Follow this up, when the plants are in bearing, with a weekly feed of dried blood in solution (1 oz. to 1 gall. of water). Do not give superphosphate, as often advised, because it tends to stimulate the development of the seeds in the fruits which is not at all desirable from the table aspect.

It is not necessary to do a lot of training. The point of the leading shoot should be nipped off when it is about 1 ft long and has made six to eight leaves; this induces branching. Do not stop any of the side-shoots, though it is permissible to cut out the weakest of them entirely, as there are usually too many of them. It is also legitimate to nip out the point of each shoot that is bearing a cucumber so as to induce the plant to devote its attention to swelling the fruit instead of making further growth beyond it. If a shoot goes on seemingly for ever without producing a cucumber, cut it back to seven leaves.

Some people train ridge cucumbers over A-shaped trellis supports or up 2 ins. square-mesh string netting, so that they are kept off the ground; but there is little point in doing this because it is only the long fruits of the frame varieties that gain in straightness if allowed to hang down. Any discoloration of the fruit where they touch the soil can be avoided by slipping a plastic tile beneath each one. These remarks do not apply to the newer Japanese cucumbers. Seeds of a few varieties are obtainable from Thompson and Morgan Ltd, Ipswich. Set out plants at 1 ft apart along a trellis about 4–6 ft high – it may be 'Weldmesh' or 'Netlon' or simply a few stout stakes linked together with several strands of soft wire. Link the top wire to the bottom wire and you have a 'mesh' trellis. The plants should be tied now and then to the trellis. When they reach the top of the supports, pinch off the growing point at the top of each plant.

Where the better known varieties are being grown on the flat, some people like to apply a straw mulch to the ground over which the plants creep and this is good practice provided that you can keep the mulching material free from slugs and woodlice.

When fine white roots appear on the surface cover them at once with a 2-ins. layer of the same compost as you used for making the mounds and press it down firmly. The compost must of course be moist.

You must of course water copiously in dry weather; but neither water nor fertilizers must be allowed to splash up against the main stem or lodge there as this might cause the stem to rot off at the collar. In order to prevent this it has long been the custom to set the plant on a slight mound so that the water will run away from the stem. This practice has, however, been misinterpreted by many people to mean that the plant should sit on a large round-topped hillock which is folly because this also causes water to run away from the roots. The top surface of the ridge or other planting place must be flat, so that water soaks down into the soil. Only a very slight convexity is permissible around the stem which should be further protected by a ring of charcoal or mortar rubble or by a zinc collar. An alternative method is cut a sod of turf, scald it to kill pests, cut a slit in it, and put it round the stem of the cucumber, grass side downwards, in the form of a collar.

In addition to watering it is necessary to syringe both sides of the foliage of the plants with tepid water on dry evenings. Apart from creating a moist atmosphere this also helps to keep away the dreaded red spider mite. It will be the fault of the red spider if the foliage becomes sickly-looking and turns a rusty colour and you can do little about it except syringe more forcibly than ever, for the mite hates water, and spray occasionally with derris or soft soap.

If the leaves become mottled with yellow and puckered and the plants then rapidly wilt, shrivel, and die, they have been infected by mosaic virus carried by aphids. Hence you will see that it is most important to keep them free from greenfly by means of a nicotine spray. Do remember, though, that nicotine is a poison. If some leaves become bleached, cut them off and spray at once with nicotine-soap wash. If some leaves develop yellow blotches or greyish brown mould as a result of damp muggy weather, cut them off and spray the plants with colloidal sulphur. If a whole plant wilts and collapses it is probably a victim of the root knot eelworm and is best taken up and burned, although it is sometimes possible to save it by exposing the roots and cutting off those with egg-shaped swellings – but it is hardly worth the trouble. As a precaution, if one plant is affected, water a quarter teaspoonful of copper sulphate into the soil close to each of the other plants.

Cut the fruits whilst still hard and green and before there is any sign of yellowing at the stem end. Gherkins for pickling should be about 4 ins. long.

Growing under Cloches

Ridge cucumbers benefit greatly by cloche protection and in the warmer parts of the country in favourable seasons it is even possible to grow the frame types under cloches.

In order to get the longest possible season dig out two trenches each 21 ins. deep, 16 ins. wide and 5 ft 6 ins. long: these trenches should be 3 ft apart. Improve the subsoil, return sufficient of the top soil mixed with manure or compost to raise the level of the bottom of the trench by 9 ins, then make a mound of good soil 6 ins. high at each end of the trench, following the instructions already given for making outdoor ridge beds. Insert four canes, one in each corner of the trench; the length of these canes must be such that they project 12 ins. above the top of the trench; join the tops together with four horizontal canes either by lashing or by using 'hortiballs'. About halfway along each trench insert a curved (90°) field drainpipe with its vertical end projecting just above soil level immediately outside the cloche line and its horizontal end entering the trench through the side-wall.

If practicable, one trench should run to the north of the other. About the middle of March cover the southernmost trench with three large barn cloches, not forgetting to close the ends, and at the same time sow seed in a heated greenhouse so that by the middle of April you have two strong, hardened, *ridge* cucumber plants to set out, one on each mound. (The dates are for the warmer south; in the north sow and plant three weeks later.) Give the cloches a light spraying with a shading compound and keep the young plants regularly ball-watered for the first fortnight, so that they never get dry at the roots.

About mid-May sow seeds of a frame variety under jam jars or preserving jars on the mounds in the second trench if you live in the south – in the north sow in a greenhouse and plant out mid-June. Cover with tall cloches, such as 'Eff' High Levels, but otherwise proceed as you did with the other trench.

A special method of training must be adopted. Remove the growing points of all plants when they have made the fourth leaf and train the resulting two laterals, one on each side of the trench, up the vertical canes and along the horizontal ones to meet the plant at the other end of the trench. Stop these laterals just beyond the fifth leaf and stop all subsequent laterals and sublaterals at the same stage unless they show fruit, in which case you stop two leaves beyond the fruit. This drastic and rather tedious curtailment of growth is essential to keep the plants within bounds; even so, after about five weeks, the ridge sorts will have grown so rampantly in a good season that the cloches will have to be removed: but every effort should be made to keep the frame cucumbers covered throughout growth even if this involves cutting away some of the foliage.

So long as the cloches remain in position over the ridge cucumbers it will normally be sufficient to water copiously *outside* the cloches during dry weather – or you may use trickle irrigation lines – with an occasional flooding of the trench through the medium of the drainpipe. But, if the frame sorts are to be kept covered, there must be regular flooding of the trench so as to produce as far as possible the same steamy atmosphere as you would get in a frame or cucumber house and thus minimize the need to resort to hand-syringing which is extraordinarily difficult to carry out under cloches. It must not be overlooked that the risk of a dry atmosphere is far greater under cloches than it is with plants growing outdoors and it nearly always spells disaster. One untoward effect of dry conditions in the air and at the root is the decay of the young fruits from the flower end. One fruit infects another and all have to be cut off and burned and the plants (if worth saving) sprayed with liver of sulphur solution (1 oz. in 3 gallons of water).

Under this plan the ridge cucumbers should begin to bear some time during June and will continue for about six weeks by which time the frame sorts will be ready and should yield supplies into September. The frame sorts may not be up to the standard of commercially-grown cucumbers because owing to fertilization by insects many of them may be bull-nosed with a swollen end and bitter taste. As the plants are parthenocarpic they bear fruits without fertilization of the female flowers and, if one had the time, one could usefully nip off all the male flowers. But this does not apply to the ridge sorts which *must* be fertilized by insects, otherwise no cucumbers!

Cucumbers in Frames

So far as the average private gardener is concerned, there is no better method of growing summer cucumbers than to put them in frames. It is quite possible to grow the ridge sorts in frames but in view of their inferior quality as compared with the 'frame' varieties I always consider this to be a waste of a good frame. The only arguments in favour of the frame culture of ridge cucumbers are: (a) that some people actually prefer the flavour of the ridge sorts; (b) that in small households a ridge cucumber can be consumed at one or two meals whereas a long frame cucumber would have to be cut in half and kept for several days; (c) that ridge cucumbers call for much less attention, and suit the busy gardener who is away at work all day, because the light is removed from the frame altogether during June and then the crop is in the same position as if it were growing in the open air; and (d) any small frame will serve your purpose.

If you do decide to grow ridge cucumbers in a frame, you should follow the general instructions already given for growing them under cloches, except as regards training. What I am now going to write will refer in the main to the 'frame' sorts only.

A good solid frame is required for the job; the base must be of brick, concrete, or really thick timber in order that as much heat can be retained as possible. The size should be 6 ft × 4 ft and this will call for one plant only: under the conditions of frame treatment the plants grow much larger and bear for a longer period than under cloches and a single plant will provide all the cucumbers you are likely to need over a period of about two and a half months. If anybody tells you to put two plants under the same light, that is evidence that he or she does not know how to grow frame cucumbers.

All plants must be greenhouse-raised and about a month old at setting-out time. The earliest are set out about the second week in April and should bear fruit until about the middle of August. A second planting in May will extend the season but in my experience no frame cucumbers are worth keeping after the third week in September. In both these cases a hotbed is essential to success: if you cannot provide one, postpone planting until June and be content with a later and shorter season.

Organic hotbeds are by far the best: they should be from 18 to 24 ins. deep, the bed of the frame being excavated to a similar depth to make room for the fermenting material. The best covering soil is a rich, light, turfy loam. Probably the frame already contains this, having been used for previous crops; if so, keep the best of it apart when you are excavating and then return it to a depth of 4 to 6 ins.

Make your hotbed of stable manure, if you can, and put it in the frame as soon as its temperature is steady at about 80° F. If you cannot get manure, use autumn leaves mixed with fresh lawn mowings, coarse weeds, and nettle-tops – the mixture, if well moistened, will generate quite a nice amount of heat. It is practicable to use electrical soil-warming in conjunction with electrical space-heating to grow cucumbers in frames – but I do not consider this to be a desirable method because the drying effect of the buried wires or cables merely adds to the grower's difficulties in maintaining a very moist root run.

For compost for making the mound in which the plant will be set I have always used a good loam obtained from a sundriesman with not too much clay in it and have mixed with it half its bulk of old hotbed manure, spent mushroom-bed compost, or rotten leafmould, whichever happened to be available, with a preference for the manure or compost which always seemed to give the best results. With this soil I have incorporated good dustings of hydrated lime, steamed bone flour, and wood ashes from the bonfire; but you do not want much of any of these things because the whole quantity of compost required for one mound is only ½ bushel or, say, a heaped-up 3-gallon bucketful. Although I incline to stick to my own mixture I must admit that I have seen good cucumbers growing in ordinary John Innes Potting Compost No. 3: one gardener I know of always uses the John Innes Compost as a base but adds to it some well rotted chopped up turf loam and mixes in also a little bone meal and hop manure.

The mound of compost is made at the back of the frame in the centre and the cucumber plant is set out in it as usual. You must now aim to maintain a minimum night temperature of 60° F. and a day temperature of 70° F.–80° F. – so set an air thermometer in the frame and watch its readings most carefully. Keep the lights closed for several days after planting; cover with mats at night until mid-June; shade from strong sunshine, applying a coat of shading compound to the outside of the light when the summer sun begins to attain its full force.

As growth increases and the nights get warmer the light can be wedged up about ½ in. during the evenings and about 2 ins. during the daytime, opening always on the leeward side if there is any wind blowing. During the earlier part of the season, air should be given only during the middle of the day, preferably during those few minutes in which the frame has to be opened daily in order to give the plant necessary attention.

Watering is of the greatest importance. Only soft water must be given and it must be of exactly the same temperature as the frame; therefore a spare can filled with water must always be kept in the frame ready for use. The greater the heat the more freely must water be supplied, and it is only in the event of the heat in the hotbed failing or a period of cold weather setting in that the plants should be allowed to become in the slightest degree dry. During hot weather they must be syringed twice or even three times a day; the sides of the frame should also be drenched with water from the syringe and the frame should be closed in the afternoon after the second watering.

As previously mentioned, water must not be allowed to splash against the neck of the cucumber plant where it emerges from the soil, since damp at this point may bring on an attack of Collar Rot.

It is therefore necessary to take the precautions already advised in the case of ridge cucumbers outdoors.

Pinch out the growing point when the plant has made three rough leaves. Nip out the points of the resultant side shoots when these are about 6 ins. long and thus get four leaders which you train into the four corners of the frame and there stop them for obvious reasons. After that do no more stopping until the fruits are showing. Then the laterals which bear fruit should be stopped one leaf beyond the fruit. Do not allow any fruit to form on the main stems.

Peg out the growths so that they cover the bed in an orderly manner and without overcrowding; remove any superfluous shoots – crowded shoots are not fruitful. If too much fruit appears at one time, remove some of it; otherwise you will get a glut for a short season and then no further crop.

Feed the plants with weak liquid manure.

Finally, keep an eye on the developing fruits, raise them clear of the soil, and do what you can to give them a clear space to extend into so that they do not grow curved.

Greenhouse Cucumbers

From the point of view of the private gardener the only advantage to be gained from growing summer cucumbers in a greenhouse instead of a frame is that the plants are somewhat easier to manage and the fruits, since they hang down from the roof, are absolutely straight. As against this it must be emphasized that the conditions required by the cucumbers are so different from those required by other plants that the cucumbers really require the whole greenhouse to themselves. Since, however, two plants will supply all the fruits required by an average household, it would be folly to devote the whole greenhouse to cucumbers unless you are in a position to sell the surplus locally. Only an inordinate passion for cucumbers and the digestion of an ostrich would otherwise enable you to dispose of all the fruit you had grown.

The only solution to this difficulty would be to grow two plants of the variety Conqueror at one end of the greenhouse, shading the roof above them, and devote the rest of the house to tomatoes. Conqueror is not a particularly good cucumber and makes an awful lot of leaf, but it will tolerate a lower temperature and drier atmospheric conditions than other indoor cucumbers – therefore you can give the tomatoes the growing conditions they require and yet still get some cucumbers. But you cannot do this in winter because Conqueror is not suitable for winter cropping and, since you cannot grow winter cucumbers in frames, you must, if you grow them at all, let them have the greenhouse to themselves – you will also be wise to work out in advance the probable cost of your heating, otherwise you will get a shock when the fuel bill comes in.

For summer crops seed can be sown in February, March, and April; for winter crops sow on 1 September for November supplies, and again on 1 October and 1 November to provide a succession – a final sowing in January will carry on the supply until the end of May. Seedlings from these autumn and winter sowings will grow much more vigorously if irradiated by mercury vapour lamps and those who are interested in this new development are recommended to get in touch with the firm of Camplex of Sawston, Cambridge. Otherwise the raising of plants for growing on in the greenhouse follows exactly the same lines as if they were to go in frames or open ground except that at the time of potting into 4½-ins. pots each plant is given a 2-ft cane.

If the greenhouse is glazed to the ground, the plants must be grown in the borders and these must be exceptionally well drained. If there is any doubt about drainage, excavate to a depth of 18 ins., put in a 9-ins. layer of clinker, and replace the soil removed. No cucumber plant must be set into soil which is at a lower temperature than 60° F. and, in an amateur's house, the most simple and satisfactory way of raising the soil temperature is to employ electrical soil-warming prior to planting and then, after planting, to switch off the soil heat and rely on the ordinary greenhouse heating apparatus plus sun heat to maintain the raised temperature. If you cannot do this, you must either put down a layer of fresh manure 18 ins. wide and 3 ins. deep, after releasing its excess ammonia (as described under 'Cultivation outdoors'), and then make up a ridge bed on top of this 1 ft high and 2 ft wide; or you must put down a 2-ft-thick layer of baled wheat straw, made quite firm, spray water on it from a hose until it is saturated to its full extent, cover with 2 ins. of soil, and make your ridge on top of that.

In the case of plant houses with solid bases, beds 4–5 ins. deep are made up on the staging and the plants set on mounds, following the lines already laid down for preparing frames for the reception of cucumbers.

In winter it is best to grow the plants in half-filled 9-ins. pots or boxes, top-dressing with 2-ins. layers of fresh compost when the roots appear on the surface. Limitation of soil prevents sourness at a season when root activity is naturally below par. I myself use boxes, 12 × 12 × 14 ins. deep, stood on ashes and each buried to the rim in an artificial mound of moist peat, which assists in maintaining a humid atmosphere.

The composts used in the greenhouse are the same as when growing in frames and the plants should be spaced 2 ft apart.

For the purpose of training it is necessary to obtain galvanized wrought iron training eyes 10 ins. long and screw these 12 ins. apart into the underside of each sash bar from eaves to ridge to ridge. Galvanized wires are passed through the eyes and strained taut from one end of the house to the other. (In metal houses it may be necessary to consult the makers as to the method of fixing the wires.) The tops of the canes are tied securely to the lowest wire, a second cane being lashed to the top of the original 2-ft cane if the latter is too short to reach the wire. The growths are tied loosely to the canes at intervals of a few inches and then trained on the inside of the wires nearest the glass.

Remove all side-shoots that form before the leader has reached the lowest wire. Stop the leader when it reaches the ridge. If fruits form in the first or second leaf joints of the laterals, stop at two leaves beyond the fruit; if no fruits appear, stop them after the second joint. Sub-laterals may form several leaves before a fruit appears and should then be stopped two leaves beyond the fruit: but in a small house, if there is no room for such development, stop them at the first joint. This applies to summer cucumbers.

It is most undesirable to stop winter cucumbers on the lines adopted in the case of summer crops. It is, of course, necessary to pinch out the points of the leaders when they reach the ridge, and it may occasionally be necessary to stop other shoots in order to prevent overcrowding and straggly growth and to ensure that the fruit is reasonably evenly distributed and matures in regular succession. But the more that can be done without cutting the better; and a great deal of cutting can be avoided if common sense is exercised when tying the growths on to the wires.

In all cases remove the older leaves when they turn yellow so that younger ones may develop and cut out weak and unfruitful growth. Remove also all male flowers unless you have gauze insect-excluders over the ventilator openings; it is essential to prevent pollination of the fruits. Do not allow any fruits to form on the main stem.

A different method entirely is used to grow the 'cordon' cucumbers. No wires are used and the growths are trained up fillis strings as if they were tomatoes. When the second rough leaf has formed the growing point is removed, care being taken not to injure the shoot at the base of the leaf. A few days later the seed leaves and the first rough leaf must be cut away, leaving only the shoot at the base of the second rough leaf; this is secured to the string. From this point onwards every time the plant makes a rough leaf the shoot at its base is stopped at one leaf. If any laterals should form, they are removed until the leader reaches to within 6 ins. of the top wire when the growing point is cut away. Thereafter a few laterals may form adventitiously. These must be stopped after the first leaf and left to hang down without tying up. Do not remove any leaves except those which have gone yellow. Cucumbers should form in bunches all the way up the stem, starting from the node below the first stop but should be limited to three or four fruits in a bunch. These usually mature in seven days from the opening of the female flower as against an average of fourteen days with standard varieties and methods of training.

One other type, the apple cucumber, best grown in pots or boxes, also demands unorthodox treatment. It is stopped above the seventh leaf on the main stem and then left well alone except in so far as it may be necessary to prevent overcrowding.

The atmosphere of a cucumber house must be what is known as a Turkish bath atmosphere; in other words, it must be consistently warm and moist. A minimum night temperature of 65° F. is essential; the cucumber will not tolerate periodical falls in night temperature to anything like the same extent as tomatoes. By day a temperature of 70–75° F. is desirable with an occasional rise to 90–95° F. under the influence of sun heat. This means that the successful culture of cucumbers in winter involves a heavy expenditure on fuel and the regular use of blinds at night, not for the purpose of shading but to conserve the indoor heat. Considerable economies can be effected, however, by lining the greenhouse with polythene sheeting which also facilitates the maintenance of a humid atmosphere. It need hardly be said that the greenhouse itself must be of the best possible construction so that there is never a suspicion of draught even under the most wintry conditions.

The best way of providing the requisite humidity is to have zinc trays filled with water placed over the heating pipes or tubes. The water in the trays should be regularly replenished. The trays can be dispensed with if the grower is prepared to syringe the plants and staging three or four times a day. If you wear spectacles they should mist over the instant you enter the greenhouse in which cucumbers are growing; if they don't, then conditions are all wrong for the cucumbers.

Some ventilation is necessary, because the air must not be entirely stagnant and there must be no prolonged overheating but it should be provided only by the use of sub-stage ventilators and and by opening the roof ventilators on the leeward side but only to the minimum extent necessary. In winter heat must always be conserved by closing the house very early in the day.

A light shading of the glass will be needed during April and heavier shading by means of lath blinds or the application of a shading compound is necessary from May to September.

No definite rules can be laid down regarding watering. The beds must never be allowed to get dry; but overwatering can quickly prove fatal. A useful tip is to thrust a cane or your fingers 8 ins. down into the bed and if the compost is moist at that level no water is required. All water must be at the same temperature as the soil in the greenhouse. Protect the neck of the plant as previously recommended.

Top-dress all surface roots with compost warmed to the temperature of the house. Feed with dried blood when the plants are in full growth (2 oz. per yd run of bed or its equivalent in solution).

In recent years a number of F.1. hybrid cucumbers have been introduced. Most of these are for greenhouse cultivation only; some are all-female flowering. An all-female flowering plant has no (or practically no) male flowers to nip off. This is an advantage since, as has already been explained under cloche cultivation above, *frame* varieties can produce misshapen and rather bitter cucumbers if the female flowers are fertilized by pollen from male cucumber flowers. On the other hand all-female flowering cucumber plants have a tendency to set far more cucumbers than is good for the general health and well-being of the plants. Therefore, it pays to reduce the number of tiny cucumbers and to leave only a reasonable number to swell. How many you leave will depend on your experience with cucumbers and the sort of plants you have in your greenhouse at the time. If the supplier includes a leaflet or gives any special instructions on the seed packet of an all-female flowering hybrid, make sure his advice is followed.

When to Cut

Cucumbers are most tender and at their best when the two sides are approximately parallel and traces of the flower remain on the tip. A pointed cucumber is not mature. For exhibition purposes cucumbers count as a salading and can obtain a maximum of 18 points: the number of fruits required to be shown is usually two. These must be fresh, young, green, straight, of uniform thickness with short necks and noses and with flowers still adhering. Yellowing, bull-nosed, irregular fruits do not stand a chance. A good stage at which to cut is when an average-sized hand can just encircle the fruit. Take care not to bruise or remove the 'bloom'.

Diseases and Pests

The troubles most likely to affect frame and greenhouse cucumbers are roughly the same as those already described in connection with cucumbers grown outdoors. They all arise out of errors in treatment or management especially in connection with watering and ventilation. Little can be done to mend matters once the damage has occurred. Strict adherence to the instructions given in this book will minimize the risk of disappointment and losses.

Special Note

Cucumbers are highly susceptible to damage by many of the newer insecticides and fungicides and readers are advised to consult a good sundries man before purchasing any compound for the spraying, dusting, or fumigation of these plants.

Dill

This herb is a native of Mediterranean countries and arrived in Britain during Roman times. Its botanical name is *Peucedanum graveolens* or *Anethum graveolens.*

Many gardeners confuse dill with fennel. They are similar but, unlike fennel, dill seldom reaches a height of more than 2 ft and rarely has more than one very upright stalk which is smooth, shiny and hollow. Fennel foliage has a pronounced aniseed aroma; the foliage of dill is similar but has more its own smell. The fresh foliage and the seeds are similar in taste to orange peel. Dill foliage is seldom dried because much of the scent and flavour is lost during the process. The yellow flowers are very small and are produced in umbels measuring from 2 ins. to 3 ins. across. Flowering occurs between June and August, depending on when seed is sown. Fennel is perennial but dill seed must be sown each season.

Although young, fresh leaves may be used to garnish salads or be boiled with potatoes and peas to give these vegetables somewhat of an aniseed flavour, dill is mainly grown for its seeds which are used to flavour vinegar for pickling gherkins and cucumbers. There are around 25,000 seeds to the ounce. To make dill vinegar soak half a teacup of the seeds in a quart of malt vinegar for three days. Strain before using the vinegar and discard the seeds. The seeds may also be used as a flavouring in cucumber sandwiches though only sparingly – too many seeds may lead to excess bitterness. In France, dill seed is sometimes used for flavouring cakes and pastry and in sauces. Oil distilled from the seeds is mixed with other essences for use in the soap industry and dill water is an old remedy for 'the wind' – particularly in infants.

To grow dill, sow the seeds at a depth of ¼ in. in a sunny position during April or May. For successional crops, sowings may be made up to July. Always sow where the plants are to grow and thin the seedlings to 12 ins. apart when they are quite small. Hoe or use a hand fork to remove weeds. As soon as the first seeds are ripe, cut the plant stems near to ground level, tie them in bunches and hang over a sheet of paper or a tray indoors. As more seeds ripen, they will fall on to the paper or tray. Always harvest dill in dry weather and try not to shake the stems too much so as to prevent the loss of seeds.

Egg Plant

See Aubergine

Endive

Endive (*Cichorium endivia*) is of the same family as chicory and is thought to have originated in Egypt. It was known to the Romans who used it as a salading and also as a boiled vegetable. In medieval times it was credited with magical properties because it is anti-scorbutic and a mild laxative – contemporary sorcerers got quite a lot of fun out of it. It was first grown in this country during the reign of Edward VI but has never become as popular with us as it has done on the Continent (although there was a time during the last century when endive-growing formed the staple industry of the little town of Isleworth in Middlesex). Like so many of the less common vegetables, endive has always been cultivated as a staple crop in the gardens of large private houses and mansions; and during recent years the increased demand for it by hotels and canteens leads one to suppose that it may be on the way to becoming generally popular with the British public. Nevertheless it is still seldom seen in the smaller private gardens or on allotments, which is rather a pity because it is invaluable as a salading during the period when good lettuces are scarce.

The most obvious explanation of this lack of interest in endive on the part of the amateur gardener is either that he is unfamiliar with it or that he and his household just do not like it. Endive, like chicory, is bitter to the taste unless it is bleached (or blanched), and it has to be admitted that much of the endive sold by greengrocers has either been poorly blanched by the grower or has lost a lot of its blanch during transport and as a result of careless handling and prolonged display in the shop. Apart from this, endive has to be sown in summer when so many gardeners neglect to make sowings because they have a host of other things to attend to, while those with quite small gardens have no land to spare for additional crops. It has to be admitted also that endive, though not difficult to grow, is an exacting crop demanding constant watchfulness and attention as well as a fair amount of forethought to ensure that heads are available just when they are wanted. Yet, despite all these snags, I would like to see much more endive grown – and well grown – by amateur gardeners who, I feel sure, would learn to appreciate its qualities and to value it as an ingredient of the salad bowl.

Soil and Manuring

Endive requires a medium to light sandy or gravelly soil rich in humus. It is more or less useless to try and grow it on heavy land because the crop is expected to stand well into the rainy season when clay is slow to part with its moisture and since endive will not tolerate wet feet it just rots off in the clay. The only way of overcoming this difficulty would be to make an artificial raised bed of light, rich, well-drained soil on top of the ordinary garden soil, using plenty of old potting compost, sand, peat, and leafmould; but as such a bed would have to be 1 to 2 ft deep few gardeners would consider it worth while to go to so much labour. On the other hand it is essential for the growing plants to be supplied with adequate moisture in summer and you may find it necessary to pack a light soil with compost, peat, and other moisture-retaining materials in order to prevent it from repeatedly drying out.

As regards manures it is most undesirable to use organic manures when preparing the land for endive; these manures should have been applied for the benefit of the previous crop and for this reason endive should, if possible, follow leeks, broccoli, or late savoys on the assumption that, as a good gardener, you did these crops well. All that need be done to prepare the vacant site for endive is to dig it over, make good any shortage of humus and dress with hoof meal (2 oz. per sq. yd). Do not use any inorganic fertilizers – inorganic nitrogen (e.g. sulphate of ammonia) in particular makes the plants susceptible to Bacterial Heart Rot by promoting lush growth.

Raising the Plants

There are two stages in the production of endive: the first stage consists in sowing the seed and growing the plants on to maturity; the second stage consists in blanching it to prepare it for the table. In theory it is possible to produce endive all the year round, but in practice few people want it except as a substitute for, and a change from, lettuce during that period of the year when good, hearted lettuce is not easy to come by. Unfortunately, whilst it is a reasonably simple business to have endive ready for consumption up to Christmas, it is by no means so simple to have it ready in January or February (when it would be most appreciated) because the plants are not hardy. Endive will stand light frost; the plain-leaved varieties will stand a short, sharp frost such as would put paid to the last of the summer lettuces; but no endive will stand severe frost. It is only in the counties of Dorset, Devon, and Cornwall therefore that there is a reasonable prospect of it passing the winter without protection outdoors – in all other areas protection will be necessary from September or October onwards when the earliest curled endive must be covered with cloches, while later batches will need frame protection.

Owing to the vagaries of our climate and the widely different conditions that may obtain, not only as between one district and another but also as between two gardens in the same district, it is most difficult to lay down rules about dates of sowing; in fact the cultivation of endive calls for a certain flair for sensing the right moment for each operation. In general terms I would say that the latter part of June is the best time to sow the decorative curled and mossy sorts, leaving the other types to be sown during the latter part of July. One thing I am certain of is that in the average garden it is useless to sow after 31 July because plants sown in August or later will not have completed their development before bad weather stops growth. It takes three months from the date of sowing for endive to reach its maturity.

Another most important thing is to secure quick germination. In the trade it is held that any sowings before June must be made on a hotbed (60° F.) in order to rule out the risk of subsequent bolting; but I would go further and say that even the June sowings ought to be made in a heated propagator if outdoor conditions are in any way unsuitable. The point is that endive is extremely prone to bolt if germination is delayed beyond three days – indeed I have known experienced growers who have scrapped a sowing if the seedlings were not visible on the fourth day and then sown again forthwith, deeming this to be far more profitable than just waiting for the seedlings to show up. (Incidentally, endive seed harvested in a good season and properly stored germinates better when it is up to four years old than when it is absolutely fresh.)

Of the many methods of raising the plants outdoors I think the following is among the best: Draw your drill very shallow and, when weather conditions are suitable, sow, say, three 2-ft runs at weekly intervals, making 6 ft in all. The seed must be sown very thinly and barely covered, the drills must be moist and protection should be given with cloches during the period of germination – the PVC type of plastic cloche is most suitable for a job of this nature. As soon as the seedlings are large enough to handle, thin to 3 ins. pricking out a few of the best of the thinnings in three stages to stand 3 ins. apart in a prepared nursery bed. Thin again to 12 ins., putting the best of this lot of thinnings into their final positions to complete the row at 12 ins. apart. Then use the plants from the nursery bed to form a second row 10 ins. from the first with the plants the same distance apart but alternating with those in the first row. This should give you the longest possible succession.

Attentions during growth consist mainly in hoeing, keeping the crop free from weeds and slugs, and seeing that it never lacks moisture. It has been said that if an endive is ever allowed to wilt, however slightly, it will become irretrievably tough, while any prolonged dryness at the root will almost certainly lead to rotting at the heart later on. The best stimulant for lagging plants is the liquid obtained by steeping poultry droppings in water.

When bad weather sets in, the crop must be protected. It is not merely a case of keeping off hard frost – the plants cannot be blanched unless they are absolutely dry, so that you have simply got to keep off rain for a suitable period beforehand. It is particularly necessary to protect the curled sorts by the beginning of November because damp and cold soon cause the leaves to get spotted. The simplest way of doing this is to cover both rows with one line of low barn cloches. Alternatively you can lift a light portable frame over a batch of plants if you have set them out in rectangular formation with this end in view. The most popular method, and perhaps the most convenient, is to tie the leaves of each plant together with raffia 4 ins. from the top, then lift with a good ball of soil and replant close together in a good solid frame, removing the ties as soon as the operation is completed. Discard any damaged plants and remove any broken leaves when effecting the transfer. Keep lights on the frames but give ample ventilation both in frames and under cloches except during fog, mist, or frost.

Hotbed Culture

If you possess a small run of brick frames and are really skilled in the management of manure hotbeds, here is a method of securing endive in January and February. Make up a hotbed in the first frame towards the end of September, cover with a bed of light sandy soil brought to within 2 ins. of the glass, and when the temperature has settled to 80° F. sow by pressing the seed into the soil, water, and throw a mat over the frame. Immediately germination has taken place, admit light and air, but cover at night. After fourteen days prick out 3 ins. apart on to another hotbed in the next frame topped with a bed of rich gritty compost 6 ins. deep and coming to within 4 ins. of the glass. At the beginning of the fourth week in November transplant finally to a 6-ins. bed of equal parts of old hotbed manure and fibrous loam over a good hotbed, setting the plants about 10 ins. apart every way (seven rows of five in a 6 × 4-ft frame) and allowing a full 6 ins. headroom. Water as necessary, ventilate as often as possible on the leeward side, and cover with thick mats at night. Do not allow water to get on to the leaves.

Blanching

This can commence as soon as the plants are fully grown. Since endive must be cut immediately the blanching is complete – otherwise the heart will quickly deteriorate and commence to rot – obviously you don't want to blanch more than a few plants at a time. There are two methods of approach to the business of blanching: one is to blanch the heart only, the other is to blanch the whole plant. If you think the former method good enough, your best plan will be to invert a plate over the centre of the plant which must itself be in a frame or under a cloche – this will work well enough in early autumn. I myself, however, prefer complete blanching and there are several ways of doing it. The one that I have always found most satisfactory is to invert a sufficiently large flower pot over the plant and then to exclude all light by placing a tile over the drainage hole. (If you intend to do this in a frame, be sure to leave sufficient headroom when preparing the frame for the reception of the endive, although of course once in position the flower pot is itself a sufficient protection against cold and damp.) If the plants are under cloches, you can remove, say, a couple of cloches and replace them by two others which have been sprayed with whitewash or fitted with asbestos cement sheets in place of glass. Cut these two off from the rest of the row by inserting asbestos sheets at right angles and throw sacks over all to exclude light – ignore the textbooks which advise against this course because light entering through the ventilating chinks between one pane and another has been proved by experience to ruin the blanch entirely. Another method with outdoor plants is to make up a sort of long tent cloche (with closed ends) out of 1-in. thick timber and place this over three plants at a time. Some gardeners heap dry hay over selected plants in frames until light is excluded; others lift plants from under cloches, pack in boxes of soil, and place in a dark cellar – this is far better than placing them, covered with sacks, under the greenhouse staging because of the risk of drips from above. (It will be apparent that it is useless for the amateur to darken a whole frame with mats as market-gardeners often do because that would result in the blanching of too many plants at once.)

Whichever method is adopted you must deal with the curled and mossy endives before you make a start on the plain-leaved types. I cannot tell you how long either kind will stand in good condition after it is fully grown, so much depends on the district and season; but I would expect a well-grown crop to stand not less than four or five weeks. As already stated, plants must be dry before blanching commences and the first step is always to tie the outer leaves over the centre 4 ins. from the top: but this by itself will *not* provide a really good blanch.

In early autumn blanching takes only from five to ten days but later on it can take at least twenty days. Be on your guard not to leave the plants too long before ascertaining whether blanching is complete. When a plant is ready, cut it off within ¼ in. of the bottom leaves about midday when the air is driest. Do not pull it up by the roots as this will scatter earth over the other plants.

As a final warning I would remind you that slugs are very fond of endive and you may have to lay bait for them on and off throughout the life of the plants and especially whilst they are under glass.

Fennel

This is a wild plant from southern Europe which may have arrived during the Roman occupation and has become naturalized in Britain. It is said to flourish mostly on chalky soils near the sea, but grows frequently on waste ground, particularly in the London area. There are two types of fennel – *Foeniculum vulgare* (syn. *F. officinalis*) and *F. vulgare* var. *dulce*. The former is a true herb, being grown for and used as a culinary flavouring and for medicinal use;

the latter is a vegetable. In English the herb is usually referred to simply as fennel. It is, however, sometimes called Fenkel, Common Fennel, Wild Fennel, or Sweet Fennel. This last name is somewhat misleading because the vegetable fennel is really Sweet Fennel. Fortunately Sweet Fennel is also known to those who know it as Florence Fennel or by its Italian name of *Finocchio*. For the sake of clarity, the herb is referred to here as 'Fennel' and the vegetable as 'Finocchio'.

FENNEL

This herb is more frequently grown than the vegetable. It is an aromatic perennial reaching a height of from 5 ft to 7 ft under cultivation. Each clump takes up at least a square foot of ground space. The stems are shiny, the light green to blue-green leaves are finely cut and the very small yellow flowers at the top of the stems are borne in umbels 3 ins. to 4 ins. in diameter. Flowering occurs in July and August and the best position for fennel in an herb garden or herb border is to the rear where it becomes a tall foil for other lower-growing herbs. Fennel is an excellent plant for a flower border. Both the ordinary green and the handsome bronze-leafed variety are much liked by flower arrangers.

Fennel is usually grown for its foliage but the seeds can be used medicinally in Fennel Tea for infants and Fennel Water (an eye wash). The foliage has a strong anise flavour and should be used sparingly. Only a small leaf should be added to milk or water in which fish is being boiled. The leaves may be used as a salad garnishing or finely chopped in a white sauce in the way parsley is used in fish sauces but again caution is necessary because of fennel's very strong flavour.

One comes across references at times to the Italian habit of using fennel stem in soups or in salads. This is a shorter form of fennel grown in southern Italy and known botanically as *F. vulgare* var. *piperitum*.

Fennel seeds should be sown in April at a depth of no more than ½ in. and preferably where the plants are to grow, although seedlings can be transplanted. The distance to allow between plants depends on how you wish to grow them. For single clumps dotted here and there, allow 5 ft or more between plants. For a close fennel 'hedge', thin seedlings to 18 ins. apart. Although fennel is a perennial, some herb specialists suggest that since the plants sometimes die after three years, it is wise to renew one's supply every third year by starting off again with a sowing of seeds. Fennel may also be propagated by division of the clumps in March when the shoots are just showing above ground. Like many garden herbs, fennel does best in a warm, sunny position and in ordinary, well-drained but not over-rich ground. Fennel is noted for resisting periods of summer drought.

Because the foliage does not dry easily, winter supplies of fennel foliage are obtained by storing in deep freeze or by digging up a clump in October and replanting in large pots or boxes of peat in a greenhouse heated during the winter at a temperature of around 55° F.

Garlic

The garlic that we use in cooking is *Allium sativum*, a member of the onion tribe, which grows wild only in the deserts of Tartary and was introduced into England from Sicily in 1548. It is not the same as our own wild garlic or ramsons (*Allium ursinum*) or crow garlic (*Allium vineale*). The belief is still widely held that garlic commends itself only to the Latin races; but I can assure you, though you may not have noticed it, that garlic is used today in all the best kitchens, hotel, restaurant, and private, not in such quantities as to proclaim itself both by its taste and by its pollution of the breath but just so much as will bring out the flavour of the other ingredients of the dishes. Many a cook has received praise which should more properly have been bestowed upon the garlic.

Therefore I consider that every lover of good food should command that garlic be used in his kitchen; but whether, if he is a gardener, he should also grow his own garlic is another matter entirely. Garlic insists on a rich, light, sandy or gravelly soil and an abundance of sunshine; it is said that the hotter the summer the larger are the clusters of bulbs and the more cloves are formed. Garlic also demands early planting because, like all onions, it is acutely sensitive to day-length, makes all its root and leaf growth during the short days and normally starts to ripen as soon as the long days begin to draw in towards the end of the summer. These conditions are unlikely to be found anywhere except in the more favoured parts of southern England and I do not consider that it is worth even trying to grow good garlic in other parts of the country. There are about 32 bulbs to the pound and 1 lb. of them will provide a fairly large household with a year's supply of garlic and in addition enough sets for replanting the following season.

If you decide to grow your own garlic, try to find a sunny site which was richly prepared for peas, spinach, or turnips, do not add any more manure, but dig it over, incorporating any available well-rotted garden compost, and then dress with bonemeal (1 oz. per sq. yd) and hoof meal (¾ oz. per sq. yd). If you live in the warm south-west, plant in early November; elsewhere, owing to the risk of severe winter frosts, delay planting until the second half of February. (When ordering the bulbs, insist upon an undertaking from the seedsman that he will deliver by mid-February; some firms, which obtain the bulbs from the Continent, are shamefully late in sending them out.)

When planting, take out a shallow flat-bottomed drill, as for garden peas, and place small heaps of sand along it at intervals of 8 ins. If you merely want to secure the biggest weight of garlic, plant the whole bulb as received from the supplier, pushing it well down into the sand and covering with 1½ ins. of soil; if on the other hand you want individual bulbs of exhibition quality, split up the planting bulbs into cloves and select for planting those on the outside of the cluster which are as nearly as possible ⅝ in. in diameter – these should be covered with only ½ in. of soil. Make the covering soil firm so that the bulbs do not rise up when they begin to root. If you have more than one row, space the rows 12 ins. apart. If the weather is bad, cover with tent or rounded plastic cloches for a few weeks.

No further attention is necessary beyond weeding and hoeing; it is only during exceptionally dry spells that garlic requires watering. Restricted leaf growth should not disappoint you: it is a sign of good bulb formation. Some gardeners tie the foliage into a knot about mid-June in the belief that this gives them larger clumps.

When the tips of the leaves yellow, it is time to lift; this will be about mid-July with spring-planted garlic and perhaps a month or so earlier if it was planted in autumn. You do not have to wait for the foliage to wither. (If garlic foliage persists in remaining rank and green while the plants are in the ground, bend the tops over in the same way as you do with onions.) When lifting, simply pull the plants up and leave them on the ground to ripen for a week, protecting with cloches if rain threatens, after which you should clean the bulbs of earth and lay them on wire netting in a frame until the foliage has withered, then hang in the sunniest place possible for a week. After that the bulbs can be separated, the dead foliage being removed, and either strung into ropes or placed in bags. For the next month or two there is no better place for them than a warm spot somewhere near the kitchen boiler.

Gherkins

See Cucumbers

Good King Henry

See Mercury

Gumbo

See Okra

Horseradish

Horseradish (*Cochlearia armoracia*) is a native of Europe which has become naturalized in Britain and can be found growing wild on light soil by the roadside or on waste land that was formerly cultivated. The decision whether it is to be included among the crops to be grown in a private garden will obviously be governed by the amount of roast beef consumed in the household and by the ability of its members to distinguish between well- and freshly-made horseradish sauce and the ready-made stuff that is sold in bottles (though, curiously enough, horseradish sauce was served with fish long before anybody thought of serving it with roast beef). Horseradish is of course of no interest to vegetarian gardeners except as a homely plaster for chilblains.

For the benefit of those who do wish to grow horseradish, it may be stated: (a) that, if grown at all, it should be well grown, not relegated to any odd corner of the garden and neglected so that it produces only worthless roots; (b) that even in the wild state horseradish will not grow on heavy, wet, clayey soil; and (c) that once it has been admitted to the garden it is unlikely, owing to its phenomenal power of spreading, that it will ever be got rid of again.

Horseradish demands an open, sunny, well-drained site and a heavily-manured medium to light soil, such as suits garlic – and by 'manured' is meant liberally dressed with actual stable or farmyard manure, though there is no objection to the use of good garden compost to eke out the manure. No fertilizers should be used prior to planting.

If you know of a nurseryman selling roots then buy only half a dozen. You certainly won't want more. They may be as little as 4 ins. long, though I prefer straight roots 8 to 12 ins. long. It is a bit uncertain what you will get if you get pieces of root with buds on, reduce the buds to one, and plant bud upwards. If there are no buds, the pieces are probably thongs of pencil thickness (or up to ½ in. across) and these need to be cut squarely across the top (or larger end) and planted top upwards – the top will then form its own bud underground. Suppliers of horseradish roots are difficult to find – you may have to look for plants growing on waste land from which you can take suitable pieces of root for replanting in the garden. If you have an allotment you may well be able to obtain roots from a fellow plot holder when he lifts his own crop in the autumn.

The usual method of planting is to bore holes with a crowbar 1 ft apart of such depth that when the piece of root has been dropped in and gone right to the bottom its top is 4 ins. below ground level; the hole is then filled up with soil. This is done in late February or early March. It is claimed, however, that the crop is less likely to spread if the holes are made semi-horizontally with the far end about 4 ins. below the surface – in this case the top is left just protruding from the upper end of the hole and the soil is not pressed round the roots.

Weeding, watering, and hoeing are the only attentions required. If you can manage it, don't leave the crop to be dug as required and do not leave it to grow for two years before lifting any, as the commercial men do. Clear the whole bed annually in autumn and store the roots; then form a fresh plantation on a fresh site the following year using thongs from your own roots similar to those that you purchased. This is the only way in which you can get high quality roots and the only way in which you can be sure of eradicating every scrap of root and preventing the crop from encroaching on to the surrounding ground. When the roots are lifted, the tops are cut off and the roots stored anywhere under cover in slightly moist sand or sifted ashes. They are taken out as required, well scrubbed, and then grated just before they are wanted for table. Oil of horseradish is very volatile and quickly evaporates. Any surplus can be shredded and dried in a slow oven and kept in a corked jar – but it will be a poor substitute for fresh horseradish.

Kale

(See also Brassicas)

The European races living north of the Mediterranean, for whom the cabbage was a staple food, christened it 'cole' or 'kale' by derivation from the Latin *caulis*, a stalk, and it is quite possible that the earliest cabbages were more stalk than anything else. Generations ago the Scots ate custocks, the pithy stalks of kale, which the prodigal gardener burns and the more knowledgeable slices and adds to the compost pile. Our modern kales still come nearest to the original wild cabbage: botanically they are *Brassica oleracea* var. *acephala* because they produce either an open head or no head at all. In most seed catalogues, including some of the highest repute, you will find kale listed under the heading 'Borecole or Kale', a splendid example of the conservatism of the trade in perpetuating an error. Borecole is merely one particular variety of 'curlies' which once formed the staple food of the Dutch peasants or Boers (*Boerenkool* or Boers' Kale): all other varieties of kale are *not* borecole.

Kales are the source of most late spring and early summer 'greens'. They will grow well in a poorer soil than would suit most other members of the cabbage family; indeed they have been known to thrive on hard, rocky ground. But they will succumb if the water-table is so high or the drainage so bad that the tips of the roots come into contact with standing water in winter and, although extremely hardy, if planted in frost pockets they may be killed outright by prolonged and persistent ground frosts, Russian kale and Hungry Gap kale may be relied upon to survive.

There are many different types of kale, as may be seen from some seed catalogues. It is very important to use only the best strains of seed and, although the plants will stand a lot of punishment, it will pay you to make a real effort to grow them well. Kale usually does excellently on ground from which potatoes have been lifted, and the kale plants may even be set between the potato rows before the potatoes are lifted provided that the rows have been spaced more widely than usual with this object in view. Alternatively, kale may follow broad beans, peas, early lettuce, or even spring cabbage – kale is much less subject to club root than other brassicas. Do not dig the ground again after the previous crop has been cleared unless conscience tells you that you have badly neglected its humus content, in which case the best remedy is to dig in green manure; otherwise simply rake the plot over and hoe in a light dressing of a balanced compound fertilizer as soon as the plants are established.

Plants are raised as already described under Brassicas. Some people consider that kale ought to be sown in the rows where it is to mature and there may be something in this. But in practice (except in the case of Hungry Gap) it is impossible to arrange for it to be done because in the average kitchen garden and allotment there is not sufficient land to spare at the time when the kale is due to be sown, so that there is no option but to start it on a seed-bed. There is no fixed date for sowing: it depends partly on when your planting land will become available, partly on where you live, and partly on when you want to cut. You can have kale of sorts in November if you like (when it is sometimes to be seen in the shops) but that is a waste of a good crop. It is poor stuff until it gets frosted and would be far more use to you in spring and early summer. The whole secret of growing good kale is to get it well established before cold weather sets in because after that it will make little growth until February or March; but at the same time you have got to prevent it from growing so proud, especially in the milder south, that it will either be damaged by the first hard frost or will bolt at the first touch of springlike weather. Curled kale is particularly liable in a mild wet winter to turn black and go to pulp after it has been frozen and this type is best left to those who live in the bleaker parts of the country.

Another point to bear in mind is that if you sow early you must plant early – kale must never be kept hanging about in the nursery bed after it is large enough to plant.

Subject to all these considerations, I would say that, if you want an early crop, you should sow in early March and plant in May; but for the main cuttings from February to April the best sowing time is from late March to mid-April except in mild districts where it is better to sow in May and plant in July in as cool a spot as possible. The 'asparagus' type can even be sown with success as late as July if it is thinned, not transplanted, and I know people in Scotland who actually sow the Scotch kales at the end of July, plant in late autumn, and cut the following June. I have also heard of a Wiltshire grower who, when a bad autumn had damaged the spring cabbage crop, sowed three rows of curly kale under cloches at the beginning of January, left the crop unthinned, and cut excellent 'spring greens' in April. Hungry Gap kale is of course always sown from June to August in the rows where it is to mature for cutting from May to June the following year, and this variety should be grown by everybody as a stand-by, since it will thrive through drought, wet, and frost when all other varieties have been killed.

Plant the Scotch kales 18 ins. square and the more vigorous growers, especially the sprouting types, 24 ins. square. Thin Hungry Gap to 9 ins. Firm planting is essential. If you buy plants from a nurseryman they must be from 4 to 6 ins. long. A dozen plants of a variety will suffice for a small household. Do not stint water during dry spells in summer whilst the plants are establishing themselves. In autumn earth the plants up to their basal leaves; this assists rooting, conserves moisture, protects the stem from frost, and holds the plant steady against rough weather. Kales of the asparagus type also appreciate protection from north and east winds. If you use chemical fertilizers top-dress with nitro-chalk in February.

Except in the case of the tree kales (grown for their leaves) and the hearting types which produce a loose, cabbagy head, the edible portions of kale are the short side-shoots which are broken off in much the same way as those of sprouting broccoli. After the first picking, other shoots develop up and down the stem and provide further supplies on the cut-and-come-again principle until either the plant is stripped or it decides to run to seed. It is desirable with the curly kales to remove and eat the top of the plant early in the year so as to stimulate the growth of these shoots. It is most important that the shoots should be taken and eaten young; otherwise they become tough and inclined to be bitter.

Avoid the larger and older leaves of Scotch kale unless you are a skilled cook, for it is difficult to render them tender. The whole head of a plant of variegated kale, if cut when clear of frost, will last for weeks in water, which should be changed fairly frequently. If Jersey kale is left to continue growing after the leaves have been eaten and then in autumn the plants are transplanted very close together against a wall or hedge, the main stems will grow up to 10 ft high during the following spring and summer. It is the dried lower portion of these stems that is manufactured into 'Jersey Walking Sticks'.

Kohl-Rabi

The 'Corinthian Turnip', as Pliny calls it, is in the nature of a curiosity of the brassica family: the name means 'cabbage-turnip'. It is regarded as a most acceptable vegetable on the Continent, especially in Austria where it is on sale at every market, but is comparatively seldom grown in Britain. Yet it can be much recommended as a substitute for turnips where these fail owing to lightness or dryness of soil or a hot, dry season and it is well worth growing on its own merits since it is popular with all who have tried it; it has a most distinctive nutty, turnip-like flavour. The

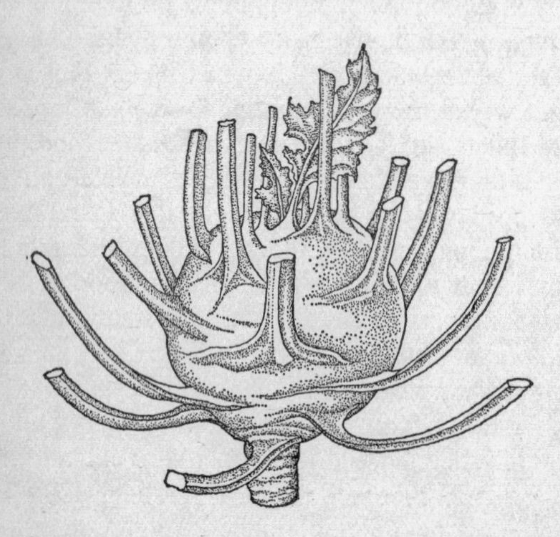

edible portion is the cricket-ball-like knob which appears just above ground level. It should be sent to the kitchen when in fact it is no larger than a cricket-ball. Do not wait for it to grow into a football. Seed may be sown any time between March and the end of July either in a seed-bed for transplanting or in rows where the plants are to remain. The plants require at least 10 ins. of space in which to reach full development, but it is a good practice to thin to 6 ins. in the first place and pull each alternate plant young as an early vegetable, thus leaving the remainder to mature at a foot apart.

Kohl-rabi will grow on any decent well-drained soil with plenty of humus in it. The ground can be prepared as if for turnips. Make the sowing drills ¾ in. deep and space the rows 18 ins. apart. No attention is needed beyond weeding, watering, and hoeing. The plant is hardy and late sowings may be left to stand outside all the winter, roots being pulled as required at any time until late spring. They will not keep in store for any length of time. It may be remarked that any animal that can eat turnip will prefer a kohl-rabi. But kohl-rabi must *not* be cooked like a turnip: it must be peeled thinly and *sliced* into ¼-in. slices before being boiled in salted water for 40 minutes – see continental recipe books.

Leeks

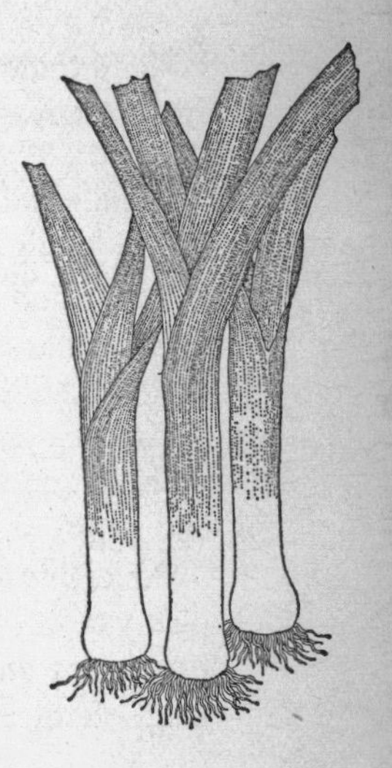

The leek is an ancient British vegetable and still grows wild in many places. It is reputed that, in the sixth century A.D., when the Ancient Britons were playing a warlike match against the Saxons, they were instructed by their captain, St David, to wear wild leeks in their caps as a distinguishing badge – presumably both sides were wearing the same-coloured jerseys. Ever since that time the leek has been the national emblem of the Welsh or Wälsch ('them furriners') as the Saxons politely called them.

(Shakespeare's Fluellen did not allow Pistol to forget this.) The leek is still a popular vegetable in Wales.

Although extensively cultivated in Egypt from Biblical times right up to the present day the Egyptian leek is a different vegetable from the one we grow over here. (It was imported into Rome and served at the table of the Emperor Nero and eighteen centuries later it was imported into Britain and sold during the Second World War as a 'wonderful novelty' under the name of the onion-leek, presumably because it has a bulb-like swelling at the base of the stem.) All our British strains are now home-raised, mainly in Scotland (where leek-growing is almost a religion) and in the north of England. There are long leeks and short (or 'pot') leeks; of the former the Musselburgh is the most famous. All the Scotch and north country leeks are immensely hardy. The London leek (or Broad Flag) is not so hardy because the warmer climate of the south does not encourage it to become so frost-resistant – in any case, southerners do not care half so much about leeks as do their brethren in colder climes although leeks are becoming more popular in the south as a consequence of the shortage of onions in the second world war.

The Old English word *leac* simply means a plant and it is difficult to see why it should have been applied to the leek in particular. Perhaps some distinguishing epithet has fallen off during the ages. Incidentally, garlic is the gar- or spear-leek.

Soil and Manuring

The leek is a very long-suffering vegetable: it will grow in almost any soil and will tolerate an almost incredible amount of ill-treatment. Nevertheless it will appreciate any kindness you may render it and, although small leeks no thicker than your finger are not to be scorned for eating purposes, you will get much finer specimens if you do the crop well and see that it never lacks food and moisture.

Preferably leeks should follow a crop for which the land received plenty of farmyard or other organic manure. You cannot do better than plant on ground vacated by spring cabbage, early peas, or winter lettuce. If your soil is short of potash dress it with a compound fertilizer rich in potash – one of the so-called 'tomato' fertilizers will do. The crop will also appreciate a dressing of agricultural salt at the rate of ½ oz. per yd run; the salt should preferably be dissolved in water to prevent the possibility of any crystals coming into contact with the plants at a later stage.

Do not plant leeks after early potatoes, since these are not lifted soon enough and leave the soil much too loose. If owing to lack of previous organic manuring the ground suffers from a shortage of humus, do not try to remedy matters by incorporating either stable or farmyard manure when preparing it for the leeks as these manures will give rise to coarse, leafy growth unless applied so long beforehand that the site can lie fallow for a considerable period and thus have time to 'digest' these organics. You would do better to use good ripe garden compost or shoddy or peat fortified with prepared hop manure, and well-rotted leafmould.

If you have good, fertile soil leeks will need no feeding. Otherwise dress them with nitrate of potash (1 oz. per sq. yd) just before finally earthing up.

Raising the Plants

Those gardeners who wish to exhibit their leeks at the autumn shows must sow not later than the beginning of February in boxes of John Innes Seed Compost in a heated greenhouse at a temperature of 55° F. When 2 ins. high, prick the seedlings out 3 ins. apart into shallow boxes or place them singly in 5-ins. pots, using John Innes Potting Compost No. 2 in each case. You may want to try the newer proprietary soil-less composts or use any special mixture you personally prefer. Take great care not to damage any roots. Commence to harden off in frames about mid-March preparatory to planting out during a favourable spell in April.

It is a different matter if the leeks are intended solely for household consumption. Some favour sowing about mid-February either in shallow boxes in frames, heated or unheated, or under cloches, two rows under tents or five rows under barns, then either pricking out into other boxes or thinning in the rows preparatory to planting out in May. But this has always seemed to me to be a needless labour so far as the growing of leeks for eating purposes is concerned, although it may be justified a month later, in March, if cold or wet weather persistently delays outdoor sowing. Ordinarily, however, the simplest course is to sow in a seed-bed in the open at any time from early March until mid-April according to the weather and the state of the ground. Thin early and plant out in successive batches between June and August, beginning when the seedlings are about 6 ins. high; this will provide a succession from November to April. But, when deciding how or when you will sow, do pause to consider when you really want your leeks. The plants mature in from 30 to 36 weeks from the time of sowing, so that the earliest plants from a February sowing will be ready in October. Now leeks are far more valuable after Christmas than before it, and in a well-cultivated garden or allotment there ought to be plenty of other vegetables available besides leeks in October and November. What is more, the leek, being biennial, makes more growth in its second season and puts on a lot of weight in the second year, especially during March and April. I therefore always advise gardeners to concentrate on the late leeks and let the early ones go hang.

I often wonder, too, whether it is worth while bothering to raise your own plants at all. Small seedling leeks are very finicky things to handle and it is much simpler to buy plants from a nurseryman. Leek plants travel well and will tolerate a substantial amount of neglect on arrival.

The alternative is to give up bothering to transplant leeks and sow them in April in the rows where they are to remain. I have done this myself, spacing the rows 12 ins. apart and thinning the plants to an inch or two apart, and everybody has agreed that I got more leeks, and more tasty ones at that, than my neighbours who went to all the trouble of setting out each plant. There are, however, two snags in connection with this method of procedure. One is that it may upset your rotation because the crop occupies the land for a longer period and you have got to find a suitable patch of ground which will become vacant well before the end of March. The other disadvantage is that, in the absence of transplanting, you cannot determine the direction in which the leaves will arch. If you are setting plants out it is an easy matter to place them so that the leaves all point along the row and not across it; in this way you get an absolutely clear alleyway in which to walk between the plants instead of having the leaves sticking out in all directions and getting entangled with your feet.

Planting Out

There are several ways of planting leeks. If you possess a really deep soil in which there is as good stuff 1 ft down as there is in the top spit, you can adopt the traditional method and dig a trench a foot deep and either 1 ft wide, in which case it will take a single row of leeks, or 1½ ft wide, in which case it will take a double row of leeks set in pairs and not alternately. This procedure is in fact very desirable on light soil which is apt to lose its moisture, but in my opinion it is neither necessary nor desirable to go to the labour of digging trenches and preparing them properly under average garden conditions and particularly in shallow soils such as are found in so many new gardens. A far simpler method of planting leeks is to make holes with a dibber about 2 ins. wide at the top and 6 ins. deep and simply drop one plant in each hole. (It will be better still if you use a trowel and make the holes 9 ins. deep and 3 ins. across at the top.) It is quite unnecessary to fill the holes in; simply fill each hole with water from a can after planting and leave the leek to look after itself. The water will wash enough soil over the base of the plant to enable it to get a hold of the ground, and the rest of the hole will fill itself in automatically under the influence of the weather during the course of the season. The only possible attention that the plants may need is a little straightening up after planting.

On very heavy soil it is really better to plant on the flat, simply drawing a shallow drill as a guide and setting the plants in it; but on land that is very wet and pasty it will be better still if you make up an artificially-raised bed of lighter soil and plant your leeks in that.

The distance at which the plants should be set apart will depend upon whether you want big leeks or smaller leeks. If you want mammoth specimens, plant at least a foot apart; if you are content with smaller leeks and more of them, plant 6 to 9 ins. apart. It is on record that in the garden of a certain noble lord the princely specimens were reserved for the purpose of winning prizes at the local village show and for supplying the servants' kitchen, while the less pretentious leeks were selected for his lordship's table. This is a policy with which I am entirely in agreement, because the smaller leeks are much more sweet and tasty and more generally appreciated than the grandiose specimens which win prizes.

Rows of pot holes should be 18 ins. apart and the actual holes at least 9 ins. apart from rim to rim. If you get them any closer, one hole is likely to collapse as you are making the next one.

When examining the seedlings, whether raised at home or purchased, select those with long necks and reject those with noticeably arching leaves, prominent middle veins to the leaves, and little or no stem or neck.

It is now the accepted practice, when planting leeks, to trim back the roots to within an inch or so of the base and to cut off the leaves square to a length of about 4 ins. so that they do not trail in the mud and decay whilst the plants are recovering from the check. The purpose of trimming the roots is simply this: under the conditions of fairly large-scale planting, such as is essential when leeks are grown to eat, it is really not practicable to spread the roots of every individual plant so that they do not bunch and to avoid injury to many of the growing tips, which are abnormally brittle, and since, if the root of a leek loses its tip, it will not fork and produce a new feeding root and thus become useless, it is better to scrap the existing root system and, by the trimming back, to shock the plant into producing a new set of roots from its basal plate, which it will do within a remarkably short period.

The foregoing planting instructions apply primarily to leeks grown for eating purposes. The exhibitor plants on the flat as being more suited to his methods of blanching and, having fewer plants to tend, does everything possible to preserve all roots intact, especially when planting from pots; he also allows the leaves to remain at their natural length, removing only those which at any time begin to decay.

Curly kale

Sprouting Broccoli

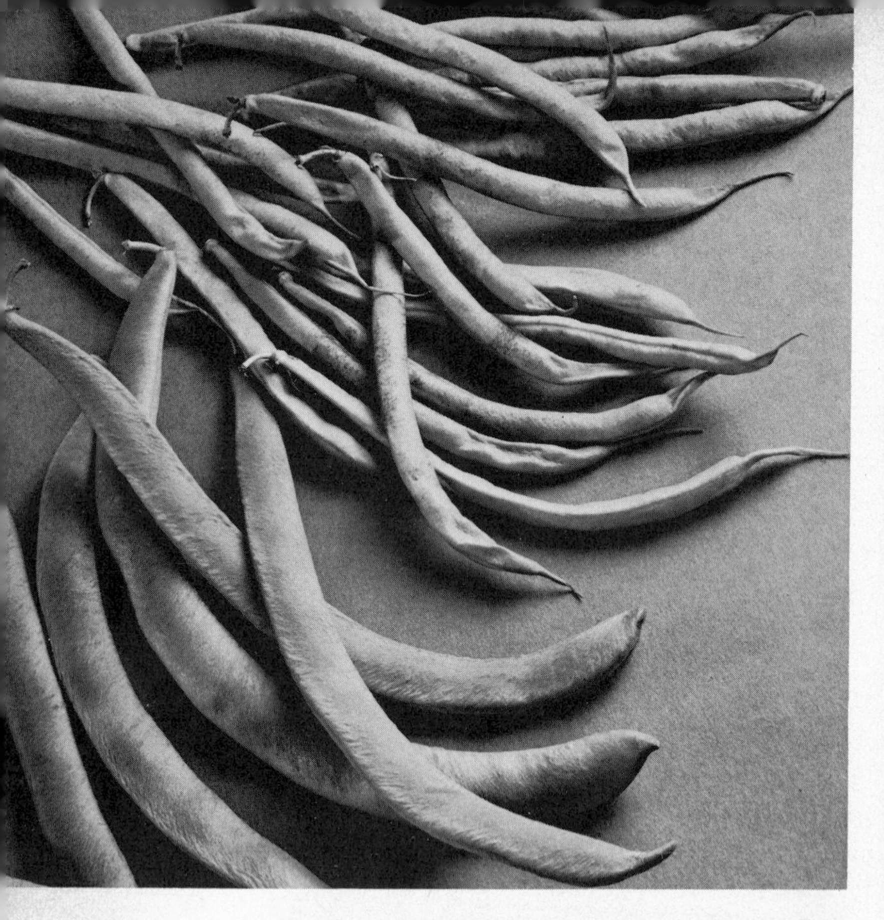

French beans
and runner beans

Broad beans

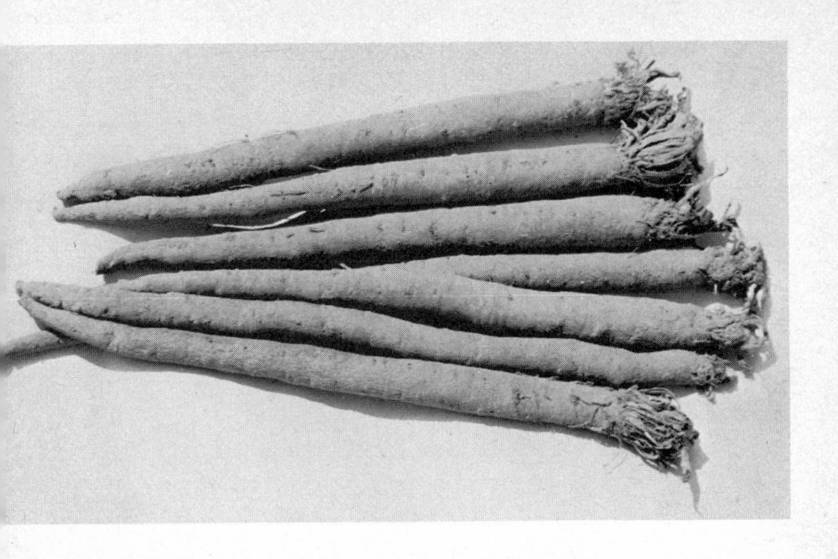

Scorzonera

Turnip and parsnip

Celeriac

Giant radish

Salsify

Hamburgh parsley

Globe artichokes

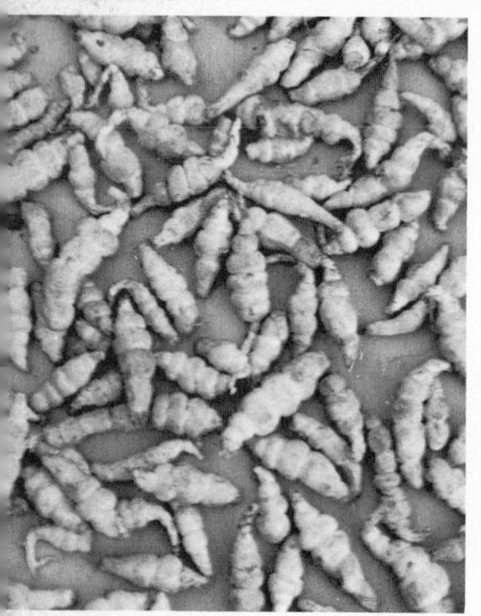

Chinese artichokes

Jerusalem artichokes

Cos lettuce

Cabbage lettuce

Chinese cabbage

Blanched seakale

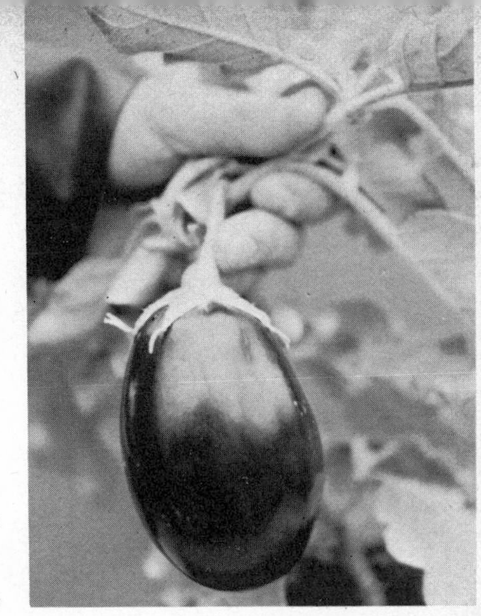

Aubergine

Courgette

Swiss chard

Chinese mustard

Vegetable marrow

Endive

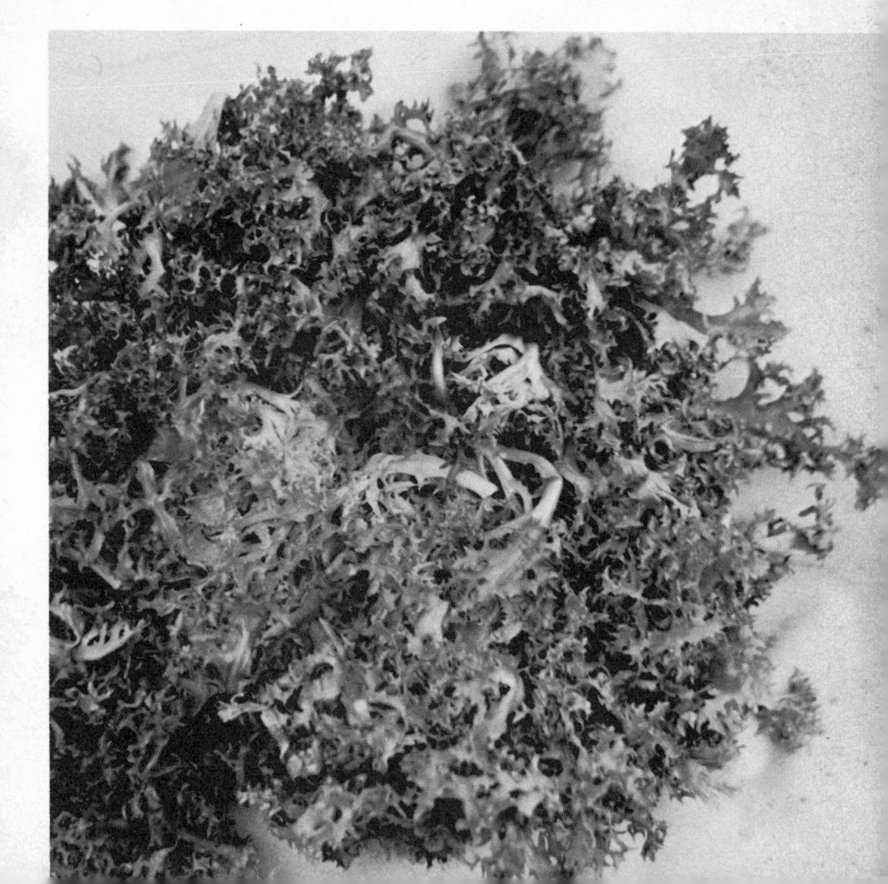

Onions, pickling onions
and garlic

Sweet corn

Blanching

The flavour of the leek tends to be too strong and bitter for most tastes unless the stems are blanched. Blanching also helps to increase the length of edible stem. For ordinary eating purposes it is usual to earth up the plants, as is done with celery, and the most important thing to remember about earthing leeks is that you will ruin any plant if you earth it up with pasty, lumpy soil. The soil must be in a dry and friable, almost powdery, condition so that it can easily be swept around the stems and will fill in every crevice; wet soil may discolour the leeks and cause decay of the stem bases. It is, however, wise to water well before earthing up as it may be difficult later on to get the water to the roots. If the plants are growing in trenches, earthing up consists of little more than filling the trench in by gentle stages so that the soil level keeps pace with the base of the lowest leaves. If the plants are in pot holes, a certain amount of extra earth can be drawn up the stems with the aid of a hoe so as to increase the length of blanch; if the plants are on the flat, soil is ridged up against the stems from both sides, an operation which nowadays is often simply and quickly performed by means of a small wheeled cultivator of the hand-propelled type – it is not necessary to have a power-driven machine.

Different methods are adopted by those who intend to exhibit their leeks. Some enthusiasts put planks along either side of the row and fill the trough so formed with old potting soil, silver sand, sifted leafmould, or granulated peat as the plants grow; others put a drainpipe or a cardboard tube, not less than 2½ ins. diameter and 12 to 15 ins. long, over each plant as it reaches maturity; others buy special paper collars and tie them round the stems with raffia, adding a second collar, when the first has been outgrown, or sometimes shifting the first collar upwards and 'earthing' up the portion already blanched with one or other of the dry materials mentioned above, an operation which is more simply and economically performed if planks are used in addition to collars. I have also heard of an expert who knocks the bottom out of a 5-ins. pot or a 2-lb. glass jam jar and inverts it over each seedling leek at planting time, subsequently dropping a cardboard tube over the plant and inside the pot, and stuffing the top to exclude light when the time comes for final blanching.

A tip given to me by one exhibitor is to sink a flowerpot to the rim 6 ins. from each leek so that water will reach the roots despite earthing up – this also enables dilute liquid manure to be given (but take care to avoid any excess of nitrogenous food).

Trimming

Apart from any top-dressing before earthing up and the subsequent blanching, the only attention needed by leeks grown for eating purposes is the periodical shortening of the leaves. The tips of the outer leaves should be snipped off just a little at planting time and successive snippings should be given about mid-June, mid-July, and the beginning of September so that the leaves never trail upon the ground. Remember that it is only the long mature leaves that must be cut, not the young ones in the centre of the plant, and never take off more than a couple of inches at a time. (*This procedure does not apply to leeks grown for exhibition.*)

Pulling

It is a good practice to eat the largest and whitest leeks first rather than to leave them to battle with the elements. But the remainder can be left in the ground and dug as required at any time after they are large enough and sufficiently blanched. Scrape a little soil away from them with a trowel or spade and then lever up with a spade or fork, taking care to drive the tool down under the root of the plant and not through the stem. Don't try to pull a leek out before it has been properly loosened from the soil; it will come in half. During winter, in the intervals between spells of severe weather, it pays to lift some of the best leeks and store them in sand in a shed. They will keep a month and be available when the ground is frozen and lifting impossible. If desired one or two plants may be left to go to seed, for the leek is a biennial. If any plants are left, however, which are not required for seed production and are not occupying land which is wanted, they can remain where they are, the flower stems being nipped out as they rise. This will result in the formation at the base of the plant of small round, whitish bulbs known as 'leek bulbs'. These can be taken away in early summer and make an excellent dish when stewed in gravy, or they may be used for any purpose for which onions or shallots are employed.

Exhibiting Leeks

Lifting is in the nature of a surgical operation, bearing in mind that you wish to retain the roots full length and intact and to avoid also any damage to leaves and stems. First of all carefully scrape away all sand, soil, leafmould, or peat; drain pipes must be skilfully drawn off; paper collars and cardboard tubes are often best left in position until after lifting, to protect the stems, and then cut down vertically with a very sharp knife so that they can be removed without injuring the foliage. When the blanched stems are exposed prior to lifting, put straw on the soil to prevent them from being sullied during handling. After lifting, wrap the whole plant at once in clean, damp paper, take it indoors, and stand it with its roots in water until it is time to prepare it for the show. Do not expose to the light or you will lose your blanch, as the stems will begin to go green. The final preparation commences with the gradual elimination of all soil from the roots by means of gentle laving, spraying, and rinsing. The leaves must then be sponged. It will be necessary to remove at least one layer of skin with its attendant outer leaves in order to get a fresh white appearance; but do not remove more than one skin if you can help it as, if the judges spot that leaves have been removed, they will suspect that you had something to hide. The final stage is to tie round each stem at the base of the leaves either a broad strand of raffia or several turns of green fillis string – this is necessary to prevent the leaves from splitting down the stem by their own weight.

The first thing the judges look for in a prize leek is solidity which carries 8 points out of 20; there must be no softness about the stem, which must not taper but must be thick in relation to its length which should be not less than 12 ins. No prizes go to thin-stemmed leeks. Condition accounts for another 8 points and means that the stems must be clean, spotless, and well blanched without a trace of discoloration or bulbing (swelling) at the base, while the foliage must be healthy. The remaining 4 points go to uniformity – you require nine matching leeks in collections and six for single dishes.

Propagating Exhibition Leeks

Although all exhibitors start off by raising plants from a specially selected strain of seed, any of them, after they have succeeded in raising prize-winning specimens, propagate vegetatively from these specimens and thus retain their own strain. This can be done either from suckers or 'pods'. The former spring from the basal plate of a large leek: they are side-shoots with a few roots of their own and are detached during December, January, or early February, treated as cuttings, and inserted 2 ins. deep in pots of light soil, after trimming off the longest leaves. 'Pods' are small living plants which appear among the ripened seeds in the seed-head of the leek: they are sometimes mistaken for sprouted seeds. They are removed carefully from the dried head in November or December and potted up in a sandy, peaty mixture. Both suckers and pods are started in a greenhouse heated to 45–50° F., potted on as required, and finally hardened for planting outdoors.

Pot Leeks

These are the small leeks so much grown in competition by the miners of Durham and Northumberland. They are not grown to produce a long white stem but are thick and stumpy with what is known as a 'tight button' or 'fast button' at the V of the lowest leaf which must be from 3 to 6 ins. from the base. The stem from base to V must be a perfect cylinder, not 'onion-ended', and a 6 ins. stem may measure as much as 14 ins. in circumference and contain 110 cu. ins., though of perfect texture and free from coarseness. Such leeks are judged by cubic content and tables are published for calculating this. Generally, the culture of these pot leeks is the same as that of other leeks but no miner would part with the secrets of producing prizewinning specimens even on his death-bed!

Diseases of Leeks

Provided that leeks are not grown on the same site year after year it is unlikely that the crop will develop any disease. The most likely trouble, especially in a wet season, is White Tip, a fungoid disease which from September onwards causes the tips of the leaves to take on a waterlogged appearance, later becoming white and papery as if bleached by frost and finally rotting off. Growth is checked, affected plants are unsightly and soon wilt after being dug. Nothing will cure the disease but its spread can be checked by spraying with Bordeaux mixture or dusting with a copper-lime dust. Diseased plants must be promptly dug up and burned.

Lettuce

The name 'lettuce' comes from the Latin *lactuca* which has reference to the milky ('lactic') sap which is so noticeable when you cut a lettuce. Few people realize that this juice is highly narcotic and forms a reliable substitute for opium. Lettuce has been a common ingredient of salads in this country since the days of Queen Elizabeth I and is also believed to provide the earliest known example of a foliage pot plant for room decoration. Nobody seems to know where the garden lettuce originated but it was certainly served at the table of Darius, King of Persia, before 500 B.C. The Romans knew only one sort of lettuce but there are actually a host of wild kinds, some with wide leaves, others with narrow erect leaves like a Cos lettuce (which clearly came to us from the Greek Island of that name) and having a loose habit of growth like the so-called American gathering lettuces. Three species of wild lettuce are actually natives of Great Britain.

It is from all these wild sorts that the hybridists have bred the many specialized varieties which figure in the seed catalogues, each being designed to grow best under certain specific conditions (e.g., in a heated greenhouse or in a cold frame or outdoors) and to heart at different seasons of the year. The aim of all our raisers has been to produce a solid-headed (i.e. 'hearted') lettuce because the public taste favours that sort. This is rather a pity, for the bleached inner leaves have none of the health-promoting value of the green ones and our American cousins are more sensible in this that they always prefer the loose-leaved sorts which contain the most vitamins. If you wish to try a loose-leaved, American lettuce several major mail order seedsmen offer seeds of Salad Bowl.

Probably more failures in lettuce-growing are due to the choice of a wrong variety than to unskilled cultivation. The reader's first step, therefore, should be to make sure that the right type is chosen for the particular job in hand. The next most important thing to bear in mind is that lettuces will not stand in good condition for more than a few weeks after they are fully hearted and mature and, if not used within a reasonable time, will bolt. Continuity of supply can therefore be ensured only by going to the trouble of making repeated small successional sowings and/or plantings. No household wants more than six lettuces ready at once.

It will assist the reader to know how lettuce is made available for cutting at the different seasons of the year. *Summer lettuce,* which may be of cabbage, cos, or American type, is available from June to August inclusive and is grown outdoors without protection from seed sown from March to June except that in some areas the earliest crop is started in cold frames in February or under cloches in March. *Early autumn lettuce,* cabbage, or cos, to fill the gap from the end of the plum season to the arrival of the first frosts, is grown outdoors from sowings made in June and July. *Late autumn lettuce,* cabbage only, can be cut in November and on into December from July/August sowings protected by cloches. *Winter lettuce,* which means hearted cabbage lettuce cut from December to March inclusive, can be obtained only by growing special forcing types of lettuce in a well-heated greenhouse (50° F.). (There *have* been cases in which hearted lettuce has been cut from a September sowing under cloches during the early months of the year but these were exceptional and the result of sheer good luck.) *It must be emphasized that there is no class of lettuce which can be grown in a cool greenhouse (i.e., a heated greenhouse in which the night temperature is below 50° F., although kept above freezing-point).* Spring lettuce, which may be taken to include very early summer lettuce and is cut over the period from mid-March to the end of May, is obtainable in a variety of ways, namely:

(1) from autumn sowings of the winter-hardy type in the open ground,
(2) from either autumn or Jan./Feb. sowings under cloches,

(3) from autumn sowings in cold (unheated) greenhouses and cold frames,
(4) from winter plantings of autumn-raised seedlings in hot-bed frames.

The Soil

The soil requirements of lettuce planted outdoors are essentially the same at all times of the year, although fertilizer requirements may vary from season to season. Dry, dusty stuff is useless, so is sour waterlogged land. The lighter sandy loams and gravelly soils and well-drained medium to heavy clays which have been thoroughly cultivated and improved over the years are all suitable provided that they contain sufficient organic material to ensure their water-holding capacity so that the plants are able to draw on a continuous supply of moisture. In practice this means that lettuce sites must have their humus content renewed annually by the addition of farmyard or stable manure, rich composted material made from straw, seaweed, or vegetable refuse, granulated peat, and green manure (lupins or mustard). But no animal manures or partly rotted material must be used when preparing the ground for the lettuces. Either it must have been worked in for the previous crop which the lettuce follows or it must be incorporated in autumn or early winter against the sowing of lettuce in late spring. It follows therefore that you cannot necessarily grow good lettuces by just dashing around at the last moment to try and find a bit of spare land for them; proper planning is necessary.

Another important factor is lime content, which must be of the order of pH 6·5 or higher.

As regards physical characteristics, the soil for lettuce must be beautifully crumbly but it must also be capable of being thoroughly consolidated. On commercial holdings I have often noticed that the best hearted lettuce was at the end of the row where everybody cut the corner and trampled the ground solid.

Bolting

This can be a great nuisance with lettuces. It can be caused by dry growing conditions and by the check occasioned by transplanting, especially if this involves any root breakage. Both these causes can be avoided by proper methods of cultivation. But there is one cause of bolting about which the gardener can do absolutely nothing: it is in the nature of lettuce to throw up flowering stems whenever the temperature rises above a certain level and when, during a heat wave, the thermometer runs up into the 70s and 80s, unless you can keep the lettuce cool, nothing will stop it from bolting, however much water you give it. Fortunately newer lettuce varieties stand up better to high summer temperatures, providing you keep the soil itself well and truly moist.

SUMMER AND AUTUMN OUTDOOR LETTUCE

The earliest sowing can be made about mid-February in shallow boxes of John Innes Seed Compost placed in a cold frame, the seedlings being planted out at the end of March. The next sowing is made on an outdoor seed-bed about the middle of March for planting out at the end of April. After that you need to make small sowings at intervals of about three weeks in drills ½ in. deep where the plants are to mature, starting in the first half of April and continuing until June: but bear in mind that most people use fewer lettuces during the soft fruit season – don't ask me why but it is an established fact – so go gently with May and June sowings. Don't transplant any seedlings after 1 May, merely thin them *in situ.* Seedlings should be transplanted or thinned when between 2 and 3 ins. high.

In a wet summer, sowings for autumn cutting can commence any time after Midsummer Day. But in a dry summer it is better to wait until the dews begin again in July and then sow successionally up to mid-August. Sowings of cabbage lettuce made in late July in the north and during the first half of August in the south can be cloched up, a few plants at a time, from early September onwards according to weather conditions and will then usually stand through November. Plant only two rows to a cloche.

Except under cloches, where the plants have to be spaced 9 to 10 ins. apart, summer and autumn lettuces are spaced 12 × 12 ins. You can reduce this to 9 ins. if you wish, but wider spacing gives a bigger, better, and earlier lettuce, and the plants are generally more healthy.

The problem of where to put summer and autumn lettuce is one that each gardener must work out for himself. In my own garden I find that the earliest crops need a sunny, warm position under a south-facing wall or fence. On the allotment I set the seedlings in a flat-bottomed drill which can be covered with sheets of glass until they are 4 or 5 ins. high, or alternatively I sow about mid-March under barn cloches, 3 rows thinned to 8 ins. between plants, and decloche not later than the middle of May. On the other hand lettuce which is to be cut between July and September definitely needs a cooler position with shade from hot sun; and, whereas the ideal position for summer lettuce is on land vacated by leeks, onions, peas, or beans, it can quite well be grown as an intercrop between tall peas or runner beans or in the shelter of the ridges formed by the soil dug out from trenches used for celery and leeks. Some gardeners use a north-facing border for summer lettuce; others allow marrow plants to trail among the lettuces and afford them some shade. As regards autumn lettuce the most important point is to shelter it from autumnal gales which can render the outer leaves horribly tough, especially in coastal areas. By the way, do not plant lettuce on ground vacated by root crops or by any members of the brassica family.

SPRING LETTUCE

Outdoor Production

This is not worth attempting by anybody who has cloches, frames, or a cold greenhouse at his disposal because the resultant lettuce will be no earlier than lettuce grown with glass protection. It is usually rather tough, and after a hard winter it is also likely to taste bitter. If the crop is grown, only the so-called winter-hardy varieties must be used and, although these will withstand snow and a reasonable amount of frost of short duration, prolonged freezing will most certainly injure and, possibly, kill the plants. In the past I have had much experience with outdoor lettuce in winter and I would recommend its cultivation only in those districts where the winters are comparatively mild without excessive rainfall and in those gardens which are protected from north and east winds and are blessed with a perfectly drained lightish soil. The crop cannot be grown on cold, heavy land where it will rot unless a special raised bed of soil is made for its reception; it is unlikely to survive in a frost-pocket. It must not follow brassicas but can follow late peas or beans or second early potatoes. The site must be sunny and well away from any site on which it is proposed to grow summer lettuce in order to minimize the risk of the spread of infection from aphids or mosaic disease, both of which are liable to attack the winter crop. The land must be well limed and in good heart as a result of previous organic manuring. No nitrogenous fertilizer should be given before planting but if you use chemical fertilizers there should be an application of superphosphate (1 oz. per sq. yd) and sulphate of potash (¾ oz. per sq. yd). Seed is sown on a seedbed between 10 August and 7 September, the latter date being applicable to sowings in the mildest areas. The seedlings are lightly thinned and planted out 9 ins. apart in rows 12 ins. apart between mid-October and mid-November. (In cold counties some delay planting out until February or early March but this increases the risk of bolting.) Hoe the rows twice before winter sets in. Then leave well alone until growth re-starts about the beginning of March when the crop may be given a side-dressing of sulphate of ammonia (¾ oz. per sq. yd), followed three weeks later by a similar dressing of Chilean potash nitrate.

Cloche Cultivation

The May King type of lettuce, grown under cloches, will normally succeed in any area of Great Britain provided that it can be kept clear of botrytis and other troubles. Its general requirements in respect of soil and manuring are much the same as for spring lettuce grown without protection. The usual practice is to sow three rows under low barn cloches during the last week in September in the coldest areas, between 10 and 20 October in the London area and about 21 October in the warm south-east. Thin to 9 ins. during November. Thinnings, if lifted carefully, can be replanted under other cloches to give a successional crop. Commence to remove the cloches, a few at a time, about the end of March, weather permitting. In Devon and Cornwall the crop will come into cut about the end of March; in the north of Scotland it will not be ready to cut until May; elsewhere cutting should commence some time in April.

Under favourable conditions during January in the south, and some time in February elsewhere, lettuces of the All The Year Round group can be sown under cloches, thinned to 2 ins. 6 to 8 weeks after sowing, thinned again to 4 ins. 14 days later (and the thinnings transplanted), and thinned finally to 8 ins. a fortnight after that. The lettuces from these sowings can be cut during May in the warmest districts, in June elsewhere. During the latter part of the growing period it will be essential to ventilate the cloches during spells of hot weather.

Frame Cultivation

Frames, usually of the Dutch light type, are used extensively in the production of lettuce for market: but their employment by the amateur gardener raises certain problems. The commercial grower fills his frames with lettuce and sends the produce to market in bulk as soon as it is ready; the amateur who devotes a 6 × 4-ft frame to lettuce will find himself with 4 dozen lettuces all maturing and demanding to be eaten over a period of a few weeks in early spring when the household requirements in the way of green saladings may be comparatively small. Successional sowing is not practicable in a single frame and, if only part of the frame is devoted to lettuce, it may be difficult to find a crop to fill the remaining space which will thrive under exactly the same conditions as the lettuces.

Perhaps the best solution to the difficulty is to sow a small quantity of seed of the May King type in a box placed in the frame between 7 and 20 October; prick out, as soon as the seedlings can be handled, 1 in. apart into a bed of John Innes Potting Compost No. 1 made up in the frame; overwinter in the frame and plant out successionally 12 ins. apart from March to April in land prepared as for summer lettuce which is in a suitably sheltered position. With the aid of a seed-raiser, however, and a spare frame, you can make successional sowings at four-day intervals between the dates mentioned, prick off into other boxes, place these in the spare frame with the light closed for seven days, then plunge to the rim in peat moss in the frame in which the seedlings will pass the winter (in boxes of course). This will give you a much longer succession. The soil in the frame (or the boxes) must come to within 4 ins. of the light. Correct ventilation is most important. While the seed is germinating, the light is kept closed. It is also kept closed for seven days after pricking out, but at all other times it is removed altogether during fine, dry weather, propped up 2 ins. at the back and ½ in. in front during wet weather prior to pricking out, and 2 ins. at the back only when the weather becomes cold and wet after pricking out has taken place, closed during fog (though this may cause very young seedlings to draw and spindle), and finally closed and matted up during severe frost. If the plants are caught by frost and the morning is sunny, prop up the lights 2 ins. at the back until the plants have thawed out. The whole object is to raise young plants which are not too lush to withstand frost and cold wind after setting out. Do not allow rain to reach the plants. If the soil is properly moist to begin with, very little watering will be necessary and any water that has to be given must not leave the foliage of the plants wet. The date of removal to the open will vary with the district and season but it is important that the plants should not be allowed to remain in the frame so long that they become drawn and too leafy.

The alternative to the foregoing procedure is to mature the lettuce in a cold frame instead of putting it out in the open. If this is done, the seedlings are raised and wintered in another frame exactly as in the previous paragraph to which perhaps I should have added a warning that, when the light is off, it is usually wise to replace it by a framework covered with wire netting, otherwise birds may take the lettuce. About the end of January or early February, the plants are set out in a prepared bed in another frame (twenty-four to a Dutch light) and the technique of ventilation is altered. No air is given for the first seven days after planting; then the light is raised ½ in. *at the front* and this opening is never varied except during windy frost. The back of the frame is never opened except to thaw the plants after they have been frozen and it is closed again as soon as thawing is complete. Later in the season during hot spells more ventilation can be given at the front but the whole aim is to admit sufficient air without allowing the escape of the moisture which condenses on the underside of the glass. The lettuces can be cut in April. If desired, carrot seed may be broadcast in the frame before the lettuces are planted finally.

If an organic hotbed will be available from 18 January onwards, seed of Cheshunt Early Giant or Cheshunt 5B can be sown in a cold frame from 10 October onwards and must be pricked out 2 ins. apart by 15 November at the latest The seedlings are grown hard during the winter, as before. If desired, they can be in boxes and half the seed can be sown at the end of September to extend the period of cutting. The plants are set out in the hotbed frame 9 × 9 ins. apart towards the end of January and will be ready for cutting from the middle to the end of March. With this type of lettuce the lights are never opened except for weeding and removal of discoloured leaves and on sunny mornings after a frosty night. No watering is done after the initial soaking of the bed. The frame is covered with mats during severe frost. Carrots, turnips, and autumn-sown cauliflowers can be grown in the same frame with the lettuces.

Exactly the same procedure can be followed in a frame containing an electrical hotbed (soil-warming cables) except that owing to the warmth being less planting should take place around Boxing Day and owing to the greater drying effect of the cables as compared with an organic hotbed the reserves of water in the frame must be greater – a bed in a 6-ft × 4-ft frame, if it has not been soaked by autumnal rains, will take 30 to 60 gallons of water. Also the current can be switched off permanently after a third of the lettuces have been cut, thus delaying the maturity of some of them – this helps to avoid a glut.

Cold Greenhouse Treatment

Many people write to me for instructions on how to grow lettuces in a small unheated greenhouse of the type that is glazed to ground level. While I do not recommend the cultivation of spring lettuce in these tiny houses because it is so much more easily managed in frames, I appreciate that there is a natural desire to put the house to some use during the period between the cutting of the last chrysanthemums and the planting of bought-in tomatoes, so I will deal with the subject here as fully as space permits.

Raise plants in frames exactly as if you were going to plant outdoors, growing them as hard as possible and keeping the roots moist but the tops as dry as possible. Choose varieties of the May King type, though Cheshunt 5B is suitable provided that it is not planted until after the middle of February. Sow in late September or early October for planting in the borders at the end of December or early in January; in mid-October for planting at the end of January and in late October for planting during February. Seedlings, which should have been pricked out to stand 1 in. apart, should be 2 ins. high at the time of planting.

After the chrysanthemums have been removed, thoroughly clean and disinfect the greenhouse and prepare the borders as for the tomatoes, giving them the usual winter flooding but omitting the tomato base fertilizer and substituting superphosphate (2 oz. per sq. yd) and sulphate of potash (1 oz. per sq. yd). It is assumed that the borders are well-drained and cannot get waterlogged in winter and that you know all about their proper preparation or are prepared to follow the instructions given under the heading of tomatoes. If you cannot grow absolutely first-class tomatoes in your borders you are not likely to have much success with early lettuce.

Plant 9 × 9 ins. (Cheshunt 5B 7 × 8 ins.), with the neck of the lettuce at soil level – if you plant too high, your lettuces will not heart up; if you plant too low and bury even part of a leaf, you may lose your crop with botrytis. Spray or dust with derris prior to planting to ensure that they are free from greenfly. Get the soil in the borders as warm as possible by planting time – soil-warming is a great help.

Water the plants in, if necessary, but try to avoid watering thereafter until late February. If you do have to water during the first two months of the year, do not allow any of the water to fall on to the leaves. Overhead watering must not start until March when the sun is more powerful. No plant must ever be allowed to flag so that its leaves go limp and lie on the soil; but cut down moisture to the minimum during really cold spells. On bright days after the beginning of March, damp the plants down overhead just sufficiently to moisten the leaves; more frequent damping will be beneficial during the last three weeks of growth, as it prevents tip-burn, but during the same period the plants must be kept drier at the roots – too much water at this stage, when the leaves start to turn inwards to form the heart, will make the lettuce too leafy and soft.

Admit as much fresh air as possible, except during fog, and use the ventilators also to prevent wide fluctuations of temperature, opening them widely if the thermometer looks like rising above 60° F. and, as a rule, closing them when it falls to 50° F. Ventilation is your best ally against mildew and other fungoid troubles – but take steps to keep birds from entering the house while the ventilators are open.

Hoe the soil occasionally and, if necessary, weed by hand; but take extreme care to prevent any soil from falling on the lettuces. Fumigate against greenfly. Remove and burn any plant that becomes affected by botrytis. If you have displayed proper skill, your lettuces will be ready in April.

WINTER LETTUCE

As previously stated, this crop demands a greenhouse of good construction and design in which a minimum temperature of 60° F. can be maintained. Since the cost of fuel will be considerable, the growing of winter lettuce in an amateur's greenhouse is a reasonably economic proposition only if the owner devotes the whole of a small house to this one crop and is in a position to sell his surplus at a good retail price to other residents in the immediate vicinity. The important thing is to choose the right varieties and to sow them at the proper times. I recommend the private gardener to limit himself to either Cheshunt Early Giant or Cheshunt 5B and to be guided by the following table which shows what can be done to obtain a succession of lettuces from December to April, the period of the greatest shortage, by devoting part of the greenhouse to maturing crops and the other part to the raising of seedlings for planting out successionally – see table on p. 224.

All sowings should be germinated in the greenhouse itself at a temperature of between 50° F. and 60° F. Seed should be sown in boxes or trays of John Innes Seed Compost and the usual current practice is to prick out the seedlings in John Innes Potting Compost No. 2 1 in. apart immediately they have germinated and to plant them finally in the beds as soon as the first pair of true leaves has developed. In the case of winter sowings the time from sowing to planting will be as much as a month. But in the case of at any rate the earlier autumn sowings the first true leaves will appear in ten

SOW	*PLANT OUT IN BEDS*	*READY FOR CUTTING*
late Sept.	early Oct.	early Dec. to Christmas
mid-Oct.	early Nov.	early Feb.
early Nov.	late Nov.	late Feb.
mid-Nov.	early Dec.	early Mar.
late Nov.	mid-Dec.	mid-Mar.
early Dec.	early Jan.	late Mar.
late Dec.	mid-Jan.	early April

days after sowing, so that it is not worth while to prick out and, provided that the seeds have been spaced out singly about 1 in. apart, the seedlings can be planted out finally direct from the seed box. I do, however, strongly recommend amateurs to adopt an alternative to the accepted procedure and prick out all seedlings, as soon as they can be handled, into 2 to 2½ ins. soil blocks which can be packed thickly together on the staging and planted out at a much later date, approximately four to nine weeks before the due date of maturity according to the time of year – the time from planting to maturity decreases of course as the season advances. Blocks are planted with the top just above soil level. By this method many more lettuces can be cut in unbroken succession because the plants occupy their full final spacing for such a much shorter period. If you have no soil block making machine, prick out into peat pots instead.

Seedling lettuces must be kept moist by watering lightly overhead with a rosed can until the leaves are an inch long; after that, only the soil around the plants must be watered, otherwise the leaves may stick together. It is only fair to say, however, that this view is not accepted by all gardeners, and commercial growers invariably water plants in soil blocks overhead with a fine rose – but then they are also highly experienced in maintaining the correct atmospheric conditions in the greenhouse.

By far the best way of growing winter lettuces in a private greenhouse is to make up a bed for them on the staging. The asbestos or other covering of the slatted staging should be surfaced with a layer of very old, crumbly manure. Over this should go a 6-ins. layer of light compost, preferably the John Innes Potting Compost No. 3, but if you want to mix your own, a combination of three parts of turfy loam with one part of peat and a half-part silver sand will meet the case.

The distance between the plants depends upon the variety. Plants of Cheshunt 5B go 7 ins. apart in rows 8 ins. apart; Cheshunt Early Giant goes 9 ins. apart in rows 10 ins. apart.

A steady temperature of 50–55° F. is what is required. Don't let it drop below 50° F. (easily arranged if the heating apparatus is efficient) or rise above 55° F. if you can possibly help it. Any amount of air can be admitted to keep the temperature down on sunny days, even to the extent of leaving the door wide open – but in that event watch out that sparrows don't enter the house and eat the lettuces. On the other hand, the house must be kept tightly closed during foggy and rainy weather, because damp is the greatest enemy of winter lettuces. If you get your house too damp, you will notice at once that the lettuces acquire a dull appearance, whereas when the house is properly ventilated the colour is always bright green. The condensation of moisture on the roof glass is an indication that you want a drier atmosphere.

During the first two or three weeks after planting out it is very desirable that the plants should grow quickly and produce a broad, healthy rosette; for if the initial growth is slow, the crop will be sub-standard. It is therefore desirable to maintain the house at 60° F. during this preliminary period; but after that, as soon as the leaves begin to turn in, the temperature should be reduced to within the limits previously stated.

Watering is the only attention that is required – no feeding is necessary. It is, of course, necessary to water the plants in immediately after planting out in order to settle the soil around the roots.

As a rule no further watering is necessary for ten to fourteen days, but after that watering will be necessary at least once a week and sometimes oftener. Provided that the air in the house is buoyant and dry, the soil really cannot be too moist. The object is to ensure that the leaves shall be continually turgid with water; in that state, the lowest leaves lift themselves clear of the soil and the air is able to circulate beneath them and keep them dry. If there is the least suspicion of dryness about the soil, the lowest leaves lie flat and their under-surfaces become covered with condensed moisture which leads to the onset of disease. It might also be stated that the moister the soil, the quicker the hearting. Water must never be applied overhead, at any rate until after the middle of February, and the use of a watering can with a very long extension spout will be found of material assistance as the plants get bigger in avoiding the splashing of water on to the leaves.

As an alternative to growing lettuces in beds of soil on the staging, it is possible to grow them in pots, but the labour of watering them and maintaining the soil in a properly moist condition is very considerable, and the method of growing in pots can hardly be recommended unless the total number of lettuces grown is very small. However, it is a common practice in America and, if you want to try it, I advise you to sow from mid-August to mid-September in sterilized John Innes Seed Compost, prick out the seedlings 1 in. apart as soon as they can be handled, place them in a cold frame, and pot off into 5-ins. pots four weeks after pricking out. After a further month in a cold frame bring into the greenhouse and grow on at a temperature of 50° F. Treat in the same way as plants in beds, taking great care not to allow the leaves of the lettuces to come in contact with water, and you should be cutting at Christmas and in early January.

When to Cut Lettuce

Lettuces are ready to cut as soon as the hearts feel solid to the touch. When the hearts begin to push outwards and upwards from the centre it is a sign that the plants are beginning to bolt, and they should be used as soon as possible. The foregoing applies to ordinary English lettuce both of the cos and cabbage varieties. In the case of American lettuces, individual leaves are pulled from each plant after the manner of spinach, since these lettuces do not form hearts.

By the way, most cos lettuces are now self-folding and need no tying. But reluctance to heart up, especially in dry weather, can sometimes be overcome by tying the outer leaves together with raffia or slipping a rubber band over them.

Pests and Diseases of Lettuces

Reference has already been made to the partiality of birds (especially sparrows) to seedling lettuces, and it should hardly be necessary to draw attention to the imperative need for controlling slugs wherever lettuces are grown. It is less well known that mice will eat lettuces; in a hard winter I once had two whole frame-loads of lettuces reduced to stumps by field mice which tunnelled under the foundations of the frames – in one of the frames after setting a trap I caught no less than twenty-three mice in a single night.

The principal insect pest of lettuce is the lettuce aphis. This not only attacks young plants, checking their growth and preventing them from hearting: it also swarms over mature lettuce exuding honey-dew which attracts dust and dirt and rendering the lettuces completely unfit for human consumption. This beastly insect usually overwinters in the egg stage on currant and gooseberry bushes; but live adults can also survive the winter buried in the hearts of outdoor lettuces. In April and May a swarm of aphids moves over to the young summer lettuces; the infestation is usually worst in a dry spring when there is no rain to wash them off the plants. Some of these aphids are destroyed when the mature lettuces are prepared for table in the kitchen; some survive on the remnants of the crop, especially 'bolters' if you add these to the compost heap without covering them immediately with other rubbish or with some soil: others migrate to autumn-sown seedlings, whether growing in the open or in frames, and may remain on the plants until they are fully grown the following spring. Attacks are not confined solely to the lettuce aphis: any species of greenfly is liable to be found on lettuces.

It is well nigh impossible to have lettuces entirely free from greenfly but well-grown plants are much less liable to infestation than weak ones. A hard winter will usually kill all living aphids and it is then up to the gardener to ensure that his lettuce plants grow rapidly without any severe checks. Spraying and powderings can help but these should be of a non-poisonous kind – after all, you and your family are going to eat the lettuces! *Nicotine-soap washes (and any other sprays containing soap as a spreader) must not be used on lettuces.* In the case of lettuce crops maturing in greenhouses and frames, if the seedlings are clean at the time of planting and the planting quarters have been suitably fumigated beforehand, there is little risk of infestation by aphids.

It may be added that aphids act as carriers for the seedborne Mosaic Disease which causes stunting and yellow mottling of the leaves. Infected seeds are comparatively rare so that infected plants are correspondingly rare unless aphids get out of control and spread the disease to other lettuces. There is no cure.

By far the most serious trouble that besets lettuces is *Botrytis cinerea*, otherwise known as Grey Mould or Red Leg. It is a fungus that attacks decaying or dead leaf tissue in the first place but once established on the plant it can spread to the healthy parts also. In addition to the visible grey mould the fungus can work its way into the stem and turn it red, after which it may rot entirely; it can also cause a slimy soft rot of the whole lettuce. There would be no botrytis if there were no decaying leaves and it follows that the disease is most likely to become epidemic when growing conditions encourage withering of the leaves and rapid multiplication of the spores of the fungus. This happens mainly in winter and early spring when outdoor lettuces may be checked by frost and wet, especially on badly drained soil, and lettuces under cloches, in frames, and in greenhouses may be affected by errors in watering and ventilation. Large outer leaves which lie flat on the ground, wilt owing to dryness at the root, and subsequently collect moisture beneath themselves are one of the principal causes of 'grey mould'. Occasionally the disease will break out in the summer as a result of wet weather, potash shortage, or 'Tip-burn' which is associated with very hot weather at a time when growth is vigorous.

Good cultivation represents the best safeguard against botrytis.

Infected seedlings with red bases or decayed seed-leaves should never be planted; when planted, the crowns of the seedlings should always be a little above soil level and only suitable varieties should be grown.

In unheated greenhouses where conditions are cold and wet, as well as outdoors in wet spring weather or in autumn when there is much rain or heavy dew Downy Mildew may be met with. This fungus usually gains a hold whilst the seedlings are still young. A preventive measure is to spray with thiram at the rate of 2 oz. per 3 galls. cold water just after the seedlings show and again before transplanting them.

Marrows

The 'vegetable' marrow, *Cucurbita pepo ovifera*, as we know it, is essentially a British institution, for the edible gourds of the same family grown on the Continent and in the U.S.A. (where they are known as 'squashes') so often lack the characteristic shape and flesh of our own humble marrow. Strange as it may seem, nobody knows where the marrow originated or when we first came to grow it.

Somebody at some time or other must have compared its flesh to the marrow in a marrowbone and added the prefix 'vegetable' for distinguishing purposes; yet prior to 1816 the name 'vegetable marrow' was applied to the fruit of the avocado pear.

It may be said at once that the growing of marrows on heaps of turf, manure, or rubbish became obsolete practice over thirty years ago because even then so few gardens remained which were of sufficient size and employed sufficient labour to permit of the accumulation of those vast heaps which never dried out completely even in an almost rainless summer. A small mound is useless owing to its lack of moisture-retaining properties: so marrows are now grown on the flat in prepared stations, 6 ft apart for trailers, 4 ft for bush sorts.

Some forethought is desirable when selecting a site for this crop. Obviously the bush types can be grown in any open, sunny situation which is convenient for watering. But the trailing kinds, which 'cover an acre', as an old gardener put it, need plenty of room and must not in any circumstances be so sited that they can smother low-growing crops, such as onions, carrots, and lettuces, or strangle the runner beans. It must be arranged that they come up against only those strong-growing plants which are able to cope with them or those early crops which are well past their peak by the time the marrows arrive. If you can give the marrows a clear start of about 5 ft they can be permitted to ramble at will among brassicas or potatoes: alternatively, they may be planted between well-spaced rows of tall early peas. Some gardeners deliberately leave gaps at the end of the potato rows for the reception of marrow plants.

In many small gardens marrows of the trailing type would be much less of a nuisance if they were trained up and over trellis-work, fences, and walls or even up the clothes posts, rather than left to their own devices and allowed to escape into the flower garden where they may climb up the dahlias – for marrows are natural climbers, a fact that is all too seldom remembered. It is just a question of giving a little assistance by tying and pinching out side-shoots till the plants have reached the desired height. You may, however, have to support the swelling fruits to prevent their weight from pulling down the whole vine and in general it is wiser to confine this method of training to the smaller-fruited varieties of marrow listed by many seedsmen because the task of rigging up a sort of network hammock in the open to cradle a large British marrow may well lead to somewhat Heath-Robinsonian results.

There is no need to go to a lot of trouble in preparing the stations. Commercial growers plant on ordinary land which has been very liberally manured. But for the average private gardener it is simplest to dig out a hole 18 ins. square and 18 ins. deep and fill it with lawn mowings, straight from the mower box, fresh, succulent, and moist with the addition of any available leaves in course of decay from the previous autumn. These, when well trodden, will compress into the lower 9 ins., leaving room for a similar depth of soil on top. Before returning the upper layers ('top spit') of excavated soil lace it liberally with any available leafmould, hop manure, granulated peat, and coarse vermiculite. It is also a good plan to incorporate remnants of John Innes Compost because this stuff does not store well and, if there is a surplus in the bags which will not be needed for potwork whilst still in good condition, it will be appreciated by the marrows. Do all this shortly before you are ready to plant so that the fermentation of the grass and leaves will provide heat to keep the plants going until summer really comes along.

Half a dozen plants should produce enough marrows to satisfy the members of an average-sized household, unless they are all vegetarians. Some experts recommend that, where more than this number are grown, a continuous trench (instead of separate stations) should be prepared for their reception but the logic of this advice wholly eludes me. Neither do I agree with those who set their plants on a slight hump: I set mine in a shallow depression made by leaving about 3 ins. at the top of the planting hole unfilled. This facilitates watering, and in well-drained soil I have never experienced trouble through water lodging round the neck of the plant.

The end of April is quite early enough to sow in a heated greenhouse or frame for planting outdoors towards the end of May when the seedlings should have made their first true leaves and should of course have been properly hardened off. Sow the seeds singly on edge $\frac{1}{4}$ to $\frac{1}{2}$ in. deep in 3-ins. pots and pot the plants on to the $4\frac{1}{2}$-ins. size before hardening off. Draughts, overwatering, and splashing the stems with water must all be avoided, and every effort should be made to preserve the seed leaves. Alternatively, seed may be sown on the prepared stations in the open about mid-May in which case you put four or five seeds 1 in. deep in each planting hole and protect by putting large flower pots over them with a stone to stop the drainage hole until the seeds germinate when you must replace each flower pot either by a cloche, a preserving jar or a 2-lb. glass jam jar. Thin bush marrows to one plant to each station; you can leave two of the trailing kinds as they will grow different ways. If the weather is cold when the cloches or jam jars have to be removed use twiggy brushwood to keep off ground winds. If you have slugs you may need to protect the plants with slug bait.

You can of course purchase marrow plants from a good nurseryman – do not buy those which have been exposed for sale in shops and become chilled in draughty positions – but, before you accept delivery, satisfy yourself that the plants have not suffered in transit, that no flowers are showing, and that they are otherwise up to standard. The stems should be straight and succulent, not thin and hard, which indicates a rootbound condition, and the leaves should be large and rich green with a prominent growing point, not small and yellowish. In the case of bush marrows plant only perfectly symmetrical seedlings. A young bush marrow with a slightly kinked stem will eventually overbalance and flounder about unless you perform miracles of staking.

If continuous cloches are available, greenhouse-raised plants can be set out under them from mid-April onwards; if you do it earlier, you risk a poor show of fruit owing to imperfect pollination. Seed may be sown beneath jam jars inside ordinary cloches from early April to early May according to district and season. By using cloches you can start cutting during the first half of June. But, if you want really early marrows, grow a trailing sort in the borders of a heated greenhouse or in a deep frame with both soil and air warming, sowing the seeds in February. In the greenhouse it is usual to plant in holes filled with a mixture of equal parts of loam and well-decayed manure. The crop can be grown alongside early tomatoes. In a frame the plants are sometimes grown in much the same way as cucumbers on mounds of good fibrous loam, enriched with old manure, over a bed of similar material, giving a total depth of about 9 ins. An average temperature of 65° F. is desirable, never falling below 55° F., and rising to 80° F. when the sun shines brightly. Give plenty of ventilation when weather permits.

It is really quite unnecessary to pinch and stop outdoor trailing marrows: what is necessary is a little common-sense training of the shoots to make them go in the desired directions and this can be done by driving short sticks in on either side of the stems at 2-ft intervals. Pegging also prevents the plants from being blown out of the ground by a strong wind before the trailers have rooted into the soil. If for some reason the plants run straight on without branching you can pinch out the growing point; you can also stop side-shoots at seven leaves if they are going too far afield, and at one leaf beyond a marrow to hasten its swelling. But all these attentions are relics of the Mammoth Harvest Festival Marrow era; if you cut your marrows small, as you ought to do, you will get all the marrows you want without any need for chopping the plants about (except in so far as is necessary to prevent them from going next door).

In a frame you must nip out the points of the leaders when they are 18 ins. long and suppress laterals which would cause overcrowding, while in the greenhouse the leader is trained up to the roof and stopped when it reaches the ridge, then fruiting laterals are pinched out at one leaf beyond the embryo fruit. In the absence of purlin posts, which are only found in very large houses, the plants are best trained up stout stakes lashed together on to wires stretched along the roof in the same way as already recommended for cucumbers. Side-shoots must be looped to the stakes and later secured to the wires. Remove all flowers from the main stem and allow fruits to develop on side-shoots only, one fruit per side-shoot, about four fruits per plant. Swelling fruits must be looped to the overhead wires to take the weight off the vines. Side-shoots that do not develop fruit and any other unwanted foliage must be removed, otherwise there will be too much shade in the greenhouse.

The bush types are preferred for cloche culture because they are earlier; but if trailers are grown under cloches you must stop leaders, sterile laterals, and sub-laterals just above the fifth leaf and bearing shoots two leaves beyond the fruits. Even this stopping will not enable the plants to be kept covered throughout growth. Both bush and trailing marrows soon fill the cloches and can be protected only till the last frosts are over.

Marrows bear male and female flowers: the former are obviously male and carry a 'core' covered with pollen; the female flowers have a baby marrow beneath them. For some time after planting only male flowers will be produced; if you get tired of the sight of these you should cut some off. In due course female flowers will be formed. Although insects should fertilize them, it is an established custom to make sure of your earliest marrows by hand-pollinating. This operation is quite simple; you take a male flower, remove the petals, and push the 'core' into the centre of the female flower. Use a different male flower for each female. *Marrow plants under glass must always be hand-pollinated.*

There has recently been a great scare about marrows tasting bitter and even becoming poisonous as a result of cross-fertilization with ornamental gourds and wild members of the cucumber family. Such cross-fertilization can only affect the seed and you are therefore warned to buy seed and plants only from reliable firms and not to save your own seed if you also grow ornamental gourds in your garden. (In South Africa it is illegal to grow an edible marrow within one mile of a wild cucurbit.)

Marrows *must* be kept watered; otherwise the fruits will fall off. Other causes of the embryo fruits shrivelling and falling off are lack of pollination and starvation due to the absence of sufficient nourishment in the soil. Never apply fertilizers or the marrows will be all seeds. Feed only with dried blood solution or soot-water. If any roots appear on the surface cover them up with mixed loam and compost.

Syringing the leaves with plain water helps to keep red spider at bay in very hot dry weather; if it actually gets a hold, plants in a greenhouse can be fumigated with an azobenzene smoke provided they are moist at the roots; but there is no insecticidal spray which can be used against red spider mite on outdoor marrows without seriously damaging the plants. If any leaves go rusty red, cut them off and burn them. Combat powdery mildew with colloidal sulphur. In autumn a few sheets of paper held down by stones will protect the plants from early frost damage.

Marrows are always best when cut small or at any rate while the skin is still sufficiently tender to be broken easily by your thumb nail. A good length for a marrow is 9 to 12 ins. As they get bigger, marrows lose flavour and become full of seeds. Those which are required for storage must be allowed to grow to their full size and ripen thoroughly before they are cut. As a rule it is best to select only one fruit from each plant for storage purposes, wait until the last moment before frost threatens and then cut, taking particular care not to bruise the skin. Mark your selected fruit by placing a stick against it; do not touch it or tie anything to it. Select only fruits that are rounded at the butt end: those with pointed ends rot off before they attain any size.

Since marrows are very susceptible to low temperatures and easily damaged by frost they are best stored in the kitchen or in a bedroom or attic where the temperature is normally between 50° F. and 65° F. Cellars and outside sheds and other damp places where the temperature is liable to fall below 45° F. are quite unsuitable. The marrows are really best hung from the ceiling in nets; but this is seldom practicable, and they usually keep in good condition until March or April if they are simply laid on a shelf or put in boxes on sacking in a single layer, not one on top of the other, so that they do not touch.

If may be added for the benefit of exhibitors that the giant marrow is no longer held to be prizeworthy at any reputable show held under R.H.S. rules which stipulate that marrows must be young, tender, shapely, and well matched. But, if you do wish to blow a marrow up to a ridiculous size, you can try sugar feeding which consists in threading some wool through the stem an inch from the fruit and letting the ends dip into a jar of sugar water which must of course be kept filled up.

Courgettes are a kind of marrow that produce a large number of fruits together, and are ideal for culling when young.

Mercury (or Good King Henry)

Chenopodium Bonus-Henricus ('Good King Harry') is a native perennial plant, allied to the familiar weeds known as Goosefoots and Fat Hen. It is extremely hardy and has been grown as a vegetable in cottage gardens in Lincolnshire from time immemorial; it has, however, remained comparatively unknown in other parts of Britain and is never sold in the shops because it loses its freshness within an hour of gathering. It forms a very useful source of 'spring greens' from March to June and the produce is taken in two stages. First, the shoots which arise from the leaf axils are taken in much the same way as those of sprouting broccoli. They are firm, fleshy, and light green with young green leaves along their whole length and embryo flower buds at the tips. If desired, they can be earthed up and blanched. If cooked and served after the manner of asparagus they form a reasonable substitute for that vegetable, whence yet another popular name for mercury – 'Poor Man's Asparagus'. Later in the season the large triangular soft green leaves are gathered and eaten as spinach, whence the plant has acquired yet another name 'Lincoln spinach' – the flavour resembles that of spinach beet.

Mercury will grow in any soil but it appreciates an annual dressing of old manure, ripe compost, or well rotted leafmould. Although one sometimes sees plants advertised for sale, it is more usual to raise one's own stock from seed. This may be sown in April or May in drills 1 ft apart and the seedlings thinned to stand 12 ins. apart; but the seeds are very hard and want a lot of moisture to germinate them so that I prefer either to start them in gentle heat in May or June, harden off, and transplant to a nursery bed preparatory to planting out finally in September or October, or to sow on a seed-bed in August, transplant in September to a nursery-bed where the seedlings will pass the winter and place in permanent positions in spring. It is wise to allow twelve plants for each member of the household and you must not expect a large crop the first year after planting.

Practically no cultural attentions are needed beyond weeding and top-dressing. Do not cut any shoots after the end of June as the plants must be allowed to build up again next year in the same way as asparagus. When you do cut, sever the shoots as close to the base as possible. Judicious removal of leaves for use as spinach can go on into August. When winter comes, any yellowed and frosted foliage should be removed in the interests of hygiene.

Once a stock of mercury has been raised from seed the quickest method of propagation is from pieces of basal stem with roots attached.

Mint

Of the few culinary herbs in common use mint is usually the most ill-treated. It is relegated to an out-of-the-way corner of the garden where it spreads all over the place, and, except that bunches are picked and taken to the kitchen so long as there are any growths to pick, it receives no attention whatever. In due course it lies down for the winter and the family has to be content with dried mint or a proprietary mint sauce until growth recommences in spring, unless of course the housewife is aware that all the best bottled mint sauce is made from *fresh* mint (and that such sauce will keep almost indefinitely).

There is of course no valid reason why every gardener should not grow mint really well. The wild mints of the European continent are found chiefly in damp ditches in rich acid soil and it follows that our cultivated mint requires a good, rich soil with plenty of well-decayed animal manure, ripe compost, and other retentive organic materials worked into both top and second spits: it also benefits by a moist situation but this does not mean that it should be grown entirely in shade – indeed it is important to give it an open position if the habit is to remain stocky and the leaves close together: and, finally, it is to some extent a lime-hater.

Mint is extremely invasive, and, as most people know, it will be all over the place in a year or two unless it is firmly dealt with. It is worth while digging a foot deep round the site of the mint bed and putting in two courses of bricks to make a wall to confine it to barracks. Furthermore, because mint is apt to deteriorate after the third year, the best gardeners make the bed of sufficient size to allow of its being divided into four sections for 1st-, 2nd-, and 3rd-year plants with one section fallow for catch-crops and then plant a new section every March, the oldest section being uprooted and the youngest stolons from the outside of the clump replanted 9 ins. apart in the fallow.

The roots of mint are best planted as soon as soil conditions are suitable which may be about the end of February or the beginning of March. As delivered, they are usually in a tangled mass and very tedious to handle, but a little patience will sort them out. The strips of root should be laid flat 9 ins. apart in drills about 2 ins. deep, spaced 12 ins. apart; the mint will soon creep and fill in the intervening spaces. After covering, firm the soil well. It is not desirable to have more than five rows in a bed because of the difficulty of carrying out weeding if all parts of the bed cannot be reached with comparative ease. Some people space the rows closer together so that three rows can be covered with a barn cloche in spring to encourage early supplies.

There is some difference of opinion as to the effect of chemical fertilizers on mint. My own view is that the crop does not desire, and is not benefited by, their application and I never use any inorganic fertilizers on my own mint.

Mint calls for no attention during the growing season except weeding and, during dry weather, watering. Special care must be taken to eradicate perennial weeds whilst they are still small. In theory, as soon as the crop has been harvested, or has died down naturally, the bed should be given a final, thorough hand-weeding and in November all old stems having been removed, it should be treated to a good dressing of manure or compost. In practice the bed is often such a jungle owing to neglect of weeding that these attentions are utterly impracticable. In that case there is nothing for it but to make a new bed. This is best done about the second week in March, the roots being lifted and divided and replanted on a fresh site.

Fresh plants of mint may be raised from cuttings taken at the end of September from late-formed basal shoots or older side-shoots

$2\frac{1}{2}$ to 3 ins. long. Strip the first inch of stem, trim beneath the joint, set the cuttings 3 ins. apart in a cold frame, and, when they start to grow, nip the points out when the shoots are 4 ins. high. An alternative, and better, method of propagation, however, is by means of runners which consist of young subterranean stems, each with a growing point, from the outside of a clump of plants not more than three years old: these are pruned to a length of 6 to 9 ins. and planted in prepared soil. Either method is superior to that of increasing stock by mere wholesale and indiscriminate division of the roots.

Forced Mint

This can be had from January to March either from spring-propagated runners or from roots lifted in November. The former are much to be preferred. Take 'Irishman's cuttings' (i.e. young leafy shoots springing from the roots), about 4 ins. long, in March or early April, if possible with a little root attached, and plant at once 6 ins. apart. Keep them moist and hoe for the first month or so; then leave them to go on growing. It is better to force the plants as maidens, but you can, if you like, take a light cut about the end of June and then feed with dried blood solution to encourage fresh growth. Cut the stems down to ground level in October or November, lift the roots and pack them closely together in boxes of rich soil with an inch or two of soil over them. Keep the boxes in a shady cold frame, do not allow them to get dry and remove about Christmas time to a warm greenhouse (60° F.) or the kitchen window-sill. A humid atmosphere is necessary to avoid attack by red spider mite. If you prefer to force roots lift them from a two-year-old bed which has not been hard cut during the previous season and plant them 6 ins. apart and 2 ins. deep in a hotbed frame or in beds or boxes in a heated greenhouse. Each root must consist of a growing point and a stout runner about 8 ins. long.

Fresh mint can of course be had at any time if there are growths to pick. Nip off about 4 ins. from the tip of each young shoot; new shoots will then appear lower down the stems for further use.

If you want dried mint, cut your plants (provided they are rust-free) almost to the ground in August before they flower, preferably after a shower whilst the rain is still on the leaves; spread them out in a single layer on a wire cakestand or on the bottom of a shallow cardboard box lined with brown paper and dry quickly at about 90° F. in a cool oven with the door ajar. When the leaves are quite brittle, strip them off the stalks, powder with a rolling pin and store in screw-topped jars. But do not use dried leaves for making mint sauce for storing, use green leaves, washed in cold water, rinsed, stripped from the stems, and put through a mincing machine. The finely minced mint should then be put into jars, preferably stone jam jars, and then covered with a mixture of 1 quart vinegar to 1 lb. sugar which has been brought to the boil, boiled for five minutes, and allowed to become quite cold before pouring on to the mint. Close the jars as when making jam. When mint sauce is required, take sufficient from the jar and add a little boiling water to it. Use at once if to accompany hot lamb but allow to become quite cold if it is intended to go with cold meat.

Rust Disease

This disease is the bane of mint. It can be identified by the orange pustules on the bases of the shoots and the rusty spores underneath the leaves, which soon cripple the plant and turn the stems into swollen and twisted masses. Mint beds that display signs of the disease must be freed of it before the mint can be used. Such beds should be cut hard back at the end of June and will be cut over again in September, if sufficient new growth has been made. Then dry straw should be worked in among the stems and a foot all round the bed and set alight, care being taken to make it burn briskly – it must not smoulder. This treatment will burn the old stems and kill disease spores without injuring the roots, but, if you prefer a less spectacular method of killing the spores, you can lift the roots in late autumn or winter and immerse them for ten minutes in hot water maintained at a temperature between 105° F. and 115° F. Then wash them in cold water at once to cool them off and replant. It is very desirable to have a reliable thermometer when you embark on this treatment and, if you keep the pan over the gas whilst the roots are in it, you will be wise to let them rest on a grid of wire netting so that they do not get overheated on the bottom of the pan. Alternatively, you can stir constantly with a stick. If on the other hand you take the pan off the gas you must put a lid on it to keep the heat of the water from falling below 105° F. Runners treated in this way make unusually luxuriant growth and should therefore be planted wider apart than usual and, of course, on a site well away from the previous infected one.

Mushrooms

Although the mushroom is regarded as a vegetable, it is in fact a fungus and its cultivation bears no resemblance to that of any other vegetable crop. It cannot be grown in the ordinary soil of the kitchen garden or allotment and the only certain method of producing a crop of mushroom is a highly scientific process which is usually carried out in buildings or in sheds which have been specially designed or adapted for the purpose. A full description of this process would occupy far more space than is available in this book and I must therefore refer any reader who wishes to grow mushrooms to my handbook on the subject, *Mushroom Growing*, published by John Gifford Ltd, 119–25 Charing Cross Road, London, W.C.2, price 25p. plus postage.

Mustard

See Cress.

Okra (or Gumbo)

Gardeners who have encountered this vegetable in the U.S.A., where it is so popular in the famous gumbo and chicken gumbo soups, have often written to ask whether it cannot be grown in this country. The answer is that seed is obtainable from Thompson & Morgan, Ipswich, but that I would not advise anybody to treat it as other than a cool greenhouse crop; if sown outdoors, it would be unlikely to succeed except in the very warmest of summers and in the humid conditions of the south-west.

Okra is a native of north Africa and was introduced into the U.S.A. about a century ago. It requires a long growing season, taking five months from sowing to maturity, and is grown only in the warm, southern states. The plants, which are from 2 to 4 ft tall bear slightly ribbed or grooved, dark green, pointed pods, about 7 ins. long, which must be gathered young before they become too large and hard and before the seeds inside them are fully developed, in much the same way as kidney beans.

Seed should be sown not later than March in a temperature of 60° F. and potted on to the 8-ins. size. The John Innes composts can be used throughout. Warmth is necessary, especially at night, during all stages of growth and plenty of moisture must be present both in the soil and in the atmosphere.

Onions

The onion shares with the pea the reputation of being one of the oldest vegetables known to mankind. 'Leeks, Onions, and Garlick' were among the good things that the Israelites bewailed that they could no longer buy from the Egyptian greengrocers after they had begun their trek towards the Promised Land. By way of contrast

Peter Treveris, writing in 1526, says: 'The Onion being eaten, yea though it be boiled, causeth headache, hurteth the eyes, and maketh a man dim-sighted, dulleth the senses, engendereth windiness and provoketh over-much sleep, especially being eaten rawe. Being rawe, they nourish not at all and but a little though they be boiled.' Clearly Mr Treveris did not like onions, though it would appear that his 'windiness' did not keep him awake. The Roman author and naturalist, Pliny, was much nearer the mark when he compiled a list of twenty-eight different human ailments for which the onion was the remedy, for the Soviet scientist, Dr B. Tokin, has shown that the onion is a most potent germ-destroyer and the American research workers, Walker, Lindgren, and Bachmann, have discovered that the acid vapour from a raw onion chewed in the mouth for five minutes has powerful bactericidal properties and renders the lining of both mouth and throat completely sterile – the anti-social effects of this practice can be countered by the use of chlorophyll!

Our English word 'onion' comes from the Latin and invites us to assume that the Romans grew mainly those members of the family which form clumps, as do garlic and shallots. They called onions *cepae* (whence the word chive) and a single bulb was a *unis*. In some curious way the word *cepae* has dropped out and left us with *unis* (one): so that we might well be justified in saying to a prize onion: 'Well, you are a one!'

Recent scientific discoveries have entirely altered our views on the cultivation of onions in this country. The onion is one of those plants which are acutely sensitive to day-length and temperature. It develops its roots and leaves during the shorter days when the hours of daylight do not exceed fifteen or sixteen and throughout this stage it requires cool, moist conditions with plenty of nourishment; but immediately the critical day-length is reached (and this differs with the variety) it ceases to make new leaves and concentrates on the formation of fleshy scales on the bulb. Thus the variety, Ailsa Craig, enters the bulbing stage on 25 May, whatever the prevailing weather conditions, simply because the day is then sixteen hours long. It follows that it is only by early sowing that it is possible to obtain really large bulbs.

While bulbing is in progress onions want warmth and moisture and must not be assisted by feeding with nitrogenous fertilizers; but they will not tolerate a really wet summer which will cause a resumption of the growth of green foliage (as will also an excess of nitrogen) and lead to thick-necked bulbs. Provided that the formation of foliage is kept in check, the time will come when the growing scales so constrict the neck of the bulbs that the flow of sap to the leaves is cut off and they topple over; but this will not happen if leaf-growth is resumed and remains erect – there is no constriction, hence the 'bull-neck' which will not keep.

The normal ripening of the bulbs will only take place in hot, dry weather and it should be clear from what has been said that, as a rule, it is easier to grow onions in the south and east of England than in other parts of Britain.

Soil and Situation

Onions prefer a medium to light soil; good crops cannot be expected from very heavy or very light soils; indeed I do not consider it possible to grow onions at all on dry sand, thin chalk, sticky clay, or very shallow soil until these staples have been very much improved; and it is certainly unwise to attempt them on newly broken meadow land because it is too spongy. Since, however, the crop can be grown on the same site year after year, it pays to go to some little trouble to convert the existing soil into one really suitable for onion-growing. In carrying out the work, it should be borne in mind that onions will not tolerate stagnant moisture, the presence of which is liable to give rise to highly infectious fungoid diseases; good drainage is, therefore, one of the first things to aim at. On the other hand, nothing is more likely to cause trouble with the onion crop than drought in summer; therefore every effort must be made to render the soil retentive of moisture while at the same time keeping the sub-soil drainage open. If the soil dries out while the onion is bulbing, the outer scales harden and set. Then, if rain comes or if you water, the inner scales swell and split the outer ones.

The site of the onion bed must be open and sunny, away from

overhanging trees and not overshadowed by other and taller crops; but it must not be subject to draughts or exposed to cold currents of air. Other things being equal, if a new bed has to be made, onions should follow peas or potatoes.

Manuring

Onions are very greedy feeders and there is no better way of preparing the land for them than by incorporating up to 4 cwt per rod of farmyard or stable manure or, preferably in my opinion, garden compost which has been enriched with animal manures. All these materials must be well rotted and dug in during the autumn so that they may have an opportunity to turn themselves into humus before the onion crop is sown or planted in spring. If they are not sufficiently decomposed by that time, they may stimulate excessive leafy growth. Onions also do well in ground which received a good dressing of manure or garden compost for a different crop in the previous season. In fact, many gardeners now prefer to include onions in a rotation of crops system instead of having a fixed site for the onion bed. Moving the onion bed round the garden is claimed to be a way of preventing certain fungal diseases of onions building up in the soil. So far as onions are concerned there is no finer nitrogenous fertilizer than household soot at least a year old applied in February at the rate of 8 oz. per sq. yd. If you are sure that your soil is short of potash, you may apply an approved tomato fertilizer shortly before preparing the bed in spring. If you use highly nitrogenous fertilizers, do not put them round onion seedlings after May as excess nitrogen late in the season is a prime cause of thick necks and mildew.

Preparing the Bed

The preparation of the onion bed is a matter calling for some artistry, for the texture of the soil must be extremely fine and crumbly, the surface perfectly level, and the whole bed as smooth and firm as though it had been finished off by rolling. But the actual use of a roller, so frequently recommended, is entirely misconceived: very light, dry soil can almost always be sufficiently consolidated by treading, and heavy ground needs firming with the lightest of touches, otherwise it will consolidate and form a crust, which is the very last thing which is wanted.

It may be of some assistance if I explain why firmness is essential in an onion bed. As most people may have noticed, when an onion seed germinates, a green loop appears above ground and it is quite often imagined by the amateur that the tip of the seedling has got stuck in the ground and needs helping out. This is far from being the case: whilst it is in what is called the 'crook' stage, the seedling is drawing food stores from the seed through its tip. In loose ground the seed may be pulled out of the ground when it will lose its moisture and the remaining food supplies will dry up; but in firm soil the seedling will suck the seed dry before it straightens up, bringing with it the little black knob which is now only the remnant of the seed coat.

A light dressing of lime immediately after sowing gives a finishing touch to the onion bed.

Sowing

Bulb onions (as opposed to spring onions and picklers) may be sown at three times of the year – in autumn outdoors, in January under glass, and outdoors again as soon as the soil is dry enough to work in March.

Autumn Sowing

This is intended to provide bulbs for consumption between July (when the previous year's crop of spring-sown onions has probably been exhausted) and December (when the current year's supply of spring-sown onions can be drawn upon from store). The varieties sown in autumn do not usually possess particularly long-keeping qualities. Autumn sowing produces larger bulbs which usually resist attack by the onion fly and ripen more readily in this fickle climate because they mature in July when the weather is usually hotter and drier than it is when the spring-sown crop matures in September. The disadvantages of autumn sowing are the risks that the seedling will either be killed by frost or will run to seed; but the former risk at any rate can be minimized by giving some winter protection.

It is no longer usual to sow in autumn in rows where the plants are to mature because this exposes the seedlings to greater risks in a severe winter, is rather a waste of land and seed, and can prevent the adequate routine preparation of the onion bed. The better course is to sow, not too thinly, in drills not more than ½ in. deep and 5 ins. apart, either on a slightly raised seed-bed under a few cloches or on a bed in a garden frame. In the former case the cloches will remain continuously in position; in the latter case the frame lights are used only to keep out cold and wet, full ventilation being given at all other times.

Having regard to what has already been said about the sensitivity of varieties of onion to different day-lengths, it will be obvious that a correct choice of variety for autumn sowing is of paramount importance. But it is equally important to sow at the right time and this is much more difficult because nobody can say definitely what is the correct date owing to the complete unpredictability of the weather. The wise gardener therefore makes two sowings, one during the last week in August, the other ten days later. In some years one of these sowings will yield plants that are too small, in other years they will be too large owing to the mildness of the autumn – any onion seedling which at the time of transplanting measures more than ¼ in. across the stem at 1 in. above ground level is likely to bolt. There have been years in which an early October sowing in the south of England has proved better than either of the others.

January Sowing

This is of interest mainly to the exhibitor who requires large fully ripened bulbs in time for the early autumn shows. It calls for a greenhouse heated to 55° F. and seed is sown in 3-ins.-deep boxes filled to within ⅞ in. of the top with a light compost such as old mushroom or cucumber bed to which a little sharp sand has been added. Space the seeds 1 in. apart, cover not more than ¼ in. deep, and place glass and newspaper over the boxes until germination takes place. When the fourth leaf begins to form, prick off singly to 3½-ins. pots and move to a cold frame as early as possible in March. The seedlings will probably need the support of slim canes.

Spring Sowing

This should be done as early in March as possible. Onion seed is rather fickle in its behaviour and may germinate well or badly, quickly or slowly, according to weather conditions. In the ordinary way it should come up in three weeks but, if sowing is delayed until the dry spell that we sometimes get in April, the seed (which has a husk that needs plenty of moisture to soften it) may lie dormant for a month or six weeks, with the result that the ultimate crop will inevitably be light and may in fact be so gappy owing to patchy germination that the whole sowing represents a dead loss. If the soil is sufficiently dry on 14 February not to stick to your boots that is the traditional day on which to sow and you will do well to follow tradition. Cloches will help to get the soil into proper condition by that date and can be replaced to cover the rows after sowing: alternatively a few cloches can be used on a seed-bed to raise plants for subsequent transplanting, but great care has to be taken to see that the soil does not dry out beneath the cloches. In districts where the spring outdoor onion sowing is habitually fraught with difficulties I advise sowing the seeds barely ¼ in. deep and ½ in. apart in boxes and germinating in a cold frame – this also should be done about mid-February. Good, fresh seed is essential to ensure good germination – you cannot rely on seed that has been kept for several months.

Purchased Plants

If it is not convenient to raise your own onion plants, you can obtain them from a nurseryman, but be sure that he supplies you with decent stuff. The points to look for are pure white unbroken roots and rich green leaves; if the roots are greyish white and broken, the plants are bad, and the same is the case if the leaves are long, drooping, and yellowish-green.

Thinning and Planting

So far as onions for the kitchen are concerned, which should range in size from that of golf ball to that of tennis ball, no larger, whether the plants are thinned or transplanted, a distance of 6 ins. apart will be ample to allow for the production of suitable bulbs. It has been amply proved that a far heavier weight of crop will be obtained by growing the plants fairly close together even though the size of individual bulbs will be smaller. The rows in this case should be 6 to 9 ins. apart. On the other hand, if large bulbs are wanted for exhibition purposes, the correct spacing is 12 ins. apart in rows 12 ins. apart.

Autumn-sown onions must be planted out during the first two weeks of March; if you leave them until April a great many of them will probably bolt. Plants raised in the greenhouse in January and those started in frames or under cloches in February are due to be planted out (after hardening off) from mid-April to early May.

The planting out of seedling onions is rather a tedious and fiddling business. It has always been regarded as an essential feature of onion growing that the bulb should sit on the soil and not be buried in it so that when transplanting onions every care was taken to bury only the roots, a sufficiently deep hole being made with a trowel to ensure that they went down straight and care being taken not to break any of them. If it was found difficult to make the onions sit upright without burying the bulblet (and this invariably happened!) either the plants were given some temporary support in the form of twiggy brushwood or they were earthed up for a few days and the earth carefully removed as soon as they were able to stand up by themselves. But nowadays both exhibitors and market growers save themselves time and trouble by allowing the base of the seedling to go ½ in. below the surface, thus giving some support to the slender stem. A trowel is used to make the holes for pot plants but plants lifted from boxes, frames, or open ground (which should have been well watered the previous day) are set out with the aid of a dibber. Holes are made of sufficient depth to take the roots at full length, the seedlings are plunged right into the holes, then pulled upwards until the embryo bulb is ½ in. below soil-level and locked in position by means of a side-stroke from the dibber which is plunged in a few inches away and thus closes up the hole.

Another method which is useful when very many onions have to be planted is to stretch the garden line along the row to be planted, nick out a slit trench of suitable depth with a sharp spade, keeping the wall against the line absolutely vertical, then simply lay the seedlings in position with their roots hanging down into the trench and the top growth lying flat on the ground. Close up the trench, tread firm, and rake, and under normal conditions, given several light overhead sprayings if the weather is dry, the plants will assume a vertical position within two or three days.

It is not desirable that the leaf-tips of newly planted onions should touch the soil as this encourages worms to take hold of them and drag the whole leaf underground; any such tips ought therefore to be snipped off with a pair of scissors.

Cultivation

The subsequent cultivation of onions consists mainly in keeping the ground regularly, but very shallowly, hoed and removing all weeds; it is most important when using the hoe not to loosen the ground in which the roots are growing, which would prevent the formation of good bulbs, not to push any soil on to the bulbs and not to nick them with the blade of the hoe. From July onwards some growers prefer to leave the onion bed unweeded on the grounds that the weeds will absorb any excess nitrogen which would impede ripening, but probably the best course is to remove the taller weeds which might shade the crop and leave only the low-growing ones. Watering sometimes presents rather a problem. Of course it is necessary to water the plants in after transplanting, but whether, in the event of dry weather, it is desirable to water is another matter. Drought, as has been said before, is a great enemy of onions, and provided watering is started before the crop is really beginning to feel the effects of drought and is kept up on a copious scale until rain comes again, then there is a good deal to be said in favour of watering. But once the onions have got really dry, and root activity has ceased, and the outer scales have begun to get tough and dryish, water, whether in the form of rain or from a can or hose, is liable to do more harm than good. One of the most common results of the sudden advent of moisture after a period of dryness is the formation of one-sided bulges on the onions or even of split bulbs; another extremely common result is the all too familiar thick neck. The moral is to let your onions grow as long as they will and to help them to do so if you can. But once growth is stopped, whether by reason of drought or from any other cause, your aim should be to get the crop off the ground as quickly as possible before the roots again get active and the onions start into second growth.

Pests and Diseases

Onion Fly

Which looks like a housefly, lays eggs in May or early June which develop into maggots which tunnel into the bulbs and cause them to rot besides feeding upon the roots and basal stems. The maggots themselves become flies about six weeks later, so that there are three broods in a season. The skins of autumn-sown onions and of those sown in heat early in the year are often too tough to allow the maggots to effect an entrance to the bulbs; hence these sowings usually escape the worst ravages of the fly when the spring sowings fall victims to it. The first symptom of attack is a yellowing of the leaf-tip and soon afterwards the whole plant succumbs to soft rot.

It is the smell from onion seedlings which attracts egg-laying female onion flies – so make sure that no onion smell, over and above the normal, guides this pest to your onion bed. Broken onion foliage, for example, emits a strong smell so take every possible precaution not to break the foliage when cultivating: it often happens when rows are being thinned and the soil is dry. Never, therefore, pull onion thinnings out of dry soil, always soak the soil with water and wait an hour or so before thinning. Never leave onion foliage or tiny, unwanted seedlings around the garden. Bury these wastes *inside* the compost heap. Onion seedlings from an autumn sowing are rarely affected by the pest. The growing of onions from sets is dealt with on p. 255.

Onion Eelworm

If the leaves of an onion swell up, becoming distorted and puffy, and the neck becomes swollen, soft, and twisted, pull it up and cut the bulb in half. If maggots are to be seen, blame the onion fly, but if the interior is 'full of wind' the trouble is 'bloat' caused by eel-worms and you must burn affected plants and abandon your onion bed so far as onion-growing is concerned for at least a couple of years.

Fungoid Diseases of Onions

In warm summers and, in the case of autumn sowings, during warm spells in autumn or spring, if the leaves go yellow and die off, the roots rot and the base of the bulb is covered with white mould, this is White Rot (or 'Mouldy Nose'), probably caused by lack of adequate organic manuring. There is nothing you can do about it except burn affected plants and start afresh with a new onion bed well away from the site of the old one. A wet season and a poorly drained soil may land you with Downy Mildew in which the leaves die from the tips downwards and are covered with a fine, downy growth, starting off grey, then turning browny-purple. Here again there is no cure and you can only do as advised for White Rot. Neck Rot of the bulbs is caused by faulty drying and storage under badly ventilated conditions. Too much nitrogen is also a cause and the bulbs most commonly affected are those that are thick-necked, soft-grown, immature, or damaged. There is no cure for this or for Onion Smut in which blisters filled with black spores appear on the leaves and bulb scales.

Lifting

Autumn-sown onions are ready for lifting about the end of July and spring-sown onions from the middle of August onwards. In a good season and under proper conditions of cultivation the bulbs will ripen naturally and the yellowing of the foliage will indicate that they are getting ready for lifting and drying. But in unfavourable seasons, and especially when heavy rains follow a period of drought, the bulbs may show reluctance to ripen. In such a case matters will be helped if the leaves are bent over at the neck of the bulb by pressing them down with a rake. If even this does not stop the growth and it is necessary to lift the bulbs green, the foliage must be left on until it has completely withered; if this is cut while it is still green, the onions will not keep. Under suitable weather conditions, the onions can be laid on the open ground to dry in the sun, and it is always best to lift them when a spell of fine weather seems reasonably likely to continue. In many years this is more likely to occur in July when the autumn-sown onions are reaching maturity than it is in August when the spring-sown onions are fully developed. If the weather is wet, the onions must be taken off the ground and laid somewhere where they can be exposed to the full force of the sun but protected from rain. A cold frame comes in useful for this purpose. In the last resort the drying of the onions can be completed indoors, use being made of sunny rooms or any shift to keep them dry, expose them to the air, and let them catch whatever sun there is. The tops will wither in due course and then, and only then, you can proceed to store them.

Storing

First remove all ailing specimens, notably those that show an embryo flower-stem, those with soft necks, and those with black dots on the skin. Use these at once in the kitchen, for they will not keep. Then take the rest, remove the withered tops and roots, but leave the loose skins on. You may now make them into 'ropes' or you can hang them up in nets or store them in shallow trays or boxes or put them in a single layer on a shelf.

The roping of onions is not as difficult as it may seem. The first step should be to grade the bulbs into sizes so that you can arrange them neatly on the 'rope' with the larger ones at the bottom and the little ones at the top. The true rope consists of three pieces of cord knotted together at one end and braided together, the necks of the onions being caught between the cords during the process of braiding. But this operation is a simple one only to those who already know how to do it. The beginner would be better advised to take a wisp of half a dozen or so pieces of long-stalked, straight straw about the thickness of his middle finger, or a bamboo cane, or a length or rope, and tie a piece of raffia half-way up this 'leg'. Then a large onion ('The Captain') is secured with the loose end of the raffia, a very small onion ('The Mouse') is secured on each side of this by further twists of the raffia and after that, as it is wound round and round the leg, the raffia takes in the neck of an onion on every second turn, the onions being placed on each side of The Captain alternately. If even this is too complicated for you, you can just tie each onion individually to the central core with a piece of fine string or a strand of raffia. The cane or straw or whatever is used can conveniently be about 2 ft long, and the job of tying the onions to it is made much simpler if it is hung up by means of a loop at one end a reasonable distance from a wall so that you have space for free movement and run no risk of bruising the bulbs.

The next thing is to find a place in which to keep the ropes or trays or boxes. Cool, dry, airy conditions are essential. A few degrees of frost won't hurt them, but you must keep them away from severe frost. I have successfully kept ropes of onions up to Christmas under the eaves of a thatched cottage and so made room for other things indoors. But in due course, when the weather got severe, they had to come indoors, so perhaps you would do better to put them in a shed or other outbuilding or in the coldest room in your house, right from the start. If you prevent the shed or room from becoming stuffy by keeping the door open most of the day during fine weather, your onions should keep perfectly until the spring. But whatever you do don't let them get damp: damp will start them sprouting and you will then have to be continually topping and tailing them if you want to keep them fit for use.

Exhibiting Onions

Large bulbs for showing, as already explained, are started in January in a heated greenhouse and spaced more widely at planting time; but after that their cultivation does not differ from that of ware onions except that nitrogenous feeds can be continued a little later, especially in the form of dilute liquid animal manure and in July a light dressing of phosphate of potash may prove helpful. Towards lifting time it is a good idea to scratch a little soil away from the base of the bulb, and to remove weeds and loose skins, so as to assist the bulbs to acquire a good colour. Loosen the roots by lifting slightly with a fork a few days before harvesting, by which time the necks should have become limp and remove to a slightly shaded greenhouse for ripening. Reject all thick or bull-necked specimens and remember that a monster bulb of a variety which naturally forms a large neck will score fewer points than a smaller bulb of a variety which makes a slim neck. Match up the required number of bulbs (six for single dishes, twelve for a collection); remove the roots with a sharp knife and smooth the basal plate with fine glass-paper; cut off the tops 2 ins. above the bulb and tie down the necks with raffia, using a clove hitch; turn the bulbs daily whilst they are ripening under glass and remove loose skins as they appear. Rough, broken skins cause loss of marks; the aim is to show bulbs with unbroken, clean, well-ripened skins but this may prove almost impossible for the earliest shows and the exhibitor must always be on his guard against over-peeling or excessive skinning which makes the onions look as if they had been prepared for cooking. Some exhibitors polish the skin with a touch of vaseline, rubbing in one direction only. Pack in wood wool when transporting to the show and stage on rings cut from a cardboard cylinder. Under R.H.S. rules 5 points each are allocated to (i) firmness and thorough ripening; (ii) size; (iii) form; and (iv) uniformity.

Growing Onions from Sets

Onion sets are small immature onions in a state of arrested development which complete their growth when replanted in spring. No special onion bed is required: any decent ground which was manured or dressed with garden compost for a previous crop will serve. Do not apply nitrogenous or general compound fertilizers. Plant sets at 4 to 6 ins. apart in drills 1 in. deep and 1 ft apart and cover lightly with soil, using a garden rake. Do this, weather permitting, about the end of the first week in March in the south, the first week in April in the midlands, and the end of April in the north. Black cotton stretched above the rows will prevent birds from pulling the sets about when the necks are visible above the soil. There is very little risk from onion fly and no special treatment of the plants is required during the summer – just keep down weeds and keep well watered during periods of drought in late June and July. Stop all watering when it can be seen that the onions have stopped swelling. The crop will ripen much earlier than crops grown from seed which is a great advantage in areas where it is difficult to harvest the latter successfully owing to weather conditions. The bulbs are usually of a good size, averaging about ¼ lb. each.

Why, in view of the obvious advantages, are onions for kitchen use not always grown from sets? The reason is that many gardeners have had bad experiences with sets, for example bolting. This may be from using a fertilizer high in nitrogen or a variety of set unsuited to our climatic conditions. Whatever the reason, it pays to buy onion sets from a supplier who can more or less guarantee from bolting.

SALAD ONIONS

The variety White Lisbon is sown from mid-July in the north to late August in the south to provide 'spring' onions from March to May, and again as soon as the ground is fit to work in February to continue the supply until the end of June, after which date few people want salad onions.

Any good soil which has been well manured organically will grow this crop provided that it is well drained; and in the case of the autumn sowing no preliminary treatment with fertilizers is necessary. In wet districts it is an advantage to make a slightly raised bed for this sowing and in all areas the plants should be covered with cloches from October onwards as an insurance against losses through severe frosts. The onions should be of lead pencil thickness by the end of November at the latest. Cloches may also be of great service in starting off the February sowing.

Seed should be sown in ½-in.-deep drills 'thickly', i.e. about sixty seeds to the foot – there are about 7,000 onion seeds to the ounce – and the rows should be spaced such a distance apart as will allow three rows to fit nicely under a barn cloche. No thinning is necessary.

In February the autumn sowing can be dressed with Chilean potash nitrate (½ oz. per sq. yd). It must also be kept weed-free.

A good place for spring sowing is an area of the garden which was dressed with garden compost for a different crop a year before.

When salad onions are pulled they should not be hauled out in bundles by grasping the tops; this bruises the foliage and spoils the appearance besides heaving the soil up and damaging the roots of plants which are to be left. The proper procedure is to water the soil, if it is at all dry, and then pull each plant out singly by grasping it at ground level.

PICKLING ONIONS

The 'silverskin' varieties of onion, used for pickling, do best on light, sandy or gravelly loams of only moderate fertility. No fertilizer should be applied unless the soil is naturally deficient in potash; but the land must not lack lime. Seed is sown in March in drills a few inches apart and the bulbs are harvested in June or July. The bed, which should be not more than 3 ft wide, should be as carefully finished off as for ordinary onions and weeding must be regularly attended to. Very shallow sowing is necessary to obtain round bulbs – too deep sowing will result in oval bulbs. Do not thin the crop at all.

OTHER TYPES OF ONION

The Tree Onion

Allium cepa aggregatum is a curious plant of Canadian origin. It is a hardy perennial which, in addition to forming offsets underground, sends up stems, up to 4 ft tall, on the tips of, and sometimes at intervals along, which are borne clusters of small 'cocktail' onions. In some cases flowers are borne as well as bunches of onions; occasionally flowers alone develop. The plant is immune against onion fly.

Any soil in good heart with plenty of humus in it will grow this curiosity and, as it will occupy the land for anything up to six years, a mulch of garden compost applied each autumn will be beneficial.

A stock is usually raised by purchasing a few of the little cocktail onions and treating them as sets which you put 1 in. deep and about 12 ins. apart in triangular groups 2 ft apart, so that one 4-ft stake will suffice to support the three plants in each triangle after they are more than 9 ins. high. This planting is usually performed in October or November but the sets must actually be put in the ground as soon as possible after you receive them from the supplier, even if this happens to be in midwinter. If you prefer you can obtain large three-year-old stock bulbs which go 4 ins. deep and 18 ins. apart or you can buy young growing plants which you put in during March.

The small sets do not produce full-sized plants of normal cropping capacity until the second season following planting. In the first year they merely produce a fair-sized single onion bulb, which you can eat if you please (but that will be the end of your tree onion!). After the first year, however, you can harvest the little 'cocktail' onions annually when they complete growth in September; and in the third and subsequent years you can lift in autumn or spring and remove all the large bottom bulbs except two. You then replant and can use the bulbs removed either to make a new plantation or for eating purposes. Some people stop the top growth at the first cluster in July but this is not essential. As a rule, in course of time, the multiplication of bottom bulbs leads to congestion and compels you to lift and divide.

The Potato Onion

The plants form clusters of large cloves on or just beneath the surface of the soil. These are flattish and of pleasantly mild flavour, and store well. This species used to be valued on soils where ordinary onions are apt to fail from seed but it prefers a mild district and is now rarely grown. This onion is believed to have been grown in Ulster until around 1960. No more was heard of it until 1972 when plants were on view to visitors at the Royal Horticultural Society's Garden, Wisley, Surrey. I would regard the potato onion as entirely superseded by sets of ordinary maincrop onions. If, however, you possess some potato onions and wish to grow them, I advise you to plant and lift at the same time as shallots, setting the bulbs 8 ins. apart with the tip of the bulb just beneath the surface. In due course they will push themselves up and sit on the soil; you can help them to do this by removing earth so as to form a shallow basin round the bulbs – but take care not to expose the roots.

All the remaining types appear to be variants of *Allium fistulosum* and are used as substitutes for salad onions produced by annual sowings.

The Welsh Onion

This onion is not Welsh at all but Siberian (Old English *waelisc*, meaning foreign). It forms an insignificant, brownish, flat onion bulb but is cultivated only for the immature sprouts (or 'chibols') which are used as spring onions and are ready very early in the year.

Stock must be raised from seed sown in February or March, as plants are seldom offered by nurserymen. When the seedlings are large enough, they can be removed to a nursery bed and then lifted in spring or autumn and planted finally 3 to 4 ins. deep and about 9 ins. apart. No attention is needed beyond an occasional hoeing. Each plant grows into a bunch of 'spring onions' which is dug up complete and split up indoors. A few clumps should be reserved for stock and lifted, split up and replanted in autumn or spring to replace those that have been eaten. Laxton & Bunyard Nurseries also offer this onion.

The Japanese Bunching Onion

This is also raised from seed, which is sown in April and the plant attains its full size in the second year. It is a bulbless perennial which resembles a very large chive plant but, unlike the chive, retains its green leaves throughout the winter. The leaves may be used as chives or the scallions (i.e., leek-like silvery white stems) used as salad onions.

Evergreen Hardy White Bunching Onion

Now a standard vegetable in the U.S.A., this onion is perennial, standing up to heavy frost, and will produce from four to six shoots from a single seed during the first season. It reaches full size in the second season and produces scallions which may be used in the same way as those of the other types just described. The plants are resistant to thrips. Sow in April or September.

Orach

(Mountain Spinach)

Garden orach (*Atriplex hortensis*) is a native of Tartary and a close relative of mercury ('Lincoln Spinach'). It was widely cultivated in this country in Tudor times prior to the introduction of true spinach which quickly replaced it in popularity. Nevertheless it makes an excellent vegetable, being used both raw in salads and cooked, and it has the additional advantage of being highly ornamental. There are green, red, and white varieties: the French esteem the white most highly, but the red is the most attractive in appearance and its young leaves are most decorative in salads. It is the older leaves that are cooked like spinach, three or four of them being sufficient for a dish for a family of five. The plants grow from 3 to 5 ft high, and seed should be sown out of doors in April or somewhat earlier in heat. The seeds are rather hard-skinned and may need soaking if the weather is dry. The plants appreciate a good soil and should be spaced 1½ ft apart. As the season advances they can be earthed up a little round the bases of the stems and it may be that staking will be necessary before autumn. No feeding is necessary.

Parsley

Parsley was known and appreciated on the Continent long before it was grown in England. Charlemagne is stated to have had a liking for cheese flavoured with parsley seeds and, long before his time,

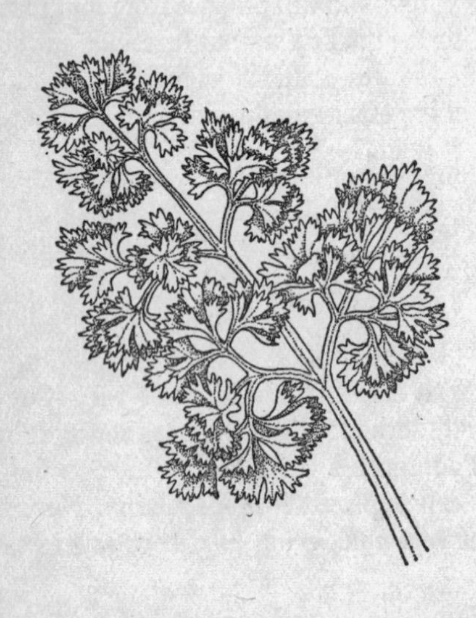

the Greeks used parsley to garnish the heads of victorious athletes and to make wreaths for funerals because it remained fresh and green for a longer period than most other plants. It probably reached us from Sardinia about the year 1500 and it is reported that Henry VIII very much enjoyed parsley sauce with his roast rabbit. For some curious reason no vegetable has been more hedged around with superstitions and, if even a few of these old wives' tales were true, many people would probably be too scared to grow parsley at all!

Any well-drained soil will grow good parsley, especially if it is on the medium to heavy side, although light soil is usually satisfactory for the winter crop which also appreciates a sunny spot which will become sunless when the days shorten, thus enabling it to escape the damage caused by rapid thawing after freezing. Parsley is very hardy but severe winters can kill the stems and leaves above ground and then of course there is no parsley to pick.

Contrary to general belief, parsley is not likely to do really well on poor, undernourished soil. If your soil is not sufficiently fertile for this crop, dress the site with a balanced fertilizer.

Parsley makes a good edging to a plot and in that position is convenient for picking; but it should not be grown as an edging against a path if it is to be given cloche protection in winter because the cloches would encroach upon the path.

Like other biennials parsley runs to seed the second year; it is only by persistent removal of flower stems that you can make any use of it in the year after sowing, so don't try. The seed has the reputation of being the slowest of all vegetable seeds to germinate – it may take eight weeks. But it usually comes up within three or four weeks if the sowing drill (which should be ½ in. deep) is lined with moist peat and covered with polythene cloches to retard loss of moisture. (Some people soak the seed in water to hurry it up, but that merely makes it stick to your fingers and refuse to be sown.)

Sown in boxes under glass in February, and planted out in April parsley will start giving you a supply about ninety days later. But once you have a stock you need sow only in March and July: the first sowing will come into pick in the summer and will probably bolt the following year but the July sowing will continue the supply until the next year's spring sowing is ready. No plant is more intolerant of overcrowding: a well-grown parsley plant is one that has never touched its neighbour from the day it was sown, and such a plant will need a foot of space. About a dozen plants are needed for an average household. Do not neglect to water them in summer during periods of really dry weather – even young parsley can be driven to bolt by prolonged spells of drought.

Pick constantly, taking a few of the best leaves from each plant. Don't strip one single plant and leave the others to grow too large; if you do, the foliage will get coarse and you will have to cut the whole plant back.

The best dried parsley comes from young leaves picked between July and September; spring-dried parsley will not keep its colour.

Parsley is dried in the same way as other herbs but requires a much higher temperature, especially at the end of the drying – it is best dried in a very hot oven. Don't do as is sometimes advised and pour boiling water over it before you start to dry it. And don't lose a moment in starting to rub it down as soon as it is dry and crisp. If you delay it will reabsorb moisture and become like indiarubber. Before rubbing down, shake it in a fine sieve to get rid of particles of earth splashed up by heavy rain.

In practice it ought not to be necessary to dry parsley. The more popular moss-curled kinds will generally continue to give pickings throughout the winter; but in bleak districts and as a general precaution it is better to cover with cloches in winter or to lift a few plants and pot them in 5-ins. pots which can be kept in a frame till mid-October and then placed in a greenhouse. Or why not make a parsley basket for the winter? It is simply a wire hanging basket with about a dozen parsley roots set in the top, bottom and sides and will be very happy in the window of a sunny kitchen – just reach up and pick!

Hamburg Parsley

As has been mentioned previously, parsley belongs to the same family as the carrot. It is not surprising therefore that there is one variety (*Carum petroselinum fusiformis*) which forms an edible root. This has always been very popular in Germany (whence the name) and was much appreciated in this country on its introduction by Philip Miller in 1727 and for a century or more afterwards: it was often sold under the name of 'Jew's Root'. Then it seemed to be entirely forgotten until its cultivation was revived during the Second World War.

Hamburg parsley is worth trying. The Germans boil the roots which have a flavour somewhat resembling that of celeriac, but some people grate them raw and serve with mayonnaise as a salad or mix with other saladings. In the seed catalogues you may find the plant listed as 'turnip-rooted' parsley which is absurd – the epithet should be 'parsnip-rooted' because the roots look more like parsnips than turnips, being similar to parsnips in colour and shape: they are chubby, about 7 to 8 ins. long and 3 ins. thick; when cooked they are tender right through, and the centre is soft and jelly-like.

Prepare the soil and sow just as you would parsnips and leave at least 6 ins. between plants. Hoeing is the only attention required; but the finest roots are those which have been abundantly supplied with moisture throughout the season – if you have time, water as copiously as you would celeriac. The roots are lifted as wanted, usually from September onwards, but, as in the case of other root vegetables, a proportion can be lifted, if desired, before frosts come, and stored in semi-moist sand, the remainder being left in the ground over the winter and used as required. The foliage remains abundant throughout the winter and may be used for flavouring.

Parsnips

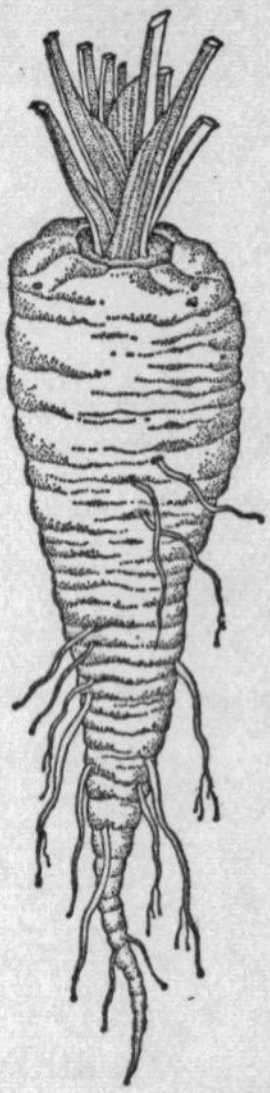

You can see wild parsnips in flower, a couple of feet high, almost anywhere on the South Downs in late summer and it is from these that all our cultivated strains have come. But parsnips have been in general use as a vegetable all over Europe for a very long time: nearly 2,000 years ago they were grown in the Rhine Valley and sent to Rome to grace the table of the Emperor Titus; in Britain they were eaten for centuries where we now eat potatoes; and there was made from them wine which some connoisseurs adjudged equal to the finest Madeira.

Parsnips ought not to be called parsnips but 'pastinacks', from the Latin *pastinaca*. Unfortunately, in the days when few people could read or write, spoken names might be only half heard and thereby suffered corruption. Somebody thought the parsnip was a sort of turnip or 'neep' and so it came to be called a pars-neep, without anybody understanding what the first syllable meant, if anything – and of course it meant nothing.

The roots of parsnips contain an even higher percentage of sugar than those of sugar beet; and if your household does not appreciate sweetness in vegetables it is little use to grow parsnips for their consumption. You should in any event consider whether, having regard to the comparatively low cost of this vegetable when purchased from the greengrocer, the household demand for it is sufficiently strong to justify your devoting to its cultivation a considerable area of land which could otherwise be put to more profitable use.

A great deal depends on your soil. You cannot grow parsnips on thin gravel soils because these will give you only small, fangy roots. But you can grow them on most ordinary well-drained soils provided that you are prepared to cultivate to whatever depth you expect your parsnips to descend, incorporating ample moisture-retaining material and removing all except the smallest stones. This of course can mean a lot of work.

Some people prefer small, short-rooted parsnips, others much larger, deeper ones. Whatever you decide on, your land must be moisture-retaining, stone-free, and well supplied with lime – no stable or farmyard manure must be used in preparing it for the parsnips, though either may have been used for a previous crop; you may use other organic materials if there is a shortage of humus but, if you use compost, make sure it is very well decomposed. If you use fertilizers dress the site with a general fertilizer.

Parsnips are traditionally sown in February, but in practice the soil is seldom in a fit condition for sowing to take place in that month, and it is usual to postpone sowing until March or April when the soil is warm and workable. It is true that the parsnip needs a long season of growth, but since it is left in the ground until required for eating (and should not be eaten until after the frosts come) it has been found possible to sow as late as May in unfavourable seasons and still obtain good roots.

Sow in drills 1 in. deep and 15 ins. apart, setting the seeds in clusters at intervals of about 8 ins. Parsnip seed germinates very slowly, and the number of seeds which do not germinate at all is greater than in the case of any other vegetable. This is because the seeds, which are rather like confetti, consist of a very thin membraneous disc which in cold, clammy soil may become covered with fungus, causing suffocation of the germ. Therefore sow at least five seeds in each cluster, thinning the resultant seedlings to one specimen, and that the strongest, when they are 2 ins. tall; and sow a pinch of lettuce between each two 'stations'. The lettuce will germinate quickly and serve to mark the positions of the parsnip row until the parsnips show up, which may be anything up to a month, and all the lettuces will be off the ground and eaten before the foliage of the parsnips requires the intervening space.

If you wish to grow long parsnips you will be well advised to use the crowbar method. This consists in making deep holes with a crowbar 1 ft apart, 3 ft deep, and 8 ins. across the top and filling them with prepared potting soil, which should be made quite firm. Then sow seeds to stations as before.

Except in particularly unfavourable seasons when a spell of wet weather follows a dry period during early autumn, and may lead to an attack of canker, parsnips are unlikely to require any attention once they have started into growth except hoeing and weeding.

Parsnips are usually left in the ground until they are wanted, but it is a good plan to lift some of the crop in November, or whenever hard weather appears to threaten, and put these roots aside for immediate use. The flavour of parsnips improves if they are left in the ground until the end of February, but after that they begin to grow again and therefore the remainder of the crop must be lifted, trimmed up by cutting off the tops close to the crowns, and stored in a shed or cellar packed head to tail and covered with sand or dry earth until wanted. In very wet soil it may be necessary to lift and store the whole crop in November but this should only be done in extreme cases as stored parsnips soon lose their flavour.

When parsnips have been grown by the crowbar method in pockets of light soil, it is often possible to pull them out after easing them slightly with a fork, which should be pushed in vertically and not on the slant. But in most cases, and particularly in heavy soil, it is necessary to dig a hole 2 ft deep at one end of the row to facilitate the removal of the roots without breaking them, each root being grasped by the shoulder and drawn sideways into the hole which is then filled up with soil excavated when making a similar hole against the next parsnip.

Reference has already been made to parsnip canker. This causes the crown of the root to crack, when it is liable to be invaded by fungi and go black and rotten. The short-rooted, broad-shouldered types of parsnip are more liable to canker than the long ones. Canker is most likely to occur when wet weather follows a dry period in autumn which caused the soil to dry out: but lack of lime, too much nitrogen, the use of undigested stable manure, and attack by carrot fly can also be responsible. The remedy is better cultivation. The later parsnips are sown the less risk there appears to be of canker. Avonresister, bred by the National Vegetable Research Station, is canker free; Tender and True from Suttons of Reading shows marked resistance to it.

Peas

The pea is probably the oldest of all cultivated vegetables. It was known at least 4,000 years ago and pea seeds have been found in the remains of Swiss lake dwellings of the Bronze Age. Dried peas were a common article of diet in Old Testament days and are referred to as 'parched pulse' in the Book of Samuel.

Actually we ought to call the plant a 'pease' from the Latin *pisum*. Our forefathers always spoke of 'pease' pudding. But spelling was not a strong point in the days before state education and the 'e' dropped off so that it became 'peas(e)'! Then some too-clever grammarian made the brilliant 'discovery' that 'peas' must be plural, so that a single seed or plant must be a 'pea'; and he had his way so that 'pea' it is for us, whether we like it or not. (The more logical Frenchman still keeps his 's' in *pois*, just to remind us that we are wrong!)

There is a wild British pea which grows by the sea and was eaten in the great famine of 1555 but it is very bitter and has played no part in the creation of our garden pea, which has been bred largely from the French and Dutch 'field' types, first introduced into England during the reign of Henry VIII.

Nowadays the British garden pea represents the finest example of the hybridist's skill in the field of vegetable plant breeding. It is vastly superior to the old field pea.

There was once a time when fresh green peas were esteemed as the most delectable of all summer vegetables and gardeners went to immense pains to grow them to perfection. But nowadays we are given canned and frozen peas all the year round so that the novelty has worn off and, although the preserved produce cannot compare with well-grown, freshly picked peas from one's own garden, the general lowering of the standards of taste and the steady increase in idleness among gardeners have led to a sharp drop in the number of private gardens and allotments in which garden peas are cultivated.

It has to be admitted that the growing of first-class peas involves a greater expenditure of time and trouble than the growing of most other vegetable crops, but results are well worth the labour if you do the job thoroughly; if you haven't the time to do it thoroughly; and are not really fond of peas, my advice would be to cut this crop out of your schemes altogether. It takes up plenty of room, so that the wastage of land is all the greater if it fails.

The essential requirements of the pea crop are good growing conditions with plenty of rain whilst the haulm is being formed and then reasonably warm, dry weather during the flowering period and whilst the pods and peas are being produced. It follows that it is usually easier to grow an early crop, especially in those years when we get a dry May, than it is to grow summer crops, for in some years July and August are terribly wet. Indeed in a cold wet summer or in a very hot, droughty one, summer peas are likely to prove a disappointment, if not a complete failure.

Deep cultivation is therefore obviously essential to the production of good peas. The soil must be retentive of moisture but well-drained through the subsoil, so that the roots can penetrate deeply and be certain of a supply of water even in the driest seasons. It is a curious thing that many enthusiastic amateurs will go to immense trouble and labour in digging two and three spits deep in order to grow sweet peas for exhibition, yet the same people never think it necessary to go to the same trouble when growing culinary peas. But exactly the same considerations apply in each case – and it is not merely a question of moisture, for peas also want their food deep down since the roots do not feed near the surface.

We have always been told that the land for peas must be liberally manured with stable or farmyard manure; but this does not mean that such manure is to be dug in when preparing the ground for sowing. By all means incorporate humus-forming and moisture-retaining materials throughout the whole body of soil; but put your old, decayed manure, rotted compost, composted straw chaff, or whatever you use, in a fat layer 4 ins. thick beneath the top soil. This of course involves taking out a trench, a labour that can be avoided, however, if you are able to site your peas over the line of last year's celery trenches, which have already got the manure where it is wanted.

Much the same principle applies to the use of fertilizers. It has been found that the best results are obtained by placing them in bands 2 ins. to the outside of, and 1 in. deeper than, the seed. In the matter of choice of suitable fertilizers, the pea is rather exceptional: it gets its nitrogen from the air and therefore does not want it in the soil; but it needs both phosphate and potash of which the latter is the more likely to be in short supply unless you keep your garden soil well supplied with nourishment in the form of garden compost prepared from a great number of different wastes. If you are worried that phosphate and potash may be required by your pea plants I suggest that you mix some superphosphate with an equal weight of sulphate of potash, taking great care that the two fertilizers are evenly combined, and put this down at the rate of 1 oz. per yd run of band 2 ins. wide. (Compound fertilizers containing *no* nitrogen are not available to amateurs, although they *are* supplied to farmers who grow peas.) As regards lime, it is important that the pH of the soil shall not be below 6·0; but peas will not tolerate alkaline conditions above pH 7·5 and it is always difficult to grow them on limestone soils.

When to Sow

Although much has been written in the textbooks about the maintenance of a regular succession of peas from May to October, I do not believe that in practice such a thing is possible in the average amateur's garden. Good peas can be grown on most *well-cultivated* soils of good texture (i.e. all except raw clay and sandy soils lacking in humus), but comparatively few gardens possess the almost ideal soil in which peas will thrive almost all the year round. If your land is light and therefore naturally well-drained, it will grow excellent early crops of peas but, however much organic material you pack into it, it is most unlikely that it will retain sufficient moisture to see the main summer crops through to maturity. On the other hand medium to heavy land in good heart, which is far less likely to dry out in summer, is apt to be too cold for the early crops, though by retaining its warmth later into the autumn it will be better for a very late one. Apart from this, owing to the area occupied by the pea crop, and taking into account the fact that peas ought not to be grown on the same patch more frequently than once in five years, it is necessary to have a very large garden if you are to maintain a regular succession, even though you may economize in space, for example, by growing both maincrop peas and early potatoes on the same plot.

Subject to what has been said, the possible sowings may be summarized as follows:

(1) Peas are extremely hardy and will withstand 20–30° F. of frost but the flowers can be severely damaged by a sharp late frost of no more than 10° F. so that you lose all the pods that the frosted flowers would have produced, though you may get plenty of pods from other flowers at a later date. Nevertheless in all areas except those in which these sharp frosts regularly occur after March – by which time even the tallest of cloches will have had to be removed – and provided the garden or allotment is not in a frost pocket, a round-seeded first early variety (preferably Meteor) can be sown under tall cloches during October in the north and November in the south with a reasonable certainty of picking peas in May.

In the warmest parts of the extreme south and in the south-west (particularly in the coastal areas bordering the Channel), skilled gardeners have for generations achieved the same result without the aid of cloches by sowing on sloping, sheltered borders of light soil facing south, running the rows from north to south in order to secure for them the most even allocation of sunlight and placing reed or wattle hurdles in strategic positions to keep off cold northerly and east winds.

(2) In areas favoured similarly to those just described the first early wrinkled varieties are sown without protection on warm soils in February or very early in March if favourable weather

has enabled the land to be got into suitable condition. Under cloches in the south the same sowing is sometimes possible in January; but if that month is cold and wet sowing will certainly have to be postponed until some time in February, while in the colder areas of the midlands and north it may well be March before you can get the seed in. Picking from this sowing will begin some time in June.

(3) The principal outdoor sowing of the first and second early varieties is due to take place about mid-March. The second earlies (also referred to as early maincrop or mid-season sorts) ordinarily give a bigger and better yield than the first and there is not much to choose as regards time taken to mature – from a level start some second earlies are no more than about five days later than the first earlies and the average time from sowing to maturity in both these classes is about twelve weeks. It is a matter of choice whether you sow one or the other or both types for successional picking during late June and July. But the weather will decide whether you can get the seed into the ground and it happens all too frequently that conditions are far from favourable at this date. In such circumstances the keen gardener will consider whether he cannot save delay by starting his peas under glass.

There are various methods of doing this. In the old days of large gardens in rural areas when turf was to be had for the asking it was standard practice to take turves from short clean pastures, lay them out grass side downwards for the birds to clean, then remove any remaining pests by sprinkling with water with a little salt in it and cut the turves to fit 4-ins.-deep boxes. Then they were sliced into 3-ins. squares and 4 seeds were sown on each square and covered with fine soil. The boxes were then placed in a cold frame. Alternatively strips of turf were laid out in a cold frame and seeds sown 1 in. apart all along the centre of them. Now, however, that few amateur gardeners have access to turves, the best practice is to sow in special long, deep boxes with slide-out bottoms; 3½-ins.-size peat pots may be used, too. Sow three pea seeds in each, spacing the seeds as near to 1 in. apart as you can. In both cases germination is effected in a frame as early as possible in March with a view to the plants being hardened and transferred to open ground by the end of April. Exhibitors make an even earlier start for the summer shows, sowing in a cool greenhouse in January or February either in boxes or peat pots. Where pots are used then only one seed is sown in each. Such sowings are transferred to the open in March or April. Squares of turf and potfuls of seedlings are planted out 1 ft apart. Strips of turf and seedlings from special boxes are planted end on to form a continuous line. The two essentials are that the roots must not suffer any disturbance – never, never must you sow peas in boxes and dig the seedlings out with a trowel as if they were beans – and there must be no undue delay in planting because peas start their existence by sending down a tap-root and in artificial containers this will all too soon reach the bottom.

(4) Maincrop peas take from fourteen to sixteen weeks to mature, i.e., at least three weeks longer than the earlies and a fortnight longer than the second earlies. They are sown during April and May to be ready in July, August, and September. You must time the sowing according to when you want to pick and the lateness of the variety chosen.

(5) If you hesitate to grow the late maincrops, which can be decidedly difficult to manage, you can sow first early varieties again in June for cropping in September and October, giving preference to a very dwarf sort which can be covered with cloches in late September.

Sowing

Peas are sown in flat-bottomed drills 6 to 8 ins. wide and 2 ins. deep. Space the seeds singly in 2 rows, 3 ins. apart each way, i.e., about eight seeds to the foot. It used to be the custom to sow much more thickly to allow for losses from birds, vermin and other causes which we are now in a much better position to prevent. In the case of the later sowings and in dry districts, it is advisable to arrange the depth of the trench or drill so that the surface will remain below the level of the surrounding ground after the seeds have been covered with 2 ins. of soil – this assists the collection of rain water and allows room for a deep mulch. As a general rule the distance between two rows of peas should be the same as the height to which the variety normally grows.

Do not make too small a sowing – it is no use getting only a spoonful of peas at each picking. The absolute minimum length of row that is worth sowing is 5 yards which should yield at least 10 lb. of peas in four pickings of 2½ lb. each.

Because of the possibility of the seeds rotting if the soil is too cold or too wet, some gardeners like to dress pea seeds with a proprietary seed dressing at sowing time. Certain seedsmen market pea seeds already 'protected' by such a dressing.

It is generally wise to protect all sowings from birds by covering the rows with small mesh chicken wire or several strands of black cotton. If you use wire mesh, don't forget to close the ends to stop birds getting in. Remove the wire mesh before the growing peas take hold of it with their tendrils and make removal impossible. Leave black cotton where it is, it will help the pea plants to climb.

In some districts field mice are very troublesome and steal the seeds. You can obtain seed dressed to protect them from rats and mice. If you have gorse in your area you can cover the sown seeds in the drills with gorse clippings. But it is always desirable where mice are prevalent to set traps in addition to whatever other precautions are taken. These should be of the breakback variety, baited with either marrow or pea seeds, but, if you keep a cat, do please take such precautions as will prevent it from getting its paw caught in the trap.

Cultivation

Immediately the peas make their appearance above ground, they are liable to attack by the pea weevil and by slugs. Pea weevil can easily be detected by the scalloping of the leaf edges; slugs eat the plant off at ground level. The critical period is that between the first appearance of the seedlings and their attaining a height of 2 or 3 ins.; during this time the plants should be dusted several times with derris dust early in the day when there is dew upon the leaves to make the dust adhere. Any good slug bait will look after slugs.

Once the peas are about 4 ins. high, any wire mesh used to protect the seeds and seedlings from attack by birds should be removed and immediate steps taken to give the plants support. Although pea sticks are becoming increasingly difficult to obtain, there is nothing really so good for growing peas. But it is no use putting in the pea sticks alone when the plants are only a few inches high. You must first hedge them in with pieces of twiggy brushwood and then fix the pea sticks firmly outside the hedge of brushwood; the young peas will then first take hold of the twiggy portion of the brushwood. A pea will not take hold of the thick bare stem at the bottom of the bough in the same way that a runner bean will curl itself round a bean pole.

It may interest readers to know that the good old-fashioned pea sticks consisted of the prunings from hazel coppices on the game preserves of large estates, which used to be sold at a nominal figure as 'throw-away' stuff. Their present scarcity and high price result partly from the decline in the number of large estates and partly from the fact that all the best hazel prunings go as crate rods to the Midlands, for packing pottery. But if you live near a modern conifer plantation you can often acquire cheaply the 'brash' from Sitka spruce and Douglas fir which makes quite good pea sticks.

The only effective substitute for brushwood and pea boughs is either wire netting or square-mesh string or nylon netting of 3-ins. or 4-ins. mesh. Either a single line of netting can be run down the middle of the trench between peas sown in a double row, or a line of netting can be erected on either side of the trench, thus forming a double line with the peas growing in between. The second method is, on the whole, the better one, because modern strains of peas do not appear to have retained their natural instinct to cling with their tendrils to the fullest extent and it does happen, when there is a single central line of netting, that the peas sprawl away from the netting instead of pulling themselves on to it as they are intended to do; if the netting is on either side of them, they have no option but to take hold of it. (It is frequently claimed that dwarf-growing peas need no support, but, while this is true in theory, it usually happens in practice that even varieties with the strongest haulms sprawl about and get dirty and are liable to be beaten flat by heavy rain unless they are supported like the taller sorts.)

Netting is useless unless it is firmly erected. It is sometimes forgotten when the net is being erected that it will, in due course, have to bear the whole weight of the pea haulm and that this haulm presents a wide flat surface to the wind. String netting should always be purchased with head and foot lines which make it easier to stretch it taut. Wire netting should be secured in slots cut in the top and bottom of galvanized tubing. The end posts should be very stout and driven in deeply; if necessary they should be secured to some object such as a tree or guyed with pegs after the manner of a flagstaff. Lighter canes should be inserted at intervals all along the line of the netting, and the netting must be tied to these canes so that there is no question of sagging.

String netting is not cheap, and it pays to erect it properly and take even more care when taking it down and storing it away for the winter. It will soon become a hopeless, unusable tangle if it is merely bundled up with bits of pea haulm sticking on it. Similar care should be taken if nylon mesh netting is used. Wire netting has a much longer life because it is so much easier to clean the haulm off it.

Watering

As the season advances, the question of moisture becomes an important one. There is nothing to which the pea so much objects as cold water from a hose pipe in warm weather. It the soil has been properly prepared, it should retain its moisture for a substantial period during dry weather. If it is obvious that, owing to the absence of rain after the pods have formed, it will be necessary to water in order to save the crop, the proper course is to get a sufficient quantity of rain water, put it to warm in the sun and then thoroughly soak the rows with it at the rate of about 2 gallons a yard. As soon as the watering is completed, mulch the plants with a 3-ins. layer of moistened peat or other suitable moisture-retaining material. Do not carry this mulch right over the roots of the plants, but leave a clear space in the centre of the row for rain water to percolate if rain subsequently falls, or for future watering if this proves unavoidable.

Pests and Diseases

A close watch must be kept for aphids during spring and early summer and also for thrips which may cause serious damage in dry weather, their presence being recognized by curious silvery markings on the leaves and pods where the insects have scraped away the tissues in order to feed upon the juices which come from the wound. Spraying with derris or a proprietary mixture of derris and pyrethrum will control aphids. A nicotine spray (but remember this is a poison) can be used against thrips. You may grow peas all your life and never meet these two pests, nor even pea moth which is responsible for maggots found inside the pods. The best defence against all three of these pests is good cultivation and lots of water applied to the roots in a dry season. It is weak plants which suffer most from pests. If you are growing mangetout peas, where the entire pod is eaten, never apply a nicotine spray or any other dangerous spray.

The only other pests of peas are birds at the time when the pods have filled, particularly the sparrows; for the sparrow is always after anything that is worth having, and, though many other small birds take the filling pods, the sparrow is always the leader of the gang. When peas are grown on the grand scale it might be practicable to cage them in as is done in the case of soft fruit. But on the smaller scale, the only practicable thing to do in districts where birds are a serious menace is to stretch two tight wires or cords on either side of the rows and throw small-mesh fish netting over them, taking care that every possible means of ingress is barred, otherwise the birds will find the way in somehow, and making sure also that the net is sufficiently far away from the peas to prevent the birds from pecking the pods through the mesh, a trick which tits are particularly adept at. However, such extreme measures should be unnecessary in the ordinary private garden and allotment. I myself have found that a few of the bird scarers made of pieces of shining metal, which not only flash in the sun but make a loud noise when moved by the least breath of wind, constitute an effective deterrent, and do not, like the nets, render the gathering of the pods as difficult for the owner as it is for the marauder. It must be admitted, however, that in built-up areas the noise of these scarers can sometimes lead to complaints by neighbours.

As regards diseases the only common trouble with peas is mildew. There are two sorts. Powdery Mildew is only met with late in the season in rather dry weather and in sheltered gardens when there is a big difference between day and night temperatures – hot days and cold nights; it is easily controlled by colloidal sulphur dust. Downy Mildew, a greyish-brown growth on the underside of the leaves, is far more serious and may cause the loss of the crop. Fortunately, however, it occurs only in extremely wet seasons and usually only on poorly drained land: it is difficult to control but copper dust should be effective in the early stages. All mildewed foliage must be burned as soon as peas are cleared or infection may be carried over to the next year.

Picking Peas

Pick the pods regularly, testing a pod here and there, as in the case of broad beans. Don't hold a basket in one hand and tug away at the pods with the other so that you crack the haulm or pull the plants out of the ground. Put the basket on the ground, then hold the stem in one hand and snap the stalk of the pod with the first finger and thumb of the other hand.

Mangetout peas are gathered when the peas can be felt in the pods before they are too large. Peas and pods are sliced together.

When all the peas have been picked and it is desired to clear the haulm, cut it off at ground level and dig in the roots which will then add nitrogen to the soil.

Exhibiting Peas

It takes a great deal of skill and ingenuity to produce fifty perfect, matching pods, well filled with tender peas, on show day. With most exhibitors it is one long story of patient watering and mulching and regular spraying with insecticides to keep the pests away. All weak and misshapen pods must be removed to allow the specimen pods more space to swell and there must be regular picking from the bines so that they are not encumbered with over-ripe and drying pods. During very hot weather it may be necessary to shade the bines with mutton-cloth. When the day of the show is at hand the chosen pods must be snipped off with scissors at the very last minute. Handle them only by the footstalk and take them to the hall carefully packed between layers of cotton wool or crepe tissue so that none of the bloom is removed from the pod. Before doing so, however, hold each pod up against a powerful light so that you can see whether it is well filled and free from maggots. Stage the pods, stalks inwards, in wheel formation in upward diminishing layers. Size counts and only really large pods qualify for the full 4 points allocated under this heading: fullness of pods and uniformity are allocated 4 points each whilst the 8 possible points for condition can be gained only by fresh, deep green specimens with bloom intact and free from markings, containing large, young, tender seeds with no maggots among them.

Growing Peas under Glass

Garden peas represent a useful catch-crop for the borders of a fair-sized greenhouse which has been cleared of chrysanthemums and will not be required very early for tomatoes. In the southernmost counties at any rate it is possible to grow them without heat; but then they will come into pick little, if any, earlier than the cloched outdoor peas. The real attraction is to be able to eat your own freshly gathered peas at a time when the only other peas available are either canned, dried, deep-frozen, or inferior imported: and for this purpose you need artificial heat and a steady temperature of 50°–55° F. Since winter lettuce demands almost identical conditions, there is no reason why peas and lettuces should not be grown together in the same greenhouse.

Sowing takes place in December or January. No special preparation of the borders is necessary: it will be sufficient to work in a little bonemeal just prior to sowing the seed in narrow drills. The best return is given by the taller first early varieties such as Gradus or Thomas Laxton, which reach 3 to 4 ft and must of course be staked in the usual way as growth advances. Overwatering must be guarded against – one good watering at the time the borders are prepared will decrease the demand for frequent replacement of moisture later on.

Peas can also be grown in 10-ins. pots, two thirds filled with a compost of two parts loam to one part of old mushroom bed with a sprinkling of lime added. In this case a dwarf variety is recommended and there is none better for the purpose than Little Marvel (20 to 24 ins.). Each pot will take 8 seeds 1½ ins. deep. Water thoroughly after sowing and stand the pots on staging or on shelves as close to the roof glass as is convenient. As the plants grow, the pots will be filled to within one inch of the rim with a top-dressing of the same compost as before. Later, a little support with twiggy brushwood will be helpful.

Peppers

See Capsicums

Potatoes

The batata (as it was originally called) was first brought to this country from Chile by the botanist Hariot who returned to the Old World in one of Drake's ships in 1586 and gave the tubers to Sir Walter Raleigh who planted them in his estate at Youghal in Southern Ireland. Nobody knows who changed the name batata to potato. In America they still call our version the White or Irish potato to distinguish it from their own 'Sweet Potato'.

Botanically, the potato is a solanum and a cousin of the tomato, the egg plant, the 'Winter Cherry', and the Deadly Nightshade among other things.

In 1792 somebody wrote: 'As to potatoes it would be idle to consider them as an article of human food which ninety-nine hundredths of the human species will not touch.' As a prophet the writer seems to have been rather wide of the mark. Previously Shakespeare had made mock of the things: 'Let the skie raine potatoes.'

The original tubers were of any old shape and full of large deep eyes. The botanists succeeded in breeding these out and immediately the Leaf Curl Virus ruined all their efforts. (This was about the time of the quotation given in the previous paragraph.) A fresh set of varieties was raised and was promptly wiped out by Blight Disease in 1845. So another start was made and then soon after 1900 Black Wart Disease appeared.

Quite undismayed, our hybridists are still trying to breed disease-proof potatoes by crossing existing types with the wild potatoes of the Andes region.

Buying Seed Potatoes

For the benefit of the complete novice it may be explained that in order to grow a crop of potatoes it is necessary to plant actual potatoes which are sold under the name of 'seed' potatoes. These are of course entirely different from potato seed which is the actual seed produced by the potato plant after flowering and is used only by plant-raisers engaged in the production of new varieties.

Leading seedsmen confine themselves to the sale of certified Scotch or Irish seed. The explanation of this is that the potato is subject to certain virus diseases and it has been found that, if potatoes are grown in England year after year from seed saved from the crop grown on the same land in the previous year, the stock degenerates and becomes extremely liable to contract these diseases. But in the colder regions of Scotland and in certain districts of Ireland, this deterioration does not occur, largely owing to the absence of greenfly, which is one of the principal agents in introducing infection into the haulm. Certain conditions of moisture and wind discourage the greenfly, and it is from districts where these conditions occur generally that virus-free seed potatoes come. It is therefore wise to purchase only Scotch or Irish seed which has been certified by the appropriate Government Department to have been grown on clean land and to be true to name. The certificate number with other relevant particulars should be found on a ticket in the bag in which the seed potatoes are sold. If it is not there, you should refuse to accept the potatoes.

It is also wise to buy fresh certified seed every year and not to replant tubers saved from your own previous year's crop; this is the only way in which to safeguard yourself against an outbreak of disease due to infection of the seed. In the course of the years that have elapsed since I wrote the original *Vegetable Grower's Handbook* I have seen so many ruined and worthless potato crops due to the repeated use of home-saved seed that I feel bound to emphasize the real importance of buying new seed each year. If, however, this bears rather heavily on your pocket, I suggest that you plant only half the area reserved for potatoes with new seed and plant the other half with home-raised seed potatoes saved from the area which was planted with new seed the previous year; in this way the same stock will not be grown upon your land more than twice. If you do this, you must select your seed potatoes *at the time of lifting* from vigorous plants which have produced really large individual crops, setting aside tubers about the size of a hen's egg. You should never pick out potatoes for planting from a clamp, and you must always order your new seed very early each year so that the merchant has a chance to deliver before frosts hold up the movement of the tubers.

It does not always follow that you will effect much economy by saving your own seed. You must remember that many of the best varieties are liable to suffer from a disease known as Dry Rot in store. If the seed merchant does the storing, any losses from this cause fall upon him but if you store your own seed you are the loser from any outbreak of this kind.

There is also the point that owing to high transport charges and packing costs no seedsman will sell less than 7 lb. of seed potatoes (and some will not accept orders for less than 14 lb.). This will not matter if you are out to keep your family in potatoes all the year round – an excellent thing to do having regard to the low quality of many of the potatoes sent by British farmers for sale in the shops – but it involves the planting of approximately 21 lb. of earlies, 56 lb. of second earlies, and 28 lb. of maincrops, and these will occupy a good 6 rods of land or well over half of a standard 10-rod allotment. It is because the small gardener lacks sufficient land for potato-growing on this scale that he usually confines himself to 'just a few earlies'.

Preparation of the Land

Potatoes naturally prefer a lightish soil and dislike a heavy, sticky clay, but they will put up some sort of show on any soil. Some varieties do better on heavy land than others. Unfortunately the poor potato has come to be looked upon as a maid-of-all-work for breaking up new land, and so the idea has got about that little preparation of the ground is really called for. That is all wrong: if you want a worth-while crop, you must dig the ground well and, if necessary, manure it organically in autumn. If it has been manured for a previous crop so much the better but unless this manuring is at a very high rate add a balanced proprietary potato fertilizer just before planting.

One of the most important things is to break up the land as finely as possible, because potatoes do not like lumpy soil. Do not use ashes or other gritty materials to improve heavy land, as these would scratch the skins of the young tubers, but rely on charred remnants from the bonfire, unsifted leafmould, and reasonably well-decayed garden compost. Rotted or organic material is always good for potato land but keep it *beneath* the top 9 ins. of soil. Use only a proprietary potato fertilizer (or potato manure), adhering strictly to the quantities advised by the makers; any excess can prove disastrous. Do not apply any other chemical fertilizers – their effect on potatoes is not yet fully understood but there is ample evidence that, when applied by amateurs without reference to the existing nutrient content of the soil, they can have most undesirable effects on the cooking, eating, and keeping qualities of the tubers.

Incidentally, if your land is infested with couch grass ('twitch') do not waste time trying to fork it out. Simply dig in the green top growth and cut it off with the hoe, as it reappears, until the haulm of the potatoes hides it from view and smothers it. Then, when you lift, dig out potatoes and twitch roots together.

It is often said that potatoes will not crop well if planted under the shade of trees, but during recent years I have seen many plantings of early varieties which have bulked very well in such positions.

Sprouting the Seed

Sprouting before planting is now regarded as essential: it makes for earliness and high yield. By adopting the practice you are enabled to detect any 'dud' or frosted specimens before you plant; you are able to regulate the number of shoots, for haulm composed of a forest of shoots is so crowded that the crop will be lighter than the land is capable of producing; you have greater latitude in the matter of planting and can afford to wait for good conditions; and you get a stronger plant.

The sprouting process consists in setting the potatoes eye-end uppermost in shallow wooden trays or seed boxes and placing them in a light frost-proof place. In due course each eye sends out a shoot. Some people experience difficulty in deciding which is the eye-end, because there are eyes both ends. But actually there are more eyes on the eye-end than on the heel-end and if you look very carefully you will see on the heel-end the little scar showing where the tuber was once attached to its parent tuber. If you find that the potatoes won't stand on their heel-ends but fall over and roll about, tilt the tray while you are putting the potatoes in and pack any vacant space with screwed-up newspaper before you restore the tray to a level position.

Another excellent method of setting up potatoes to sprout is to put them in the depressions of the papier-mâché egg-trays in which eggs are usually supplied these days in supermarkets or delivered by the milkman.

The job of finding a light frost-proof place is not always easy. Most modern sectional sheds and garages have poky windows and are by no means frost-proof. It is far better to place the sprouting trays near the window of an unoccupied bedroom or a box-room or beneath the skylight of an attic, provided that you open the window or skylight on sunny days and cover the trays with newspapers when there is sharp frost at night. I myself use a cold frame for the purpose and mat it heavily during frosty nights. If the frost seems likely to be severe and prolonged, I bring the trays indoors temporarily. On sunny days I take the light off the frame: sprouting potatoes want a temperature of about 40° F., not higher, and frames soon heat up in the sun. So unfortunately does an unheated greenhouse while a heated greenhouse is totally unsuited for the job. Too much heat makes for spindly shoots: you want short, plump, sturdy shoots. In the light of these points you will probably be able to work out the best plan for sprouting your own sets to suit your own particular conditions. Keep a watch for greenfly during sprouting and, if necessary, spray with soft soap or derris. Destroy any sets which show signs of disease – tubers with damaged skins are particularly liable to go rotten during sprouting.

Of course, all sprouting is intended to be started early in the year – late January or February – when you should normally get delivery of your seed potatoes from the seed merchant. But sometimes, owing to late ordering, frosts, transport delays, and other causes, people don't receive their seed potatoes until planting time – and it's too late to start sprouting them then. So the only thing to do is to plant the sets as they are, remembering to set them upright with the eye-end at the top; if you let them fall on their sides you will get a forest of unwanted, crowded growths coming up later.

Whether you intend to sprout the sets or not, you must not leave them for any substantial period in the bag in which they are delivered to you. Unpack them at once, put them in a single layer in a box, and give them light and air.

The only exception to the general rules given above arises out of the fact that some varieties (e.g. Di Vernon) begin to sprout very early so that the shoots are much too long by planting time: they should be only 1 to 1½ ins. With such varieties it is quite legitimate to hold them back for a period by keeping them in a cold, dark place so as to discourage precocious shoot formation.

Cutting Large Tubers

Until 1939 seed potatoes were nice little chaps about the size of a bantam's egg, and there was no need whatever to cut them in two; the practice of cutting the seed was confined to those who saved their own, and had only large tubers, and to those enthusiasts who had nothing better to do than vie with one another to see who could grow the biggest crop from the least number of tubers – an achievement of no value to anybody when there is no shortage of seed potatoes.

But now under Government regulations the public is forced to accept seed potatoes for planting which will pass through a 2¼-ins. riddle. The question then arises whether the largest tubers should be cut into two or more pieces and the answer is that, if you have a sufficient number of uncut tubers to plant the whole of your rows, no purpose is served by cutting any of them up because that will merely land you with a surplus of either whole tubers or parts of tubers which you have no room to plant. But if you are actually short of seed it will certainly pay you to provide the required number of additional 'sets' by cutting up some of the largest tubers at planting time, not beforehand. The total yield from the pieces will be much bigger than would be the case if the tuber were planted whole. The cutting should be done lengthwise, and each portion must possess at least two strong sprouts. Dust the cut surfaces with plaster of paris, Keen's cement, or flowers of sulphur in order to check loss of moisture, or, alternatively, put the two cut portions together and cover with a damp cloth until you plant. It is usually considered inadvisable to cut the variety Majestic, but it *can* be done without damage to the tuber as a result of bleeding if, after cutting, you cover the cut portions with a damp cloth for four or five days before you plant (and keep the cloth moist). Do not expose cut tubers to hot sun or drying wind at planting time and do not plant freshly cut tubers in very dry soil. Either wait until the cut surface has healed or water the drills.

Planting

In sheltered, sunny gardens and on light soil in the south of England it is sometimes possible to plant the earlies towards the end of February, but the usual dates of planting are mid-March in the south, the end of March in the midlands, and mid-April in the north and in Scotland. Traditionally the second earlies are planted in the southern half of the country, at any rate, during the first two weeks of April whilst the maincrops are got in any time from then on to the beginning of May – if planted after the middle of May yields will fall very sharply. But in this imperfect world the actual planting dates will depend on the weather, the progress made with your digging, and your available spare time. Some people count on getting the earlies in at Easter. But whatever you do, don't plant when heavy ground is wet and sticky; wait a bit until it is reasonably dry.

The snag about early planting is that the young growths are liable to be injured by late frosts. Few people have the time or are sufficiently enthusiastic to dash off to an allotment on a chilly evening when frost threatens in order to cover the potato crop up, especially as all the coverings have to be taken off the next morning. Those who *have* the time can keep straw or dry bracken piled handy to strew over the tops; or pots or cloches may be put over them; or wattle hurdles may be laid on pegs previously driven in so that they cover but do not crush the haulm. The most the average grower can find time for is to hoe earth over the shoots repeatedly as they break soil, leaving just the top leaves to 'see daylight'; this keeps off frost but unfortunately also slows down growth.

In sheltered gardens in the south of England it is possible to grow several rows of potatoes between early peas sown on 6-ins. high ridges. The peas are sown in February and staked with brushwood and the potatoes are put in about 1 March. The protection afforded by the ridges and brushwood keep ground winds off the potatoes and these will be unaffected by the comparatively light frosts we get in April and May.

As regards planting distances, so much depends on the vigour of the variety that it might be said that the distance between rows may be anything from 24 to 36 ins. and the distance between tubers anything from 12 to 18 ins. Experiments have shown, however, that, if you want the maximum yield from a given area (and have sufficient planting sets), you must plant rather closely, e.g. 12 ins. between sets and 24 ins. between the rows; but, if you are short of sets and want the maximum yield from each individual plant, you must space fairly widely, the optimum distance being 18 ins. apart in rows 2 ft 6 ins. apart. Much depends on the season, especially if it is warm and wet; for in that event plants growing widely apart will produce very large potatoes, which may not be what you want, whereas if planted closer together, they would yield smaller tubers of more uniform size.

My advice is that you experiment and plant at what experience proves to be the best distances for the particular variety you are growing.

If the sets have been sprouted, leave only two strong sprouts on each eye-end. The accepted method of planting is to take out flat-bottomed drills with a draw-hoe or spade and set the tubers upright in them, preferably on a layer of peat or leafmould. On light land the drills should be 6 ins. deep; on heavy land about 4 ins. Some people prefer a V-shaped drill, but it is easier for the beginner to draw a flat one. When planting sprouted tubers take great care not to break the sprouts off: always carry them to the planting site in their sprouting trays, not bundled into a sack or tipped higgledy-piggledy into a trug basket, and, when they have been placed in position, crumble soil or moist peat over each until it can no longer be seen.

One recommended method of potato planting is to draw a V-shaped drill a full 6 ins. deep, firm the sides, and then plant the tubers with a trowel in 6-ins.-deep holes in the bottom of the V. This means that the sets are much deeper than usual and that the first earthing consists in filling the drill with the soil already removed, leaving the surface level.

Do not plant potatoes with a dibber except on light, dry soil and even then a drill is better.

Some people, hard pressed for time, like to plant the sets as they dig the ground in spring. There is no objection to that – but use a line to keep the rows straight.

Finally there is the 'lazy-bed' method of planting. This is primarily intended to meet the case of waterlogged soil. Having dug the ground, you lay the tubers on the surface, preferably on a little well-rotted manure, and cover them with the soil obtained by digging trenches at 6-ft intervals. Lazy-bed planting is not intended to save those people trouble who are content merely to scratch the ground over and are themselves too lazy to dig the plot throughout.

Earthing up

The object of this process is threefold: firstly to keep the haulm upright, secondly to prevent the potatoes from coming out of the soil and turning green, and thirdly to protect the tubers from Blight. You do the job with a draw hoe and pull the soil up the stems of the plants. You can straddle the row as you work or you can stand between two rows and work over the tops of the plants.

You cannot earth up with lumpy soil. You must first break up the soil between the rows until it is powdery – this can only be done if it is reasonably dry. You can take the opportunity of working in a second dressing of potato fertilizer while you are preparing the soil, so that you earth up with fertilized soil.

Start earthing up when the haulm is 9 ins. high and draw up about 5 ins. of soil. Further soil may be drawn up about three weeks later; but never leave less than 5 or 6 ins. of haulm exposed, and do not attempt to continue earthing after the haulm has grown so much that you cannot walk between the rows without bruising it. The secret of successful earthing up is to start early and end early.

Leave the ridges with sloping sides. In a dry season leave a V-shaped hollow at the apex to catch the rain. In a wet season, round off the tops of the ridges to throw off rain. Don't make the slope of the sides too flat, or the top will be too narrow – the top should be fairly broad and the sides steep. Keep the soil of the ridges hoed to prevent a crust forming.

Spraying

The greatest enemy of the potato crop is blight (*Phytophthora infestans*). This is the fungoid disease which in the year 1846, by wiping out the potato crop, caused famine in Ireland, reduced its population by two millions of people as a result of the consequential starvation and emigration, and converted the politicians of this country from the protection of home agriculture to free trade.

Blight is still with us and probably always will be. It may attack any variety of potato whether or not it is marked 'Immune' in the catalogues – this immunity refers only to immunity from Wart Disease which occurs only in Scotland. The onset of blight is first marked by the appearance of dark brown or olive-black blotches on the leaves; then the whole of the foliage goes black and rotten; finally, if the infection is allowed to spread to the tubers, these may rot in store or after replanting or they may produce infected shoots and spread the disease in the following year. Blight rarely occurs in a dry summer and the disease is more common in the wetter, western half of Britain than in the drier east. If blight is a great hazard where you live you would be well advised to spray fortnightly with fungicides like Bordeaux Mixture, maneb and zineb. You need not spray the earlies but you *must* spray the maincrops. In the south-west spray at the end of June; in the south the first week in July; in the midlands and on the east coast the second week in July; and elsewhere at the end of July. The disease is most prevalent in a wet, muggy summer and if such occurs you should give a second spraying a fortnight after the first; but this should not be necessary in a dry season. The explanation of this is that the spores of the fungus cannot germinate without water and nowadays much help can be got from the B.B.C. which gives warning over the radio when weather conditions are suitable for the spreading of the disease so that spraying is necessary. As has already been said, earlies need not be sprayed. This is because the haulm is already dying and the potatoes are being lifted for use before blight is usually around. The first early, Arran Pilot, is a useful potato to choose if blight is common in your part of the country. You can start digging it in June and will keep on digging roots right through August. By late August or early September, the haulm will die. You can then dig the rest of the crop, dry and store it. Arran Pilot potatoes keep well in store until January.

Other steps you can take to combat the disease are (1) buy certified clean seed; (2) destroy all 'volunteers', i.e. tubers which got left in the ground when you dug last year's potatoes and in the next year grow up on their own; (3) lift in dry weather either fourteen days after the tops are quite dead or, if the tops are green, ten days after cutting them off at soil level. Add 'clean' potato foliage to the compost heap; burn diseased foliage; (4) burn any blighted tubers that are found in your store or clamp or if you can't burn them bury them in a deep pit.

Lifting

The haulm is green when you start digging first earlies like Arran Pilot and the foliage may be still green, too, when you start digging second earlies for use in August. Potatoes for storing are not dug until the haulm is dead, brown and brittle. As a rule the haulm of first and second earlies dies in August or early in September. Maincrop plants die down in September. If you are in any doubt whether the maincrop is ready for lifting, grub up one or two tubers and note whether the skins have set. If the skins do not rub off easily, the potatoes are ready to lift.

Lifting is facilitated if the haulm is first cut off with a sickle. Choose a dry day for the lifting and use a fork. The longer the prongs of the fork, the easier will be the lifting – there are special potato forks on the market which are designed for this particular purpose. Use discretion in driving the fork down or you will spear the potatoes; get the fork right under them, then dump the load a foot or so away and proceed to the next plant.

Do not leave the tubers on the ground any longer than is necessary to enable the skins to dry. On a fine day this will only take a few hours; in damp weather it may take two days. If rain threatens, protect the tubers from it or else move them under cover.

Storing

Before storing, examine all the tubers carefully and remove any which show signs of disease; these will not keep. Watch out especially for any that have brown blotches where the skin rubs off easily, exposing brown flesh underneath.

If you have not a very large crop, and possess a well-built shed, you should store your potatoes in the shed. You may put them directly on the floor, but it is better to cover the floor with a layer of straw, bracken, or sacking and spread the potatoes on that. They should not go more than 2½ ft deep to prevent sweating and should be covered over with straw, bracken, or sacking so as to exclude all light and prevent greening. Let as much air into the shed as you can on suitable occasions, but take great care to prevent the tubers from getting frozen. You can throw frame mats or old sacking over the heap during hard frosts or even light a small stove in the shed.

If you have no shed, but possess a cellar, you may store the potatoes there, provided that it is a fresh and airy cellar. Damp dungeons will not do. During the first few months of storage you should keep the door open (and the window too whenever the weather permits). You may put the tubers on a *dry* earth floor; but if the floor is damp, spread them on straw in a layer not more than 10 ins. deep, or put them in boxes stood on bricks. Cover them over to keep the light out and protect from frost, as already recommended in the case of tubers stored in sheds.

In the last resort, the household larder will serve as a potato store. Except that it is usually more convenient to put the tubers in bags or boxes, the rules for storing in a larder are no different from those governing storage in sheds or cellars.

All stored tubers should be examined fortnightly and any showing traces of disease should be at once removed.

Growing Potatoes under Glass

Potatoes are a pure luxury when grown under glass; but if you have sets saved from your own crop and room to spare in the greenhouse there is no reason why you should not treat yourself to this luxury. You can start in the middle of November and will get your first 'new' potatoes in about 10 weeks.

Sprout the sets before planting and rub off all except the two strongest shoots. The sprouting trays should be lined with moist peat and the same material should be packed between the sets.

Pots ranging from 8 to 12 ins. in diameter are most suitable. One set is sufficient for each pot, but some people prefer to put three into the 12-ins. size. Or you can get five sets into a box 4 × 1 × 1 ft deep.

You can use an ordinary compost of loam, leafmould (or preferably old mushroom-bed manure) plus sand, and a little bonemeal.

But far better results are obtained from a mixture of equal parts of *either* old potting soil and sphagnum peat *or* loam and sphagnum peat with a dash of sand. If you have any superphosphate of lime and sulphate of potash you can add to each barrowful of compost a 5-ins. potful of these two fertilizers mixed in the ratio of 3 to 2.

Only half fill the pots and cover the sets with an inch or two of compost. Add more compost (or plain granulated peat) as the haulm grows until the pots are full. Don't ram the soil, but make it only moderately firm. Water sparingly, especially at the outset. Insert a few short pea-sticks, or use canes and raffia, to keep the haulm upright. Nitrogenous fertilizers are to be avoided (they spoil the table quality), but a stimulant consisting mainly of potash and phosphates will do good.

A high temperature is not desirable: 45–50° F. is a good level to aim at, with plenty of fresh air when the weather permits. But a higher temperature of 60–65° F. can be used at the outset to encourage growth. An occasional dusting with sulphur will keep the haulm free from disease.

You don't gather the crop all at once. Carefully turn each plant out of its pot, take the biggest tubers which are usually found congregated round the outside of the ball of soil; fill the hollows thus created with fresh soil and replace the plant in its pot to go on growing. (This operation can only be performed successfully if you start with an absolutely clean pot.)

Early potatoes may also be forced in heated frames by planting sprouted sets 3 ins. deep and 9 to 12 ins. apart in rows 12 to 15 ins. apart. This may be done any time from December onwards. No great warmth is either necessary or desirable, and a hotbed which is already beginning to lose its heat will prove more satisfactory than a freshly-made bed. The compost used for filling the frame should be 9 to 12 ins. deep and consist of three parts of light sandy loam mixed with one part of peat or leafmould. Air should be given whenever possible, but the frame should always be closed early in the afternoon. Water should be given in great moderation and should be at the same temperature as the frame; no water must be given after the haulm has begun to turn yellow. No earthing up is necessary in the ordinary sense of the term, but a top-dressing of warmed soil can be added to the soil in the frame when the haulm is about 9 ins. high.

Exhibiting Potatoes

The method of raising potatoes for show purposes is really no different from that of growing good potatoes for the kitchen except that special care is necessary. Start with sprouted egg-sized tubers, no cutting allowed. Plant in March in trenches 2 ft wide, 6 ins. deep, and 3 ft apart, lined with well-rotted manure or compost. Set the tubers 2 ft apart on a mixture of sifted peat, leafmould, old crumbly manure, and discarded potting soil and cover with the same mixture. Do not let any potato fertilizer touch the tubers; do not walk on the trenches when earthing up; use stakes and string to keep the haulm upright; thin out weak, spindly shoots as they appear; keep the ridges well hoed up to prevent greening; turn a fine spray from the hose on to the ridges during dry spells; take all the usual precautions against soil pests, slugs, blight, and scab.

Headaches begin when lifting time comes along. Do not believe anybody who cheerfully assures you that a 30-ft row of each variety will see you through. You require either twelve (for a collection) or six (for a single dish) average-sized, shallow-eyed, *matching* tubers of good shape – not specimens that narrow down abruptly at the stem end or that have the rose end narrower than the other – and, believe me, you can dig a whole row easily without finding more than five such specimens.

It is most important not to leave the tubers so long in the ground that they become too large and heavy and possibly ill-shaped. Sometimes you find the specimens you want while digging for household use and, provided the ground is free from slugs and other pests, can rebury them until wanted – but don't forget to mark the site where they are! Otherwise it is generally necessary to lift the whole crop in August. Handle the tubers as carefully as if they were eggs, place them in a bucket lined with sacks and cover with fine, soft, dry sand or, better still, dry vermiculite. Store in a cool, dark place – it is essential to avoid greening and, by the way, the smooth-skinned varieties 'green' more rapidly than the netted ones.

Skins are usually still very tender at this season, so take extreme care in washing, using a soft sponge and water containing some shredded soap. Be prepared for a few unpleasant surprises when the dirt comes off! Dry by patting with a soft cloth, then wrap in tissue and keep dark until you stage – rose end outwards.

Pointing by the judges is at the rate of a maximum of 4 points each for (1) *condition* – must be clean and clear-skinned, undamaged with no speckles or patches on the skin; (2) *size* which must be medium, not very small or very large; (3) *shapeliness*; (4) *eyes* which must be few and shallow; (5) *uniformity*.

Potato Scab

Potato Scab can be a nightmare to the exhibitor and a headache to the farmer who cannot get a good price for badly scabbed tubers either as ware or as seed, because affected tubers are more liable to rot in store than those with sound skins. Scab is also a blow to the *amour-propre* of the gardener who can take no pride in produce that looks mangy; but from the purely practical outlook of the housewife all that is wrong with a scabbed potato is that you have got to peel it before you can cook it, and you may have to peel deeply which involves wastage.

There are two types of scab, Common Scab and Powdery Scab; but, except in severe cases and where there is accompanying malformation, I doubt whether the average gardener could distinguish one from the other. Both types are caused by micro-organisms in the soil, Common Scab being due to a species of Actinomyces which is most prevalent in dry seasons and Powdery Scab to *Spongospora subterranea* which revels in wet weather and poorly-drained soil. It is a proven fact that you cannot get scabbing in sterilized soil and this should dispose once and for all of the old wives' tale that it is caused by the presence of lime, ashes, or other gritty substances which tickle the poor potato's skin. The real reason why lime has been blamed is the fact that actinomyces strikes most viciously in chalky soils or in land which has been rendered alkaline by excessive applications of lime or soot or by the use of unbalanced fertilizers.

The actual scabbing, which takes the form of the development of spots of loose corky tissue on the otherwise smooth skin of the potato, is in the case of Common Scab merely the tuber's way of expressing its resentment to attack by actinomyces (just as you or I may get bumps on our faces after we have been savaged by gnats), but in the case of Powdery Scab the disfigurement is an actual fungoid growth.

Now, curiously enough, actinomyces, which feeds upon decaying vegetable matter under neutral or acid soil conditions, has no particular liking for the potato and only attacks it when deprived of its accustomed natural food. That is why Common Scab is most prevalent on light sandy or gravelly soils which are hungry and poor in their content of live organic material. The remedy is obvious: incorporate more organic matter. If the area is large enough, sow a crop of rye, mustard, or vetches and dig it in while it is green – or use a cultivator. In the smaller garden dig in green bracken or nettles in autumn or dig in just before planting time decayed leaves, spent hops, garden compost, or lawn mowings (1 barrowload to 4 sq. yds). Alternatively, spread grass in and around the drills when the potatoes are planted and cover it in when you earth up – but do not line the drills with great wads of new-mown grass as it may heat up and cook your potatoes prematurely.

It may be pointed out that in cases where lawn mowings and compost have been used plentifully without getting rid of scab the presence of the scab must be due, not to a hungry soil, but to an alkaline one, and in such circumstances it is necessary to discontinue liming and the use of soot or any alkaline fertilizer and counteract the alkalinity by applying heavier dressings of garden compost to which no lime was added when it was being prepared. It may take a few years to reduce the soil alkalinity and in extreme cases it is desirable to keep potatoes off the affected land for as long an interval as possible. Heavy applications of garden compost will not cure Potato Scab when this is due to bad drainage – that is why it is often worst at the ends of the rows where the soil gets most consolidated.

Finally, remember that some varieties are much more resistant to scab than others; do not plant scabbed seed unless it has been previously disinfected with Burgundy Mixture; and do not throw peelings from scabbed ware potatoes on to the compost heap or put them in a pig bin unless you have boiled them.

Other Potato Troubles

Potatoes are subject to various virus diseases, notably Mosaic and 'Curl' or Leaf Roll in which the leaves curl and become harsh and leathery and the plant is stunted. You can avoid these diseases if you purchase certified seed and do not persist in saving your own.

Dry rot has already been referred to. It is a fungus which gains entry to the tuber through wounds at lifting time and, after making sunken brown patches covered with tufts of white mould, causes the tubers to shrink and become hollow, hard, and dry. In the case of bought seed you can detect affected tubers in the sprouting tray and either burn or bury them: in the case of your own crop, avoid wounding, bruising, and abrasion at lifting time.

Do not ever plant a tuber (or any part of a tuber) showing signs of dry rot as it will only result in a gappy crop. Gaps can also be caused by planting sets affected with either Black Scurf, which looks like bits of dirt which won't wash off, and Stem Canker; but neither fungus is likely to trouble you if your land is properly drained and you buy certified seed and sprout it before planting. A much more serious cause of stunted or dying plants and diseased tubers is the eelworm in the form of either the potato root eelworm or the potato stem eelworm. There is no means of killing these microscopic pests except by starving them out and when they cause land to become 'potato-sick', it is nearly always due to the same site having been used for potatoes year after year. If you practise a proper four-year rotation for potatoes in your garden or on your allotment, you have little to fear. But as additional precautions you should always destroy self-sown potato plants ('volunteers' or 'groundkeepers') and you should never grow outdoor tomatoes as part of a rotation with potatoes.

Wart Disease causes warty, tumour-like growths on the tubers, light in colour and resembling cauliflower curds at the outset, but later on becoming brown or black and putrid. Recent regulations prohibit the growing in gardens and allotments of susceptible potato varieties. There is, therefore, little likelihood of your meeting this very serious disease provided that you plant only certified 'seed'.

Lastly, there are one or two physiological troubles which affect the potato and the most common occurs in years when a dry period is succeeded by a spell of very wet weather and some potatoes are apt to develop hollow hearts while others indulge in what is known as 'second-growth' and, instead of the main tubers continuing to swell, large numbers of fresh tubers form, resembling strings of beads and lacking size or usefulness. Alternatively, the main tubers may begin to grow secondary potatoes out of themselves and thus become malformed – most 'freak' potatoes owe their origin to this cause. One effect of wet weather on some varieties is that the potatoes stop growing and all the energies of the plant go into the formation of leafy top-growth – you then get only a light crop of small tubers; this is particularly apt to occur in heavy soils. Some varieties have a definite tendency towards one or other of these forms of non-productiveness; but they will not necessarily give way to this tendency, as it all depends on the weather.

Soapiness in cooked potatoes is a more or less inevitable result of lifting the tubers before they are fully mature; and a sweet taste can result from storing at a temperature below 45° F. The latter can sometimes be eliminated by keeping the potatoes in a very warm kitchen for a week before cooking them.

Nobody has yet discovered why some potatoes go black when cooked but it has been suggested that it results from errors in manuring and in particular the misguided and unnecessary use of excessive or unbalanced amounts of chemical fertilizers. It is possible, however, to prevent most tubers from blackening if they are peeled on the day previous to that on which they are to be eaten, placed in a bowl and covered with clean, cold water. On the following morning change the water and, when the time comes to cook them, put the potatoes straight into boiling water to which a little vinegar has been added, *not* into cold water which is then boiled up. Immediately they are cooked, remove them from the saucepan, strain and mash, and serve as soon as possible. Do not leave them in the pan unmashed for even a minute.

Pumpkins

See Squashes

Radishes

Radishes have been cultivated in China and Japan from time immemorial and, after finding their way to Europe (where the Greeks had them in the days of Aristophanes), have been eaten in England since long before 1500. Their Latin name *radix* means just 'root' and it is curious that radishes of all vegetables should alone have been called 'roots' whilst other root vegetables acquired distinctive names.

In theory you can grow radishes in any month of the year but I have difficulty in believing that many readers have such a passion for this somewhat indigestible salading that they really want a continuous supply of it, although admittedly some housewives use it extensively as a garnish. Apart from this, however, radishes simply will not form bulbs either during the very short days of December or when the temperature remains consistently above 55–60° F. throughout the twenty-four hours, as it often does outdoors in summer and under glass in spring. So far as outdoor radishes are concerned, therefore, I advise against sowing between the beginning of June and the middle of August, or without protection after the third week in September, and except in particularly favoured areas I cannot see that any useful purpose is served by sowing under cloches in November or December.

This crop appears to be the despair of many amateur gardeners. They complain bitterly that they sow with infinite care and get nothing but small stringy roots, while their next-door neighbour simply throws the seed in anyhow and gets an abundance of delicate, succulent, nicely shaped radishes! I think that there would be fewer complaints of this nature and fewer failures if only growers would appreciate that the radish needs to be sown very thinly on rich soil and grown quickly with the aid of ample moisture and some protection from severe frost as well as from the scorch of the summer sun. The ground must be broken up to an extremely fine tilth; there must not be a single lump in the top 6 ins. Do not add any animal manure, but work in half a bucketful of sifted leafmould or very ripe sifted garden compost, and give a 4-oz. dressing of hoof and horn meal to every sq. yd. Granulated peat may be used to increase the moisture-holding capacity of the soil (one of the finer grades is the most suitable for this purpose; alternatively fine vermiculite can be used). The soil must contain adequate lime and, if a stimulant is needed to speed up growth after a check, there is nothing better than Peruvian guano.

About 6,000 radish seeds go to the ounce and a packet of 500–600 seeds ought to be sufficient to sow 30 ft of row and should produce at least 300 good radishes (i.e. 2 dozen small bunches or 1 dozen large ones). Pulling from each sowing will not extend over more than a fortnight. It will be obvious therefore that a steady supply of radishes without wastage involves the making of small, successional sowings at intervals of approximately fourteen days, the area devoted to each sowing being calculated in accordance with household requirements.

Some people advocate sowing broadcast by scattering the seed haphazard over the prepared bed; but I do not recommend this practice to the amateur because the broadcasting of radish seed is in the nature of a skilled operation which, unless capably performed, merely adds to the labour of thinning. Other enthusiasts tell us that we should space out each seed separately, a chore which would be practicable if one were growing a dozen or two plants; but since radishes are useless unless you have plenty of them, the individual spacing of the seeds is a mere counsel of perfection. Therefore sow as thinly as possible (twelve to fifteen seeds to the foot) in ½-in.-deep drills 4 ins. apart and thin the seedlings almost as soon as they can be handled; in even the most carefully prepared drill some seeds are bound to roll up against others and one simply cannot afford the time to steer them all into their exact positions. The really important thing, when sowing radish seed, is to make sure that the bottom of the drill is absolutely level, so that all the seeds are covered with exactly the same depth of soil, which should never be more than ¾ in.

In the mildest parts of the country the first unprotected outdoor sowings can often be made in February on a sheltered south-facing border backing on a wall or fence and preferably sloping towards the sun – branches of evergreen, laid lightly over the drills on very cold nights, will serve as a protection in case frost should develop. It is a common practice in Worcestershire to sow even earlier, at the very beginning of January, on warm sunny banks and in sheltered situations between fruit trees. Screens are erected to keep off cold winds and the beds are covered with wheat straw immediately after sowing. The straw is raked off to the side of the bed as soon as the seedlings appear but is replaced temporarily on frosty nights and sometimes left in position on extremely cold days. The 'strawed' radishes, as they are called, are ready in about eight weeks if the weather is mild and damp; but if there is a cold, dry spell it may be the end of March before pulling can begin and most amateurs would do better to rely on cloches for the earliest radishes.

You can get five rows of radishes under a low barn cloche, sowing any time from January to March in the south and from February to April (or May) in the colder parts of the country; but it is the general practice to treat radishes as a catch-crop and either to sow between rows of early lettuces or peas under cloches or to mix the seed with that of lettuce, carrot, or onion, when sowing those vegetables, so that the radishes both mark the position of the rows and serve to thin out the principal crop. Another dodge to which cloche users resort is to sow radishes in the 4-ins. gap between the two lines of cloches in a double row. Here they get much protection from the wind and receive plenty of moisture from the rain which runs down the outside of the cloches, though they are of course not covered overhead; but the arrangement has never commended itself to me personally because I find it difficult to get at the radishes without damaging either the adjacent crops or the cloches.

If you have no cloches but possess a small cold frame you can sow in late February in drills 6 ins. apart and, given favourable weather as well as abundant light and ventilation, the radishes should be ready to pull in six to eight weeks. Similarly, you can sow in the borders of an unheated greenhouse after they have been cleared of chrysanthemums and prepared for summer tomatoes. But the best of all ways of getting early radishes is to sow in a hotbed frame in January and February in association with carrots, as this will give you radishes in about three weeks from the date of sowing and, as I have said before, the quicker its growth the better the radish. But you have to watch radishes grown in heat very carefully as they very soon pass their prime and the whole sowing must be pulled within a few days.

Early summer radishes can be grown wherever you can find a convenient spot for them – land prepared for planting with winter and spring greens is always a good place for them. For later sowings some shade is necessary but this does not mean that you can sow under a hedge or anything like that. Such a site would be too dry and the seedlings would draw up too much. One of the best places is in the shade of peas and beans; but when inter-cropping in this way take care to choose a place where the radishes will not interfere with your walking about, hoeing, weeding, and so on. At the end of the summer an open site again becomes essential and you may care to sow under cloches in September and October, if you want radishes as late in the year as your district permits.

In many gardens birds wreak havoc with radish sowings other than those under glass. They pull out both the seeds and the very small seedlings but show little interest in the larger plants. Protection may be given by means of small-mesh wire netting or black cotton, or bird scarers may be used, but quite an effective dodge is to strew lawn mowings over the plot when these are available.

After April the flea beetle may be troublesome, and you must either use derris dust or, in dry weather, keep the radishes well watered. If you encourage the plants to grow quickly there will be little flea beetle damage. Apart from that, nothing is likely to go wrong with your radishes if you keep them always moist and protect early sowings from chill and checks. As a rule, watering will be needed in the case of all sowings after February, whether outdoors or under glass.

Radishes must not be left in the ground after they reach a usable size, especially if the soil is inclined to be dry. If allowed to make further growth they get woody and hot-tasting and become hollow inside.

GIANT RADISHES

These are slow growing and attain a considerable size. Seed is sown in July or August in drills 6 ins. apart and the plants are thinned to stand 6 or 9 ins. apart. The roots may be left in the ground to be dug as required or may be lifted and stored in sand in November and December. They keep for a considerable period and are eaten sliced, not whole. These sorts also require plenty of moisture, otherwise they get tough and stringy and excessively hot in flavour. A dressing of soot helps the young seedlings and nitro-chalk in September (3 oz. per 30 ft run of drill) will hurry them on so that they make good before winter.

Rosemary

In botany this herb has retained its original Latin name of *rosmarinus* (sea dew). The type more usually grown is *Rosmarinus officinalis*, a decorative shrub with leaves, green on the upper side and greyish white beneath. The flowers are blue or blue/mauve. Flowering starts in March or April and continues on and off until September. To some the scent of crushed rosemary foliage is something like ginger; to others there is a nutmeg cum pine needles aroma. The flavour of the leaves is rather bitter with a hint of camphor. It is believed that the Saxons knew rosemary but somehow it became 'lost' in Britain until Queen Philippa's mother, the Countess of Hainault, sent plants to England during the fourteenth century. According to legend, the flowers were originally white, but changed to blue during the Flight into Egypt when the Blessed Virgin hung her freshly-washed sky-blue cloak over a rosemary bush to dry.

In ancient times rosemary tea was recommended for failing eyesight and Culpeper (1616–54) mentions this use of rosemary, and adds that it helps a weak memory and quickens the senses.

Oil of rosemary is contained in Eau de Cologne. The oil is also used in the soap industry. The leaves were often used at funerals in lieu of the more expensive incense, thus the old French name for the herb was 'incensier'. Rosemary was also carried in posies to ward off plague and fevers. The leaves may be used in a wet or dry pot-pourri mixture and after drying may be mixed with dried mint, thyme and tansy and freshly ground cloves as a moth deterrent in the wardrobe.

The best site for rosemary is a sunny, sheltered spot. The soil should drain well and preferably be somewhat sandy. If your soil is chalky rosemary will not reach its maximum height of 6 ft but the foliage should be more fragrant. Rosemary can be propagated from seeds sown in spring but it is more usual to start off with rooted cuttings. If you cannot obtain these locally, write to Dorwest Herb Growers, Shipton Gorge, Bridport, Dorset. When you have an established bush you can propagate from it quite easily by taking 6 ins. to 9 ins. cuttings of mature shoots in September or March and planting them where they are to grow.

As well as being grown as single specimens, rosemary may be used as a yard-high, evergreen hedge. Plant young bushes at 18 ins. apart in March or April. To keep the hedge compact and at the same time to ensure that there will be flowers in the following season, cut back all shoots by a few inches in late May or June. Dry the clippings and then strip off the leaves for use.

Most herb plants are singularly free from any pest or disease troubles and rosemary is no exception.

Rhubarb

'Rha-barbarum' was the name given by the Romans to the purgative root which they imported from the barbarians who lived by the river Rha (or Volga); but the plant is known to have been cultivated in China as early as 2700 B.C. It was used solely for medicinal purposes until the eighteenth century when some brave housewife tried using the stalks in tarts. Their food value is not high. The leaves are highly charged with oxalic acid and killed off a great many people who ate them during the First World War.

Although, from the point of view of the average household, rhubarb is the most important permanent kitchen garden crop, it is all too often relegated to a dark, out-of-the-way corner and there neglected until senile decay sets in; but this is not the way to grow good rhubarb. The crop demands good, deeply-dug soil, enriched with stable manure or garden compost, wood ashes, and bonemeal, in an open situation with some shelter from north and east winds; and the roots should be planted in November, February, or March, 3 ft apart, with 2 ins. of soil over the crowns. The planting holes should be big enough to take the roots easily without being bent or cramped. After planting, tread the soil firm and prick over the surface so as to leave it tidy. About half a dozen plants will keep you well supplied with natural rhubarb for many years to come provided that you treat them properly; but if you want to get earlier pullings of rhubarb by covering the crowns where they grow you will need more roots because such forced roots will only yield light pullings the following summer.

It is possible to raise your own stock of rhubarb from seed, though this is not a course that I ordinarily advise because, like all perennials, when raised from seed, rhubarb does not come absolutely true to its parentage and you need to be somewhat of an expert to rogue the seedlings properly. Raising the seedlings is also rather a troublesome job and the days are long past when the Royal Society would give you a solid gold medal if you could induce one hundred rhubarb seeds, smuggled from China with the aid of the Tsar of Russia, to germinate and grow.

However, if you elect to take this course because of the financial saving involved, I advise you to sow seeds 1 in. apart either in a heated greenhouse in February or in a cold frame in March, pricking out when the seedlings have made four leaves, either into 4-ins. pots or, at 6 ins. apart, into fairly deep boxes or into a made-up bed in a frame or into the open ground under cloches. The seedlings are planted out in temporary quarters outdoors without protection about the third week in April and at the end of the season the vulgar-looking and unpromising wasters are destroyed, the remaining plants being set out permanently the following spring. You can of course also sow in 1-in.-deep drills outdoors in late March or April when you will get a multitude of seedlings which will not be big enough to rogue until the following year. You thus lose a year in making your permanent plantation, though you can pull a lot of edible stalks from the rejected specimens before you throw them away. Otherwise you must wait until your permanent plantation is a year old before you pull any sticks, unless you grow what is known as 'perpetual' rhubarb which is not a first-class rhubarb but a good second-rater which will give pullings in the second year after sowing. Incidentally, pullings of this type of rhubarb can be had at most seasons of the year (but not from the same plants) if you give protection in autumn and winter – cold makes the stalks stringy and tough.

So much for rhubarb from seed, and I still hold that the best method of starting a rhubarb plantation is to buy one-year-old planting roots of named varieties. These must not be pulled the first year, and should be asked to provide only a few sticks the second year – but you do know what you've got!

Rhubarb is a gross feeder. The plants should be mulched with well-rotted stable manure or with garden compost applied generously, after pulling has ceased each season.

Don't impoverish your rhubarb plantation by underfeeding and overpulling. It is a shame to go on pulling until there is nothing left to pull. Pulling should be limited to a period of three months from the date the first sticks were ready; indeed it is a good old rule that you should stop pulling rhubarb as soon as the gooseberries come in. Remove all flower stems that may appear and if you want stalks for making wine, grow separate plants for this purpose and don't pull before summer. When the leaves begin to yellow, however, you may take the stalks for jam.

Always gather rhubarb by grasping the stem low down and pulling outwards and twisting simultaneously; the stick should come away complete with its basal bud. Spread the pulling over all the plants; don't leave any plant with less than three or four strong stems; and don't pull young stems with partially unopened leaves.

However well rhubarb is treated, the day will come when the quality of the sticks begins to fall off. The clumps must then be lifted and divided, preferably by sawing them up, the strongest of the divisions, each with one or two buds, being replanted in the fallow. It is well to anticipate this evil day by excavating and dividing some of the older plants – no light job! – before the operation becomes inevitable; then there will be no gap in supplies whilst the divisions are re-establishing themselves.

Forced Rhubarb

So far I have dealt only with 'natural' rhubarb, i.e. rhubarb grown naturally out of doors. You can get earlier supplies from the outdoor plantation by covering the crowns in December, preferably after a hard frost or two, with tubs, barrels, or boxes not less than 2 ft deep and heaping a mixture of manure and dead leaves over all; or you can simply cover with grape barrels, large boxes or old, clean metal drums without any fermenting material. In the former case your tubs, barrels, or boxes must have movable lids so that you can inspect without scraping away all the manure and leaves, and pulling will be brought forward by at least five weeks; in the latter case the date of first pulling will be advanced by approximately three weeks.

It is a different matter if you force the roots indoors and this method can be a somewhat expensive and unprofitable business unless you go the right way about it. Some people buy forcing roots from a nurseryman. These roots are not cheap and with the cost of the fuel used for forcing them in your greenhouse, the results are not profitable.

On the other hand, from a properly laid out plantation, you can have plenty of forced rhubarb at practically no cost at all subject to a waiting period of two, or at most three, years from the date of planting.

Mark out a patch of ground six yards square and divide it into four strips, each 4½ ft wide. Label them 1st year, 2nd year, and 3rd year and leave the fourth blank. Move the labels on every year so that they correspond with the actual age of the plants.

Now buy roots of an early variety of rhubarb, known to be suitable for forcing. If these turn out to be small divisions with a single bud apiece, you will need seven of them; plant six in the strip labelled 1st year, spacing them 32 ins. apart, and put the other in the unlabelled strip. If, however, you can obtain strong two-year-old roots, buy eight of them and plant six in the 2nd-year strip; then split up the others to give you six plants for the 1st-year strip. Alternatively, if you want to save money, you can purchase only two two-year-old roots and split them all up; this should give you seven divisions each with one bud but, of course, you will then wait an extra year for your first plants for forcing.

During the following year you will pull no rhubarb and can use the vacant area of the plot for other crops until November, when you must buy and plant another six roots in what will now be the new 1st-year strip. By the second year you will have either eighteen plants made up of six each three-year, two-year, and one-year, or thirteen plants made up of seven two-year and six one-year, all according to the number and age of those you started off with. In the former case you will force five of the three-year-olds and propagate from the sixth; in the latter case you will allow five of the two-year-olds to grow on and will propagate from the other two. (You can get more divisions from a three-year root than from a two-year one.) But you can take a light pulling from both second- and third-year plants during the summer.

Once you have built up your stock of eighteen plants of three different ages it becomes a routine matter of forcing five three-year-olds every winter and using the sixth to provide new stock. A different strip has a rest from rhubarb each year to allow for digging and manuring and to avoid soil sickness.

The best place for forcing rhubarb is beneath the staging of a heated greenhouse. It is desirable to drape sacking so as to cut off as much daylight as possible, as this improves the quality of the sticks. Direct heat from hot-water pipes must be screened off by means of boards. Either stand the roots close together on a few inches of manure and soil and then cover with fine soil until only an inch of the crown remains exposed, or pack the roots in deep boxes with some damp moss, moist peat, or old potting soil and invert a second box over the first to exclude light. If no greenhouse is available a place may be found for these boxes in the dwelling-house. A steady temperature of 45–50° F. is needed until growth is well away, when the crop may be finished at 60° F. Above 60° F. the sticks lose colour and firmness.

Watering must receive regular attention. Incidentally, it is generally recommended that the roots for forcing should be lifted and left exposed on the ground to all manner of weather conditions, including frost, for some weeks before being brought indoors.

Roots should be forced successionally from December to April and it takes about five to seven weeks from the commencement of forcing before the first sticks are ready to pull. Do not waste time by replanting forced roots: any attempt to re-establish them nearly always results in failure. The roots will rot down well if placed right inside a fairly large compost heap.

Sage

Salvia officinalis is a native of the sunny Mediterranean and was introduced into Britain in 1597 but, as might be expected, it thrives only in the warmer parts of the country; in cold areas it will do no more than exist, rather miserably. There are flowering and non-flowering sorts and the latter are by far the best economic proposition from the culinary point of view because any plant that flowers must inevitably do so at the expense of leaf production.

Like most plants from southern Europe, sage does best in a light, well-drained soil which, if it is at all acidic, should be dressed with ground chalk (lime). Sage will not grow on cold, wet clay but, since it does not root deeply, it should be easy to make up a suitable bed for it, preferably in a position close to a path so as to avoid the necessity for trampling over cultivated ground every time you want to pick. Dig in garden compost when preparing the site and, if you have any, some shoddy.

It is possible to raise your own plants from seed sown under glass in February or March or in very shallow drills in the open ground in April or May; but the seedlings will not come true to type, and you will get a mixed selection consisting almost entirely of narrow-leaved specimens which will go to flower the following spring. Furthermore, since the seedlings must be pricked out 4 ins. apart and grown in a nursery bed until the spring of the year following sowing, when they are planted out finally, there is a long wait before you secure any pickings unless (as some people do) you treat the crop as an annual one and raise a fresh batch of plants every year. By far the better course is to buy plants of a guaranteed broad-leaved, non-flowering strain from a nurseryman specializing in herbs, and set them out a foot apart in spring, pinching off the ends of the shoots immediately after planting to ensure a bushy habit. Give the bushes a dressing of general fertilizer annually in June and discard them after three years, for they deteriorate quickly and get leggy and unsightly. You can keep up a stock by rooting 2-ins.-long cuttings in sandy soil in the open in May – there is an old adage: 'Plant sage in May, It grows night and day.' The cuttings should be taken with a 'heel' (i.e., the whole shoot should be removed with a portion of the main stem attached) and when they have rooted and are 5 ins. high the tops should be nipped out to induce them to branch. Another, and even easier, way of raising new plants from the old ones is to sift earth over a straggly bush in March so that only the green tips are left visible; then each branch will form roots and can be cut off and planted separately in June.

Sprigs of fresh sage can of course be picked at almost any time of the year when they are available. But if you want the leaves for drying it is best to cut the whole bush over twice, using a lino knife, once in June and again in August or early September: this prevents the bushes from becoming very woody. Do not cut any stem more than half-way back – the bunches sold by the greengrocer consist of long branches solely in order to make it easier to tie them together and these branches are not cut until the very end of the summer at the earliest, sometimes not until autumn is well advanced. After the second cut, apply a dressing of manure or compost between the bushes. The June cutting can often be dried by prolonged exposure to bright sunshine if you spread it out on sheets of newspaper and take it under cover every evening. The September cutting is best treated in the same way as mint and dried in a cool oven at about 90° F., either laid out thinly on a wire cake stand or tied together in quite small bunches. When it is brittle dry, strip off the leaves, powder with a rolling pin, and store in screw-topped jars.

Salsify and Scorzonera

These two vegetables are taken together because, from the gardener's point of view, they need identical treatment, while from the culinary aspect scorzonera is merely black salsify, by which name it is often known. Yet the two plants are botanically distinct and probably of different origin, though both acquired their names in Italy. The leek-leaved salsify (more properly *sassify* of uncertain derivation) is *Tragopogon porrifolius*, a native of Algeria and a relative of our wild Goat's-beard or Jack-go-to-Bed-at-Noon, *Tragopogon pratensis*, a biennial which is common in grassy places in England. *Scorzonera hispanica* on the other hand is a native of Spain. Neither has been cultivated in Britain for more than a couple of hundred years and neither is grown here except in private gardens. Salsify is biennial and scorzonera is perennial.

Both these roots may be regarded as an alternative to parsnips, from which, however, salsify differs entirely in flavour, the roots having a taste very similar to that of oysters when prepared for the table, whence the alternative name of 'vegetable oyster'; some people prefer the flavour of salsify to that of parsnips whereas some favour scorzonera which has the familiar sweet taste of parsnips. Salsify has a cream-coloured root and slender, almost grassy foliage; scorzonera has black-skinned, white-fleshed roots and pointed, oblong-shaped leaves. Good specimens of salsify are 9 ins. long and 2 ins. thick at the top; scorzonera roots are longer and not so thick.

The only practical way of growing either of these vegetables in an average garden soil is to adopt the 'crowbar' method as described for parsnips, since absolutely straight roots are essential. Sow in April or May, spacing the prepared holes 9 ins. apart and sowing three seeds 1 in. deep in each, afterwards reducing the seedlings to one per station when they are 2 ins. high. If desired, these small seedlings can be very carefully transplanted. The crop is usually ready from October onwards and in wet districts is best lifted and stored for winter use. But on light, dry land the roots may be left in the ground until required, like parsnips, and some roots of salsify may even be left until spring, when they will put up flowering shoots which can be covered with pots and fermenting material and blanched or used green. These shoots are known as 'chards' and are cut when 5 or 6 ins. long and cooked for eating after the manner of asparagus.

If scorzonera does not form sufficiently large roots the first year, it can be left to grow on for a second season.

Savoy

See Cabbage

Seakale

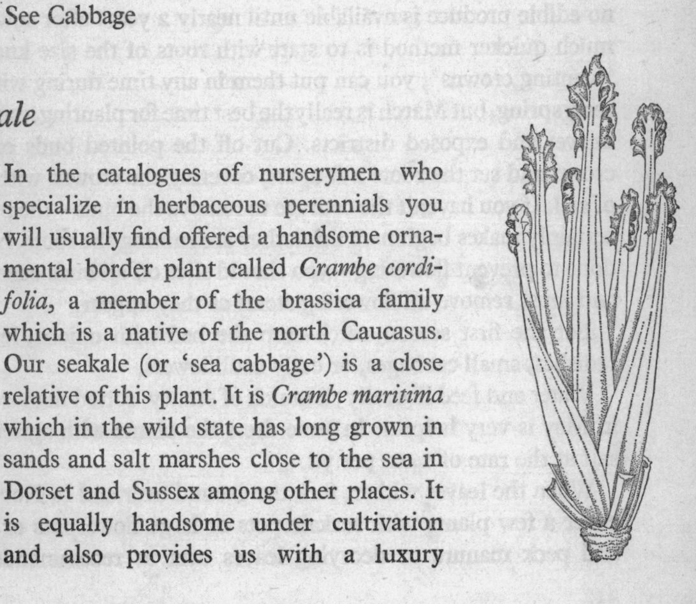

In the catalogues of nurserymen who specialize in herbaceous perennials you will usually find offered a handsome ornamental border plant called *Crambe cordifolia*, a member of the brassica family which is a native of the north Caucasus. Our seakale (or 'sea cabbage') is a close relative of this plant. It is *Crambe maritima* which in the wild state has long grown in sands and salt marshes close to the sea in Dorset and Sussex among other places. It is equally handsome under cultivation and also provides us with a luxury vegetable when its young growths are bleached or blanched in total darkness.

Seakale needs a sunny, very well-drained site, and the soil must be exceptionally rich. Bulky organic manures are best when preparing the land in winter and nothing suits seakale better than composted seaweed, if available, though farmyard manure and good garden compost will give equally good results provided that you use enough of them – at least 1½ cwt. per rod. Failing these use shoddy in conjunction with hoof and horn meal (2 oz. per sq. yd) and see that the ground is not short of lime. If you are using shoddy and fertilizers rather than manure or compost, give a dressing of Growmore fertilizer about 14 days before sowing or planting and expect to have to top-dress with sulphate of ammonia (½ oz. per sq. yd) three times during the growing season, finishing about the end of July.

The cheapest method of obtaining a stock of seakale is to sow in March or April in 1-in.-deep drills a foot apart. Thin to 6 ins. and leave till the following February or March when the roots can be dug up and put in permanent quarters. By this method, of course, no edible produce is available until nearly 2 years after sowing. A much quicker method is to start with roots of the size known as 'planting crowns'; you can put them in any time during winter or early spring, but March is really the best time for planting, especially in wet and exposed districts. Cut off the pointed buds on each crown and set the roots 2 ft apart, covering the crowns with 2 ins. of soil. If you haven't the courage to remove the buds – the practice certainly makes beginners think they are ruining the roots, but it is done to prevent flowering – you should slice off all buds except one and must remove all flowering stems as they appear.

For the first season, catch-crop the bed with onions, lettuces, radishes, small cabbages, or early cauliflowers.

Water and feed liberally; a mulch of strawy, rotted manure early in May is very helpful. In June dress the plants with agricultural salt at the rate of 1 oz. per yd.

When the leaves wither, fork the ground over and in November cover a few plants with seakale pots or large flowerpots or boxes and pack manure or decaying leaves over as recommended for rhubarb. (Experienced growers systematically collect clean leaves in advance and store them for this purpose.) This will bring along the blanched crop of growth used for eating. Another way is to surround the bed with boards and cover it a foot deep with leaves which the boards prevent from blowing about. This is a good plan when you have many trees and lots of leaves to sweep up; but the first way is better in that it allows you to blanch a few plants at a time and so get a longer season. Yet another way of blanching individual plants is to surround each one with a cylinder of wire netting or with two barn cloches resting on their ends, secure to stakes, and then fill up the enclosed space with leaves to the depth of a foot or so.

After cutting the crop and removing the coverings, put some leaves over the crowns to protect them from chill and, when the weather becomes warm, cut off all remaining small blanched shoots and cut out all except the three strongest buds. Then fork some manure or garden compost in between the rows.

If you want crowns for forcing indoors, the procedure is different. When the leaves wither you lift the roots. You will find that each has formed a lot of side-roots or thongs. Cut these off, select the straightest and most unblemished specimens as thick as or a little thicker than a lead pencil, and cut into lengths 3 to 6 ins. long. Cut the top end level and the bottom end slantwise so that you will know which is which; then tie in bundles and store in damp sand, coal ash, or fine soil until March when you replant as for bought roots and subsequently thin the growths to one. These provide your replacements. The main roots, from which you cut the thongs, are the ones you force; you store them in sand, with the crowns exposed, until you want them and throw them away after forcing.

Seakale is forced in very much the same way as rhubarb. The roots may be potted or boxed up any time from November onwards. Use 9-ins. pots, or boxes of at least the same capacity (with holes bored at the bottom for drainage), and set the roots upright 4 ins. apart with the crowns exposed. A 9-ins. pot takes six roots. Any material within reason can be used for packing round the roots – potting soil, leafmould, peat, or even half-rotted manure. Moisture and humidity are needed as for rhubarb; but temperature must be more carefully watched – 45° F. is enough and 55° F. the top limit; if you go to 60° F. you will find your seakale thin and wiry. Absolute darkness is also necessary in the case of seakale: otherwise it is bitter. It is best to invert empty pots over the pots containing the roots (or empty boxes over the boxes if that is what you're using).

Early crops take about seven weeks to mature, but after Christmas the seakale is ready in five to six weeks after planting. The roots are useless after forcing and should be thrown away.

Seakale is ready for cutting when the blanched growth is 7 to 9 ins. high. A small portion of the woody crown, about ½ in. thick, should be removed along with the top growth. It is not necessary to cut the whole of the growth in one operation: the larger outer leaves can be cut first, each with its little piece of crown attached, and the inner leaves can then be left to grow taller before cutting.

Shallots

When the Crusaders returned from Syria in the Middle Ages, they brought with them specimens of an onion which they had met with in the town of Ascalon. The latter place-name in time became corrupted into 'eschalot' and thus we got our shallot.

This crop prefers a light to medium soil, well-drained and fairly loose – it is not at all easy to grow good shallots on heavy land. Although a rich soil is desirable, the richness should come mainly from manures given to a previous crop. Do not use any animal manures or balanced fertilizers when preparing the ground; use only well-rotted compost, leafmould, and bonemeal. Shallots must not follow brassicas or lettuce or any crop subject to botrytis.

It is quite practicable to raise shallots from seed. If large bulbs are wanted (e.g., for exhibition), seed must be sown in heat in January and the seedlings hardened off in due course for planting out at the end of April; otherwise you sow outdoors in March in ½-in.-deep drills, 8 ins. apart, and thin the seedlings to 6 ins. apart in the rows. As in the case of all seed-raised crops there will be considerable variation in the seedlings and one objection to the seedling bulbs is that they cannot be replanted the following year as 'sets' because they will merely bolt. The explanation of this is that some stocks of shallot produce flowers and others don't; you can only get seed from the flowering sort and this will naturally produce plants of the flowering type because of its parentage. Therefore it is the almost universal practice to grow shallots from bulbs which have been produced as offsets.

These bulbs are traditionally planted on the shortest day and taken up on the longest. Few people ever do this, although if the ground is ready and in good condition there is everything to be gained by planting on 21 December, for the shallot is hardy and will get on with the job of making roots during the winter. Generally, planting is delayed till February or March when the ground is in good working condition. Fairly small sets, running twenty to twenty-five to the lb., are the best; if you plant bigger ones you will get a multitude of small cloves instead of the five or six large bulbs which most people aim at. Put them in 6 ins. apart, using a trowel to make a slight hollow so that they are buried to half their depth only. Do not *push* them into the ground, as so often advised, because this consolidates the soil beneath them and increases the risk of frost lifting them as well as encouraging them to 'jump' out of the ground when they begin to form roots – and of course you cannot press them back again without damaging the roots. Remove all loose skin and cut off the long, dry tops before planting, otherwise worms may drag these into the soil, thereby displacing the bulbs. Birds also seem to be fascinated by the long tops and use them to pull the bulbs out of the ground and throw them about, and cats have been known to scratch them up. Soot, applied liberally along the row is a fairly effective deterrent to worms, birds, and cats; but, if you have a few wire pea-guards or tent cloches to spare, it is always wise to place them over newly planted shallots for a week or two until the bulbs have anchored themselves to the ground.

Once the bulbs have started growth, the crop needs little attention beyond weeding and an occasional careful hoeing. As the crop matures draw the earth away from the bulbs with your fingers so as not to injure the roots and cut off any incipient flower-heads.

Lift in July when the foliage turns yellow, leaving them to ripen in a shady place outdoors for a few days, if the weather is dry, before removing them to a shed to complete their drying. Do not dry in a greenhouse or frame because the bulbs, once lifted, are subject to sun scorch which damages the base. If the weather is wet and the shallots refuse to ripen in the ground you must lift and ripen them under cover throughout. Leave a fairly long tail of dead foliage on each bulb when splitting up the clump and cleaning them up. Shallots can be kept for months in any dry and airy, frostproof place in shallow trays: or you may tie them in bundles and hang them up. But whatever you do, don't use bags to keep them in, or they will soon heat up.

It is sometimes advised that a second crop of shallots should be secured in the autumn of the same year by replanting immediately the bulbs lifted in July. It is only in an exceptional season that this experiment will succeed – as a rule the weather is too dry to induce the bulbs to start rooting and they remain dormant until October when, if they do grow, you get a large percentage of bolters and, in many cases in which the experiment has been tried, a crop of comparatively poor quality.

Shallots for Exhibition

Exhibitors have their own special strains and use planting sets just over 1 in. in diameter. The ground is prepared the previous autumn with as much care, and on the same lines, as an onion bed, though a little less rich, reliance being placed on organic manures such as bone flour, hoof and horn meal, and bonfire ash. The sets are started into growth in December in a cool greenhouse in boxes of John Innes Potting Compost No. 2 and later planted out, as soon as the weather is suitable, 12 ins. apart in rows 15 ins. apart. When top growth is well advanced in April a little light feeding is indulged in, using dilute liquid manure and sootwater, but great care has to be taken not to feed too much, as this would lead to thick necks.

When the bulbs have been dried, and the loose skins and dry tops removed, choose twice the number required to be staged and set them 3 ins. apart in a box of dry sand, turning them frequently to achieve an even nut-brown colour. Finally tie down the necks with thin raffia and a clove-hitch knot, after trimming to within 1½ ins. of the base, and stage on a plate of dry, sifted sand (in which the bulbs must not be left for more than 3 days in case they start to put out roots). Some exhibitors pare the root plate with a razor blade but this must be most carefully done if the sets are wanted for replanting the following year.

It should be noted that shallots are always staged as single bulbs, not clusters and that in a class for table shallots you need the same qualities as in the onions for which shallots serve as substitutes, namely: size, good shape, thin necks, and perfect ripening. Much smaller bulbs are wanted in a class for pickling and where these are exhibited at shows the bulbs should not exceed one inch in diameter.

Spinach

Spinacia oleracea is of Persian origin. It was first cultivated solely for its medicinal properties, but by 1551 it was being eaten by the monks on feast days and was known throughout England.

Spinach is one of the most wholesome and health-giving of vegetables; yet some people think it tastes like soot. The gardener probably thinks of it as the vegetable which holds the world's record for bolting. But summer spinach would not bolt so readily if only it were grown on well-prepared land and thinned early; it is the starved plants that are the first to bolt. Good rich soil with plenty of humus in it is essential; if you can sow on an old sweet corn or ridge cucumber bed, so much the better. In any case it is up to you to see that the ground is amply supplied with moisture-holding organic matter such as garden compost, leafmould, and shoddy. The moisture problem can also be eased by scooping out two trenches 2 ins. deep and 1 ft apart and sowing the seeds in 1-in.-deep drills drawn along the middle of each trench. This enables water to be given by flooding the gully and also conserves later applications of dilute liquid manure, when this is available.

Each corky seed capsule contains two or three seeds and it should be sufficient to drop a couple of capsules into the drill at intervals of 6 ins. Thin the seedlings to one at each station and when the young plants touch one another, remove each alternate one for use in the kitchen and leave the rest to mature at 12 ins. apart. Ordinarily spinach takes about 9 weeks from sowing to maturity in summer if it does not lack moisture; but as it is unlikely to stand more than 2 or 3 weeks after picking commences successional sowings must be made at those intervals to ensure regular supplies.

The first sowing can be made in March and sowings may be made successionally until the middle of June – there is no point in sowing after that, since there are so many other vegetables to be had in June and July. The later sowings need some shade and are never happier than when grown between two rows of fairly tall peas.

Since only a few leaves are gathered from each plant at any one time, it is necessary to sow an ample breadth to ensure a sufficient return. Too many beginners sow a single row for a large family and then cannot get a dishful or must strip the plants bare (and kill them) in order to do so. The total weight of leaves that you can hope for from successive pickings is only 5 oz. per plant, so you must work out your requirements from that.

Winter spinach is a more simple proposition: it is likely to get all the moisture it needs in the form of rainfall and it is therefore largely a matter of finding a really well-drained site for it and, if necessary, making a raised bed if there is any risk of waterlogging in winter. Trenches are unnecessary and it is better to sow continuously along the row, to allow for casualties, and to thin finally to no more than 9 ins. apart. Cloche protection makes all the difference to this crop by keeping off snow, sleet, and continuous heavy rain.

Seed should be sown from July to September except in urban districts where autumnal fogs destroy the plants in the seed-leaf stage if sowing is delayed beyond the middle of August. The season of gathering is from November to April. Take only the biggest leaves so as not to damage the plants.

If the soil is quite fertile, no fertilizer stimulants should be needed, though some gardeners like to give an early spring dressing of nitro-chalk (1 oz. per sq. yd) to help the plant spurt.

Both winter and summer spinach are gathered in much the same way. You first eat the thinnings, if any, which are pulled up whole and the roots cut off. When the main plants are ready, you take a few leaves from each. Do not strip the plants; allow as many leaves to remain as you take off. Gather the largest, fully formed leaves, but take them while they are still young and tender: it is folly to leave them to get old and tough. Take the leaves only not the stems; if you cannot nick them off with your finger and thumb without tearing the main stems, use a pair of scissors rather than spoil the plants.

NEW ZEALAND SPINACH

This is not a true spinach but a plant (*Tetragonia expansa*) with edible leaves which somewhat resemble, and can be used as a substitute for, those of summer spinach. These leaves lack the tang of ordinary spinach but on the other hand they also contain oxalic acid, as do the leaves of both summer and winter spinach, and are wisely shunned by all sufferers from rheumatism. From the gardener's point of view the principal advantage of New Zealand spinach is that it tolerates burning heat, and will therefore thrive without bolting where ordinary summer spinach will not grow. It is rather tender and must be sown in a greenhouse or a garden frame in March or under cloches or even jam jars *in situ* in April and in the former case it is planted out in May. The growth spreads and rambles along the surface of the ground so that each plant needs 3 ft of space. Light soil is necessary and the plants do well in a sunny position on a heap of discarded potting soil. Nip off any buds from the ends of the shoots and pinch long-jointed shoots; in dry weather water freely. The leaves are taken in the same way as those of ordinary spinach but owing to their being spread out over the area of a large mat it is a most laborious job to pick them. Nevertheless the plant is extremely prolific.

PERPETUAL SPINACH

A much better substitute for true spinach is provided by what is variously known as 'perpetual spinach' or 'spinach beet', which is in fact merely one of the perennial leaf beets which produces green leaves in abundance and a root that, unlike the usual beetroots, has no culinary value at all. The leaves from this plant are much larger and more fleshy than those of spinach and in many families they are appreciated as being much less trouble to gather and cook and far more substantial as a second vegetable. They do not 'cook down' to anything like the same extent as the leaves of spinach and are usually eaten with avidity by children who will not touch ordinary spinach.

This plant requires a really rich well-drained soil. Seed may be sown in March or September in drills 1 in. deep; but a well tended plantation of spinach beet will last a whole year, so that, on the whole, the March sowing is the more important one. The plants should be thinned to stand 8 to 12 ins. apart and little attention is required beyond weeding and hoeing and watering in very dry weather.

When gathering, cut off the leaves and stems close to the ground. Ordinarily you take a few from each plant but, if there are more leaves ready than you want, you must still cut them all and not allow some to grow old on the plant as this will slow down further leaf production and old leaves make poor eating. Some gardeners entirely strip very strong plants in early autumn and then give them six to eight weeks to make new foliage. Do not gather any leaves while frost is on them.

One 30-ft row is enough for an average family.

Squashes

(Including Pumpkins)

The squash is merely the American counterpart of our vegetable marrow, and squashes, marrows, and pumpkins are all members of the large family of cucurbitaceous gourds. It follows therefore that in the main essentials the cultivation of squashes and pumpkins is exactly the same as the cultivation of marrows about which I have already written fully. The big snag, however, is that some squashes (notably those for winter eating) are far better adapted to the American climate than to our own. In our short and uncertain summers only the more rapid-growing sorts get a long enough season for their proper development when sown outdoors – and then only when there is a reasonably long spell of warm weather. It pays, therefore, to extend the growing period by sowing in pots under glass. Use peat pots to prevent any shock at transplanting, remembering to tear off any *dry* portions of the pots.

It is commonly said that the word 'squash' means 'marrow', which is untrue: it is an abbreviation of the American Indian *askutasquash*, itself a perfect example of the misnomer as it means, 'eaten raw and uncooked'.

There are two sorts of squashes, winter and summer. Winter squashes originated in tropical America and must be allowed to ripen on the plants; they are harvested after the first frosts and eaten, in various ways, from store. The pumpkin is cultivated similarly and its origin is also believed to be tropical America. Summer squashes, which were first found growing in the more temperate parts of America, are eaten young and immature, like our marrows; indeed, if you let them grow too long, you may need a hacksaw to cut them. Many of them are called marrows as, for example, the Custard Marrow *alias* Yellow Bush Scallop *alias* Patty Pan Squash, and the Argentine Marrow *alias* Zapallito de Tronco *alias* Avocadella which somebody once advised me to boil, bisect, deseed, and fill with dry sherry, a suggestion which may possess more appeal to those afflicted with the palsy who cannot hold amontillado in a glass without slopping it all over the place. A certain very truthful New Yorker once assured me that even an American woman, if blind-folded, could not distinguish one variety of summer squash from another by taste alone. The difference is solely in the shape, often ridiculous, and in the knobbiness. So far as the plants themselves are concerned, you get both bush and trailing types as in the case of our own marrows.

Under good growing conditions the earliest squashes commence to bear fruit within fifty days from sowing while the latest varieties take ninety days to reach the fruiting stage. Accordingly the best course with the early sorts is to prepare stations as for marrows and sow about mid-May in the south and early in June further north, covering each sowing temporarily with either a jam jar, a cloche or a light portable frame. Alternatively, sow in peat pots in a greenhouse. With the latest sorts you can also sow in peat pots in the greenhouse but, better still, sow on a hotbed in April and remove the frame lights in June.

Stations for bush varieties should be 3 ft apart, those for trailers at least 6 ft apart unless you choose to train the latter up posts, fences, walls, or trelliswork and tie the growths from time to time to wires. When trained in this way the leader must be stopped when it reaches the limit of its support but apart from this it is undesirable to do any stopping unless a trailer sends out its leader to an unreasonable distance without producing any profitable return. Bush varieties are of course never stopped. Trailers in hotbed frames are just allowed to ramble out over the sides.

Abundant supplies of water are needed at all stages of growth and mulching can be of great help in conserving moisture in the soil; but feeding with liquid manure is not recommended because it seems merely to encourage extra leafage.

Except that mice are very partial to the seeds the only pests likely to trouble squashes are aphids and these can be dealt with by means of a suitable insecticide spray – do not use any pesticides which are known to damage cucurbits. You are more likely to get trouble with aphids if you allow the plants to be short of moisture at the roots.

The Americans cut and eat the summer squashes while they are still quite young, in the same way as the best people do our own vegetable marrows. In this country the fruits are usually available during August and September. The winter varieties are left until the first frosts, as already stated, and owing to the greater thickness of their skins are not quite so sensitive in the matter of storage as marrows and can be hung in net bags anywhere where they are safe from frosts and damp. Dryness is what they need most; they should be gathered dry and stored dry.

PUMPKINS

The pumpkin is rather a flavourless thing and is usually cooked with apples, lemons, and other fruits to render it more attractive: I am convinced that we in this country will never acquire the Americans' taste for this vegetable, however much pumpkins may continue to be grown by rural communities in other parts of Europe. Nevertheless there is a certain attraction about growing a giant pumpkin either for exhibition purposes or for charity or solely for the sake of prestige, so I will give concise instructions for the production of, at any rate, one monster pumpkin.

Pumpkins do not come absolutely true from seed, so buy the best strain you can and sow several seeds 1 in. apart and ½ in. deep on a mound of rich compost over a manure hotbed in a 6 × 4-ft frame. Shade the light until germination takes place, then thin to the strongest seedling. (If you prefer, and have a greenhouse heated to 55° F., you can raise a good plant in that, sowing in a 3½-ins. pot, as you do marrows, and then set your plant in the frame in the same way as you would cucumber plants.) As the plant grows, give it some shade from hot sun and syringe both the plant and the inside of the frame daily, just as if it were a frame cucumber but with the difference that you must give plenty of ventilation and can remove the light entirely by the end of June. Keep the soil continually moist.

When flowers appear, fertilize a sufficient number of female blooms by pressing the male blooms into them until you have got three developing fruits. Note which of these is the fastest grower and then remove the other two when they are 10 ins. long and fit to use in the kitchen. After that remove all flowers or small fruits that may appear; stop the leaders and stop all secondary growths at two leaves to secure an abundance of young foliage; peg down the growths to induce them to root into the soil.

Water liberally and feed lavishly with dilute liquid manure. Keep your prize fruit clear of the ground by slipping something smooth and strong beneath it, such as a plastic tile – not glass which would break under the weight – and take immense care not to let it get scratched even by the leaf-hairs as, when young, it will have a very tender skin.

When fully grown, pull the pumpkin off the vine complete with its stem and put it in a sunny place, protected from rain, to ripen for a week or ten days: but, whatever you do, don't hang it up by the stem which will not bear the weight – carry it around in a strong net. I am not prepared to forecast what the weight will be but you can consider yourself a proud man if your pumpkin weighs as much as 40 lb. even though there have been rare occasions when a giant specimen has topped the scale at 1 cwt or thereabouts.

Swede

See Turnips

Sweet Corn

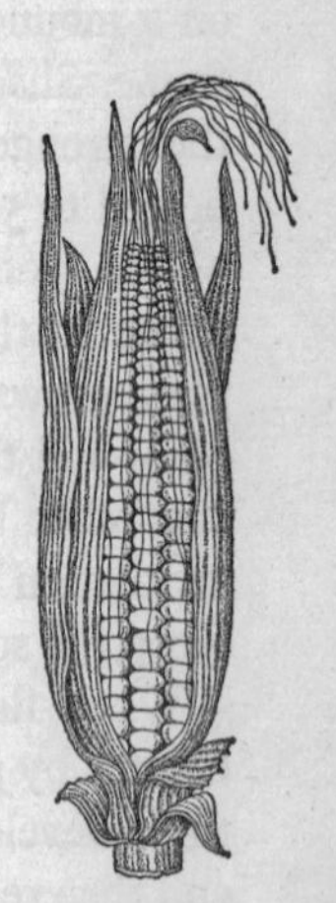

Often known as Indian corn, and the source of cornflour, maize (*Zea Mays*) is a grass which produces its seeds in tightly packed cobs. There are three main types. 'Sweet corn' has a high sugar content and the seeds are eaten in the immature state and can be very delicious. Flint and Dent maizes are starchy, tough, and lacking in flavour, and are food for poultry, pigs, and cattle.

As a plant, sweet corn has certain peculiar characteristics. It makes its growth only during the hours of darkness; it insists on producing a certain number of leaves before it will flower; and its flowers are unisexual – the male flowers appear in spikes at the top of the plant and the female flowers grow lower down.

Obviously we are up against difficulties in growing such a subject in this country, particularly in the northern counties where in summer the nights are very short indeed. If we sow early, while the nights are still long, soil and weather will be too cold (and the plants will not stand frost). If we sow under glass, maize tends to resent transplanting and in many cases remains stunted. If we defer sowing until early summer we are up against short nights and an ingenious pest known as the frit fly, which eats out the growing point.

Man's ingenuity has resolved these difficulties in two ways. In the first place, varieties have been bred which are of dwarf habit, having few leaves to make before they flower, and grow very rapidly; in the second place, cloches have been invented to keep the seedlings warm.

An open sunny site is essential, and there must be protection from high wind. In exposed gardens it pays to grow the crop in trenches about 6 ins. deep. Fresh manuring is inadvisable because any excess of nitrogen will induce an over-abundance of leafy growth. Use a general fertilizer on land that is in good heart and was manured for a previous different crop. Better still would be a generous mulch of garden compost over the whole bed.

The plants must be grown in rectangular blocks, not in long lines, in order to facilitate fertilization by the wind which blows pollen from the male flowers on to the silks. Seed should have been sown under barn cloches about the second or third week in April in the south, and about a fortnight later farther north, drawing two drills 9 ins. apart and setting two or three seeds 1 in. deep at intervals along each drill, later thinning each cluster to one plant. Varieties like Kelvedon Glory, North Star, and First of All can go at 9 ins. apart.

In colder districts where the plants have to be started in heat under glass, seed should be sown singly in 3½ ins. peat pots or in soil blocks. This is the only satisfactory way, as seedlings in clay or plastic pots rapidly become potbound and you cannot transplant from boxes.

Decloche at the end of May and earth up slightly. Keep the surface of the soil hoed and see that the plants do not lack moisture at any time – but do not over-water as this again makes for excessive leafage. An occasional shake during still weather will assist pollination. Feed moderately with tomato fertilizer. It is generally considered unnecessary to remove side-shoots.

Otherwise, apart from hoeing, the crop will take care of itself. But it is as well to earth up about 8 ins. of stem when the plants are 3 to 4 ft high to give additional support against strong winds; and you must be prepared for the fact that an abnormally cold, wet summer will most surely discourage even the best variety of sweet corn.

Each plant has male and female portions; the former are long, unattractive flower-spikes situated at the top of the plant, while the latter grow lower down and end in bunches of long, silky hairs, popularly known as 'silks'. It is the duty of these silks to catch the pollen; cobs then form beneath the silks.

The first silks should appear towards the end of June and from that time it will take two or three weeks for the cobs to develop and reach the stage at which they must be used. This is when the content of the grain or seed resembles clotted cream, as can be ascertained by unfolding the outer 'wrapper' of the cob and pressing a grain between the thumb-nails; at an earlier stage the content is watery and later it becomes doughy (and inedible). You should get one or two cobs from each plant.

Cut the cobs off with a knife or pull them away with a gentle jerk, taking only so many as you will use at once. Cook for about five minutes in unsalted boiling water; if you boil too long the corn hardens and it will be several hours before further boiling renders it tender again. The haulm of the plants makes excellent garden compost.

Swiss Chard

This name is applied to the leaf beet (*Beta cicla*) which is also known as silver beet or seakale beet. It is not a commercial crop because it is bulky and wilts about 24 hours after pulling: but it deserves to be much more widely grown in private gardens and on allotments because it is an excellent vegetable and provides a variety of dishes. The smallest and most tender leaves can be used in salads; the large green leaves are cooked as spinach (and actually taste better, and boil down less, than those of spinach beet): the fleshy white stems, up to 3 ins. across, can be used as a substitute for seakale or cooked in bundles like asparagus, while, if the plant (which is biennial) is allowed to throw up flower stems in the second year, these can be cooked and eaten in the same way as the shoots of sprouting broccoli.

Any soil will grow this crop provided that it is well-drained, in good heart, and has been well manured organically. Sow from mid-March to the end of April and again in August in drills 1½ ins. deep and 18 ins. apart, dropping in two seeds at intervals of 9 ins. and afterwards thinning the seedlings to one at each station. Water liberally throughout the growing season and feed with dilute liquid organic manure. The first sowing will begin to yield in late summer and continue until the end of October but, being perfectly hardy, the plants will stand the winter and yield further supplies in spring before going to seed in June. The second sowing will be ready for use during the following May and June.

Swiss chard is gathered by breaking off a few stems close to the base of each plant but no plant should be completely stripped of its leaves as this would kill it.

Thyme

A thyme plantation needs a well-drained, open, sunny position and does best in light, sandy, or gravelly soil. Generally speaking, it needs the same conditions and treatment as sage. It makes a good kitchen-garden edging. There are three types:

(1) Narrow-leaved French black thyme with grey foliage.
(2) Broad-leaved English black thyme with green foliage.
(3) Lemon thyme, identical with (2) except that it has a strong smell of lemon.

You should grow all of these. The best dried thyme consists of 1 part French thyme mixed with 2 parts of English black. Lemon thyme is wanted to make 'mixed herbs' and has plenty of uses of its own. Buy plants but make sure that you get what you ask for – some nurserymen seem to think that 'lemon' refers to colour, not scent.

Lime the ground well before planting 1–1½ ft apart in rows 2 ft apart. It will prolong the life of the bed if you dig in some manure between the plants every autumn; but, even so, the bushes will need replacement after five years. To increase stock take 2-ins. cuttings of the long tops of the shoots and root in a frame; or earth up a leggy bush as recommended for sage; or divide up an old bush and plant the divisions very deeply so that only the green tips show.

In order to prevent the bushes from getting leggy they should be cut over twice, once at the end of May or beginning of June before the flowers open and again in late August. Thyme is very easy to dry but less easy to powder. Rub it through a coarse sieve first, then through a finer sieve, and finally through a hair sieve.

Tomatoes

The tomato, which derives its name from the Mexican Indian word *tomatl*, is no new thing, for the Greek physician, Galen, knew all about it in A.D. 200. It was not until 1400 years later that it found its way to this country from Peru and began to be cultivated here

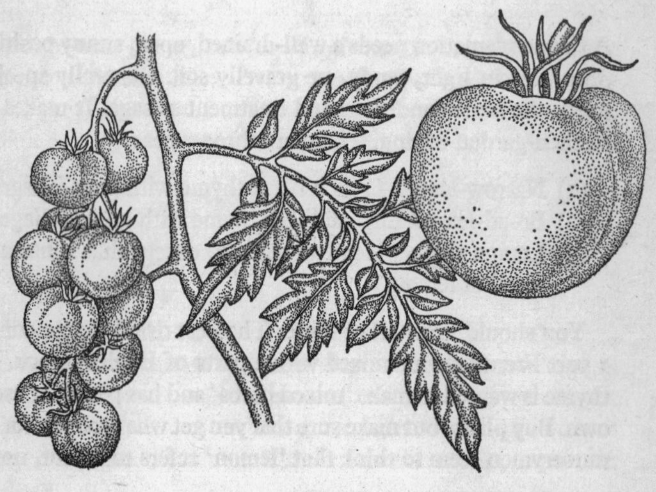

as an ornamental plant under the title of Love Apple. Nobody would eat the fruits because they were regarded as poisonous or at any rate most unwholesome

It was much the same in North America where a Frenchman, living in Philadelphia, started a campaign to popularize the tomato in 1788 and met with no success at all. It is only during the last hundred years that tomatoes have come to be accepted as an important item in our diet.

There are literally hundreds of varieties of the wild tomato plant bearing fruits which range in size and shape from large, unshapely, rough, corrugated dumplings to the grape-like currant tomatoes, no bigger than ordinary red currants. Some species bear fruits shaped like plums or cherries or little pears; some bear red fruits, others yellow ones; some make tall plants, others have a dwarf, bushy habit.

Out of this welter of wild species our hybridists have evolved the familiar modern tomato; but it cannot be too strongly emphasized that the tomato is still a tropical plant, accustomed to grow naturally under very sunny, warm, equable conditions, and that no amount of plant-breeding is ever likely to convert it into a hardy plant, fully tolerant of our colder and exceptionally capricious climate. Unless therefore it is grown under glass, its cultivation in this country must remain something of a gamble, while even under glass it can hardly be termed a straightforward crop which can be grown according to certain cut-and-dried rules like other vegetables.

Nevertheless, despite all the difficulties, it would seem that today almost everybody who gardens has a shot at tomato-growing – it has become a habit, in some cases almost a bad habit; and, judging from the many letters which they write to the press, there is still disagreement among the general body of gardeners on almost every single point connected with it. This of course is unavoidable in a country with so many different local soils and climates and a type of weather which can seldom be forecast with accuracy from day to day. It should be obvious, however, that in a general handbook of this small compass I cannot possibly deal with all the niceties of cultivation and with all the dozens of variant practices which have been adopted successfully by individuals to suit their own particular circumstances. If you want to make a thorough study of tomato-growing, you must consult one or more of the specialist books – most of them obtainable from public libraries – which devote themselves exclusively to this one subject. I can only set out briefly the basic principles of tomato-growing in the light of my own personal experience: and, in doing this, I must assume that, if you intend to grow under glass, you know all about the management of greenhouses, frames, and cloches, and the various operations that have to be performed in connection with them – if you do not, you must learn these things from other books, as they are quite outside my present scope.

Raising the Plants

Whether you are going to grow your tomatoes under glass or outdoors, with protection or without it, the method of raising the plants remains the same. The seeds are spaced out singly about ¾ in. apart in a seed box containing John Innes Seed Compost, covered ¼ in. deep, and germinated in a heated greenhouse or propagating frame at a temperature of 65°–70° F. As soon as the seed leaves have opened fully, which is usually 2–4 days after germination, each seedling is transferred separately either to a 3½-ins. pot of John Innes Potting Compost No. 2 or preferably (unless it is to be pot-grown throughout) to a soil block made from the same compost. From this stage onwards the temperature is dropped to 60°–65° F. with a further drop of about 5° F. on dull days, thus linking temperature with weather conditions. Ventilation must be given whenever possible but nothing must be done to cause any fall in the temperature of the soil in the pots or blocks. After approximately six weeks, unless the plants are fruited in the same greenhouse as that in which they have been raised, they must be gradually hardened off to withstand the temperature of their final growing quarters.

When seed is sown under poor light conditions, especially between October and January, it is necessary to sow greatly in excess of one's ultimate requirements in the matter of plants because it is often found that a high percentage of winter-sown seedlings turn out to be rogues. These rogues (often known as feather-legs or jacks) form their rough leaves prematurely and these leaves are usually ragged and close together, while the plants have a dwarf fern-like appearance. All such rogues should be discarded, for they will never give satisfactory crops, at any rate on the first two trusses. It is curious that this should happen, because it is nothing to do with the quality of the seed; seed from the same packet, sown in spring, will produce seedlings entirely free from rogues.

Apart from this elimination of rogues, it is always necessary to select only the best seedlings for planting and specimens with twisted seed leaves ought always to be thrown out at the earliest possible stage.

The poor quality of many tomatoes can often be attributed to starting off with poor plants. Only the best plants raised in ideal conditions are really worth growing on. It is all very well if you have the heat and the necessary greenhouse facilities for raising first-class tomato plants yourself: but if everybody were in that position most tomatoes would also be fruited in a heated greenhouse. In fact comparatively few gardeners have proper facilities for raising tomato plants from seed, and I always advise the others to buy first-class plants from a nurseryman, for this will not only save them much work and worry, to say the least of it, but is actually cheaper than the cost of the fuel that would be needed to heat even a small greenhouse for no other purpose than that of raising, say, a mere dozen tomato plants.

Of course, I know that many enthusiasts claim to do wonders in raising tomatoes without artificial heat (except perhaps for a small propagator) on window sills, in cold greenhouses, in frames, or even under cloches. Sometimes these claims are justified: but more frequently they prove to be examples of the natural admiration of a parent for his unprepossessing offspring. I do admit, however, that if a tomato has to be started under rather cool conditions it may still make a first-quality plant if it is grown on cool – it is a fluctuating temperature that upsets a young tomato, especially if the fluctuations are sudden and severe, as so often happens when the only source of warmth is the sun. I would add to this that nothing I have said above is intended to discourage the skilled amateur from raising his own plants in an unheated greenhouse in late May if by that date weather conditions have rendered the use of artificial heat unnecessary except perhaps occasionally at night.

Amateurs are often at a loss to know when a tomato plant is ready for planting out and it is important that they should have this knowledge, whether they raise the plants themselves or buy them from nurserymen. Generally speaking, a well-grown tomato plant, ready for planting, is about 9 ins. high, sturdy, short-jointed, succulent, and dark green in colour with the seed leaves intact, green, and turgid. You should reject long-jointed, firm, and wiry plants, indicating that they have become pot-bound, and also those with bluish-green foliage, which is a sign that they have suffered from chill. It does not necessarily follow that a plant should not be planted until the first bunch of bloom is well developed – it rather depends upon the conditions under which the plants are going to be grown. If they are going into a warm, rather rich soil in a comfortably-warmed house, they are all the better for a little starvation in pots – they will not then be so apt to produce foliage at the expense of fruit. In other words, if the plants are going into thoroughly favourable quarters, the first truss of bloom should be allowed to develop before they are planted. But if the house is on the chilly side and the compost none too good, or if they are going into frames, under cloches, or into the open ground, it is a much better practice to plant before the first truss of bloom has developed. If put out by unskilled amateurs just as the flowers are about to open, a check is liable to occur if a cold spell follows, and although the fruit will set all right upon the first bunch, the fruit above may decline to follow suit. The drain made upon the plant by the first bunch seems to stunt the plant and prevent the other fruits from growing until the first ones have been removed.

Here are a few final hints about purchased plants: do not buy plants of unknown variety; do not buy plants from boxes; do not buy plants which have stood in cold draughts on hawkers' barrows or outside shops; tell your nurseryman how you propose to grow the plants so that he may know when to send them and to what extent he has got to harden them – other things being equal, buy from a local nurseryman rather than from a distant mail order firm, thus sparing the plants the rigours of a long journey.

Tomatoes in the Greenhouse

The tomato must have sunshine and warmth: therefore a greenhouse is still the best home for it, provided that the house stands on an open site, is of fair size, well ventilated, and capable of being maintained at a minimum of 55° F. at night however cold it is outside.

If the house is overshadowed by a high wall or trees, there is nothing for it but to delay planting until outdoor weather conditions allow you to ventilate freely, as this partly offsets the disadvantage of shade. Small box-like houses with only a single ventilator, usually on the windward side of the roof, and a temperature which even the best heating arrangements cannot keep reasonably steady, will not grow good tomatoes; and those with small unheated houses, often unsuitable and sometimes filthy dirty, would do far better to grow their tomatoes outdoors under cloches. It is also possible to grow excellent tomatoes in cold frames, but surprisingly few people think of doing so.

As regards the method of culture if the greenhouse is glazed to ground level, by all means grow your tomatoes in the soil borders provided that these borders are well-drained, properly prepared, annually sterilized, periodically renewed, well charged with water by previous flooding, and adequately warmed at planting time. If you are not able to go to all that trouble, I strongly advise you to adopt the ring culture method.

If your greenhouse stands on brick walls or a timber base, you must either raise your beds to the level of the window sills or make up beds on the staging. Either method is far better than growing in pots or boxes in summer, at any rate if you are out at work all day. If you must use pots in summer, I would have nothing less than the 16-ins. size, which will take two plants, while boxes should be at least 18 × 12 × 12 ins. But in winter it is actually preferable for the amateur to grow his tomatoes in pots which need not exceed the 10-ins. size.

The table on p. 334 shows how it is possible to grow tomatoes in a greenhouse for picking at any desired season of the year; but I must add a warning that it is useless to attempt a crop of winter tomatoes except in those districts (such as the south coast) which normally enjoy large amounts of winter sunshine and in any case this luxury crop will cost the gardener a lot of money in terms of fuel. The only method of heating that is reasonably economical in winter, taking

PICKING SEASON COMMENCES	*SOW*	*PLANT*	*METHOD OF CULTIVATION*
1. January	Early July	—	Heated greenhouse. Pot culture throughout (Sunny areas only)
2. February to March	Early August to early September	—	As above
3. April	Mid-October	—	As above: final potting into 10–12 ins. pots between 7 and 15 January
4. May to June	Mid-November to end December	Mid-February to 7 March	In borders, raised beds or stage beds in a *heated greenhouse*
5. July	From 3rd week in February to end March	Mid-April to mid-May	Borders, beds, ring culture, pots, boxes in *cold greenhouse*
6. October	2nd or 3rd week in May	Mid-June to mid-July	As above
7. Late autumn, extending over Christmas and New Year	Mid-May	—	Hardened in frames, put into 10-ins. pots at the beginning of July and stood outdoors in a double row, 14 ins. apart, 18 ins. between rows. Taken into *heated* greenhouse (min. 50° F. nights) mid to end September

into account the high temperature needed, is the solid fuel boiler with hot water pipes. Gas boilers, electric immersion heaters, and electric tubular heaters are practical propositions only after the end of March, while no form of convector (which includes the popular types of oil heater) can be recommended except for occasional use in late spring and early autumn.

Soil and Manuring

Although it is none of my business in this book to teach the greenhouse-owner how to manage his greenhouse borders, the fact has to be faced that far too many beginners buy a greenhouse with the express intention of using it mainly for growing tomatoes and lightly assume that the obvious place to plant those tomatoes is in the soil on which the house has been erected. I feel that it is only fair to warn such people that the cultivation of tomatoes in beds and borders on the floor of the house is only practicable when the glass comes almost down to the ground, as in dutch light type houses, and that, even then, it does not follow in the least that the existing soil is capable of growing anything. Lack of adequate drainage is one of the most common causes of failure, the greenhouse having been set on a damp site which gets waterlogged during certain periods of the year, and in such a case artificially raised borders provide the only solution. Then I have come across cases in which an owner has suddenly decided, perhaps after a period of some years, to dispense with staging and use the soil borders which were formerly beneath the staging and have long since become sour and unhealthy. I have also seen amateurs trying to grow tomatoes in stiff yellow clay or thin sand. All such soils spell failure from the outset.

Nevertheless, given a properly drained site, it is always possible to dig out an unsuitable soil and replace it with new, imported soil, but the beginner must not imagine that this somewhat considerable labour represents the end of the matter. All soil in greenhouse borders tends to sicken after a few years, especially if it is used over and over again for the same crop; and when that crop is tomatoes the position can soon become serious because our modern strains of hybrid tomatoes are highly susceptible to a considerable number of soil-borne viruses. It is all very well for the commercial man with his large glasshouses and capital resources to steam-sterilize the soil in the borders every year. The amateur cannot do this and must resort to the laborious alternative of digging out the soil and then sterilizing it with formalin.

For this reason I strongly recommend amateurs to grow their tomatoes by the ring method instead of in soil borders. All you have to do is to remove 6 ins. of soil and fill in the bottom of the excavation with rough clinker, then cover with 4 ins. of weathered ashes and top up with pea gravel. The actual plants are grown in bottomless containers of 9 or 10 ins. diameter stood on the ash bed. Bottomless pots of various materials are now readily obtainable from sundriesmen or you can make your own out of cardboard cartons, wire netting, wooden boxes, halved apple barrels, or concrete. When grown in this way the plants make two root systems: the container is filled with feeding roots only and all liquid fertilizers are applied to the container only; the other set of roots is concerned solely with the taking up of water from the ash bed which is kept constantly moist. At the end of the season the ashes are well raked over and the beds are sterilized with Jeyes' Fluid. An even newer way of growing tomatoes in containers rather than in the soil of the greenhouse borders was introduced in 1972. This is the 'Tom-Bag' system. Tom-Bags are polythene sacks filled with Alexpeat tomato compost.

So far as the more experienced grower with established borders is concerned the very best manure for tomatoes is strawy horse manure from racing stables, applied at the rate of one bushel to every four square yards. Do not use cow manure. If you can only get horse manure rich in droppings, add some clean wheat straw to it. If you cannot get any horse manure at all, use wheat straw by itself cut into foot lengths and set almost vertically in both top and bottom spits, a pailful to each yard. Dust each layer with hoof and horn meal as the straw is being placed in position. Other alternatives are wool shoddy, or composted seaweed, or spent hops from a brewery if they are available locally. Garden compost is excellent, too, but do apply it generously.

If your borders consist of rather light, sandy stuff, stiffen them up in autumn with fresh lawn mowings (½ bushel to the yd) or sow them with rye grass which you dig in while it is green.

When the time comes to renew the soil in the borders, if you have good loamy stuff in the garden and a spare patch of ground from which to dig it, by all means use it and fill in the excavation with the soil removed from the greenhouse; but you must give the imported soil a better texture by mixing it liberally with leafmould, coconut fibre refuse, and horticultural vermiculite. If on the other hand you have to buy soil try to get a bulk delivery of good top spit from immediately under the turf of a meadow which is to be used for building. Many builders are only too glad to get rid of this material, as they have got to cart it from the site anyway, and you will often find advertisements in the local newspaper offering it for sale.

The job of effecting the changeover need not be very arduous if you take out a barrowload of old soil and return with a barrowload of new. Use sacks to prevent the two lots of soil from coming into contact with one another either in the barrow or in the greenhouse. This is just a precaution to prevent infection.

The new soil will, of course, need to be dressed with manure or garden compost after it is all in the greenhouse. If you come across any wireworms in it, pick them out. This may mean that other wireworms are present. It may be a good idea to set baits to catch them. Pieces of carrot or potato on skewers buried a few inches in the soil make good baits. Inspect periodically and remove any wireworms.

One important job in connection with tomato borders is to see that they are sufficiently watered before the season starts. Dryness, especially in the subsoil, can spell ruin to the crop and, after manuring in autumn, you may have to flood the borders in winter three times at the rate of anything from 5 to 16 gallons a square yard before you have got enough moisture in them to see you through a hot summer.

Any lime deficiency in the new material should be rectified by a dressing in early spring after checking up with a soil testing set. Then apply a proprietary tomato-base fertilizer a month before planting the crop. No tomato fertilizer need be applied if you have used lots of varied garden compost.

In the absence of soil borders, when the floor of the greenhouse is covered with concrete, ash beds (for ring culture) can easily be made up on the concrete and they can equally well be made up on a strong staging in plant houses with solid bases. If, however, you prefer a soil bed on the staging I suggest you secure a fairly heavy loam and mix it with about one quarter of its bulk of decayed stable manure or spent mushroom bed, together with a small quantity of lime rubble and the appropriate amount of tomato-base fertilizer. Go easy with the manure, as any excess will delay fruiting and result in a superfluity of leaves.

When preparing the staging to receive a soil bed the first thing to do is to increase the width of the boards nailed along the edges so that they project a good 9 ins. above the level of the slats. Then the asbestos or other covering over the slats is surfaced with a 2-ins. layer of coke or anthracite or similar material. Over this is placed a 4-ins. layer of compost. Plants for planting in the compost just described should be rather smaller than usual, not more than 5 or 6 ins. high. As the roots fill the 4-ins. layer of compost, more is added until the final layer is brought within an inch of the top of the boards. The essential advantage of this method of cultivation is that it is easy to control feeding and watering, because the root system is spreading out near the surface of the soil. Indeed the roots can often be seen on the surface, and thus food in the form of top dressings of soil and fertilizers reaches them at once, thereby preventing the tops of the plants from becoming thin and keeping the top bunches of fruit up to a good size.

Lastly, in the case of tomatoes fruited in pots or boxes or other containers, I strongly recommend the use of John Innes Potting Compost No. 3 in preference to any fancy mixtures.

Planting and Subsequent Cultivation

Set the plants 12 to 18 ins. apart according to the vigour of the variety; if in a double row, allow 18 ins. between rows. Do not plant less than 6 ins. away from the edge of the border or bed and keep the nearest plants at least 9 ins. away from the hot-water pipes. The soil ball (or soil block) must be set slightly below the surface level of the bed and watered in immediately after planting. The temperature of the soil must not be below 57° F. and many greenhouse owners make the error of assuming that it will be raised to this level almost immediately the heating apparatus is brought into action. This is not the case: it can easily take a month for the soil to attain the same temperature as the air, whether the latter has been warmed by artificial heat or by the sun. Electric soil-warming cables will, however, do the same job in a couple of days and ought always to be employed for winter and spring plantings if current is available in the greenhouse. They are used merely to raise the temperature to the required minimum, not to keep it there afterwards, which would tend to dry out the beds, and the ordinary greenhouse heating apparatus will look after that aspect once the beds have been warmed up.

As regards air temperatures the average day temperature should be 60°–62° F. But temperature must be correlated to outside weather conditions. In dry but not sunny winter weather, a rise to 65° F. by means of pipe heat is desirable by day, and the thermometer may even be allowed to run up to 80° F. when the weather is sunny. At night, 55° F. should be regarded as a good minimum with a maximum of 57° F. up to the end of February, 61° F. in March, and 65° F. thereafter. But no harm will be done to the plants if in exceptionally severe weather the air temperature falls temporarily to 45° F. provided that the soil is maintained at 55°–60° F. It is much wiser to allow the air temperature to fall occasionally, provided that the house is dry, than to endeavour to force it up, regardless of outside weather conditions, by keeping the water pipes near boiling point. Scalding hot pipes not only dry the air of the house to a greater extent than is permissible but involve great wastage of fuel.

All greenhouse tomatoes should be grown as single-stemmed cordons, the side-shoots in the axils of the leaves being nicked out when they are as small as possible – large wounds might lead to an outbreak of botrytis. If you are a cigarette smoker, do not remove side-shoots with nicotine-stained fingers as this may transmit disease to the tomatoes; they are relatives of the tobacco plant. Use a sharp knife and wipe it with a cloth soaked in weak disinfectant before you move on to the next plant.

A short stake should be set against each plant at planting time and the plant tied to it. Use split bamboos or plain wood sticks, sterilized, and not ordinary bamboos which harbour pests of every description. When the plant reaches the end of the stake, tie soft, thick fillis string from the top of the stake to a wire running along the rafters of the house and twine this lightly round the plant as it grows.

The growths of winter tomatoes are much more brittle than would be the case if the same plants were growing in summer: therefore take particular care when staking, tying, and otherwise supporting the stems and trusses.

Winter tomatoes in pots should be limited to four trusses which are about as much as they can carry: but in summer there is no need to pinch out the growing point unless space is restricted and you cannot allow the plants to extend further: they will always bear a dozen or more trusses if you will let them. If you do stop the leader, don't do so nearer than 3 leaves to the top truss, otherwise that truss may fail to set. The best rule if space is unrestricted is to leave the plants alone if they are vigorous all the way to the top; but if the top growth is getting thin and weak and there is a heavy set of fruit on the first four trusses, pinch out the top and allow a lateral from above or below the fourth truss to take its place as leader.

If plants fruiting in pots show signs of requiring increased root space, e.g. by the appearance of roots on the surface, a zinc collar can be put around the rim of each pot and a top-dressing of good compost applied.

The correct feeding of tomatoes under glass is a complex business which has to take into account the nature of the soil, the variety grown, the progress made by the plants and day-to-day weather conditions. The average amateur cannot possibly cope with all these details in the same way as a specialist and I advise him to stick to a good liquid proprietary tomato feed from the time the first truss of fruit is beginning to colour and in addition to watch out for shortage of nitrogen, easily spotted from the fact that the growth is pale and thin, with rapidly maturing fruit and sometimes yellow areas between the veins of the leaves. The remedy is to water with a solution of dried blood. Do not confuse the pale thin growth referred to with the thin woody stem of the 'lean' plant – such plants are often the real good doers and need no extra nitrogen.

It is the fat plants with thick stems and luxuriant foliage that produce only large bunches of small fruit.

The knowledge of when to water and when not to water is the hallmark of the good tomato-grower. No real watering should be necessary for a few weeks after planting in borders or on benches if the soil was properly moist to start with. If water is needed, apply it only in sufficient amount to soak the ball of soil which came out of the pot; don't water the whole bed and sour the areas of soil in which there are as yet no roots. The less watering you can manage with while the plants are establishing themselves the better: excess of water leads to soft, sappy growth. On the other hand it is just as fatal to let the roots get dry as to over-water. More dropping of flowers and other failures are due to lack of water than to any other cause. Remember therefore, before you start to grow tomatoes, that when the plants need water, they must be thoroughly soaked, not merely sprinkled, and that in July and August they may need soaking twice a day and that each plant may need a gallon of water to itself. You cannot grow good tomatoes if your other duties keep you away from them during the whole of a hot summer's day and there is nobody at home to tend them for you.

Mulching helps to save watering. Cover the beds or stages with a few inches of peat when the plants are 4 ft high, or if they are in pots or boxes heap peat around and over them.

Much loss of water can be avoided by lightly spraying overhead when the sun is bright at about 11 a.m. Still more can be avoided by shading and ventilation. Blinds are a boon to the owner of a small greenhouse – they can be used to protect the plants from the fierce light of a scorching summer sun and they can be drawn at night so that they will cut off the rays of the early morning sun which heat small houses up and dry them out before the gardener is up and about.

As regards ventilation, the house must never be stuffy. A crack of air should always be admitted by the roof ventilator at night, unless you have only one ventilator and that faces in the direction from which a cold wind is blowing. Draughts must be avoided at all costs; it is better to let the sun run the thermometer up to 80° F. with the ventilators closed than to open them and let in an icy east wind. If the plants flag a bit in bright sun after a spell of dull weather, that is natural, and does *not* necessarily mean that they want water. When weather conditions obviously make it impossible to ventilate, you should change the air once or twice a day by opening the ventilators for just a couple of minutes and then closing them again.

In winter ventilation demands special care and judgement in view of the probably wide difference between indoor and outdoor temperatures. The aim should be to keep the air buoyant and dryish at all times. This can usually be achieved by intelligent use of the sub-stage and roof ventilators only. The air of a tomato house in winter should always strike one as warm and fresh, never fuggy and never so moist as to mist your spectacles over, if you wear them. On fine winter and spring days it is often possible to give the house a thorough airing without setting up a draught.

Although tomatoes want a brisk dry atmosphere there must be moisture in the air during the period immediately following planting and at all times whilst any fruit is setting. Unless there is sufficient moisture to render the stigmata of the flowers sticky there will be no fertilization and you get what is known as 'dry set'. The best way of preventing this is to spray the foliage and trusses overhead with water in a mist-like spray on bright days sometime between 10 a.m. and 3 p.m. During the heat of summer this spraying will be supplemented by the damping down of the greenhouse which forms part of the ordinary greenhouse routine. But in winter the use of a syringe involves risks and demands great care if an outbreak of mildew is to be avoided and, when there is difficulty in getting the first truss to set, it can often be overcome by raising the pipe heat during the critical period and increasing the ventilation during the day, then watering early in the afternoon and closing the ventilators before the usual time. This procedure will give rise to the consistently warm conditions which favour the free production of pollen while at the same time creating sufficient moisture to render the stigmata receptive.

In order to ensure that the pollen reaches the stamens, you can tap the flower trusses sharply with your finger or a pencil; a little cloud of pollen will fill the surrounding air after each tap. Or you can bring a small piece of glass into contact with each flower and give it a slight upward pressure, so that pollen falls on to it and will then be taken up by the stigmata. But an even better way is to transfer pollen from one flower to another by means of a small pledget of cotton wool. And in the last resort you can use a tomato setting spray strictly in accordance with the makers' instructions. Whatever you do, the two cardinal points to remember are (a) that too low a temperature means no ripe pollen and (b) that too dry an atmosphere means that the pollen will not adhere to the stigmata.

Do not defoliate your plants at the end of the season unless, owing to inadequate ventilation, it is difficult to maintain a good circulation of air and prevent an outbreak of leaf mould. Under such circumstances it is legitimate to remove odd leaves here and there to facilitate air movement but only if it has proved impossible to tie them back out of the way. Never halve a leaf under the impression that this is better than total removal – it will merely lead the plant to misdirect its energy into an attempt to replace the loss.

Tomatoes in Frames

Tomatoes may be grown either in a double span-roofed frame sited in a reasonably open but fairly sheltered place, and running north and south, or in a single lean-to backing on a south-facing wall or fence.

Fill the frame with a mixture of four parts good loamy soil to one part each of well-rotted manure, mortar rubble, and sharp sand, with the addition of a 5-ins. potful of tomato base manure to every barrowload. The finished level of the bed must leave the plants a good 10 ins. of headroom and, if the frame is shallow, you will have to excavate to get sufficient depth of soil before making up the bed. On the other hand a glass-sided frame will have to be raised up on a plinth. Give the bed a thorough soaking, replace the lights, and leave it to warm up for a week or two. At planting time, which will be about the middle of April, surface up with a good dressing of garden compost mixed with moist granulated peat with the addition of a liberal sprinkling of fine bonemeal.

If you intend to remove the light altogether when the plants get too tall for the frame, set them either 1½ ft apart all ways and fill the frame or 1 ft apart in double rows 15 ins. apart and leave yourself more room for giving necessary attentions. Support the plants with short sticks at planting time; keep the lights closed and shade until they are established; harden off gradually before finally removing the lights and then replace the sticks with 5-ft stakes to which the plants are secured.

On the other hand, if you grow the plants with glass protection throughout, you have a choice of two methods. Cordon-training is the most popular. Use a single lean-to frame and set the plants in a single row 15 ins. apart at the back of the frame after turning it round so that the low end is at the back against the wall or fence and the deep end faces south into the garden. Strain wires or stretch strings (which may need periodical tightening) from back to front of the frame 6 ins. below the light and train the plants to them, tying in the main growth, not too tightly, every fifth or sixth day, and removing all side-shoots. Instead of wires or strings, you can use bamboo canes set at an angle from the base of each plant and tied to nails driven into the opposite end of the frame. Since the wires or canes will follow the upward slope of the frame and the tips of the plants will naturally curve towards the south, there will be far less risk of the growths snapping when they are tied down to their supports than there would have been if the frame sloped the other way.

By leaving the light pulled slightly back, rain will flow naturally into the end of the frame where the plants are, thus saving much watering. Ventilation and shading must be given as weather conditions demand, but the former should be as liberal as possible so long as draughts are avoided.

The second method of frame culture consists in using a dwarf or bush variety of tomato and in this case it will be found advantageous to fix a layer of wire-netting about 6 ins. above soil level and train the young plants to grow up through it. In this way the whole of the growth including the fruits, will be held clear of the soil and there will be little likelihood of rotting or damage by slugs and other pests. Seeds of dwarf bush tomatoes like The Amateur should not be sown in the greenhouse until early April. This sowing will lead to good, strong plants for setting out in frames in late

May. Dwarf bush plants need no stakes, nor do you have to pinch out side shoots.

Tomatoes under Cloches

A sunny site is essential, preferably with shelter from the north and east: there is no better position than under a south wall. Except in very light or very shallow soil, take out a trench 6 ins. deep, 12 ins. wide at the top, and 6 ins. wide at the bottom, the sides sloping at an angle of 45°. The strip should have been limed in autumn and dug and manured in winter on the same lines as already advocated for greenhouse borders. In spring work in plenty of peat to assist in keeping the soil moist after the cloches go on. At the same time, you may if you consider it necessary, apply a tomato-base fertilizer.

Plant during the first half of April in warm districts, and the second half of April elsewhere, setting the plants 18 ins. apart if to be grown as single-stemmed cordons and decloched at the end of May, 24 ins. apart if to be kept cloched throughout growth, and 2½ to 3 ft apart if the bush types are grown. Give an initial ball-watering, repeating this, if necessary, once or twice during the first week after planting.

Remove the cloches from the single-stemmed cordons before the plants touch the roof glass, stake them, and thereafter treat as ordinary outdoor tomatoes

Tall, or elevated, cloches are essential if the plants are to be kept covered throughout growth and there are then two alternative methods of training. One method is to train the leader up a diagonal stake and then train the first good side-shoot up a short vertical stake about 20 ins. tall. You should get three trusses off the leader and two off the lateral. The other method is to take the leader up vertically to a wire strained from end to end of the cloche row about 3 ins. below the apex and then carefully train the leader at right angles horizontally along the wire.

In all other respects the cultivation of tomatoes under cloches is the same as for outdoor crops except that it is a common practice to assist the ripening of the fruit on decloched plants by removing the stakes early in September, laying the plants down on dry peat and then covering them again with cloches.

Outdoor Tomatoes

Outdoor plants raised from April-sown seed are set out from late May until mid-June, and they crop from September onwards. In this uncertain climate a south-facing wall often represents the only hope of securing a decent crop. If the soil is not all that could be desired, make a raised bed with the aid of planks or bricks. Do the same if your only suitable wall is a house-wall with a path right up against it. Such a raised bed warms up more quickly than the main body of garden soil. A fence is no substitute for a wall if there are cracks between the boards: you must first cover it with roofing felt. Do not plant up against hedges where the soil is dry and hungry. If you must choose an open site, it must be protected from draughts: wattle hurdles can be a great help.

In small gardens where there is really no suitable bed in which to grow tomatoes, they can be grown in pots of the 10-ins. or 12-ins. size, placed against a hedge, building, or fence where they will catch as much sun as possible but will not be subject to draughts. The only precaution that has to be taken when growing plants in pots is to see that they never lack water.

The preparation of an outdoor tomato bed ought to be carried out before winter is over, the ground being deeply dug and enriched with bulky organic manures, such as strawy horse manure, garden compost, chopped wheat straw, composted straw, or wool shoddy, following the instructions already given for the manuring of greenhouse borders to which reference should be made. If the soil is newly broken or at all acid, it should receive a dressing of ½ lb. hydrated lime, if heavy, or 1 lb. carbonate of lime to the sq. yd, if light, early in the season. Then a proprietary tomato base fertilizer may be applied, if considered necessary, before planting.

If the nights are chilly at the time of planting out, although the weather generally is good, cover the plants with pots for the first few nights, but remember to take them off again in the day-time. The planting distance should be 15 ins. apart for cordons, and 2 ft apart for bush types, with 2 ft 6 ins. between rows. Bury the ball of soil an inch below the surface but do not cover it for the first 14 days. Water the plants in their pots *before* planting but do not water *after* planting unless the weather is dry; they are usually better without water until they have taken hold of the ground.

Staking should be attended to immediately after planting. A separate 4-ft stake is used for each plant and the plant is tied to it with soft fillis string or moistened raffia. When making the ties, do not forget that the stems grow thicker and that allowance must be made for this expansion. It is usual to see the plants secured to vertical stakes but this is not the best procedure. If the tomatoes are growing against a wall, the stakes should be inclined at an angle of 45° towards the wall so that the trusses hang clear of the foliage and thus receive more light and air as well as some additional protection late in the season. The same effect can be achieved, when the site is an open one, by inclining several stakes to form a structure on the lines of a wigwam.

Experiments carried out at one of the Vegetable Research Stations have proved that there is nothing to be gained by growing outdoor tomatoes on more than one stem, if they are standard varieties, and that the usual method of treating them as single-stemmed cordons is still the best. In my experience, however, there is room for some revision of the stereotyped method of applying the treatment to *outdoor* plants. No plant is benefited by the reduction of its leafage to the absolute minimum, seeing that the leaves are the factories in which the whole of its food supplies are processed; and the removal of side-shoots by nicking them out whilst they are still barely visible not only calls for knack and eternal vigilance but may, at the best, prevent the main stem from thickening and, at the worst, damage it and leave a scar which could become infected with disease. My own practice, therefore, is to allow the side-shoots to grow to a length of about 3 ins. and then stop them at one leaf. Indeed I have on occasion gone further and allowed the king shoots which form above the truss to develop and carry one truss of fruit, thereby greatly increasing the crop.

When leaves form on the trusses, as happens frequently in varieties of the Ailsa Craig type, they should always be retained except when there is a tendency to run on and form a further truss, when stopping is essential.

It might be added for the benefit of the complete novice that the side-shoots grow out of the axils of the leaves, and should not be confused with the fruit trusses, which take their origin from the stem *between* the leaves.

The question inevitably arises to what extent the plants shall be allowed to continue their upward growth if they are to ripen the maximum number of good-sized fruits. Every grower must decide what to do for himself having regard to the district, season, and variety – the latter an important factor. (Many amateurs take credit for themselves which should properly be bestowed upon the variety and strain.) The general rule is to stop at the fourth or fifth truss, but I am opposed to the ruthless decapitation of the plants which merely goads them into an endeavour to make fresh growth. It is often sufficient simply to pinch out the unwanted flower trusses. But, if the tops *are* removed, at least two leaves must be left above the top ripening truss, it being borne in mind that food from the leaf factory travels downwards, not upwards (as so many think it does!). One certain thing is that, wherever the garden is situated, the growing points ought to be removed by mid-September at the latest.

If you grow the dwarf or bush types, you must carefully distinguish between them for training purposes. A dwarf tomato, such as Histon Early, is precisely what its name implies. Its natural tendency to extend upwards ceases when it is about 2 ft tall, otherwise it is a normal tomato plant, which can be grown on one, two, or three stems, as you please. A bush tomato is an entirely different proposition. Its main stem is short and ends in a flower truss, all the remaining fruit being carried on laterals and sub-laterals. Theoretically a true bush can be left untrained but the result is often a headache. The raiser of Stonor's Dwarf Gem used to grow it on four laterals which were pulled down by the truss on the end and eventually the whole plant lay down like a starfish with the fifth bunch of fruit in the centre. As he once said to me: 'No doubt many an amateur will get into a tangle!'

I have had most success with bushes by fan-training them to strings attached to overhead wires, removing unwanted shoots when the plants were about 15 ins. high; and in the case of the Amateur it seems to be almost essential after planting to cover with a bottomless box to which has been nailed some wire netting of 1½-ins. mesh so that the plants grow through the mesh and deposit their trusses on the wire.

If the weather is dry, watering must be regularly attended to, and it is very desirable that the soil around the plants should be covered with a mulch, leaving space around the stems for watering and feeding. Littery stable manure, granulated peat, or clean straw can be used for mulching according to what is most easily obtainable. If you make use of a proprietary liquid tomato fertilizer, feed the plants with it from July onwards.

There is usually a certain amount of difference of opinion concerning the best way to treat tomatoes as the end of the season approaches; but on one point there ought not to be any dispute whatever – the removal of leaves. It is wrong to deprive a tomato plant of any foliage that is still doing its job. By all means remove leaves that are diseased or have become yellow and unserviceable, by detaching them from the socket, not by cutting and leaving a stump. You may do the same with the lowest leaves if they trail on the ground. A muddy leaf is unhygienic and in such a position may impede the free circulation of air. Otherwise, let well alone. The foliage functions in step with the roots: for every leaf removed there is a corresponding decrease in root development and a reduction in the quantity of water supplied to the plant by its roots: and this inevitably leads to a falling off in the quality and flavour of the ripening fruit.

It used to be thought that the absence of leaves encouraged the ripening process by allowing sunshine to fall upon the trusses. This is a complete fallacy. Tomatoes will ripen in total darkness. The governing factor is temperature, not light, and, although sunshine may appear to accelerate the colouring of the fruit, it may also cause greenback and other troubles. A sun-ripened tomato is definitely poorer eating than one ripened in shade.

Towards the end of the season, when the days are warm but nights begin to get cold, it is desirable to give the ripening fruit some protection. If the plants are growing in the open it is often possible to make a framework of stakes or bean poles and drape sacking over it on cold evenings. If the plants are growing against a wall or fence and you possess some frames which are not occupied, you can easily take the frame lights and lean them against the wall or fence. These little aids may make all the difference to the amount of fruit you are able to gather ripe.

Fisons Gro-Bags (introduced in 1974) could be of great use in the production of tomatoes on patios, balconies of flats and in other positions where there is no suitable bed in which tomatoes may be grown.

Gathering and Ripening Tomatoes

If a tomato fruit is to be really worth eating it must be left on the plant until it is fully coloured, though still firm, and then gathered early in the morning, complete with footstalk and calyx, removed at once to a shelf in a warm kitchen where it will be out of the sun and left for at least twenty-four hours to finish before it is eaten. This advice is, however, often in the nature of a counsel of perfection for the grower of outdoor tomatoes whose plants carry a sprinkling of large, fully developed green fruits which by their presence are seriously hampering the swelling of a large number of smaller fruits. In such a case it is best to remove the bigger specimens and ripen them indoors; but loss of flavour and skin thickness will be reduced to a minimum if removal can be delayed until the fruit has reached the pink or orange stage (or in the case of Mr Stonor's varieties until the green colour has almost entirely bleached out).

When outdoor weather conditions, or the prospect of severe frost, make it obvious that all further ripening must be carried out artificially, the proper course is to cut off each truss intact and take it indoors. It serves no purpose whatever to take the whole plant. Partially developed fruits will not ripen and should be detached and made into chutney: but all fully developed healthy fruits, whatever their size, can be ripened without shrivelling if they are properly treated.

Undoubtedly the best flavoured tomatoes are those which are ripened quickly on the slatted shelves of a heated airing cupboard at a temperature of 70° F. provided that the air is neither too dry nor so moist as to give rise to sweating and condensation.

Nevertheless if it is desired to extend the season of ripening and use over as long a period as possible, and it does not matter if the quality is suitable only for frying, the green fruits can be placed between layers of cotton wool in a drawer at a temperature of 50° F. It must be understood that, once picked, the green tomato fruit concentrates on the ripening of its seed at the expense of edibility, and, while cut off from further water supplies, tends to breathe out water vapour like a leaf. The purpose of the cotton wool is to check the loss of water but, if the wool becomes too moist as a result of sweating, it must be replaced by another dry piece.

Tomato Troubles

Commercial growers of tomatoes have many diseases and pests to contend with, but amateurs who grow tomatoes on a much smaller scale are far less likely to have their crops attacked and I shall deal therefore only with those troubles which they may reasonably expect to encounter on one occasion or another.

Blight

Often attacks the tomato, which is of course a close relative of the potato. This will only happen when the plants are grown out of doors and in wet summers, but it is always wise to take precautions against it, even when the plants are in frames, because it absolutely ruins the crop, causing dark brown blotches to appear on the fruits, followed by white downy growth and rotting, while the leaves and stems are similarly affected. Therefore all tomato plants should be sprayed with Bordeaux mixture in July, if the weather is wet, or in August, if the season is normal, in exactly the same way as potatoes. It is always wise to grow tomatoes as far away from the potato patch as possible.

Blossom End Rot

Causes the end of the tomato opposite to the stalk end to become blackish-brown, shrunken, and leathery, and finally to putrefy. There is no cure and the trouble would never arise if the plants were regularly watered. The appearance of blossom end rot means that you have let the plants dry out and then tried to save the situation by copious watering.

Blotchy Ripening

Is caused by malnutrition and deficiency of potash. The fruit ripens patchily, part red and part green. As a rule only the bottom bunches are affected and that principally on plants grown in small greenhouses which get chilled at night and far too warm by day. The remedies are to exercise better control of greenhouse temperatures and to top-dress with sulphate of potash.

Curling of the Leaves

Does not mean that there is anything wrong with the plants; it is a sign that they are doing well, in fact too well, and that their nitrogen supply must be reduced until the crop begins to hang heavily upon the plants. After that it is practically impossible to feed with too much nitrogen.

'Dry Set'

Under certain atmospheric conditions the flowers of the tomato plant are not fertilized so that the embryo fruit at the base of each flower fails to swell and, if it does not drop off the plant, will merely ripen into a tiny, seedless chat. This phenomenon is known as 'dry set'.

Imagine the flower to take the form of a chubby umbrella with the sacs of pollen suspended at the top where the ribs join the shaft. Then the stigma, which forms the end of the pistil, will correspond with the handle which you hold. This stigma may be compared to a gummed label: no pollen will adhere to it when it is dry: but when it is moistened it becomes sticky.

Assuming that there has been sufficient sunshine to ripen the pollen properly and that the plants are strong and healthy so that there is no shortage of pollen, all that is needed is sufficient movement in the air to dislodge the pollen so that it floats around airborne and sufficient humidity to ensure stickiness in the stigma to which the pollen will then adhere. But these conditions may not obtain when the weather is very hot and dry and there is not even a light breeze.

The remedy in such circumstances is to supply moisture and create movement. Spraying the plants with water will do both by shaking the flowers, scattering the pollen, and wetting the stigma. Since pollen is waterproof and readily water-borne, the fertilization may be effected by actual drops of pollen-laden water. Alternatively, particularly under glass, the soil and other surroundings of the plants may be thoroughly wetted to create a moist atmosphere and pollen may then be transferred from one flower to another by means of a pledget of cotton wool or by bringing a small piece of glass into contact with the open flowers into which pollen will fall and from which it will be taken up by the stigmata. (Nature prefers that one flower shall fertilize another but in the last resort it is quite capable of fertilizing itself.)

If these measures fail, it is possible to induce swelling of the embryo fruit by spraying it within two weeks of the flowers falling with a tomato setting solution containing beta-naphthoxyacetic acid (N.O.A.). This operation, which is carried out by means of an atomizer, needs to be very carefully performed. The whole of the fruitlet must be wetted and nothing but the fruitlet. In no circumstances must the same fruitlets be sprayed more than once or they may develop into inflated wind-bags. Strict adherence to the manufacturer's instructions is essential.

Greenback

Is not a disease but a blemish, usually caused either by lack of potash or by the unnecessary practice of cutting away the foliage so that the ripening fruit is scalded by the sun. A patch at the back of the fruit refuses to ripen and remains yellow or green and hard. Many varieties of tomato are immune to greenback.

Leaf Mould

Is rarely met with on plants grown in the open, but is often severe under glass. It comes on quite suddenly, often in June and July; but it may start in April or May and is common at the end of the season. The symptoms are pale, yellowish patches on the upper surface of the leaves with a light greyish or pale brown velvety mould on the corresponding areas on the underside. The lower leaves are generally attacked first.

The cause is a stagnant moist atmosphere, especially at night, and the disease is often very prevalent in districts where the early summer is characterized by moist warmth or the autumn by dank chill after sunset. The best preventive is to give ample ventilation at night. It is no good opening the top ventilators alone; there must be a circulation of air; and the greenhouse should never be boxed up.

If the disease breaks out, remove and burn all leaves below the fourth truss as soon as this truss has been picked. Water carefully and avoid feeding with an excess of nitrogen unbalanced by equivalent potash. If the disease spreads, and the attack occurs when the plants are young, spray with a proprietary fungicide based on copper or on zineb. Sulphur sprays, such as lime-sulphur and liver of sulphur solution, should be used only in the warm, sunny districts of the south.

In districts where the disease is prevalent every year, it is best to grow only resistant varieties.

Lop-sided Fruits

Naturally pollinated tomatoes are sometimes seedless, hollow, and flat on one side. This is because each grain of pollen makes only one seed and if, owing to shortage of pollen or any other reason, the grains are not evenly distributed over the stigma, a lop-sided fruit will result.

Splitting of Fruit

Is caused either by excessive moisture in the atmosphere or by letting the plants get dry and then endeavouring to rectify matters by heavy watering.

Finally here are eight cardinal rules for avoiding trouble with tomatoes:

(1) Buy only the best seed of the most disease-resistant strains.
(2) Don't sow or plant too early, especially if your greenhouse is unheated.
(3) Use sterilized soil and clean utensils.
(4) See that the greenhouse or frame is spotlessly clean and observe cleanliness throughout cultivation.

(5) Pay particular attention to ventilation, avoiding draughts, chills, and stuffiness.
(6) Water carefully, avoiding an excess but never allowing the plants to get dry at the roots; and aim at maintaining a dry, buoyant atmosphere.
(7) Exercise care in the application of manures and fertilizers.
(8) Spare no pains to rid the house of all insect pests.

Turnips and Swedes

The Turn-Neep is a round 'neep' or turnip and it is also a cabbage. When you eat 'turnip tops' you are eating another variety of 'cabbage greens'. It is just a question of those mysterious things called chromosomes which inhabit plant cells. The more familiar members of the cabbage family have eighteen chromosomes in a cell; but a few thousand years ago some developed twenty chromosomes and became turnips.

Turnips have been grown for human consumption from very ancient times. They were first cultivated for table purposes in this country in the neighbourhood of London about A.D. 1650. Nowadays far more turnips are grown for stock feeding than for culinary purposes. Norfolk was the first county to grow turnips extensively for cattle and the practice spread thence to the county of Moray in Scotland.

The quick-growing sorts with tender, cylindrical, or spherical roots have been developed mainly by the French and the Italians. They do not keep. It is to our own English and Scottish farmers that we owe the fine round main-crop sorts which can be stored during winter.

Few varieties of turnip are reliably hardy; some are only half-hardy. The plant's demand for cool, moist growing conditions, with absolute freedom from checks, renders it a difficult subject to cultivate in gardens during summer.

The true turnip has white flesh, though the exterior skin may be coloured. Yellow-fleshed varieties are really in the nature of 'sports' and are often of finer flavour than the white. The giant turnip, known as a swede, which originated in Sweden about 1781, is a hybrid between a turnip and some other cabbage, has thirty-eight chromosomes in a cell, and is the blood-brother of asparagus kale and Hungry Gap kale! It is hardier, milder, and sweeter than an ordinary turnip; it seldom gets woody or pithy, but it is a rather slow grower.

Soil and Situation

Turnips require a well-drained soil, liberally supplied with organic matter, and so far as spring and summer sowings are concerned it is almost essential to prepare the land in winter by incorporating farmyard manure or shoddy and then dressing with a fertilizer rich in phosphates and potash during February. There should be no need to dress with these fertilizers if you added plenty of well-made garden compost when you prepared the site. It is impossible to grow summer turnips on gravel soil. Winter (or main-crop) turnips are easier to manage and will usually succeed on land manured for a previous crop, such as early potatoes, particularly if the site is dressed with super-phosphate, sulphate of potash, and mortar rubble. Heavy and extremely light soils should both be improved by forking in a liberal body of fully-rotted compost from the compost heap.

Sowing

There are three main sowing periods: the first is from mid-March to mid-April, and usually succeeds unless the spring is abnormally cold or dry; the second is in May to provide summer turnips, and it is a pure waste of time and seed to attempt this sowing in the drier parts of Britain where scorching sun and drought are to be expected during June and July; the third sowing period is from mid-July to the end of August for main-crop or winter turnips – this is the most important and most useful sowing and should be attempted everywhere. Turnips are also sown in August and September to provide 'turnip tops' in winter and spring.

Sow continuously in ½-in.-deep drills 1 ft apart the whole length of the row and thin with a hoe. Summer turnips stand 4 to 6 ins. apart; winter turnips need more room and may be given 9 to 10 ins.

Remember that two turnip seedlings have a cunning habit of huddling together and looking like one, so inspect carefully after hoeing in case any further hand-thinning is necessary. Turnips sown to provide 'tops' only do not need thinning – simply hand-weed the rows.

Cultivation

The whole secret of growing turnips is to grow them quickly; they should mature in eight to ten weeks from the date of sowing, and to make this possible they must have cool, moist conditions and freedom from checks of all kinds. One of the most important factors is the control of the turnip flea beetle which must be effected by dusting the rows frequently with derris as soon as the seed leaves manifest themselves above ground.

Cultivation of Swedes

Swede turnips are hardier than ordinary turnips and will succeed where turnips are unsatisfactory. They are milder and sweeter than turnips and seldom get woody, but take much longer to mature (usually twenty to twenty-six weeks from the date of sowing). The recommended sowing times are, in the north, the beginning of May, and, in the south, the end of May or the beginning of June. Sow in 1-in.-deep drills 15 ins. apart, thinning to 12 ins. apart. Dust seedlings with derris as for ordinary turnips, hoe, and, during dry spells, water. An occasional dusting of soot is beneficial to young swedes.

When to Pull Turnips and Swedes

Pull the summer sorts (which do not keep) before or when they are the size of a tennis ball. Winter turnips can usually be left in the ground and pulled as required, at any rate in the south of England; but it is often politic to lift some of the crop between September and November, when the outer leaves show signs of ripening off, with a view to storage, as during a hard frost it is impossible to pull the roots out of the soil. In the colder areas of the north it may be wiser to lift all turnips in autumn; but swedes can always remain in the ground until Christmas when the whole crop should be lifted.

When lifting from the ground for immediate use, lift systematically; don't choose the biggest to pull first. In this way the ground which is cleared may be dug before winter, and any turnips that remain will be all together and will give a good crop of spring greens before they are finally disposed of.

Storing Turnips and Swedes

Cut the tops off close – but not *too* close; leave just a trace of green neck. Shorten the roots slightly, but do not remove them or cut them close – if you do the turnips will not keep. Then store in any of the ways recommended for carrots.

Growing Turnips in Frames

The 'Milan' and other forcing sorts can be sown in heated frames in mid-January and mid-February in holes ½ in. deep and 5 ins. apart, putting two seeds in each hole and subsequently thinning the seedlings to stand singly. Keep the frames closed at first, but ventilate and water as growth proceeds. At least 6 ins. of rich, light compost is required in the frame, and the bed must be really warm, a temperature of 65° F. being essential. The crop matures in about two months. These sowings are often made in conjunction with sowings of lettuces and carrots. The same varieties may also be sown in cold frames about the beginning of March.

Early Turnips under Cloches

It is possible to sow the early varieties of turnips about mid-March, one row under tent cloches or three rows under barns, provided that the soil is of suitable character. Thin to 6 ins. apart, protect against the flea beetle, and keep covered for five or six weeks. A sowing of the same varieties can also be made about the end of July and covered with cloches from September onwards.

Forcing Swedes

The blanched top growth of swedes provides a most tasty dish during winter, the leaves being boiled when they are large enough. Roots may be lifted from the open or taken from store any time from December onwards and any top growth cut off; they are then packed in boxes and forced in darkness in exactly the same way as seakale and chicory. It is not necessary to choose the best roots for forcing; the unshapely and undersized ones will do equally well.

Vegetable Marrow

See Marrow

FURTHER READING

Growing Food for Health and Pleasure: Harold Hart (Gateway Book Co., Croydon)

Fresh Food from Small Gardens: Brian Furner (Stuart & Watkins, London)

Organic Vegetable Growing: Brian Furner (Macdonald, London)

About Organic Gardening: G. J. Binding (Thorsons Publishers, London)

The Modern Greenhouse: J. S. Dakers (Cassell & Co., London)

All About Greenhouses: Arthur J. Simons (John Gifford, London)

Gardening with Cloches: Louis N. Flawn (John Gifford, London)

ADDRESS LIST

The following are reliable sources of supply for vegetable seeds, including uncommon varieties. They all produce a catalogue.

Alexander & Brown, The Scottish Seed House, Perth, Scotland
Samuel Dobie & Son Ltd, Upper Dee Mills, Llangollen, Denbighshire, Wales
S. E. Marshall & Co. Ltd, Oldfield Lane, Wisbech, Cambridgeshire
Suttons Seeds, The Royal Seed Establishment, Reading, Berkshire
Thompson & Morgan (Ipswich) Ltd, London Road, Ipswich, Suffolk
W. J. Unwin Ltd, Histon, Cambridge
G. Winfield & Son Ltd, 26 Westgate Street, Gloucester

ACKNOWLEDGEMENTS

Grateful thanks are due to the following photographers for permission to reproduce the pictures contained in the inset. To Brian Furner for the pictures of broad beans, scorzonera, celeriac, giant radish, Hamburg parsley, salsify, Chinese artichokes, globe artichokes, blanched seakale, Chinese mustard, aubergine, zucchini, endive, and sweet corn. To John Gay for pictures of French beans and runner beans, turnip and parsnip, Jerusalem artichokes, Chinese cabbage, onions, pickling onions, and garlic. To Pat Brindley for pictures of broccoli, cabbage lettuce, curly kale, Swiss chard, and vegetable marrow. To Harry Smith for the picture of the cos lettuce.

The Penguin Book of Basic Gardening

Alan Gemmell

Gardening can be a chore or a delight, a backbreaking task or a source of endless satisfaction; but to own a garden for the first time can be an exciting experience if you know what to do with it. In this Penguin Handbook Alan Gemmell has produced a clear and simple plan for basic gardening, including fruit, flower, shrub and vegetable growing.

Working on the premise that most people want a garden which looks alright and is interesting, but which will not take up vast amounts of spare time, the author deals first with the fundamentals – soil, fertilizers, necessary tools, planning and design – and then continues with advice on what to grow, when to grow and how to grow it, from the perfect lawn to the flourishing vegetable patch.

Soft Fruit Growing

E. G. Gilbert

Published in collaboration with the Royal Horticultural Society, this book is a complete and authoritative illustrated guide to growing soft fruit in all British soils and conditions. Whether you are an experienced professional market gardener or an amateur with only a small plot or allotment, you will find in this book all the latest ideas on how to grow the best strawberries, raspberries, black, red and white currants, blackberries, gooseberries, blueberries and outside vines. E. G. Gilbert, who is Plantations Officer at the Long Ashton Agricultural Research Station, has also included essential information on soil variations, and advice on planting, pruning and pest control. He offers this book as a companion to Raymond Bush's classic handbook, *Tree Fruit Growing*, which he has recently revised. Together the two books give the gardener, in a form handy for easy reference, all the advice he is likely to need on any aspect of fruit growing.

The Vegetarian Epicure

Anna Thomas

'Good food is a celebration of life'

The Vegetarian Epicure is the answer to all those who consider vegetarian food boring and fit only for rabbits. In Anna Thomas's imaginative and skilful hands vegetarian cookery is turned, on the contrary, into a rich, exciting and varied way of eating that should appeal not only to the confirmed vegetarian but to the confirmed meat-eater as well.

Included are over 200 Lucullan recipes covering:

Bread
Soups
Sauces
Salads and Dressings
Vegetables
Eggs, Omelettes and Soufflés
Crêpes and Pancakes
Cheese
Rice and Other Grains
Pasta
Curries and Indian Preparations
Sweets

Penguin Handbooks of Cookery and Wine

The Penguin Cookery Book *Bee Nilson*
Cooking for Special Diets *Bee Nilson*
Cooking in a Bedsitter *Katharine Whitehorn*
Cooking with Wine *Robin McDouall*
Danish Cooking *Nika Standen Hazelton*
French Country Cooking *Elizabeth David*
French Provincial Cooking *Elizabeth David*
Fresh from the Freezer *Marye Cameron-Smith*
Good Food on a Budget *Georgina Horley*
A Penguin Book of Herbs and Spices *Rosemary Hemphill*
Indian Cookery *Dharamjit Singh*
Italian Food *Elizabeth David*
Jewish Cookery *Florence Greenberg*
Leave it to Cook: The Slow Cooking Method
Stella Atterbury
Mastering the Art of French Cooking *Simone Beck et al.*
Modern Vegetarian Cooking *Walter and Jenny Fliess*
The Penguin Salad Book *Edited by Elizabeth Craig*
The Penguin Book of Sauces *Ambrose Heath*
The Slimmer's Cookbook *G. W. Chappell and John Yudkin*
South East Asian Food *Rosemary Brissenden*
Spices, Salt and Aromatics in the English Kitchen
Elizabeth David
Summer Cooking *Elizabeth David*
The Penguin Book of Wines *Allan Sichel*